ORSON SCOTT CARD

RED PROPHET

TALES OF ALVIN MAKER

RED PROPHET
TALES OF ALVIN MAKER

It's an alternate universe where historical events take a decidedly different turn and where folk magic is very real. The early America of this universe has the murderous Governor William Henry Harrison plotting to build an empire on the blood of slain Native American Reds. But two Red brothers, the warrior Ta-Kumsaw and the prophet Tenskwa-Tawa, have ideas of their own in regards to the future of the nation. Ideas that don't even align with each other's! Factoring into all of this is Alvin Miller, a young boy with magical abilities that are potentially limitless. He's the focal point in a frantic race to prevent the war that's brewing between the Native American Reds and the white settlers in North America. A war set in motion by Governor Harrison's dark plotting as well as the fears and prejudices that dwell within the hearts of even decent men...

WRITER **ORSON SCOTT CARD**   ADAPTATION **ROLAND BERNARD BROWN**
ARTWORK **RENATO ARLEM** (CHAPTERS 1-3) & **MIGUEL MONTENEGRO** (CHAPTERS 3-6)
COLORS **DAVID CURIEL** (CHAPTERS 1-3) & **ZONA I** (CHAPTERS 3-6)
LETTERS **BILL TORTOLINI**   EDITOR **MATT HANSEN**

Assistant Editors Cory Levine & John Denning
Editors, Special Projects: Jennifer Grünwald & Mark D. Beazley
Senior Editor, Special Projects Jeff Youngquist
Vice President of Development Ruwan Jayatilleke
Senior Vice President of Sales David Gabriel
Vice President of Creative Tom Marvelli

Editor in Chief Joe Quesada
Publisher Dan Buckley

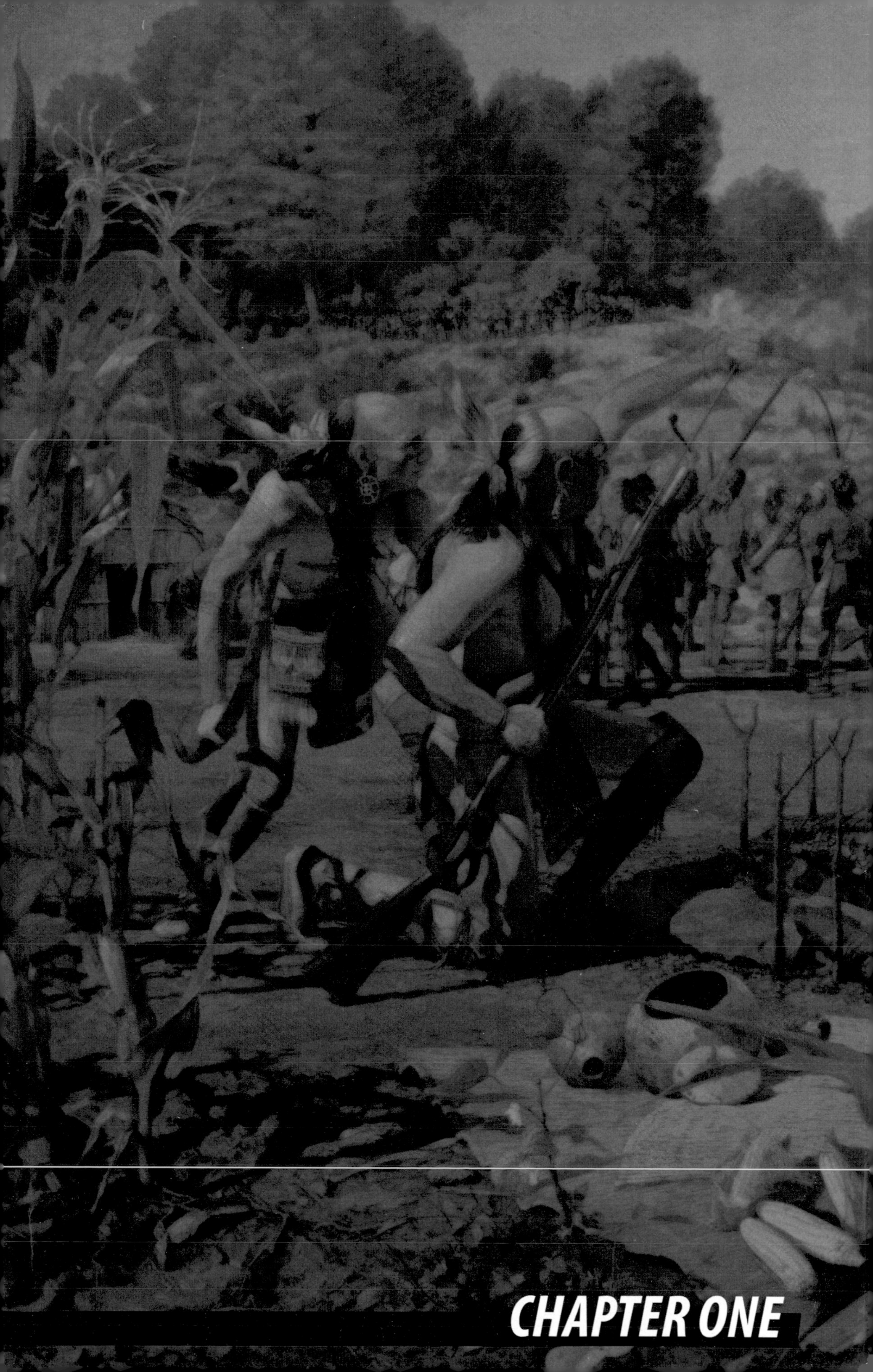

CHAPTER ONE

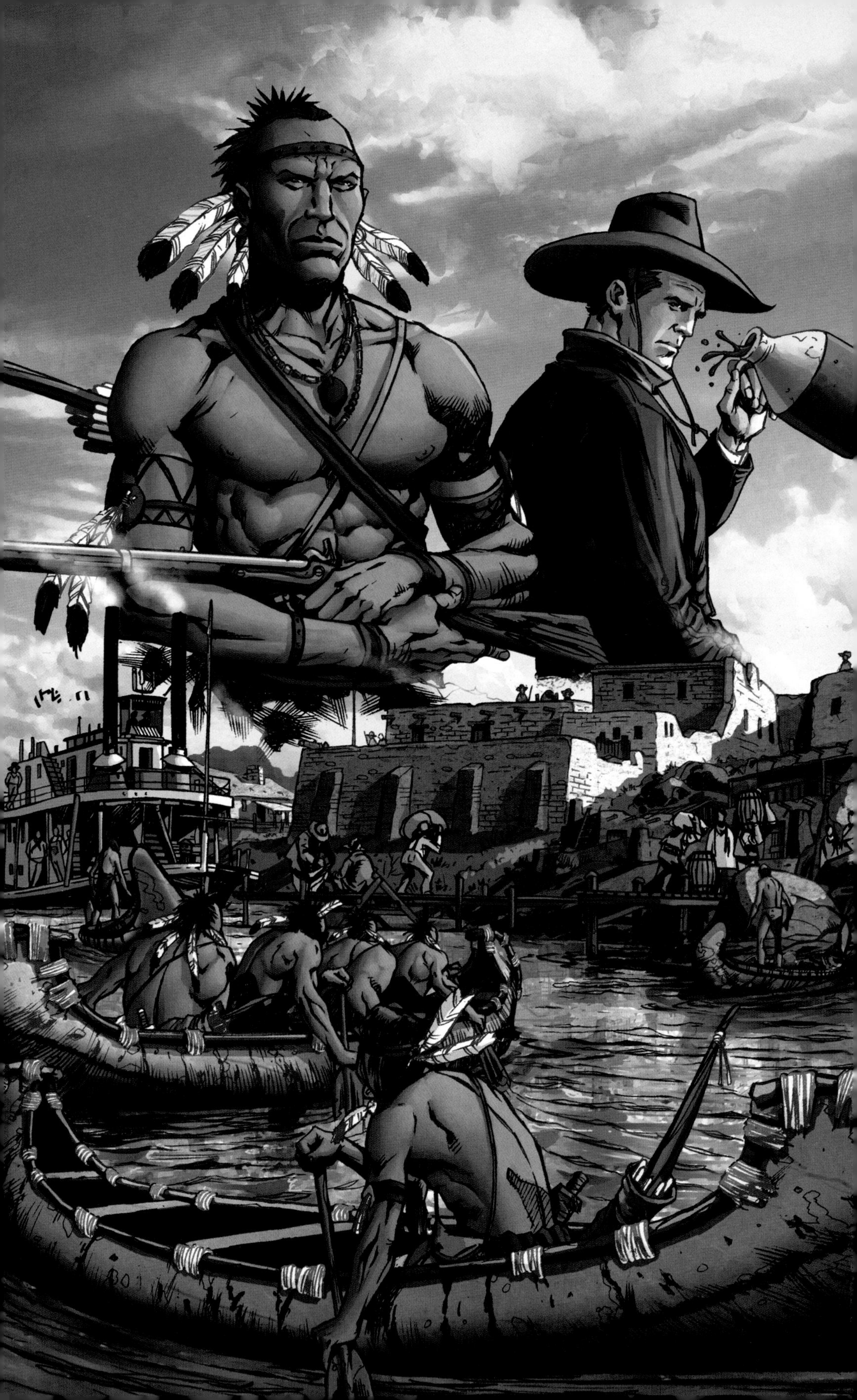

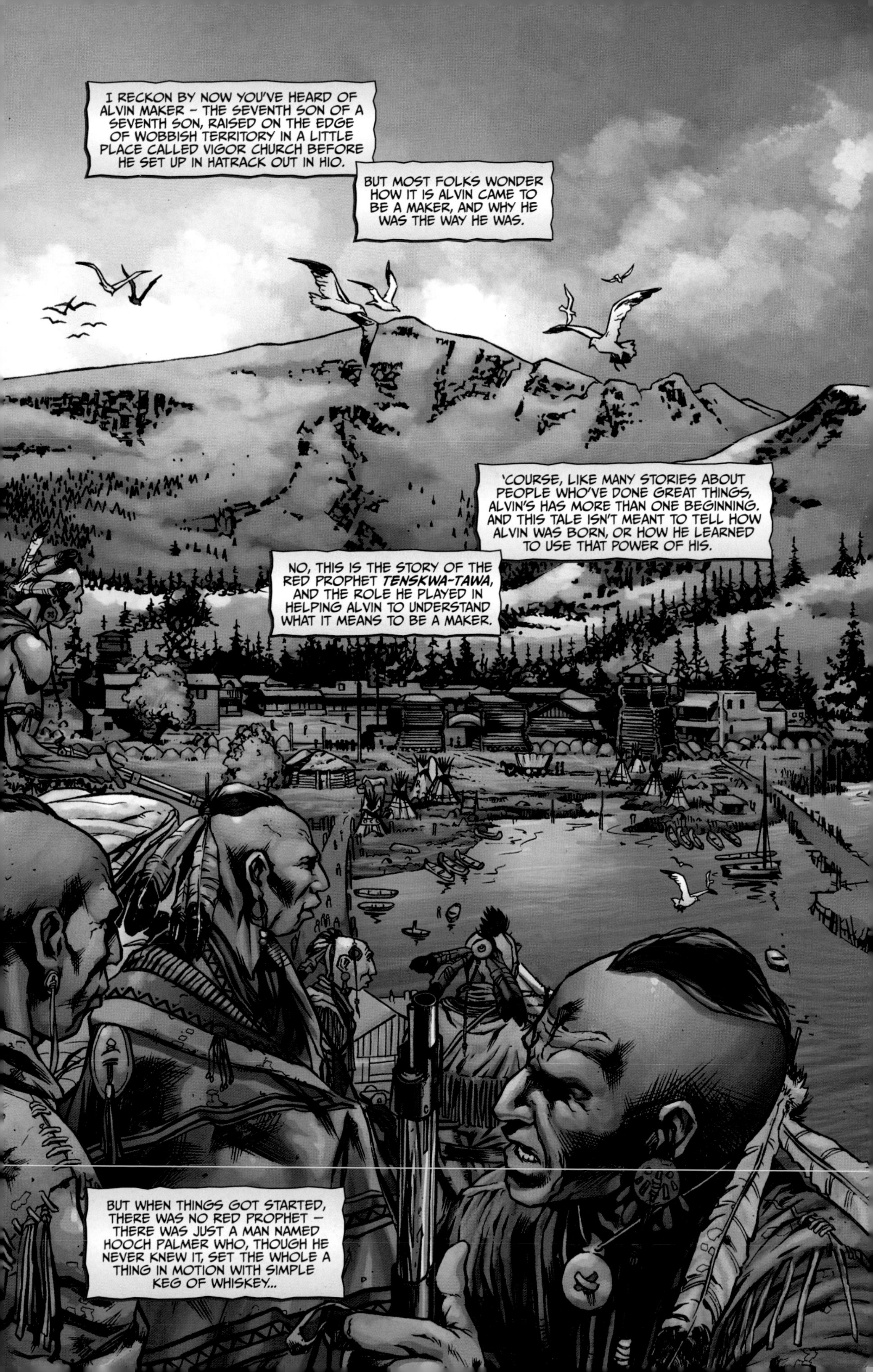

I RECKON BY NOW YOU'VE HEARD OF ALVIN MAKER – THE SEVENTH SON OF A SEVENTH SON, RAISED ON THE EDGE OF WOBBISH TERRITORY IN A LITTLE PLACE CALLED VIGOR CHURCH BEFORE HE SET UP IN HATRACK OUT IN HIO.
BUT MOST FOLKS WONDER HOW IT IS ALVIN CAME TO BE A MAKER, AND WHY HE WAS THE WAY HE WAS.
'COURSE, LIKE MANY STORIES ABOUT PEOPLE WHO'VE DONE GREAT THINGS, ALVIN'S HAS MORE THAN ONE BEGINNING. AND THIS TALE ISN'T MEANT TO TELL HOW ALVIN WAS BORN, OR HOW HE LEARNED TO USE THAT POWER OF HIS.
NO, THIS IS THE STORY OF THE RED PROPHET *TENSKWA-TAWA*, AND THE ROLE HE PLAYED IN HELPING ALVIN TO UNDERSTAND WHAT IT MEANS TO BE A MAKER.
BUT WHEN THINGS GOT STARTED, THERE WAS NO RED PROPHET – THERE WAS JUST A MAN NAMED HOOCH PALMER WHO, THOUGH HE NEVER KNEW IT, SET THE WHOLE A THING IN MOTION WITH SIMPLE KEG OF WHISKEY...

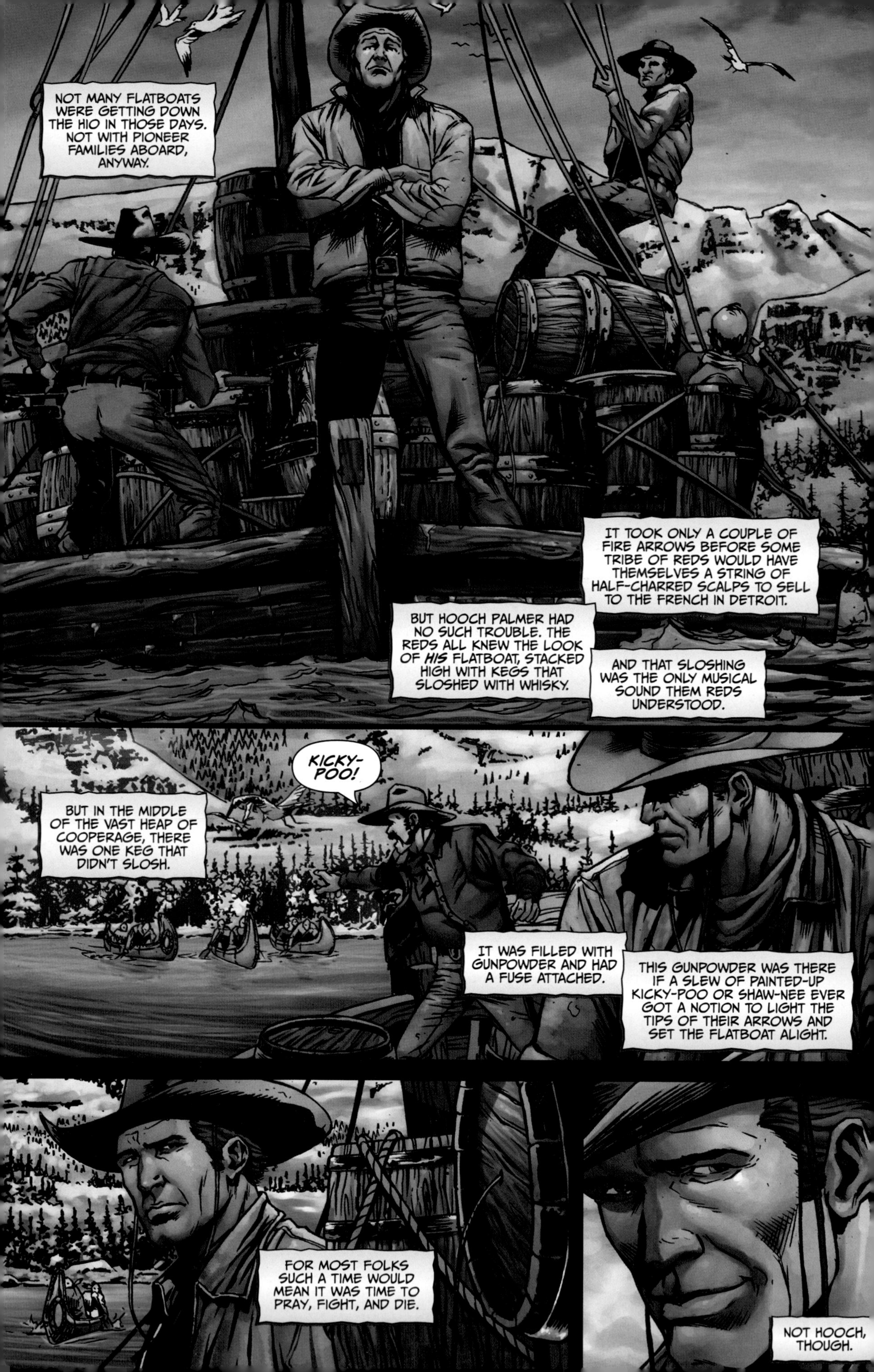
NOT MANY FLATBOATS WERE GETTING DOWN THE HIO IN THOSE DAYS. NOT WITH PIONEER FAMILIES ABOARD, ANYWAY.
IT TOOK ONLY A COUPLE OF FIRE ARROWS BEFORE SOME TRIBE OF REDS WOULD HAVE THEMSELVES A STRING OF HALF-CHARRED SCALPS TO SELL TO THE FRENCH IN DETROIT.
BUT HOOCH PALMER HAD NO SUCH TROUBLE. THE REDS ALL KNEW THE LOOK OF *HIS* FLATBOAT, STACKED HIGH WITH KEGS THAT SLOSHED WITH WHISKY.
AND THAT SLOSHING WAS THE ONLY MUSICAL SOUND THEM REDS UNDERSTOOD.
KICKY-POO!
BUT IN THE MIDDLE OF THE VAST HEAP OF COOPERAGE, THERE WAS ONE KEG THAT DIDN'T SLOSH.
IT WAS FILLED WITH GUNPOWDER AND HAD A FUSE ATTACHED.
THIS GUNPOWDER WAS THERE IF A SLEW OF PAINTED-UP KICKY-POO OR SHAW-NEE EVER GOT A NOTION TO LIGHT THE TIPS OF THEIR ARROWS AND SET THE FLATBOAT ALIGHT.
FOR MOST FOLKS SUCH A TIME WOULD MEAN IT WAS TIME TO PRAY, FIGHT, AND DIE.
NOT HOOCH, THOUGH.

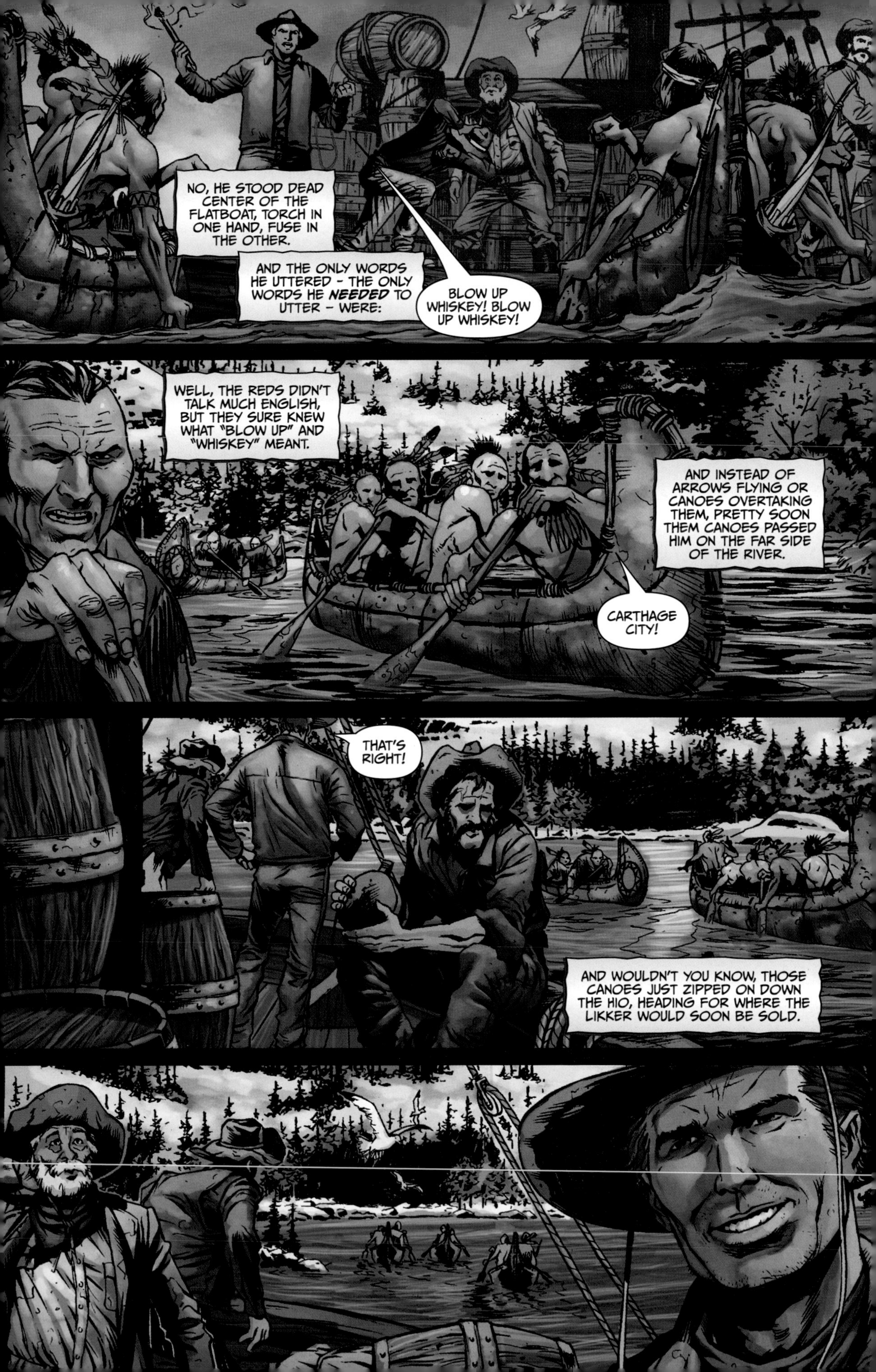
NO, HE STOOD DEAD CENTER OF THE FLATBOAT, TORCH IN ONE HAND, FUSE IN THE OTHER.
AND THE ONLY WORDS HE UTTERED - THE ONLY WORDS HE *NEEDED* TO UTTER - WERE:
BLOW UP WHISKEY! BLOW UP WHISKEY!
WELL, THE REDS DIDN'T TALK MUCH ENGLISH, BUT THEY SURE KNEW WHAT "BLOW UP" AND "WHISKEY" MEANT.
AND INSTEAD OF ARROWS FLYING OR CANOES OVERTAKING THEM, PRETTY SOON THEM CANOES PASSED HIM ON THE FAR SIDE OF THE RIVER.
CARTHAGE CITY!
THAT'S RIGHT!
AND WOULDN'T YOU KNOW, THOSE CANOES JUST ZIPPED ON DOWN THE HIO, HEADING FOR WHERE THE LIKKER WOULD SOON BE SOLD.

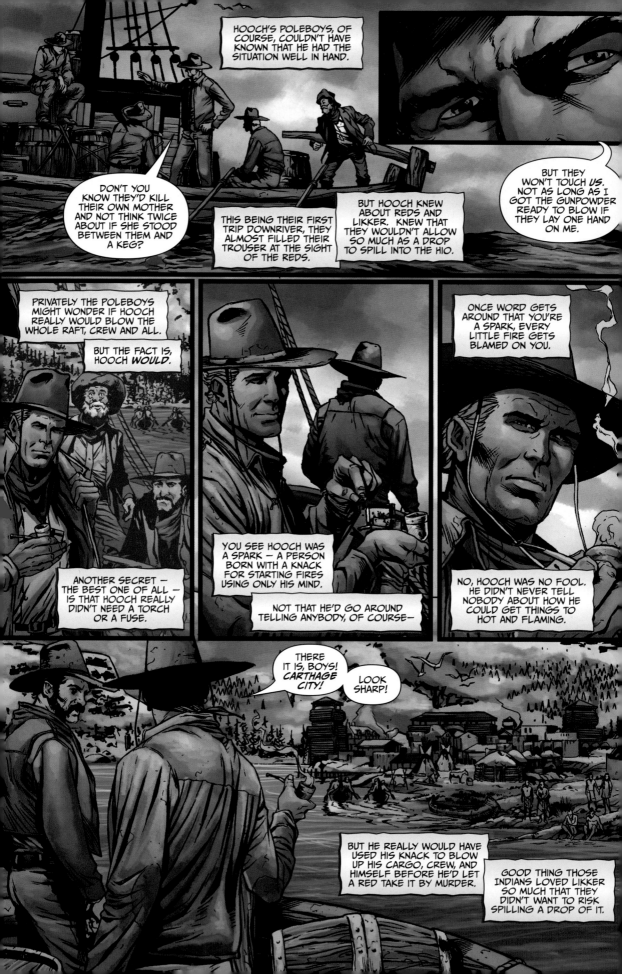

HOOCH'S POLEBOYS, OF COURSE, COULDN'T HAVE KNOWN THAT HE HAD THE SITUATION WELL IN HAND.

DON'T YOU KNOW THEY'D KILL THEIR OWN MOTHER AND NOT THINK TWICE ABOUT IF SHE STOOD BETWEEN THEM AND A KEG?

THIS BEING THEIR FIRST TRIP DOWNRIVER, THEY ALMOST FILLED THEIR TROUSER AT THE SIGHT OF THE REDS.

BUT HOOCH KNEW ABOUT REDS AND LIKKER. KNEW THAT THEY WOULDN'T ALLOW SO MUCH AS A DROP TO SPILL INTO THE HIO.

BUT THEY WON'T TOUCH US. NOT AS LONG AS I GOT THE GUNPOWDER READY TO BLOW IF THEY LAY ONE HAND ON ME.

PRIVATELY THE POLEBOYS MIGHT WONDER IF HOOCH REALLY WOULD BLOW THE WHOLE RAFT, CREW AND ALL.

BUT THE FACT IS, HOOCH WOULD.

ONCE WORD GETS AROUND THAT YOU'RE A SPARK, EVERY LITTLE FIRE GETS BLAMED ON YOU.

ANOTHER SECRET — THE BEST ONE OF ALL — IS THAT HOOCH REALLY DIDN'T NEED A TORCH OR A FUSE.

YOU SEE HOOCH WAS A SPARK — A PERSON BORN WITH A KNACK FOR STARTING FIRES USING ONLY HIS MIND.

NOT THAT HE'D GO AROUND TELLING ANYBODY, OF COURSE—

NO, HOOCH WAS NO FOOL. HE DIDN'T NEVER TELL NOBODY ABOUT HOW HE COULD GET THINGS TO HOT AND FLAMING.

THERE IT IS, BOYS! CARTHAGE CITY!

LOOK SHARP!

BUT HE REALLY WOULD HAVE USED HIS KNACK TO BLOW UP HIS CARGO, CREW, AND HIMSELF BEFORE HE'D LET A RED TAKE IT BY MURDER.

GOOD THING THOSE INDIANS LOVED LIKKER SO MUCH THAT THEY DIDN'T WANT TO RISK SPILLING A DROP OF IT.

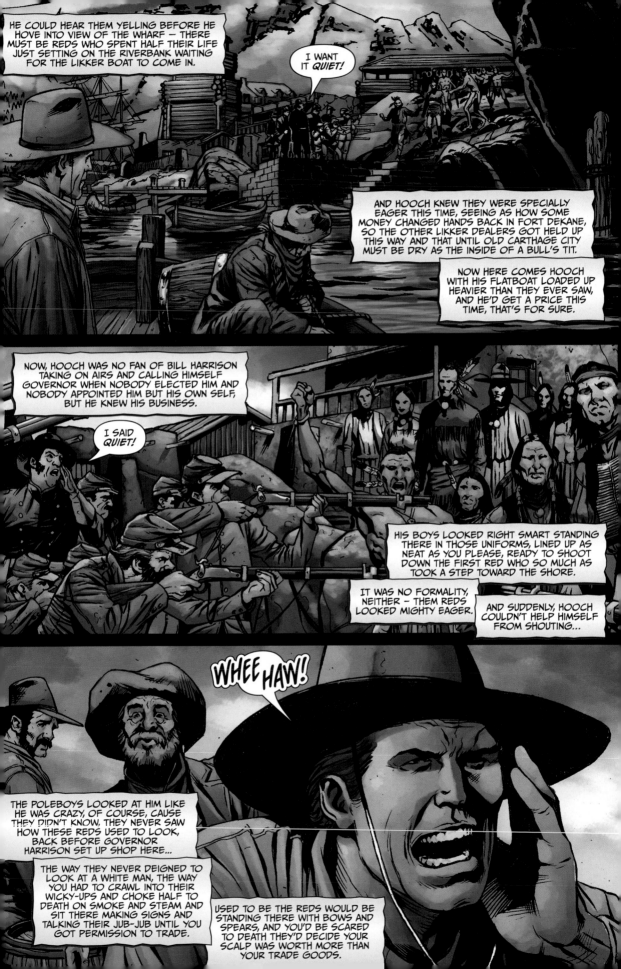

HE COULD HEAR THEM YELLING BEFORE HE HOVE INTO VIEW OF THE WHARF — THERE MUST BE REDS WHO SPENT HALF THEIR LIFE JUST SETTING ON THE RIVERBANK WAITING FOR THE LIKKER BOAT TO COME IN.

I WANT IT *QUIET!*

AND HOOCH KNEW THEY WERE SPECIALLY EAGER THIS TIME, SEEING AS HOW SOME MONEY CHANGED HANDS BACK IN FORT DEKANE, SO THE OTHER LIKKER DEALERS GOT HELD UP THIS WAY AND THAT UNTIL OLD CARTHAGE CITY MUST BE DRY AS THE INSIDE OF A BULL'S TIT.

NOW HERE COMES HOOCH WITH HIS FLATBOAT LOADED UP HEAVIER THAN THEY EVER SAW, AND HE'D GET A PRICE THIS TIME, THAT'S FOR SURE.

NOW, HOOCH WAS NO FAN OF BILL HARRISON TAKING ON AIRS AND CALLING HIMSELF GOVERNOR WHEN NOBODY ELECTED HIM AND NOBODY APPOINTED HIM BUT HIS OWN SELF, BUT HE KNEW HIS BUSINESS.

I SAID *QUIET!*

HIS BOYS LOOKED RIGHT SMART STANDING THERE IN THOSE UNIFORMS, LINED UP AS NEAT AS YOU PLEASE, READY TO SHOOT DOWN THE FIRST RED WHO SO MUCH AS TOOK A STEP TOWARD THE SHORE.

IT WAS NO FORMALITY, NEITHER — THEM REDS LOOKED MIGHTY EAGER.

AND SUDDENLY, HOOCH COULDN'T HELP HIMSELF FROM SHOUTING...

WHEE HAW!

THE POLEBOYS LOOKED AT HIM LIKE HE WAS CRAZY, OF COURSE, CAUSE THEY DIDN'T KNOW. THEY NEVER SAW HOW THESE REDS USED TO LOOK, BACK BEFORE GOVERNOR HARRISON SET UP SHOP HERE...

THE WAY THEY NEVER DEIGNED TO LOOK AT A WHITE MAN, THE WAY YOU HAD TO CRAWL INTO THEIR WICKY-UPS AND CHOKE HALF TO DEATH ON SMOKE AND STEAM AND SIT THERE MAKING SIGNS AND TALKING THEIR JUB-JUB UNTIL YOU GOT PERMISSION TO TRADE.

USED TO BE THE REDS WOULD BE STANDING THERE WITH BOWS AND SPEARS, AND YOU'D BE SCARED TO DEATH THEY'D DECIDE YOUR SCALP WAS WORTH MORE THAN YOUR TRADE GOODS.

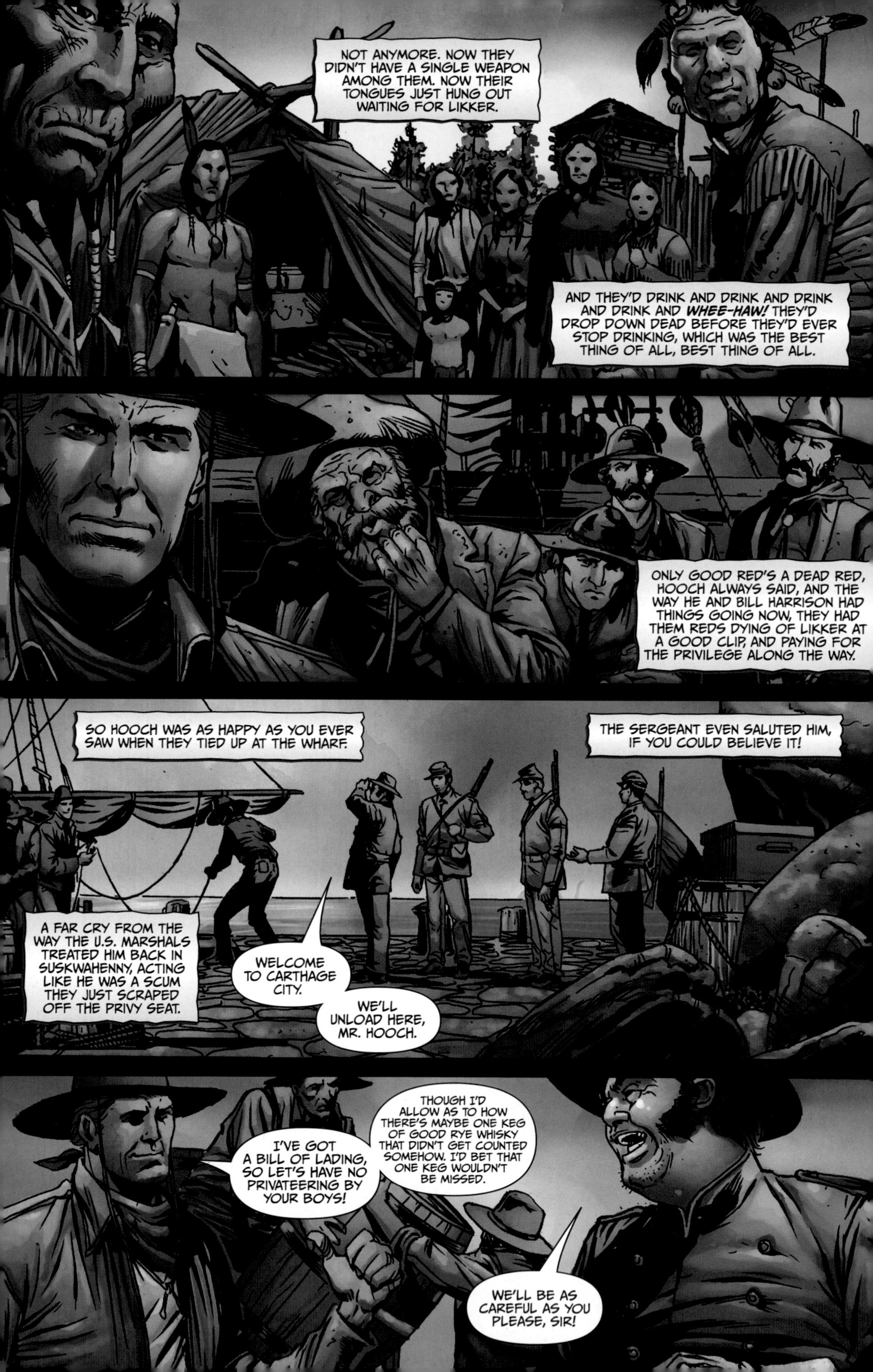
NOT ANYMORE. NOW THEY DIDN'T HAVE A SINGLE WEAPON AMONG THEM. NOW THEIR TONGUES JUST HUNG OUT WAITING FOR LIKKER.
AND THEY'D DRINK AND DRINK AND DRINK AND DRINK AND *WHEE-HAW!* THEY'D DROP DOWN DEAD BEFORE THEY'D EVER STOP DRINKING, WHICH WAS THE BEST THING OF ALL, BEST THING OF ALL.
ONLY GOOD RED'S A DEAD RED, HOOCH ALWAYS SAID, AND THE WAY HE AND BILL HARRISON HAD THINGS GOING NOW, THEY HAD THEM REDS DYING OF LIKKER AT A GOOD CLIP, AND PAYING FOR THE PRIVILEGE ALONG THE WAY.
SO HOOCH WAS AS HAPPY AS YOU EVER SAW WHEN THEY TIED UP AT THE WHARF.
THE SERGEANT EVEN SALUTED HIM, IF YOU COULD BELIEVE IT!
A FAR CRY FROM THE WAY THE U.S. MARSHALS TREATED HIM BACK IN SUSKWAHENNY, ACTING LIKE HE WAS A SCUM THEY JUST SCRAPED OFF THE PRIVY SEAT.
WELCOME TO CARTHAGE CITY.
WE'LL UNLOAD HERE, MR. HOOCH.
I'VE GOT A BILL OF LADING, SO LET'S HAVE NO PRIVATEERING BY YOUR BOYS!
THOUGH I'D ALLOW AS TO HOW THERE'S MAYBE ONE KEG OF GOOD RYE WHISKY THAT DIDN'T GET COUNTED SOMEHOW. I'D BET THAT ONE KEG WOULDN'T BE MISSED.
WE'LL BE AS CAREFUL AS YOU PLEASE, SIR!

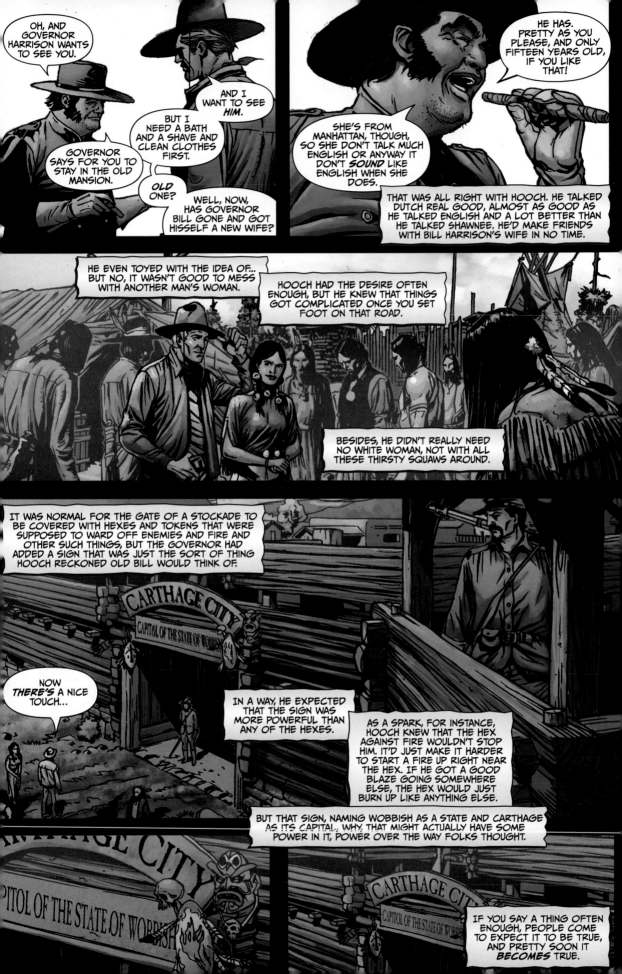

OH, AND GOVERNOR HARRISON WANTS TO SEE YOU.

AND I WANT TO SEE *HIM*.

BUT I NEED A BATH AND A SHAVE AND CLEAN CLOTHES FIRST.

GOVERNOR SAYS FOR YOU TO STAY IN THE OLD MANSION.

OLD ONE?

WELL, NOW, HAS GOVERNOR BILL GONE AND GOT HISSELF A NEW WIFE?

HE HAS. PRETTY AS YOU PLEASE, AND ONLY FIFTEEN YEARS OLD, IF YOU LIKE THAT!

SHE'S FROM MANHATTAN, THOUGH, SO SHE DON'T TALK MUCH ENGLISH OR ANYWAY IT DON'T *SOUND* LIKE ENGLISH WHEN SHE DOES.

THAT WAS ALL RIGHT WITH HOOCH. HE TALKED DUTCH REAL GOOD, ALMOST AS GOOD AS HE TALKED ENGLISH AND A LOT BETTER THAN HE TALKED SHAWNEE. HE'D MAKE FRIENDS WITH BILL HARRISON'S WIFE IN NO TIME.

HE EVEN TOYED WITH THE IDEA OF... BUT NO, IT WASN'T GOOD TO MESS WITH ANOTHER MAN'S WOMAN.

HOOCH HAD THE DESIRE OFTEN ENOUGH, BUT HE KNEW THAT THINGS GOT COMPLICATED ONCE YOU SET FOOT ON THAT ROAD.

BESIDES, HE DIDN'T REALLY NEED NO WHITE WOMAN, NOT WITH ALL THESE THIRSTY SQUAWS AROUND.

IT WAS NORMAL FOR THE GATE OF A STOCKADE TO BE COVERED WITH HEXES AND TOKENS THAT WERE SUPPOSED TO WARD OFF ENEMIES AND FIRE AND OTHER SUCH THINGS, BUT THE GOVERNOR HAD ADDED A SIGN THAT WAS JUST THE SORT OF THING HOOCH RECKONED OLD BILL WOULD THINK OF.

CARTHAGE CITY
CAPITOL OF THE STATE OF WOBBISH

NOW *THERE'S* A NICE TOUCH...

IN A WAY, HE EXPECTED THAT THE SIGN WAS MORE POWERFUL THAN ANY OF THE HEXES.

AS A SPARK, FOR INSTANCE, HOOCH KNEW THAT THE HEX AGAINST FIRE WOULDN'T STOP HIM. IT'D JUST MAKE IT HARDER TO START A FIRE UP RIGHT NEAR THE HEX. IF HE GOT A GOOD BLAZE GOING SOMEWHERE ELSE, THE HEX WOULD JUST BURN UP LIKE ANYTHING ELSE.

BUT THAT SIGN, NAMING WOBBISH AS A STATE AND CARTHAGE AS ITS *CAPITAL*, WHY, THAT MIGHT ACTUALLY HAVE SOME POWER IN IT, POWER OVER THE WAY FOLKS THOUGHT.

CARTHAGE CITY
CAPITOL OF THE STATE OF WOBBISH

IF YOU SAY A THING OFTEN ENOUGH, PEOPLE COME TO EXPECT IT TO BE TRUE, AND PRETTY SOON IT *BECOMES* TRUE.

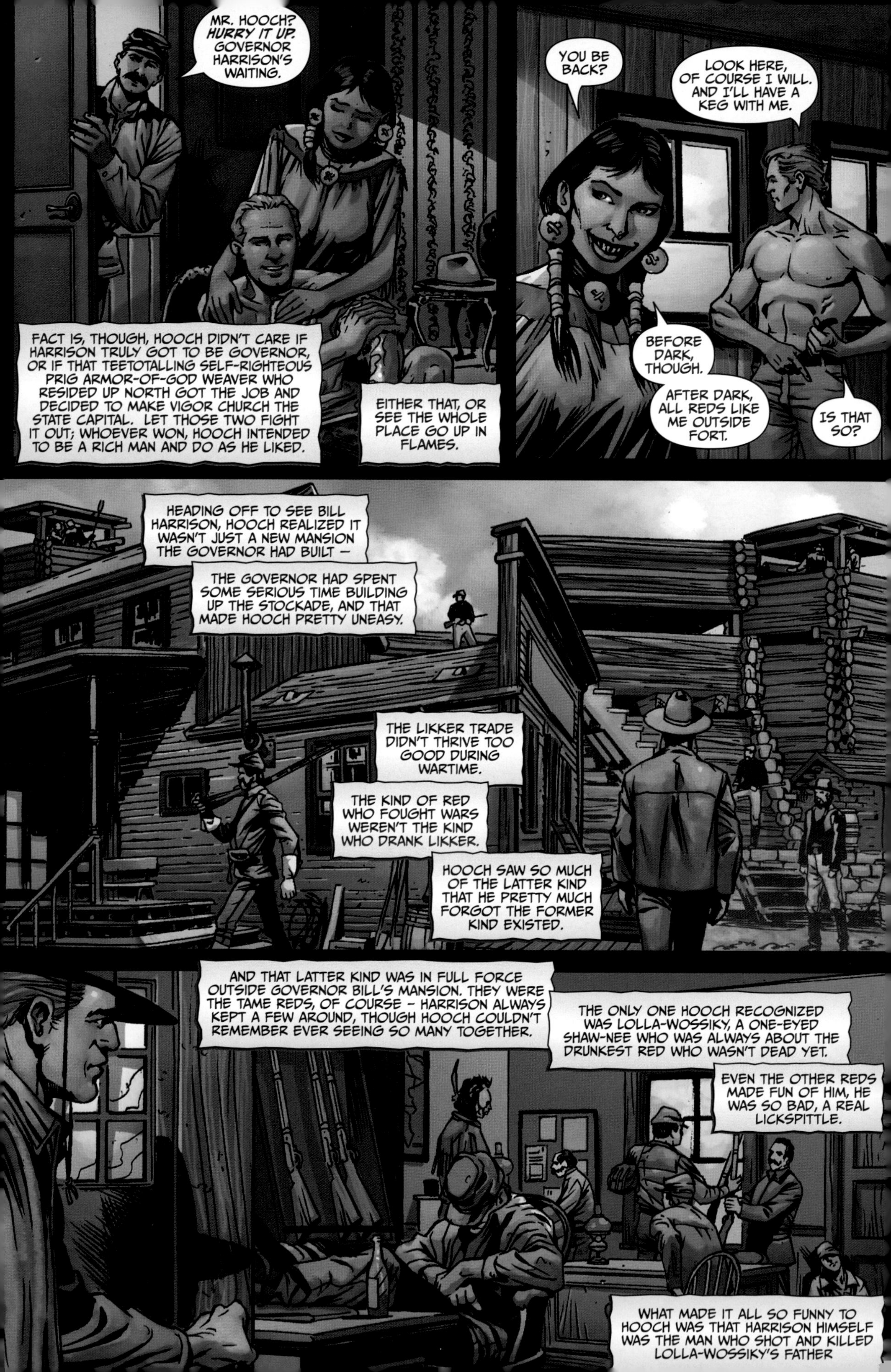

MR. HOOCH? *HURRY IT UP.* GOVERNOR HARRISON'S WAITING.
FACT IS, THOUGH, HOOCH DIDN'T CARE IF HARRISON TRULY GOT TO BE GOVERNOR, OR IF THAT TEETOTALLING SELF-RIGHTEOUS PRIG ARMOR-OF-GOD WEAVER WHO RESIDED UP NORTH GOT THE JOB AND DECIDED TO MAKE VIGOR CHURCH THE STATE CAPITAL. LET THOSE TWO FIGHT IT OUT; WHOEVER WON, HOOCH INTENDED TO BE A RICH MAN AND DO AS HE LIKED.
EITHER THAT, OR SEE THE WHOLE PLACE GO UP IN FLAMES.
YOU BE BACK?
LOOK HERE, OF COURSE I WILL. AND I'LL HAVE A KEG WITH ME.
BEFORE DARK, THOUGH.
AFTER DARK, ALL REDS LIKE ME OUTSIDE FORT.
IS THAT SO?
HEADING OFF TO SEE BILL HARRISON, HOOCH REALIZED IT WASN'T JUST A NEW MANSION THE GOVERNOR HAD BUILT –
THE GOVERNOR HAD SPENT SOME SERIOUS TIME BUILDING UP THE STOCKADE, AND THAT MADE HOOCH PRETTY UNEASY.
THE LIKKER TRADE DIDN'T THRIVE TOO GOOD DURING WARTIME.
THE KIND OF RED WHO FOUGHT WARS WEREN'T THE KIND WHO DRANK LIKKER.
HOOCH SAW SO MUCH OF THE LATTER KIND THAT HE PRETTY MUCH FORGOT THE FORMER KIND EXISTED.
AND THAT LATTER KIND WAS IN FULL FORCE OUTSIDE GOVERNOR BILL'S MANSION. THEY WERE THE TAME REDS, OF COURSE – HARRISON ALWAYS KEPT A FEW AROUND, THOUGH HOOCH COULDN'T REMEMBER EVER SEEING SO MANY TOGETHER.
THE ONLY ONE HOOCH RECOGNIZED WAS LOLLA-WOSSIKY, A ONE-EYED SHAW-NEE WHO WAS ALWAYS ABOUT THE DRUNKEST RED WHO WASN'T DEAD YET.
EVEN THE OTHER REDS MADE FUN OF HIM, HE WAS SO BAD, A REAL LICKSPITTLE.
WHAT MADE IT ALL SO FUNNY TO HOOCH WAS THAT HARRISON HIMSELF WAS THE MAN WHO SHOT AND KILLED LOLLA-WOSSIKY'S FATHER

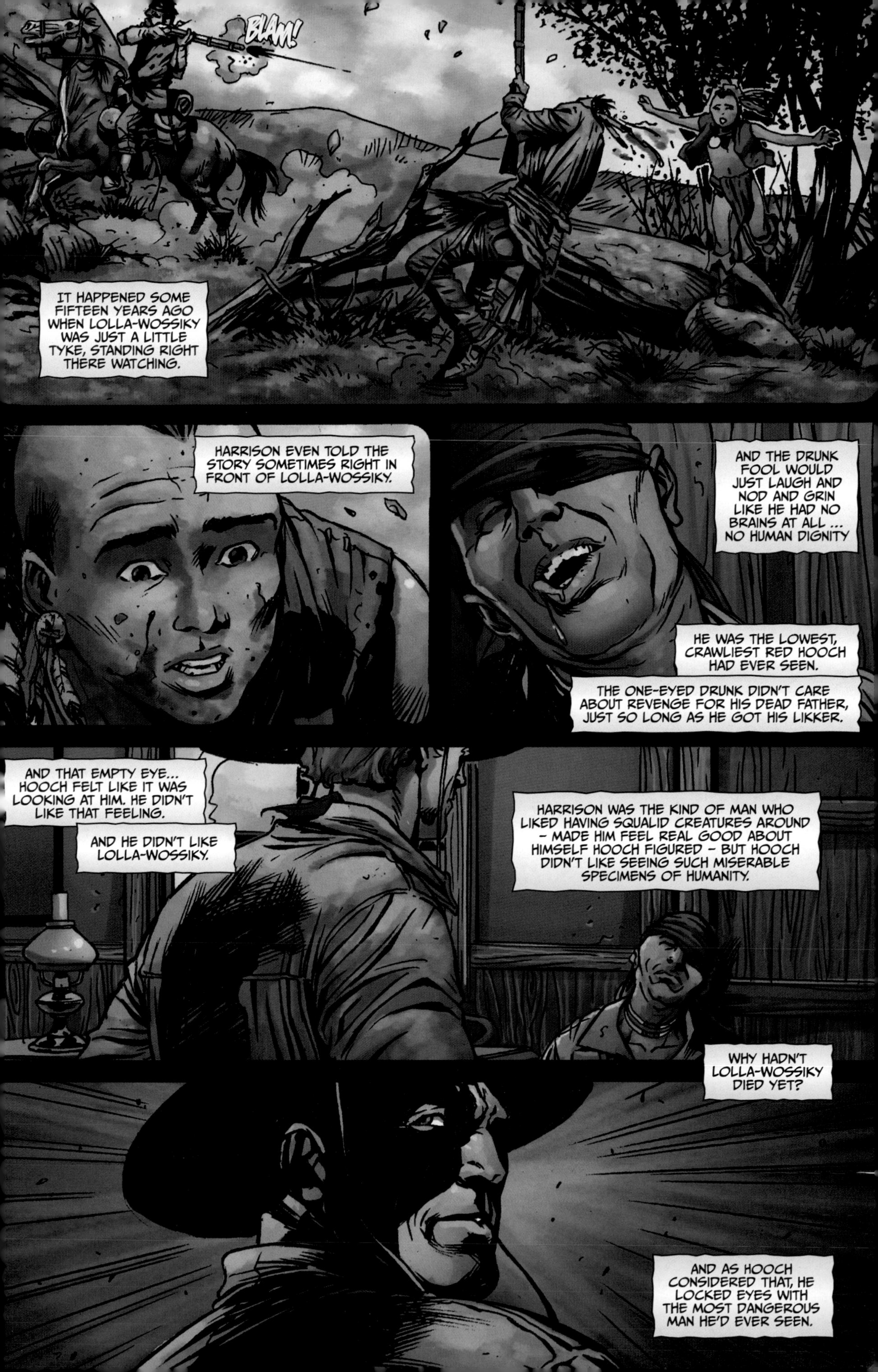
BLAM!
IT HAPPENED SOME FIFTEEN YEARS AGO WHEN LOLLA-WOSSIKY WAS JUST A LITTLE TYKE, STANDING RIGHT THERE WATCHING.
HARRISON EVEN TOLD THE STORY SOMETIMES RIGHT IN FRONT OF LOLLA-WOSSIKY.
AND THE DRUNK FOOL WOULD JUST LAUGH AND NOD AND GRIN LIKE HE HAD NO BRAINS AT ALL ... NO HUMAN DIGNITY
HE WAS THE LOWEST, CRAWLIEST RED HOOCH HAD EVER SEEN.
THE ONE-EYED DRUNK DIDN'T CARE ABOUT REVENGE FOR HIS DEAD FATHER, JUST SO LONG AS HE GOT HIS LIKKER.
AND THAT EMPTY EYE... HOOCH FELT LIKE IT WAS LOOKING AT HIM. HE DIDN'T LIKE THAT FEELING.
AND HE DIDN'T LIKE LOLLA-WOSSIKY.
HARRISON WAS THE KIND OF MAN WHO LIKED HAVING SQUALID CREATURES AROUND – MADE HIM FEEL REAL GOOD ABOUT HIMSELF HOOCH FIGURED – BUT HOOCH DIDN'T LIKE SEEING SUCH MISERABLE SPECIMENS OF HUMANITY.
WHY HADN'T LOLLA-WOSSIKY DIED YET?
AND AS HOOCH CONSIDERED THAT, HE LOCKED EYES WITH THE MOST DANGEROUS MAN HE'D EVER SEEN.

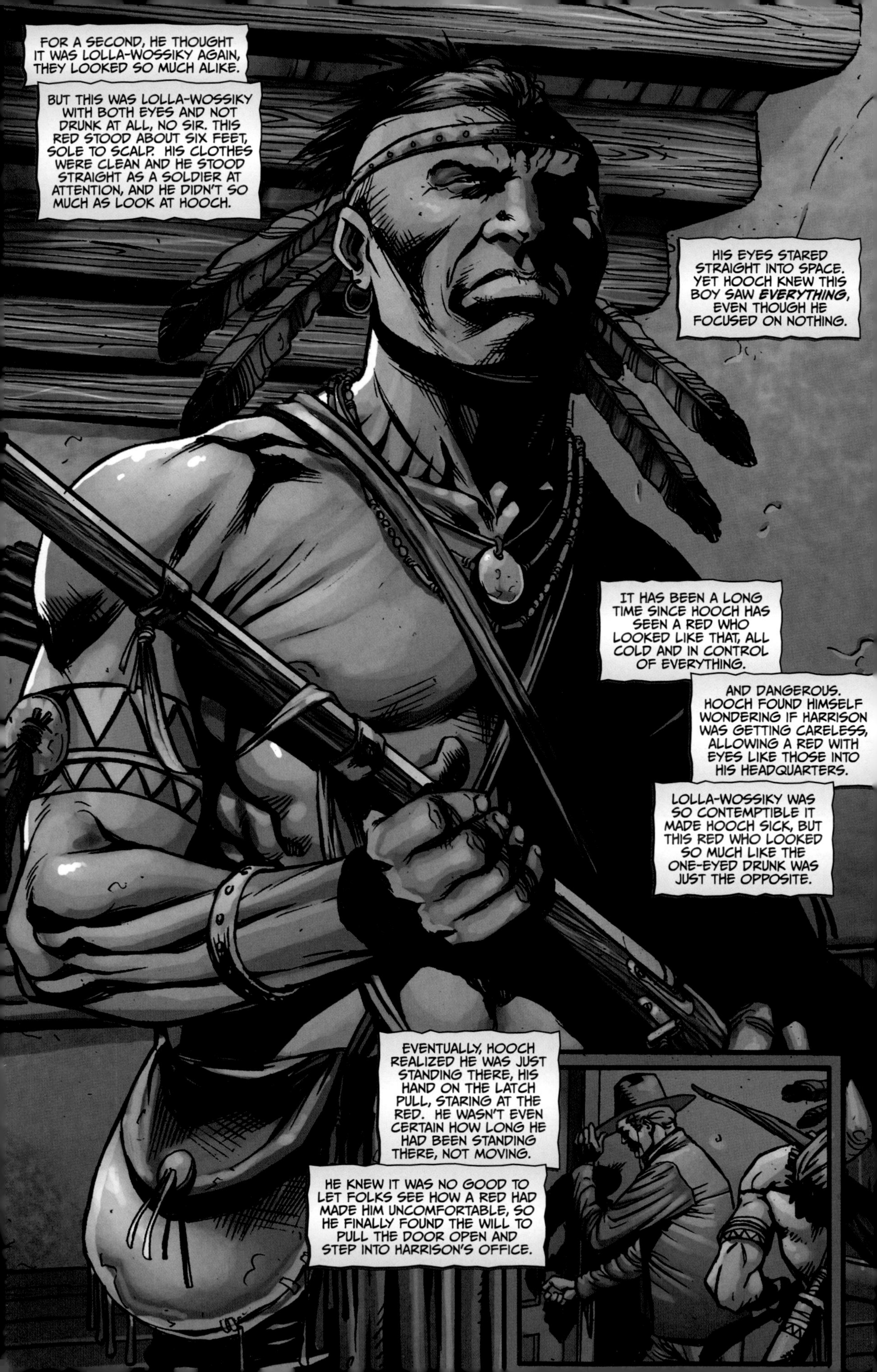
FOR A SECOND, HE THOUGHT IT WAS LOLLA-WOSSIKY AGAIN, THEY LOOKED SO MUCH ALIKE.
BUT THIS WAS LOLLA-WOSSIKY WITH BOTH EYES AND NOT DRUNK AT ALL, NO SIR. THIS RED STOOD ABOUT SIX FEET, SOLE TO SCALP. HIS CLOTHES WERE CLEAN AND HE STOOD STRAIGHT AS A SOLDIER AT ATTENTION, AND HE DIDN'T SO MUCH AS LOOK AT HOOCH.
HIS EYES STARED STRAIGHT INTO SPACE. YET HOOCH KNEW THIS BOY SAW ***EVERYTHING***, EVEN THOUGH HE FOCUSED ON NOTHING.
IT HAS BEEN A LONG TIME SINCE HOOCH HAS SEEN A RED WHO LOOKED LIKE THAT, ALL COLD AND IN CONTROL OF EVERYTHING.
AND DANGEROUS. HOOCH FOUND HIMSELF WONDERING IF HARRISON WAS GETTING CARELESS, ALLOWING A RED WITH EYES LIKE THOSE INTO HIS HEADQUARTERS.
LOLLA-WOSSIKY WAS SO CONTEMPTIBLE IT MADE HOOCH SICK, BUT THIS RED WHO LOOKED SO MUCH LIKE THE ONE-EYED DRUNK WAS JUST THE OPPOSITE.
EVENTUALLY, HOOCH REALIZED HE WAS JUST STANDING THERE, HIS HAND ON THE LATCH PULL, STARING AT THE RED. HE WASN'T EVEN CERTAIN HOW LONG HE HAD BEEN STANDING THERE, NOT MOVING.
HE KNEW IT WAS NO GOOD TO LET FOLKS SEE HOW A RED HAD MADE HIM UNCOMFORTABLE, SO HE FINALLY FOUND THE WILL TO PULL THE DOOR OPEN AND STEP INTO HARRISON'S OFFICE.

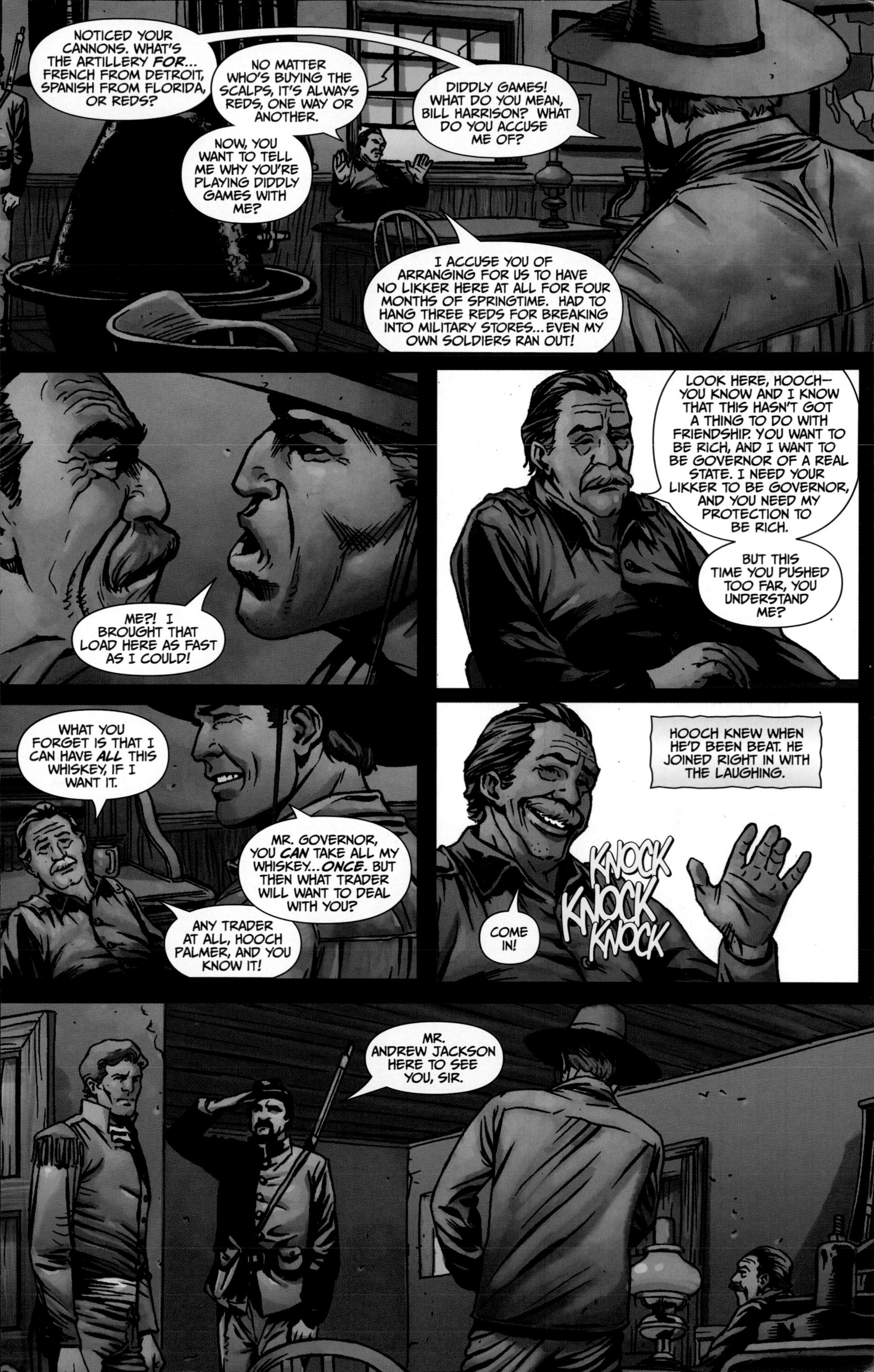
NOTICED YOUR CANNONS. WHAT'S THE ARTILLERY *FOR*... FRENCH FROM DETROIT, SPANISH FROM FLORIDA, OR REDS?
NO MATTER WHO'S BUYING THE SCALPS, IT'S ALWAYS REDS, ONE WAY OR ANOTHER.
NOW, YOU WANT TO TELL ME WHY YOU'RE PLAYING DIDDLY GAMES WITH ME?
DIDDLY GAMES! WHAT DO YOU MEAN, BILL HARRISON? WHAT DO YOU ACCUSE ME OF?
I ACCUSE YOU OF ARRANGING FOR US TO HAVE NO LIKKER HERE AT ALL FOR FOUR MONTHS OF SPRINGTIME. HAD TO HANG THREE REDS FOR BREAKING INTO MILITARY STORES... EVEN MY OWN SOLDIERS RAN OUT!
ME?! I BROUGHT THAT LOAD HERE AS FAST AS I COULD!
LOOK HERE, HOOCH— YOU KNOW AND I KNOW THAT THIS HASN'T GOT A THING TO DO WITH FRIENDSHIP. YOU WANT TO BE RICH, AND I WANT TO BE GOVERNOR OF A REAL STATE. I NEED YOUR LIKKER TO BE GOVERNOR, AND YOU NEED MY PROTECTION TO BE RICH.
BUT THIS TIME YOU PUSHED TOO FAR, YOU UNDERSTAND ME?
WHAT YOU FORGET IS THAT I CAN HAVE *ALL* THIS WHISKEY, IF I WANT IT.
MR. GOVERNOR, YOU ***CAN*** TAKE ALL MY WHISKEY... ***ONCE.*** BUT THEN WHAT TRADER WILL WANT TO DEAL WITH YOU?
ANY TRADER AT ALL, HOOCH PALMER, AND YOU KNOW IT!
HOOCH KNEW WHEN HE'D BEEN BEAT. HE JOINED RIGHT IN WITH THE LAUGHING.
KNOCK
KNOCK
KNOCK
COME IN!
MR. ANDREW JACKSON HERE TO SEE YOU, SIR.

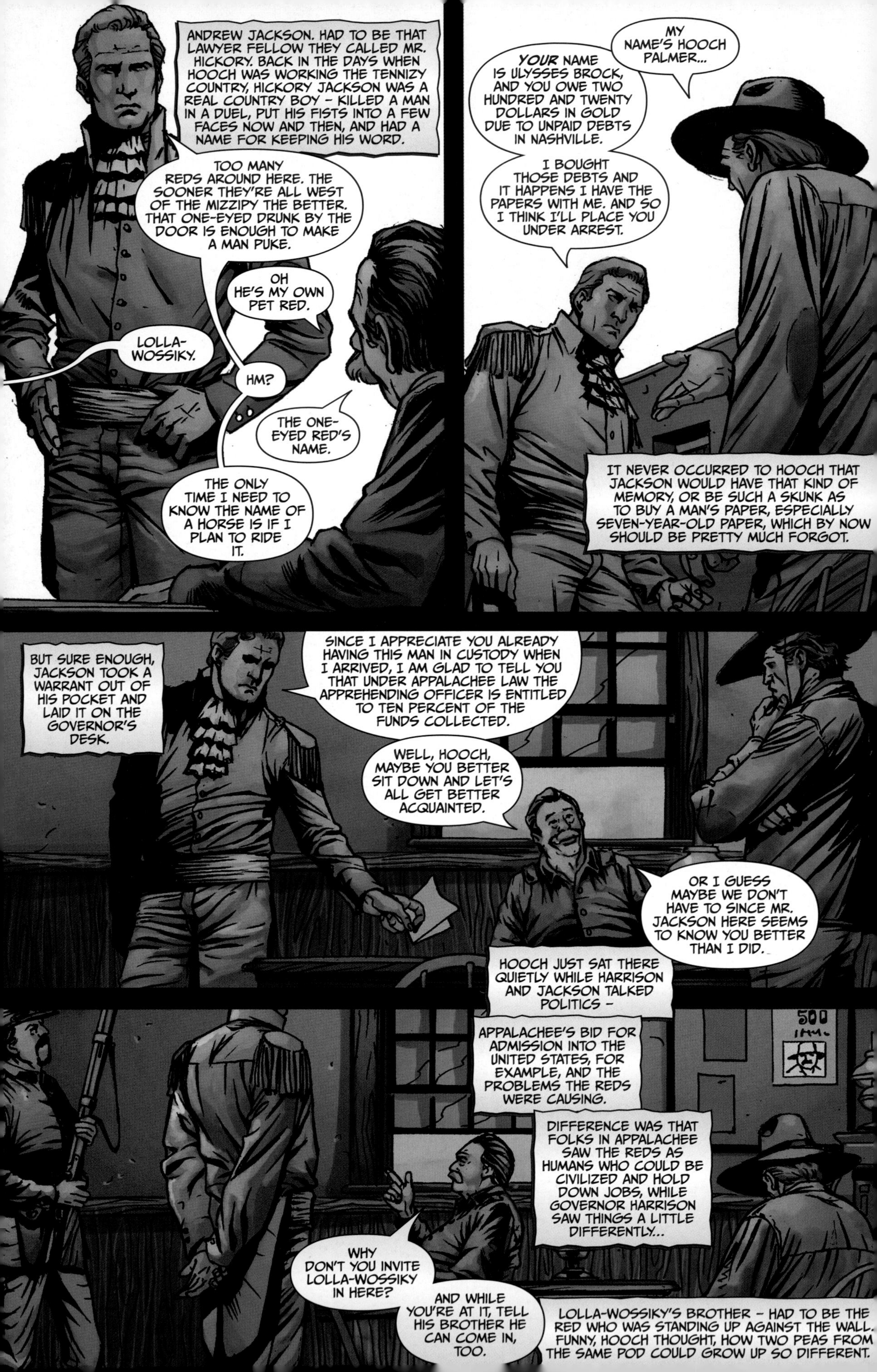

ANDREW JACKSON. HAD TO BE THAT LAWYER FELLOW THEY CALLED MR. HICKORY. BACK IN THE DAYS WHEN HOOCH WAS WORKING THE TENNIZY COUNTRY, HICKORY JACKSON WAS A REAL COUNTRY BOY - KILLED A MAN IN A DUEL, PUT HIS FISTS INTO A FEW FACES NOW AND THEN, AND HAD A NAME FOR KEEPING HIS WORD.
TOO MANY REDS AROUND HERE. THE SOONER THEY'RE ALL WEST OF THE MIZZIPY THE BETTER. THAT ONE-EYED DRUNK BY THE DOOR IS ENOUGH TO MAKE A MAN PUKE.
OH HE'S MY OWN PET RED.
LOLLA-WOSSIKY.
HM?
THE ONE-EYED RED'S NAME.
THE ONLY TIME I NEED TO KNOW THE NAME OF A HORSE IS IF I PLAN TO RIDE IT.
MY NAME'S HOOCH PALMER...
YOUR NAME IS ULYSSES BROCK, AND YOU OWE TWO HUNDRED AND TWENTY DOLLARS IN GOLD DUE TO UNPAID DEBTS IN NASHVILLE.
I BOUGHT THOSE DEBTS AND IT HAPPENS I HAVE THE PAPERS WITH ME. AND SO I THINK I'LL PLACE YOU UNDER ARREST.
IT NEVER OCCURRED TO HOOCH THAT JACKSON WOULD HAVE THAT KIND OF MEMORY, OR BE SUCH A SKUNK AS TO BUY A MAN'S PAPER, ESPECIALLY SEVEN-YEAR-OLD PAPER, WHICH BY NOW SHOULD BE PRETTY MUCH FORGOT.
BUT SURE ENOUGH, JACKSON TOOK A WARRANT OUT OF HIS POCKET AND LAID IT ON THE GOVERNOR'S DESK.
SINCE I APPRECIATE YOU ALREADY HAVING THIS MAN IN CUSTODY WHEN I ARRIVED, I AM GLAD TO TELL YOU THAT UNDER APPALACHEE LAW THE APPREHENDING OFFICER IS ENTITLED TO TEN PERCENT OF THE FUNDS COLLECTED.
WELL, HOOCH, MAYBE YOU BETTER SIT DOWN AND LET'S ALL GET BETTER ACQUAINTED.
OR I GUESS MAYBE WE DON'T HAVE TO SINCE MR. JACKSON HERE SEEMS TO KNOW YOU BETTER THAN I DID.
HOOCH JUST SAT THERE QUIETLY WHILE HARRISON AND JACKSON TALKED POLITICS -
APPALACHEE'S BID FOR ADMISSION INTO THE UNITED STATES, FOR EXAMPLE, AND THE PROBLEMS THE REDS WERE CAUSING.
500
DIFFERENCE WAS THAT FOLKS IN APPALACHEE SAW THE REDS AS HUMANS WHO COULD BE CIVILIZED AND HOLD DOWN JOBS, WHILE GOVERNOR HARRISON SAW THINGS A LITTLE DIFFERENTLY...
WHY DON'T YOU INVITE LOLLA-WOSSIKY IN HERE?
AND WHILE YOU'RE AT IT, TELL HIS BROTHER HE CAN COME IN, TOO.
LOLLA-WOSSIKY'S BROTHER - HAD TO BE THE RED WHO WAS STANDING UP AGAINST THE WALL. FUNNY, HOOCH THOUGHT, HOW TWO PEAS FROM THE SAME POD COULD GROW UP SO DIFFERENT.

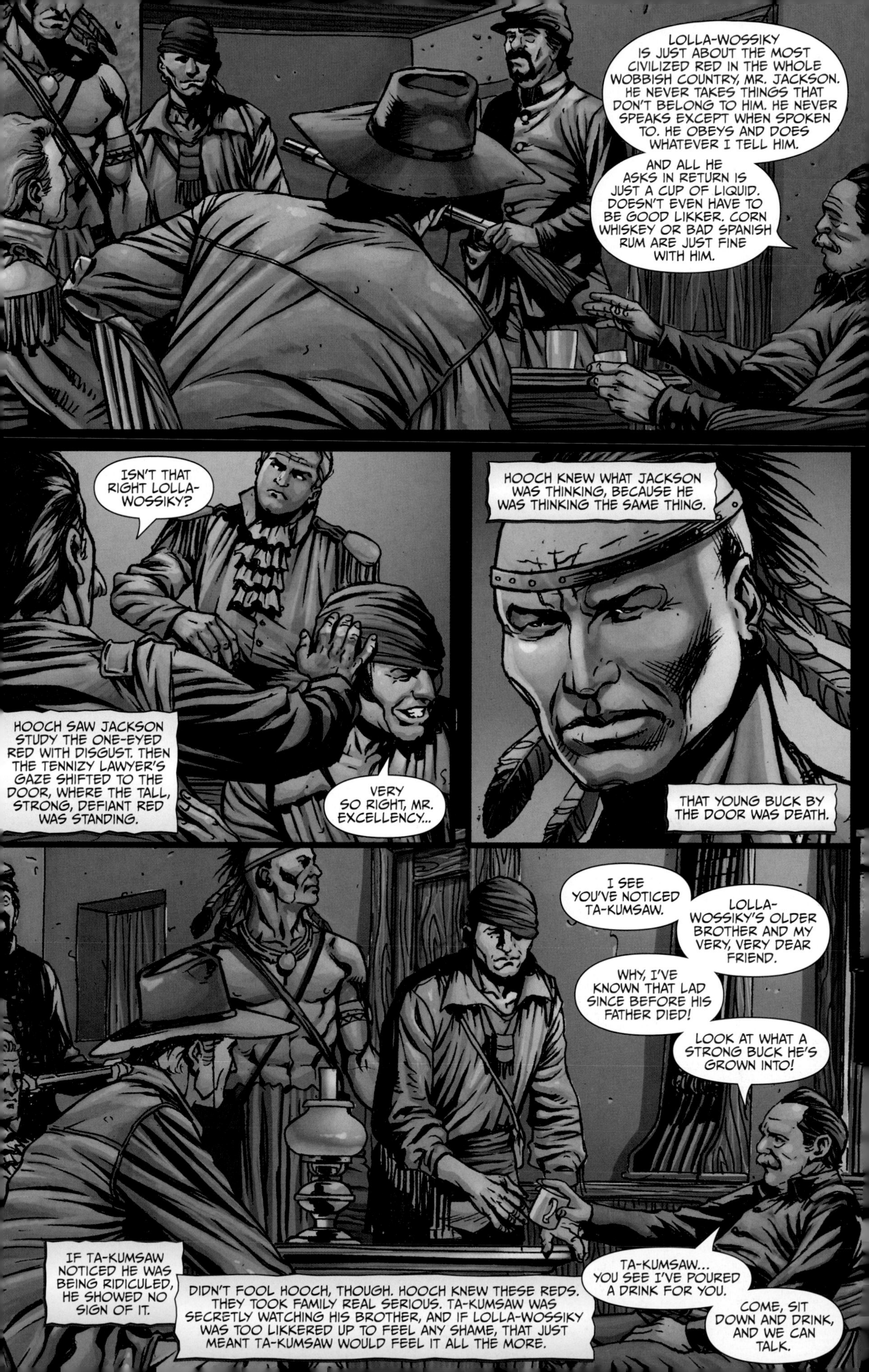
LOLLA-WOSSIKY IS JUST ABOUT THE MOST CIVILIZED RED IN THE WHOLE WOBBISH COUNTRY, MR. JACKSON. HE NEVER TAKES THINGS THAT DON'T BELONG TO HIM. HE NEVER SPEAKS EXCEPT WHEN SPOKEN TO. HE OBEYS AND DOES WHATEVER I TELL HIM.
AND ALL HE ASKS IN RETURN IS JUST A CUP OF LIQUID. DOESN'T EVEN HAVE TO BE GOOD LIKKER. CORN WHISKEY OR BAD SPANISH RUM ARE JUST FINE WITH HIM.
ISN'T THAT RIGHT LOLLA-WOSSIKY?
HOOCH SAW JACKSON STUDY THE ONE-EYED RED WITH DISGUST. THEN THE TENNIZY LAWYER'S GAZE SHIFTED TO THE DOOR, WHERE THE TALL, STRONG, DEFIANT RED WAS STANDING.
VERY SO RIGHT, MR. EXCELLENCY...
HOOCH KNEW WHAT JACKSON WAS THINKING, BECAUSE HE WAS THINKING THE SAME THING.
THAT YOUNG BUCK BY THE DOOR WAS DEATH.
I SEE YOU'VE NOTICED TA-KUMSAW.
LOLLA-WOSSIKY'S OLDER BROTHER AND MY VERY, VERY DEAR FRIEND.
WHY, I'VE KNOWN THAT LAD SINCE BEFORE HIS FATHER DIED!
LOOK AT WHAT A STRONG BUCK HE'S GROWN INTO!
IF TA-KUMSAW NOTICED HE WAS BEING RIDICULED, HE SHOWED NO SIGN OF IT.
DIDN'T FOOL HOOCH, THOUGH. HOOCH KNEW THESE REDS. THEY TOOK FAMILY REAL SERIOUS. TA-KUMSAW WAS SECRETLY WATCHING HIS BROTHER, AND IF LOLLA-WOSSIKY WAS TOO LIKKERED UP TO FEEL ANY SHAME, THAT JUST MEANT TA-KUMSAW WOULD FEEL IT ALL THE MORE.
TA-KUMSAW... YOU SEE I'VE POURED A DRINK FOR YOU.
COME, SIT DOWN AND DRINK, AND WE CAN TALK.

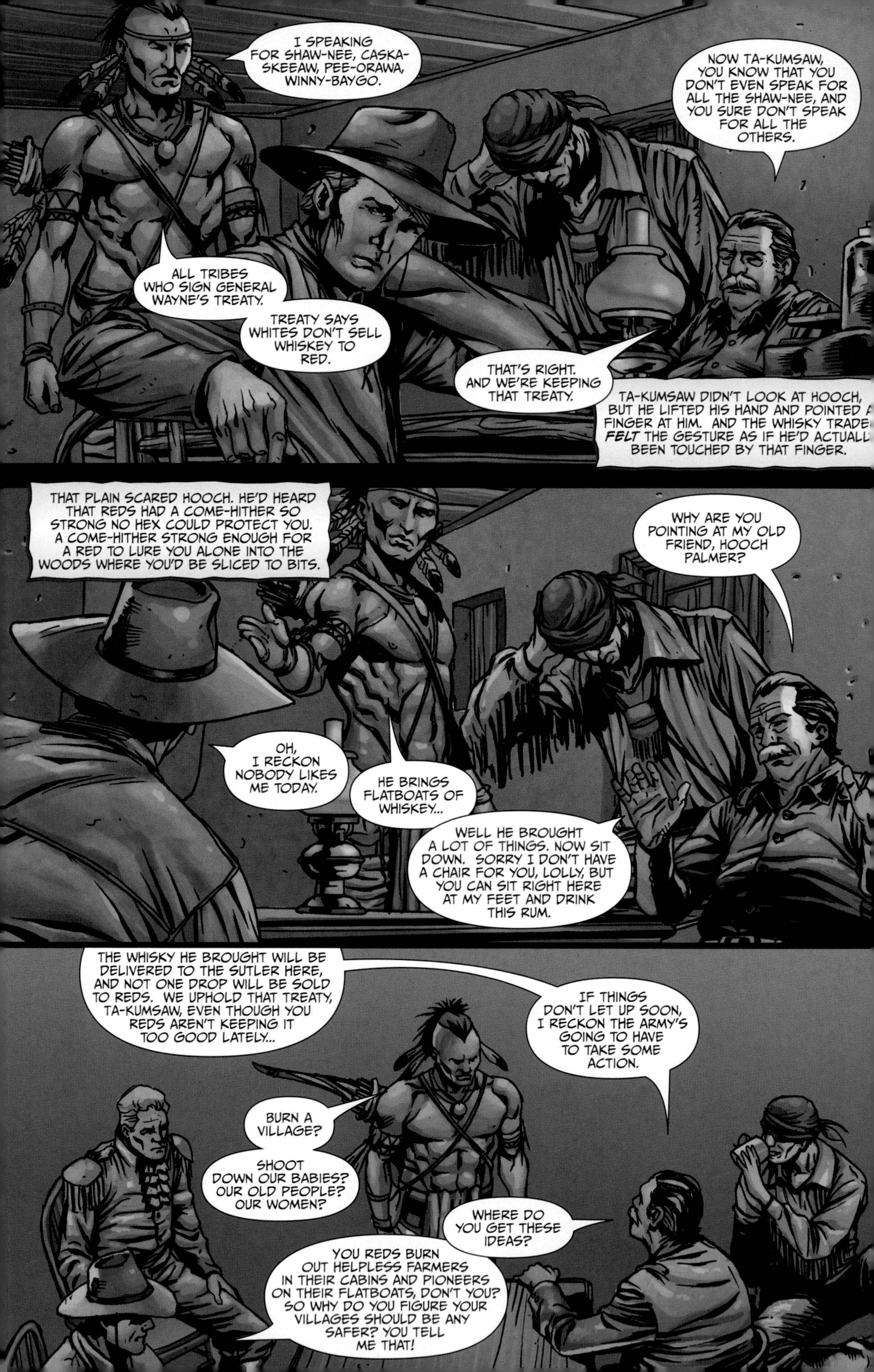

I SPEAKING FOR SHAW-NEE, CASKA-SKEEAW, PEE-ORAWA, WINNY-BAYGO.
NOW TA-KUMSAW, YOU KNOW THAT YOU DON'T EVEN SPEAK FOR ALL THE SHAW-NEE, AND YOU SURE DON'T SPEAK FOR ALL THE OTHERS.
ALL TRIBES WHO SIGN GENERAL WAYNE'S TREATY.
TREATY SAYS WHITES DON'T SELL WHISKEY TO RED.
THAT'S RIGHT. AND WE'RE KEEPING THAT TREATY.
TA-KUMSAW DIDN'T LOOK AT HOOCH, BUT HE LIFTED HIS HAND AND POINTED A FINGER AT HIM. AND THE WHISKY TRADE FELT THE GESTURE AS IF HE'D ACTUALL BEEN TOUCHED BY THAT FINGER.
THAT PLAIN SCARED HOOCH. HE'D HEARD THAT REDS HAD A COME-HITHER SO STRONG NO HEX COULD PROTECT YOU. A COME-HITHER STRONG ENOUGH FOR A RED TO LURE YOU ALONE INTO THE WOODS WHERE YOU'D BE SLICED TO BITS.
WHY ARE YOU POINTING AT MY OLD FRIEND, HOOCH PALMER?
OH, I RECKON NOBODY LIKES ME TODAY.
HE BRINGS FLATBOATS OF WHISKEY...
WELL HE BROUGHT A LOT OF THINGS. NOW SIT DOWN. SORRY I DON'T HAVE A CHAIR FOR YOU, LOLLY, BUT YOU CAN SIT RIGHT HERE AT MY FEET AND DRINK THIS RUM.
THE WHISKY HE BROUGHT WILL BE DELIVERED TO THE SUTLER HERE, AND NOT ONE DROP WILL BE SOLD TO REDS. WE UPHOLD THAT TREATY, TA-KUMSAW, EVEN THOUGH YOU REDS AREN'T KEEPING IT TOO GOOD LATELY...
IF THINGS DON'T LET UP SOON, I RECKON THE ARMY'S GOING TO HAVE TO TAKE SOME ACTION.
BURN A VILLAGE?
SHOOT DOWN OUR BABIES? OUR OLD PEOPLE? OUR WOMEN?
WHERE DO YOU GET THESE IDEAS?
YOU REDS BURN OUT HELPLESS FARMERS IN THEIR CABINS AND PIONEERS ON THEIR FLATBOATS, DON'T YOU? SO WHY DO YOU FIGURE YOUR VILLAGES SHOULD BE ANY SAFER? YOU TELL ME THAT!

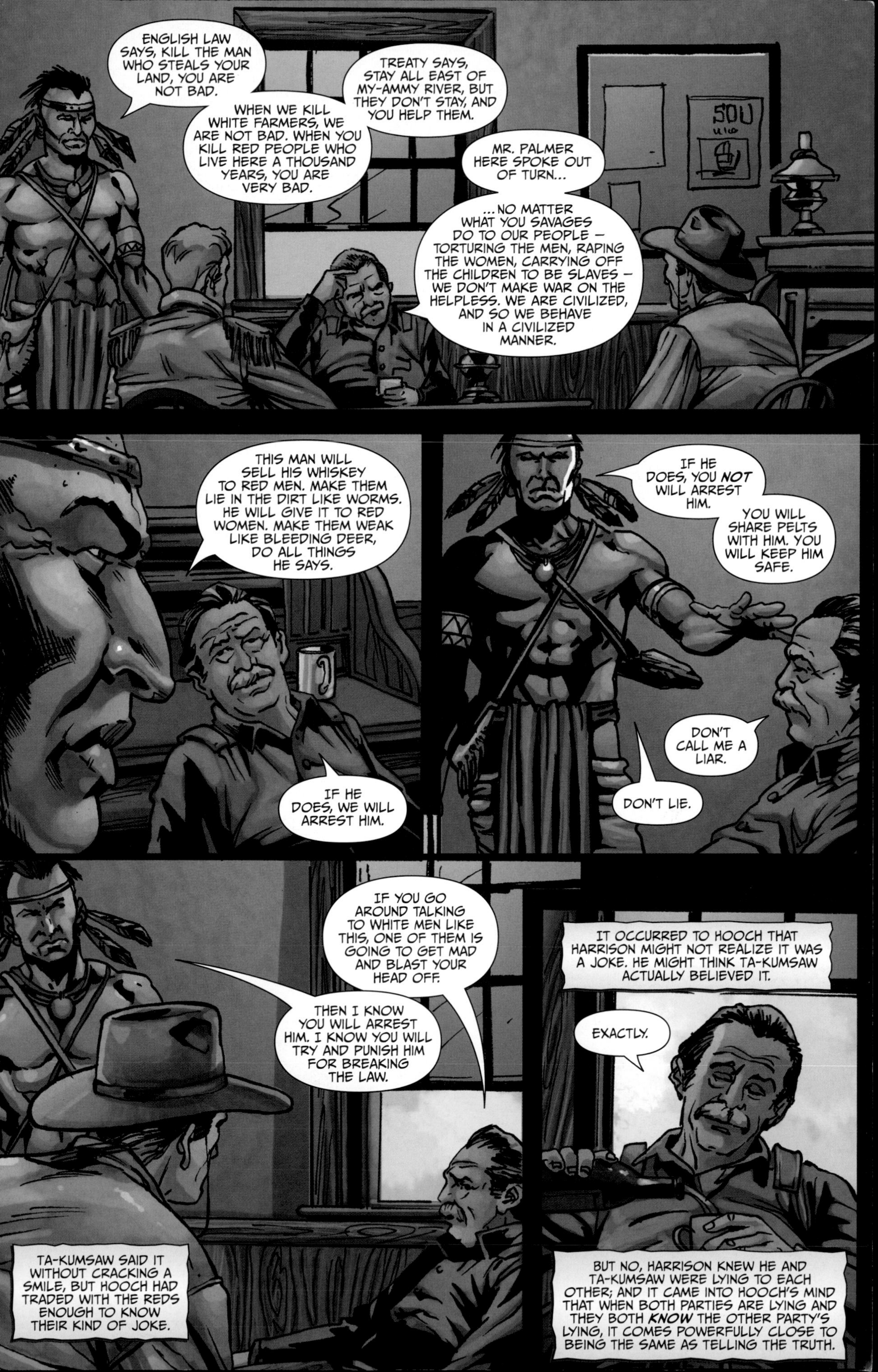
ENGLISH LAW SAYS, KILL THE MAN WHO STEALS YOUR LAND, YOU ARE NOT BAD.
WHEN WE KILL WHITE FARMERS, WE ARE NOT BAD. WHEN YOU KILL RED PEOPLE WHO LIVE HERE A THOUSAND YEARS, YOU ARE VERY BAD.
TREATY SAYS, STAY ALL EAST OF MY-AMMY RIVER, BUT THEY DON'T STAY, AND YOU HELP THEM.
MR. PALMER HERE SPOKE OUT OF TURN...
...NO MATTER WHAT YOU SAVAGES DO TO OUR PEOPLE – TORTURING THE MEN, RAPING THE WOMEN, CARRYING OFF THE CHILDREN TO BE SLAVES – WE DON'T MAKE WAR ON THE HELPLESS. WE ARE CIVILIZED, AND SO WE BEHAVE IN A CIVILIZED MANNER.
THIS MAN WILL SELL HIS WHISKEY TO RED MEN. MAKE THEM LIE IN THE DIRT LIKE WORMS. HE WILL GIVE IT TO RED WOMEN. MAKE THEM WEAK LIKE BLEEDING DEER, DO ALL THINGS HE SAYS.
IF HE DOES, WE WILL ARREST HIM.
IF HE DOES, YOU ***NOT*** WILL ARREST HIM.
YOU WILL SHARE PELTS WITH HIM. YOU WILL KEEP HIM SAFE.
DON'T CALL ME A LIAR.
DON'T LIE.
IF YOU GO AROUND TALKING TO WHITE MEN LIKE THIS, ONE OF THEM IS GOING TO GET MAD AND BLAST YOUR HEAD OFF.
THEN I KNOW YOU WILL ARREST HIM. I KNOW YOU WILL TRY AND PUNISH HIM FOR BREAKING THE LAW.
TA-KUMSAW SAID IT WITHOUT CRACKING A SMILE, BUT HOOCH HAD TRADED WITH THE REDS ENOUGH TO KNOW THEIR KIND OF JOKE.
IT OCCURRED TO HOOCH THAT HARRISON MIGHT NOT REALIZE IT WAS A JOKE. HE MIGHT THINK TA-KUMSAW ACTUALLY BELIEVED IT.
EXACTLY.
BUT NO, HARRISON KNEW HE AND TA-KUMSAW WERE LYING TO EACH OTHER; AND IT CAME INTO HOOCH'S MIND THAT WHEN BOTH PARTIES ARE LYING AND THEY BOTH ***KNOW*** THE OTHER PARTY'S LYING, IT COMES POWERFULLY CLOSE TO BEING THE SAME AS TELLING THE TRUTH.

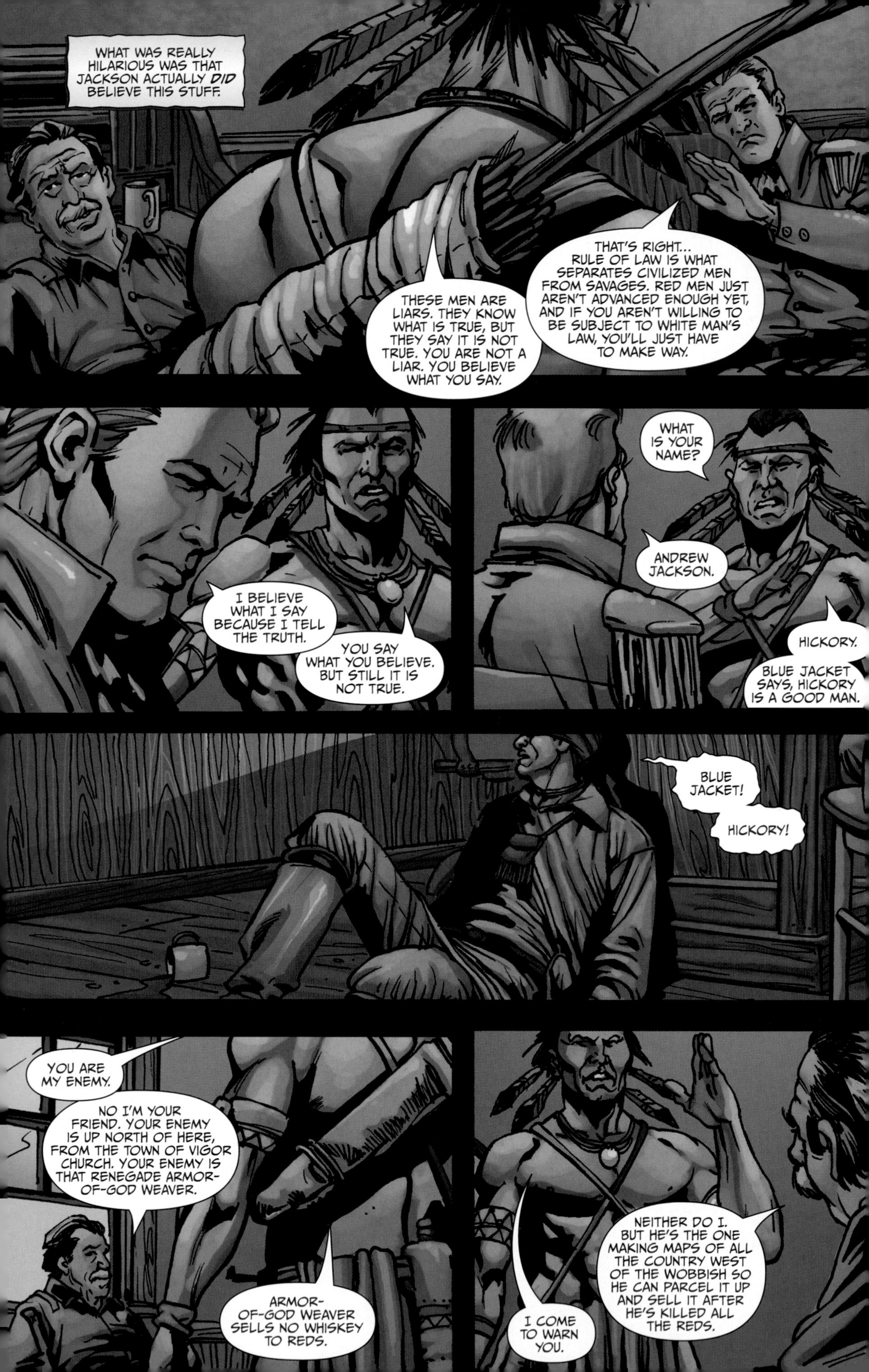

WHAT WAS REALLY HILARIOUS WAS THAT JACKSON ACTUALLY *DID* BELIEVE THIS STUFF.
THESE MEN ARE LIARS. THEY KNOW WHAT IS TRUE, BUT THEY SAY IT IS NOT TRUE. YOU ARE NOT A LIAR. YOU BELIEVE WHAT YOU SAY.
THAT'S RIGHT... RULE OF LAW IS WHAT SEPARATES CIVILIZED MEN FROM SAVAGES. RED MEN JUST AREN'T ADVANCED ENOUGH YET, AND IF YOU AREN'T WILLING TO BE SUBJECT TO WHITE MAN'S LAW, YOU'LL JUST HAVE TO MAKE WAY.
I BELIEVE WHAT I SAY BECAUSE I TELL THE TRUTH.
YOU SAY WHAT YOU BELIEVE. BUT STILL IT IS NOT TRUE.
WHAT IS YOUR NAME?
ANDREW JACKSON.
HICKORY.
BLUE JACKET SAYS, HICKORY IS A GOOD MAN.
BLUE JACKET!
HICKORY!
YOU ARE MY ENEMY.
NO I'M YOUR FRIEND. YOUR ENEMY IS UP NORTH OF HERE, FROM THE TOWN OF VIGOR CHURCH. YOUR ENEMY IS THAT RENEGADE ARMOR-OF-GOD WEAVER.
ARMOR-OF-GOD WEAVER SELLS NO WHISKEY TO REDS.
NEITHER DO I. BUT HE'S THE ONE MAKING MAPS OF ALL THE COUNTRY WEST OF THE WOBBISH SO HE CAN PARCEL IT UP AND SELL IT AFTER HE'S KILLED ALL THE REDS.
I COME TO WARN YOU.

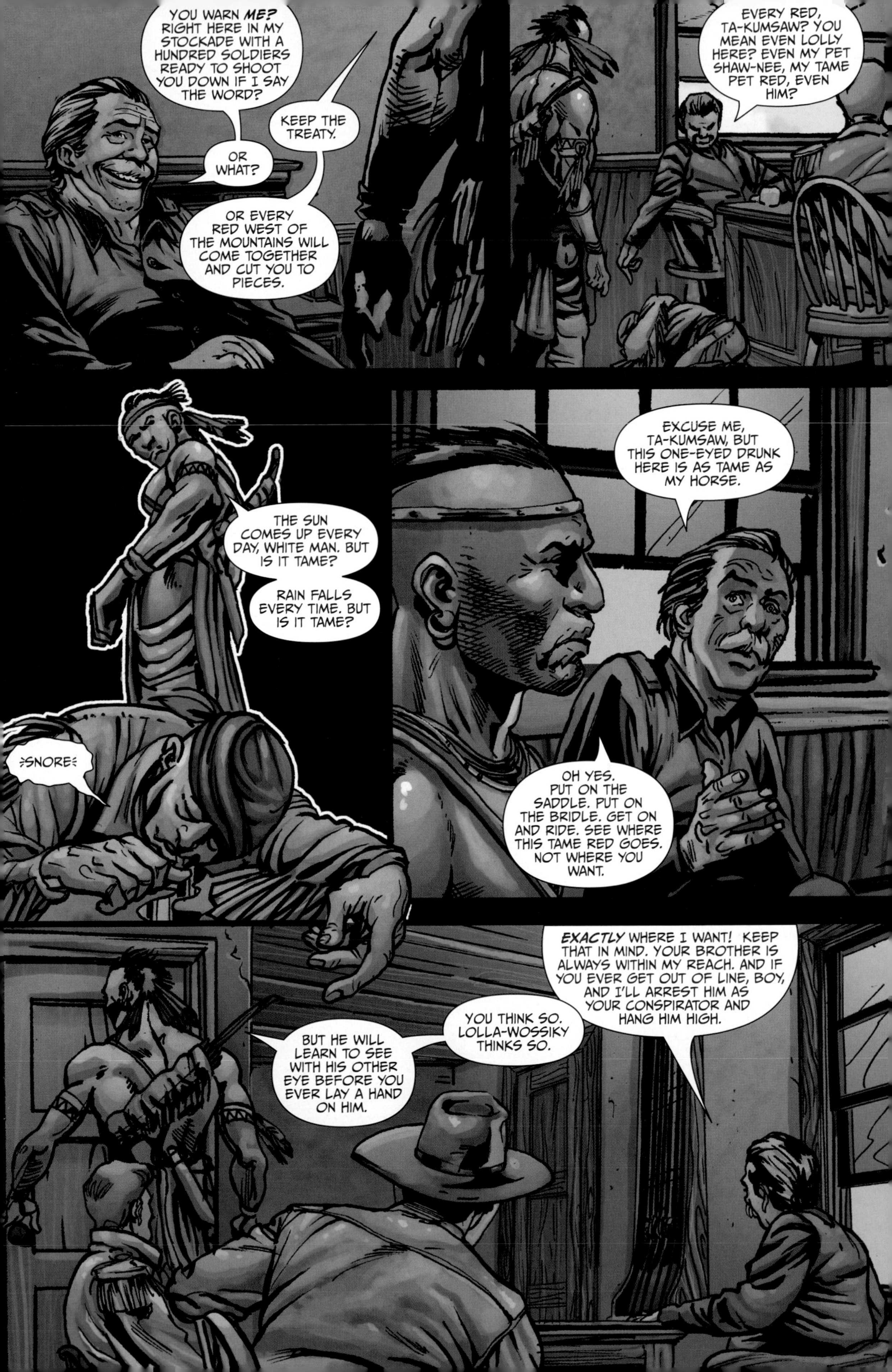
YOU WARN *ME?* RIGHT HERE IN MY STOCKADE WITH A HUNDRED SOLDIERS READY TO SHOOT YOU DOWN IF I SAY THE WORD?
OR WHAT?
KEEP THE TREATY.
OR EVERY RED WEST OF THE MOUNTAINS WILL COME TOGETHER AND CUT YOU TO PIECES.
EVERY RED, TA-KUMSAW? YOU MEAN EVEN LOLLY HERE? EVEN MY PET SHAW-NEE, MY TAME PET RED, EVEN HIM?
THE SUN COMES UP EVERY DAY, WHITE MAN. BUT IS IT TAME?
RAIN FALLS EVERY TIME. BUT IS IT TAME?
≷SNORE≶
EXCUSE ME, TA-KUMSAW, BUT THIS ONE-EYED DRUNK HERE IS AS TAME AS MY HORSE.
OH YES. PUT ON THE SADDLE. PUT ON THE BRIDLE. GET ON AND RIDE. SEE WHERE THIS TAME RED GOES. NOT WHERE YOU WANT.
EXACTLY WHERE I WANT! KEEP THAT IN MIND. YOUR BROTHER IS ALWAYS WITHIN MY REACH. AND IF YOU EVER GET OUT OF LINE, BOY, AND I'LL ARREST HIM AS YOUR CONSPIRATOR AND HANG HIM HIGH.
YOU THINK SO. LOLLA-WOSSIKY THINKS SO.
BUT HE WILL LEARN TO SEE WITH HIS OTHER EYE BEFORE YOU EVER LAY A HAND ON HIM.

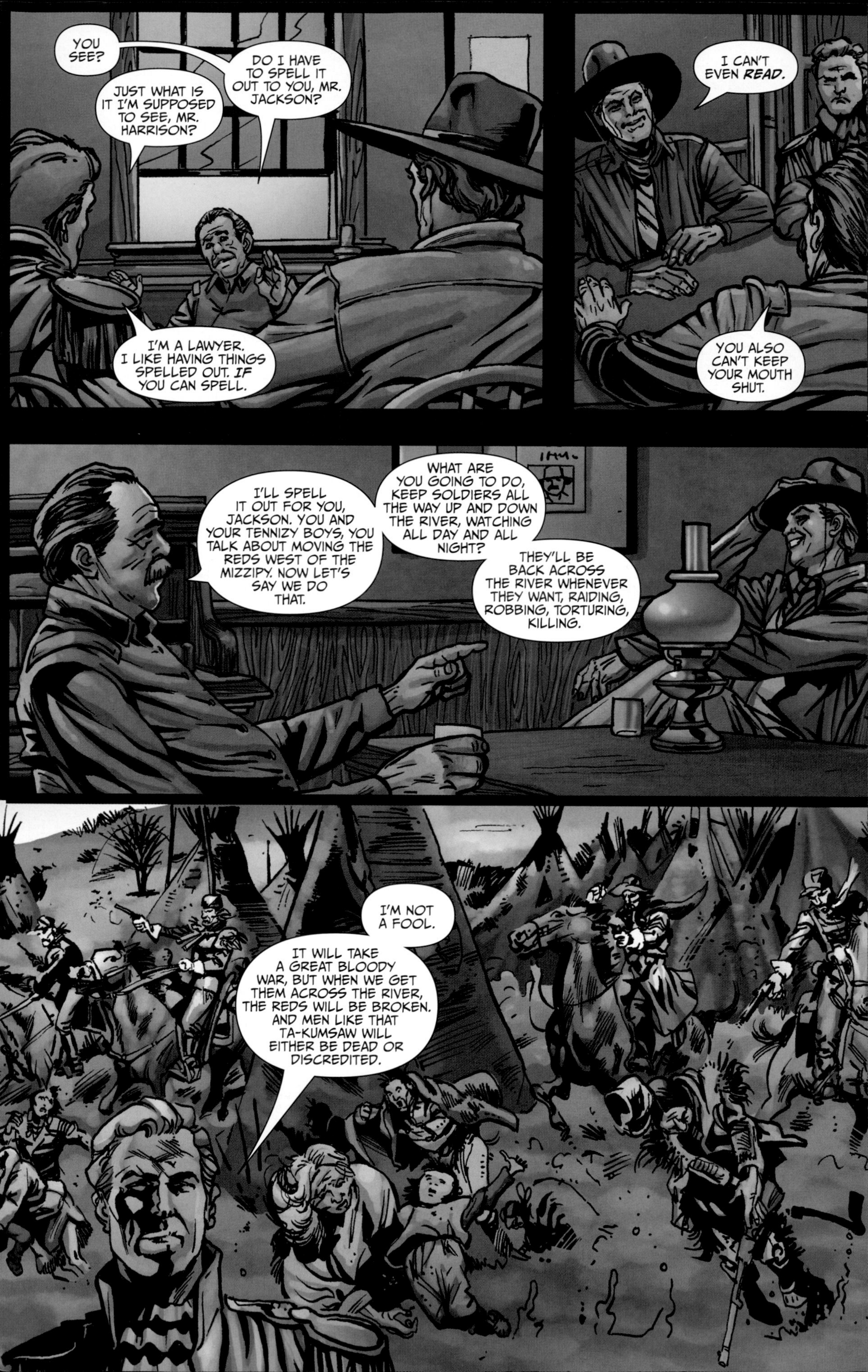
YOU SEE?
JUST WHAT IS IT I'M SUPPOSED TO SEE, MR. HARRISON?
DO I HAVE TO SPELL IT OUT TO YOU, MR. JACKSON?
I'M A LAWYER. I LIKE HAVING THINGS SPELLED OUT. *IF* YOU CAN SPELL.
I CAN'T EVEN *READ.*
YOU ALSO CAN'T KEEP YOUR MOUTH SHUT.
I'LL SPELL IT OUT FOR YOU, JACKSON. YOU AND YOUR TENNIZY BOYS, YOU TALK ABOUT MOVING THE REDS WEST OF THE MIZZIPY. NOW LET'S SAY WE DO THAT.
WHAT ARE YOU GOING TO DO, KEEP SOLDIERS ALL THE WAY UP AND DOWN THE RIVER, WATCHING ALL DAY AND ALL NIGHT?
THEY'LL BE BACK ACROSS THE RIVER WHENEVER THEY WANT, RAIDING, ROBBING, TORTURING, KILLING.
I'M NOT A FOOL.
IT WILL TAKE A GREAT BLOODY WAR, BUT WHEN WE GET THEM ACROSS THE RIVER, THE REDS WILL BE BROKEN. AND MEN LIKE THAT TA-KUMSAW WILL EITHER BE DEAD OR DISCREDITED.

YOUR WAY WILL SEE A LOT OF WHITE BOYS DEAD. AND WHITE WOMEN AND CHILDREN, TOO. BUT I HAVE A BETTER IDEA.

TWO YEARS AGO THERE WERE A THOUSAND PEE-ANKASHAW LIVING EAST OF THE MY-AMMY RIVER.

THEN THEY STARTED GETTING LIKKERED UP. THEY STOPPED WORKING, THEY STOPPED EATING, THEY GOT SO WEAK THAT THE FIRST LITTLE SICKNESS THAT CAME THROUGH HERE, IT WIPED THEM OUT.

IF THERE'S A PEE-ANKASHAW LEFT ALIVE HERE, I DON'T KNOW ABOUT IT.

SAME THING HAPPENED UP NORTH, TO THE CHIPPY-WA, ONLY IT WAS THE FRENCH TRADERS DONE IT TO THEM.

AND THE BEST THING ABOUT LIKKER IS, IT KILLS OFF THE REDS AND NOT A WHITE MAN DIES.

I RECKON I'LL HAVE TO TAKE THREE BATHS WHEN I GET HOME. EVEN THEN I STILL WON'T FEEL CLEAN.

DON'T GET HIGH AND MIGHTY WITH ME, YOU HYPOCRITE!

YOU WANT THEM ALL DEAD, *JUST LIKE I DO!* THERE'S NO DIFFERENCE BETWEEN US.

THE ASSASSIN, MR. HARRISON, *THE POISONER,* HE CAN'T SEE THE DIFFERENCE BETWEEN HIMSELF AND A SOLDIER. BUT THE SOLDIER CAN.

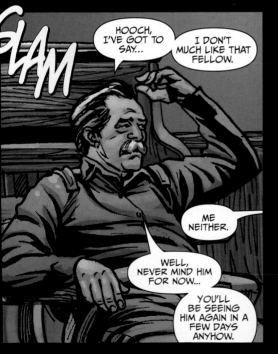

SLAM

HOOCH, I'VE GOT TO SAY...

I DON'T MUCH LIKE THAT FELLOW.

ME NEITHER.

WELL, NEVER MIND HIM FOR NOW...

YOU'LL BE SEEING HIM AGAIN IN A FEW DAYS ANYHOW.

HUH?

AT YOUR TRIAL, HOOCH.

OR DID YOU FORGET THE LITTLE MATTER ABOUT THE DEBT YOU OWE?

SEND IN CORPORAL WITHERS AND FOUR SOLDIERS AT ONCE.

WE NEED TO ESCORT MR. PALMER TO HIS NEW ROOM...

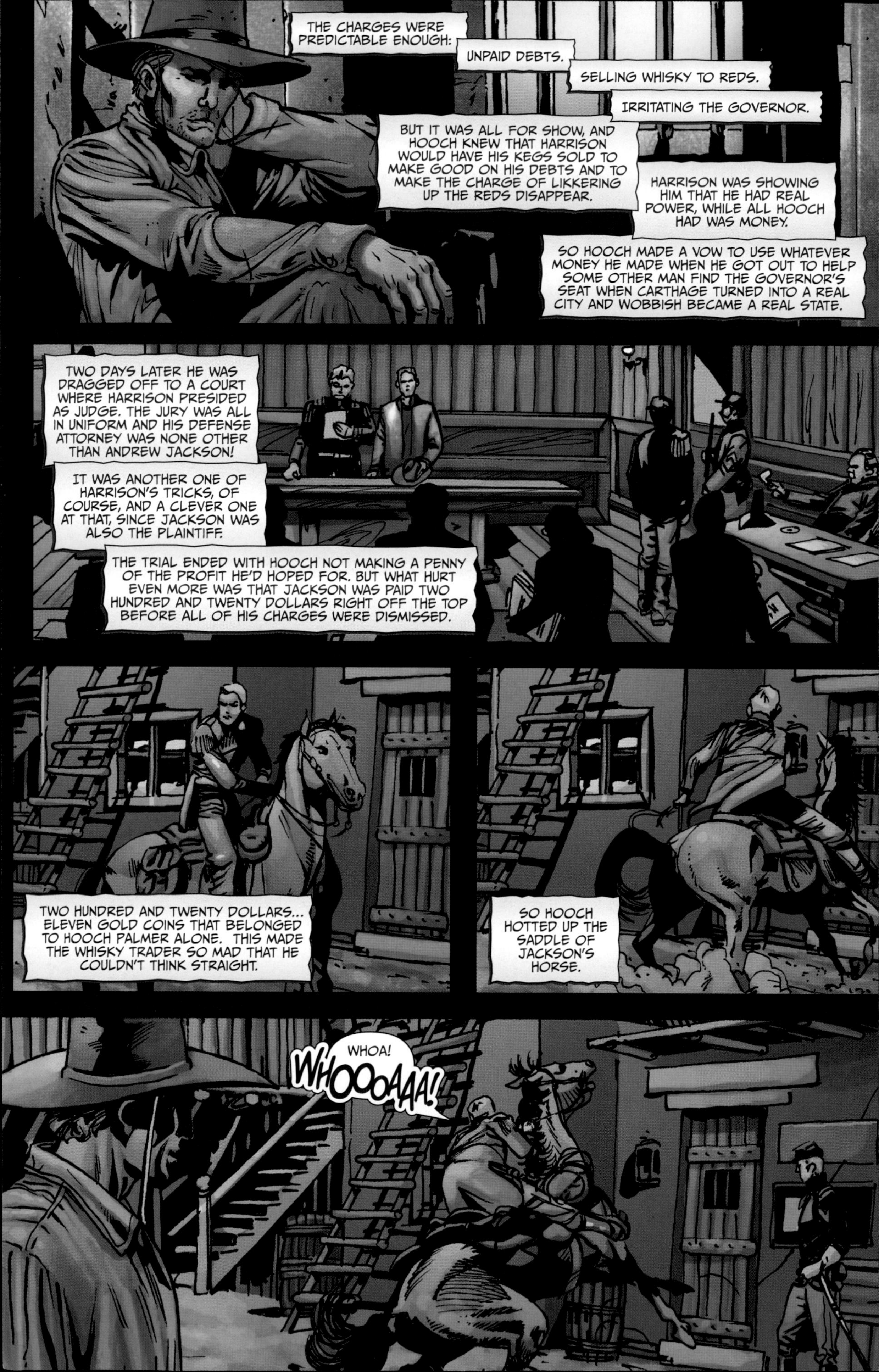

THE CHARGES WERE PREDICTABLE ENOUGH:
UNPAID DEBTS.
SELLING WHISKY TO REDS.
IRRITATING THE GOVERNOR.
BUT IT WAS ALL FOR SHOW, AND HOOCH KNEW THAT HARRISON WOULD HAVE HIS KEGS SOLD TO MAKE GOOD ON HIS DEBTS AND TO MAKE THE CHARGE OF LIKKERING UP THE REDS DISAPPEAR.
HARRISON WAS SHOWING HIM THAT HE HAD REAL POWER, WHILE ALL HOOCH HAD WAS MONEY.
SO HOOCH MADE A VOW TO USE WHATEVER MONEY HE MADE WHEN HE GOT OUT TO HELP SOME OTHER MAN FIND THE GOVERNOR'S SEAT WHEN CARTHAGE TURNED INTO A REAL CITY AND WOBBISH BECAME A REAL STATE.
TWO DAYS LATER HE WAS DRAGGED OFF TO A COURT WHERE HARRISON PRESIDED AS JUDGE. THE JURY WAS ALL IN UNIFORM AND HIS DEFENSE ATTORNEY WAS NONE OTHER THAN ANDREW JACKSON!
IT WAS ANOTHER ONE OF HARRISON'S TRICKS, OF COURSE, AND A CLEVER ONE AT THAT, SINCE JACKSON WAS ALSO THE PLAINTIFF.
THE TRIAL ENDED WITH HOOCH NOT MAKING A PENNY OF THE PROFIT HE'D HOPED FOR. BUT WHAT HURT EVEN MORE WAS THAT JACKSON WAS PAID TWO HUNDRED AND TWENTY DOLLARS RIGHT OFF THE TOP BEFORE ALL OF HIS CHARGES WERE DISMISSED.
TWO HUNDRED AND TWENTY DOLLARS... ELEVEN GOLD COINS THAT BELONGED TO HOOCH PALMER ALONE. THIS MADE THE WHISKY TRADER SO MAD THAT HE COULDN'T THINK STRAIGHT.
SO HOOCH HOTTED UP THE SADDLE OF JACKSON'S HORSE.
WHOA!
WHOOOOAAA!

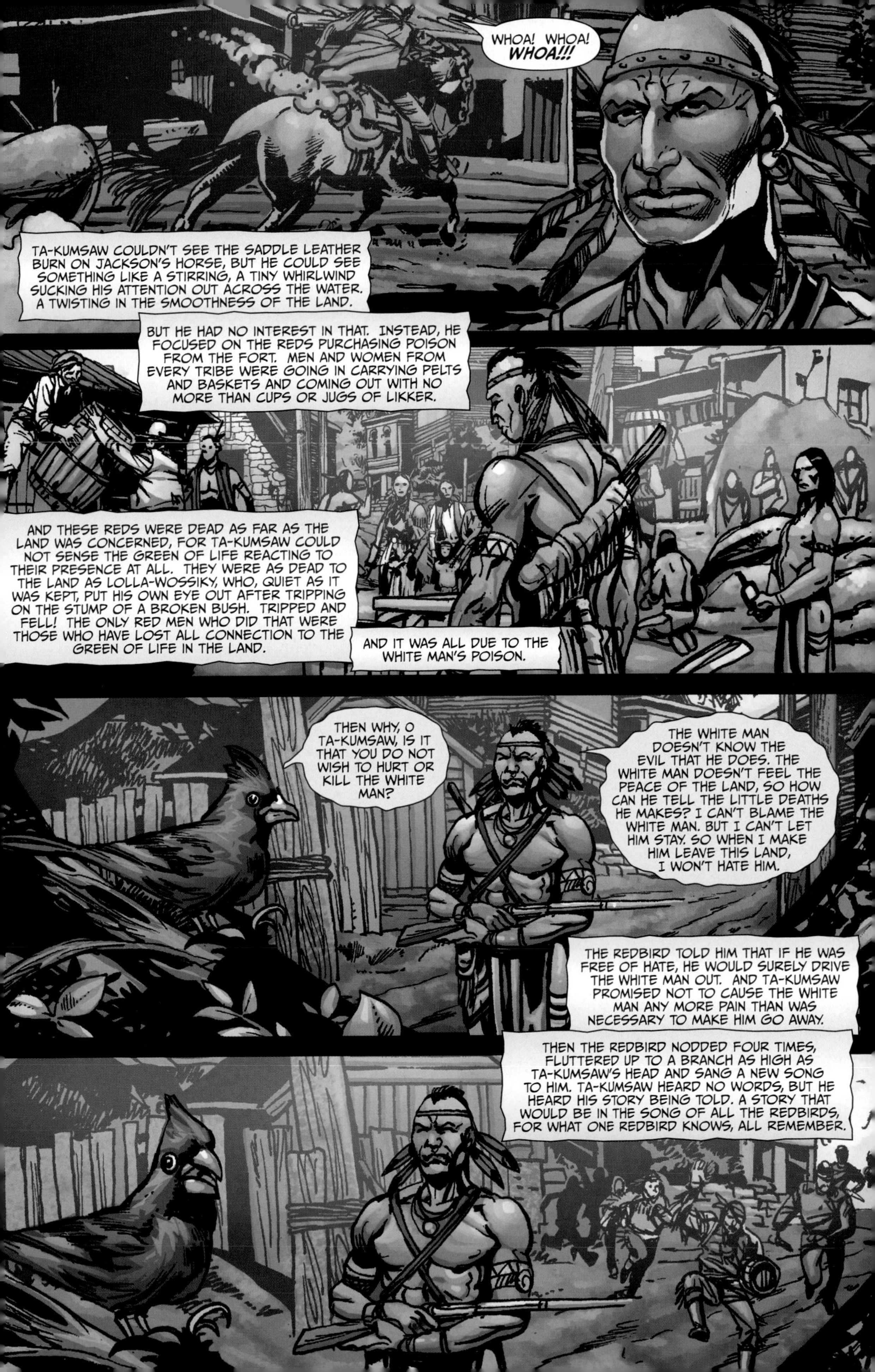
WHOA! WHOA! WHOA!!!
TA-KUMSAW COULDN'T SEE THE SADDLE LEATHER BURN ON JACKSON'S HORSE, BUT HE COULD SEE SOMETHING LIKE A STIRRING, A TINY WHIRLWIND SUCKING HIS ATTENTION OUT ACROSS THE WATER. A TWISTING IN THE SMOOTHNESS OF THE LAND.
BUT HE HAD NO INTEREST IN THAT. INSTEAD, HE FOCUSED ON THE REDS PURCHASING POISON FROM THE FORT. MEN AND WOMEN FROM EVERY TRIBE WERE GOING IN CARRYING PELTS AND BASKETS AND COMING OUT WITH NO MORE THAN CUPS OR JUGS OF LIKKER.
AND THESE REDS WERE DEAD AS FAR AS THE LAND WAS CONCERNED, FOR TA-KUMSAW COULD NOT SENSE THE GREEN OF LIFE REACTING TO THEIR PRESENCE AT ALL. THEY WERE AS DEAD TO THE LAND AS LOLLA-WOSSIKY, WHO, QUIET AS IT WAS KEPT, PUT HIS OWN EYE OUT AFTER TRIPPING ON THE STUMP OF A BROKEN BUSH. TRIPPED AND FELL! THE ONLY RED MEN WHO DID THAT WERE THOSE WHO HAVE LOST ALL CONNECTION TO THE GREEN OF LIFE IN THE LAND.
AND IT WAS ALL DUE TO THE WHITE MAN'S POISON.
THEN WHY, O TA-KUMSAW, IS IT THAT YOU DO NOT WISH TO HURT OR KILL THE WHITE MAN?
THE WHITE MAN DOESN'T KNOW THE EVIL THAT HE DOES. THE WHITE MAN DOESN'T FEEL THE PEACE OF THE LAND, SO HOW CAN HE TELL THE LITTLE DEATHS HE MAKES? I CAN'T BLAME THE WHITE MAN. BUT I CAN'T LET HIM STAY. SO WHEN I MAKE HIM LEAVE THIS LAND, I WON'T HATE HIM.
THE REDBIRD TOLD HIM THAT IF HE WAS FREE OF HATE, HE WOULD SURELY DRIVE THE WHITE MAN OUT. AND TA-KUMSAW PROMISED NOT TO CAUSE THE WHITE MAN ANY MORE PAIN THAN WAS NECESSARY TO MAKE HIM GO AWAY.
THEN THE REDBIRD NODDED FOUR TIMES, FLUTTERED UP TO A BRANCH AS HIGH AS TA-KUMSAW'S HEAD AND SANG A NEW SONG TO HIM. TA-KUMSAW HEARD NO WORDS, BUT HE HEARD HIS STORY BEING TOLD. A STORY THAT WOULD BE IN THE SONG OF ALL THE REDBIRDS, FOR WHAT ONE REDBIRD KNOWS, ALL REMEMBER.

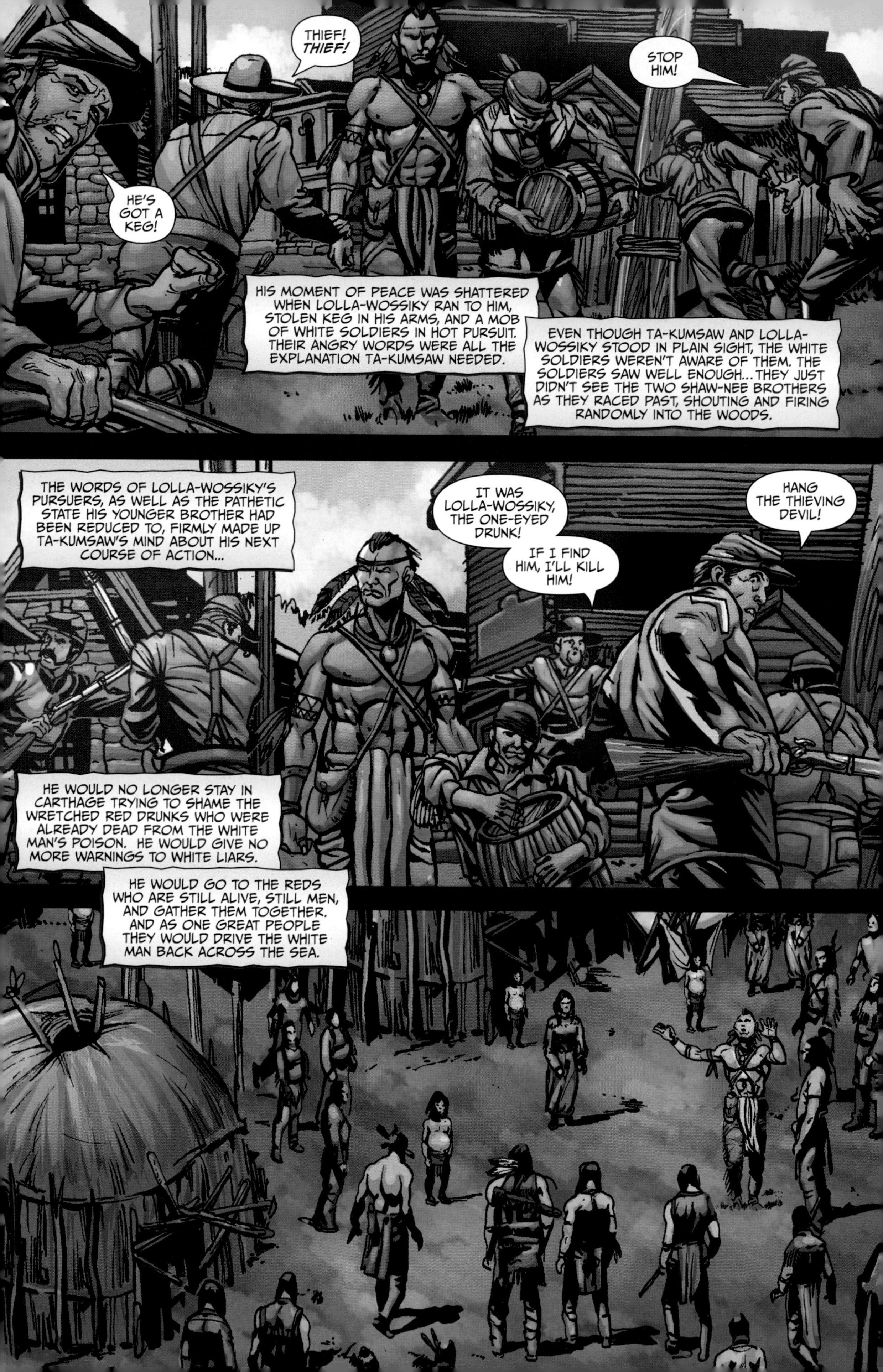
THIEF! *THIEF!*
STOP HIM!
HE'S GOT A KEG!
HIS MOMENT OF PEACE WAS SHATTERED WHEN LOLLA-WOSSIKY RAN TO HIM, STOLEN KEG IN HIS ARMS, AND A MOB OF WHITE SOLDIERS IN HOT PURSUIT. THEIR ANGRY WORDS WERE ALL THE EXPLANATION TA-KUMSAW NEEDED.
EVEN THOUGH TA-KUMSAW AND LOLLA-WOSSIKY STOOD IN PLAIN SIGHT, THE WHITE SOLDIERS WEREN'T AWARE OF THEM. THE SOLDIERS SAW WELL ENOUGH... THEY JUST DIDN'T SEE THE TWO SHAW-NEE BROTHERS AS THEY RACED PAST, SHOUTING AND FIRING RANDOMLY INTO THE WOODS.
THE WORDS OF LOLLA-WOSSIKY'S PURSUERS, AS WELL AS THE PATHETIC STATE HIS YOUNGER BROTHER HAD BEEN REDUCED TO, FIRMLY MADE UP TA-KUMSAW'S MIND ABOUT HIS NEXT COURSE OF ACTION...
IT WAS LOLLA-WOSSIKY, THE ONE-EYED DRUNK!
IF I FIND HIM, I'LL KILL HIM!
HANG THE THIEVING DEVIL!
HE WOULD NO LONGER STAY IN CARTHAGE TRYING TO SHAME THE WRETCHED RED DRUNKS WHO WERE ALREADY DEAD FROM THE WHITE MAN'S POISON. HE WOULD GIVE NO MORE WARNINGS TO WHITE LIARS.
HE WOULD GO TO THE REDS WHO ARE STILL ALIVE, STILL MEN, AND GATHER THEM TOGETHER. AND AS ONE GREAT PEOPLE THEY WOULD DRIVE THE WHITE MAN BACK ACROSS THE SEA.

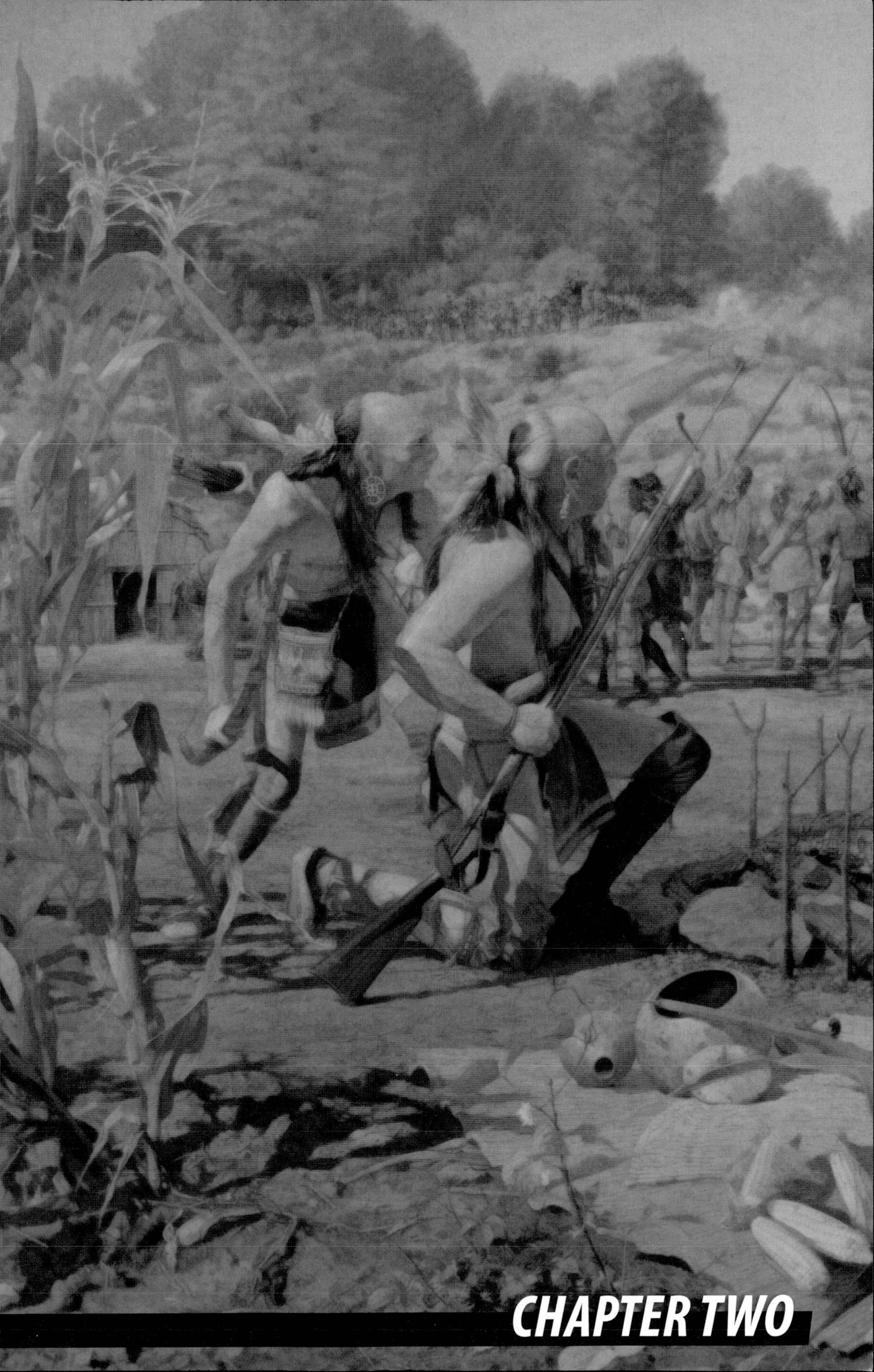

CHAPTER TWO

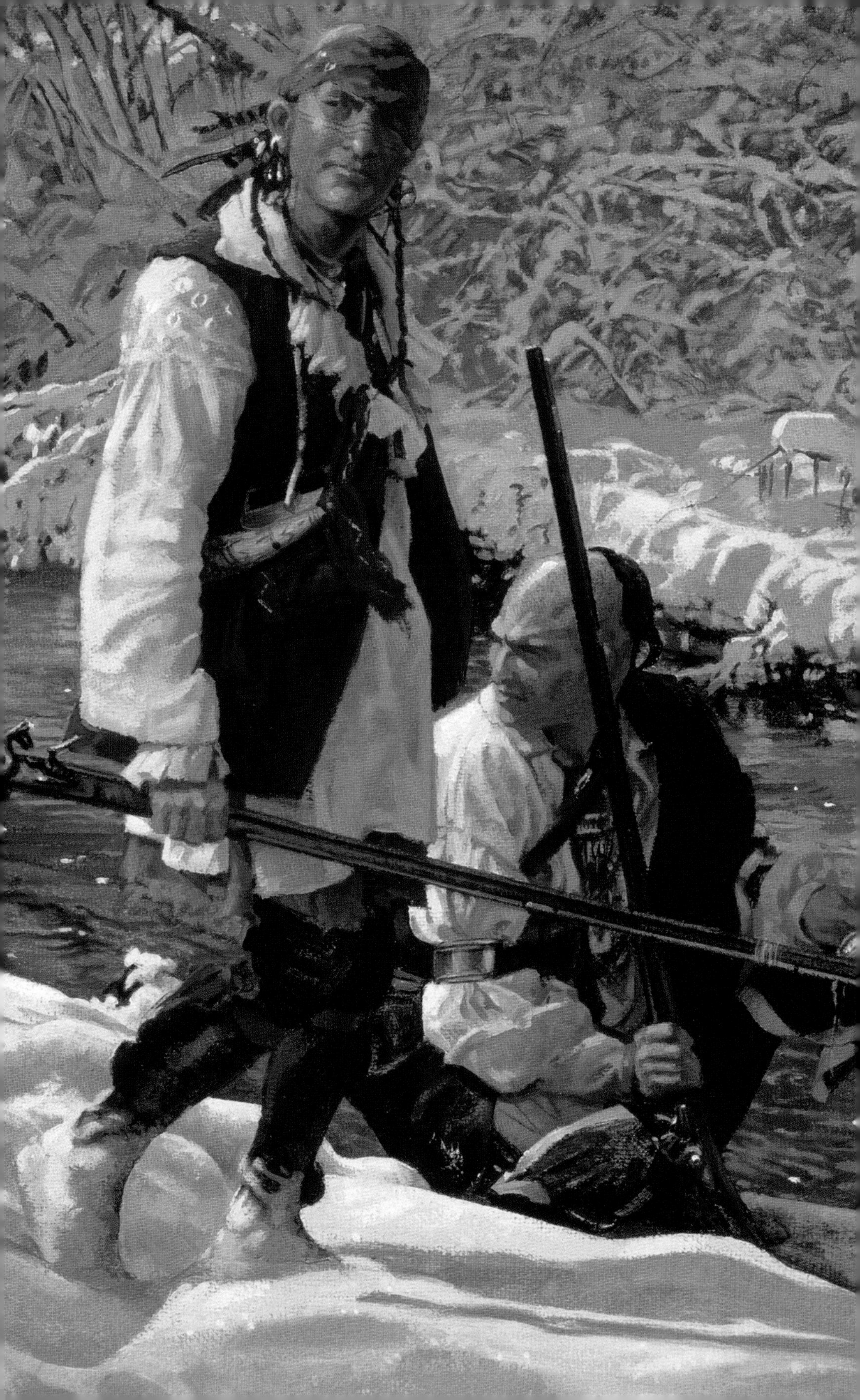

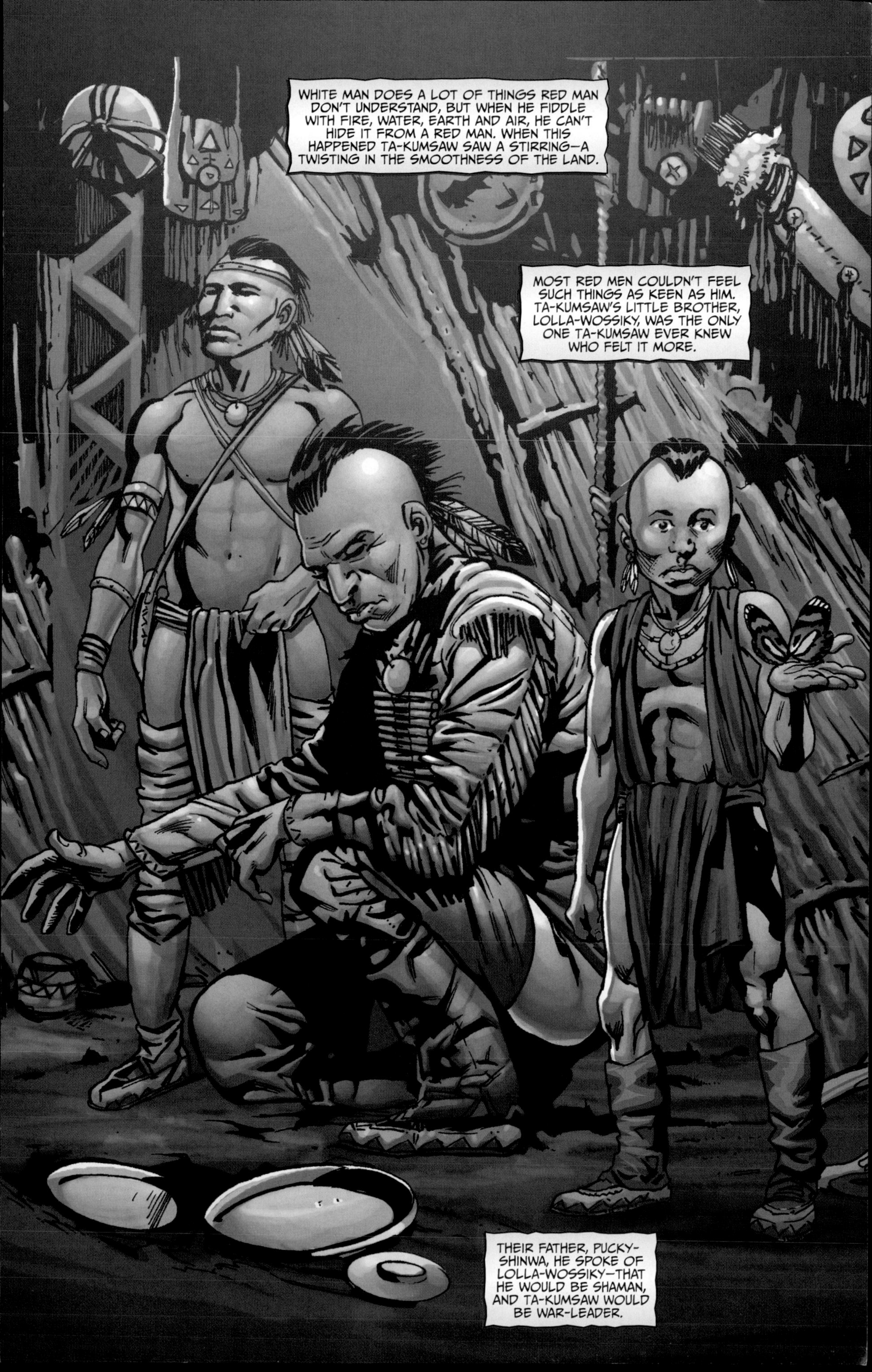
WHITE MAN DOES A LOT OF THINGS RED MAN DON'T UNDERSTAND, BUT WHEN HE FIDDLE WITH FIRE, WATER, EARTH AND AIR, HE CAN'T HIDE IT FROM A RED MAN. WHEN THIS HAPPENED TA-KUMSAW SAW A STIRRING—A TWISTING IN THE SMOOTHNESS OF THE LAND.
MOST RED MEN COULDN'T FEEL SUCH THINGS AS KEEN AS HIM. TA-KUMSAW'S LITTLE BROTHER, LOLLA-WOSSIKY, WAS THE ONLY ONE TA-KUMSAW EVER KNEW WHO FELT IT MORE.
THEIR FATHER, PUCKY-SHINWA, HE SPOKE OF LOLLA-WOSSIKY—THAT HE WOULD BE SHAMAN, AND TA-KUMSAW WOULD BE WAR-LEADER.

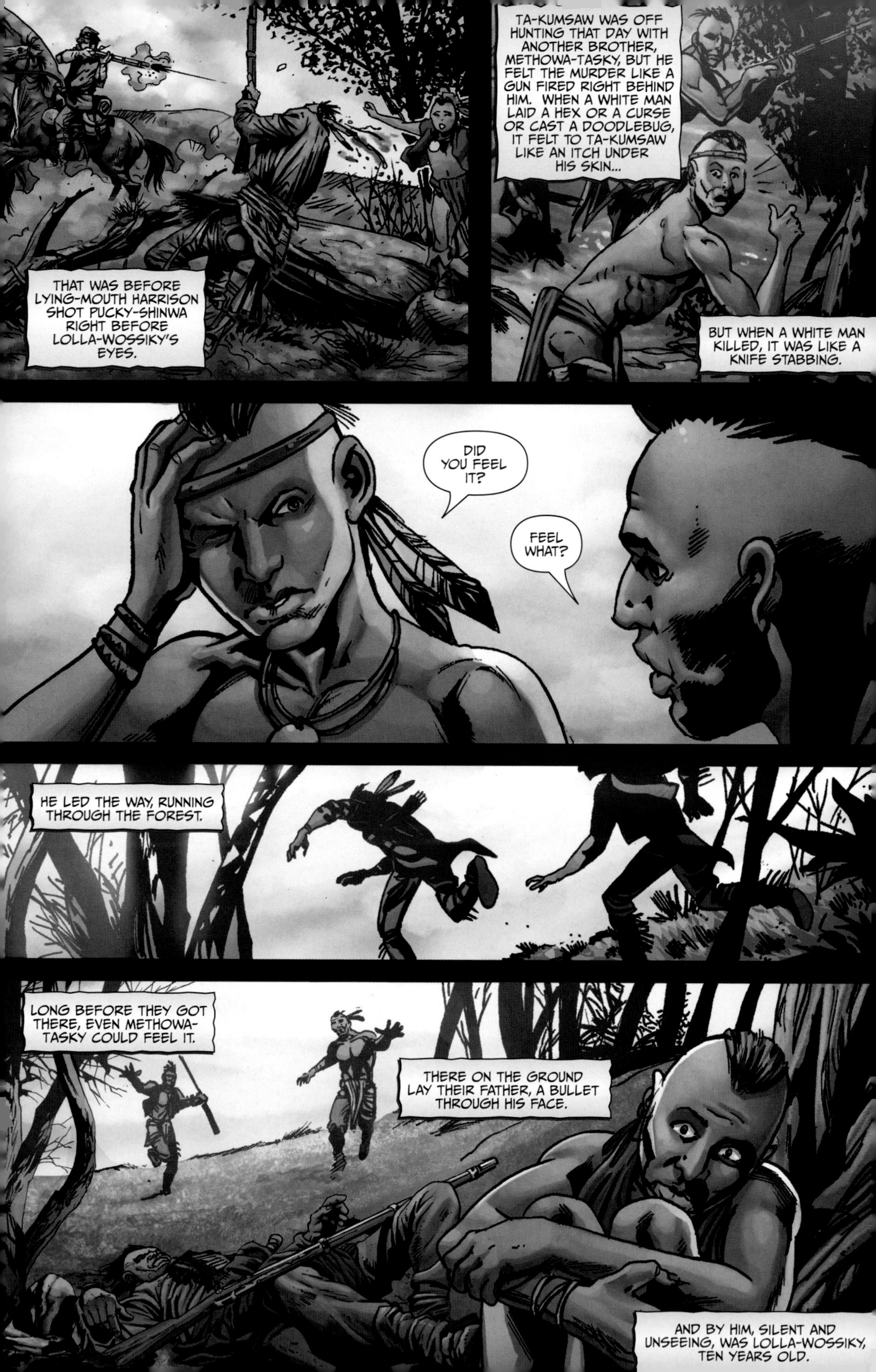

THAT WAS BEFORE LYING-MOUTH HARRISON SHOT PUCKY-SHINWA RIGHT BEFORE LOLLA-WOSSIKY'S EYES.
TA-KUMSAW WAS OFF HUNTING THAT DAY WITH ANOTHER BROTHER, METHOWA-TASKY, BUT HE FELT THE MURDER LIKE A GUN FIRED RIGHT BEHIND HIM. WHEN A WHITE MAN LAID A HEX OR A CURSE OR CAST A DOODLEBUG, IT FELT TO TA-KUMSAW LIKE AN ITCH UNDER HIS SKIN...
BUT WHEN A WHITE MAN KILLED, IT WAS LIKE A KNIFE STABBING.
DID YOU FEEL IT?
FEEL WHAT?
HE LED THE WAY, RUNNING THROUGH THE FOREST.
LONG BEFORE THEY GOT THERE, EVEN METHOWA-TASKY COULD FEEL IT.
THERE ON THE GROUND LAY THEIR FATHER, A BULLET THROUGH HIS FACE.
AND BY HIM, SILENT AND UNSEEING, WAS LOLLA-WOSSIKY, TEN YEARS OLD.

TA-KUMSAW CARRIED HIS FATHER'S BODY HOME ACROSS HIS SHOULDERS, LIKE A DEER. METHOWA-TASKY LED LOLLA-WOSSIKY BY THE HAND, FOR OTHERWISE THE BOY WOULD NOT MOVE.

MOTHER GREETED THEM WITH WAILS OF GRIEF, FOR SHE ALSO FELT THE DEATH, BUT DID NOT KNOW IT WAS HER OWN HUSBAND UNTIL HER SONS BROUGHT HIM BACK.

SHE TIED HER HUSBAND'S CORPSE TO TA-KUMSAW'S BACK; THEN TA-KUMSAW CLIMBED THE TALLEST TREE AND BOUND HIS FATHER'S CORPSE TO THE HIGHEST BRANCH HE COULD REACH.

THIS IS HOW TA-KUMSAW GAVE HIS FATHER BACK TO THE LAND.

BUT WHAT COULD THEY DO WITH LOLLA-WOSSIKY? HE SAID NOTHING, HE WOULDN'T EAT UNLESS SOMEONE FED HIM, AND IF YOU DIDN'T TAKE HIS HAND AND LEAD HIM, HE WOULD STAY IN ONE PLACE FOREVER.

LOLLA-WOSSIKY WAS THE ONLY SHAW-NEE WHO EVER FELT THE DEATH OF BEES WHEN THE AIR GREW BITTER COLD EACH WINTER. HE WOULD CRY FOR THEM.

IF TA-KUMSAW FELT THAT MURDER LIKE A KNIFE WOUND, HALF A DAY'S JOURNEY AWAY, WHAT DID LOLLA-WOSSIKY FEEL, STANDING SO CLOSE AND ALREADY SO SENSITIVE?

AFTER A FEW YEARS LOLLA-WOSSIKY BEGAN TO SPEAK AGAIN, BUT THE FIRE HAD GONE FROM HIS EYES AND HE WAS CARELESS.

HE PUT HIS OWN EYE OUT BY ACCIDENT, BECAUSE HE TRIPPED AND FELL ON THE SHORT JAGGED STUMP OF A BROKEN BUSH.

IT WAS LIKE LOLLA-WOSSIKY LOST ALL FEELING FOR THE LAND; HE WAS AS DULL AS A WHITE MAN.

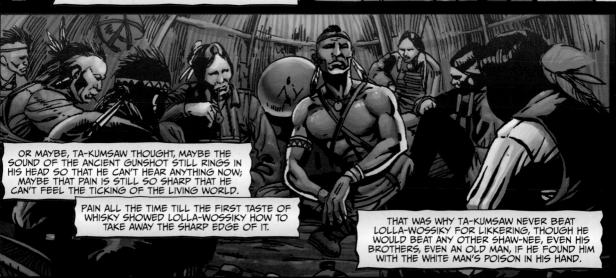

OR MAYBE, TA-KUMSAW THOUGHT, MAYBE THE SOUND OF THE ANCIENT GUNSHOT STILL RINGS IN HIS HEAD SO THAT HE CAN'T HEAR ANYTHING NOW; MAYBE THAT PAIN IS STILL SO SHARP THAT HE CAN'T FEEL THE TICKING OF THE LIVING WORLD.

PAIN ALL THE TIME TILL THE FIRST TASTE OF WHISKY SHOWED LOLLA-WOSSIKY HOW TO TAKE AWAY THE SHARP EDGE OF IT.

THAT WAS WHY TA-KUMSAW NEVER BEAT LOLLA-WOSSIKY FOR LIKKERING, THOUGH HE WOULD BEAT ANY OTHER SHAW-NEE, EVEN HIS BROTHERS, EVEN AN OLD MAN, IF HE FOUND HIM WITH THE WHITE MAN'S POISON IN HIS HAND.

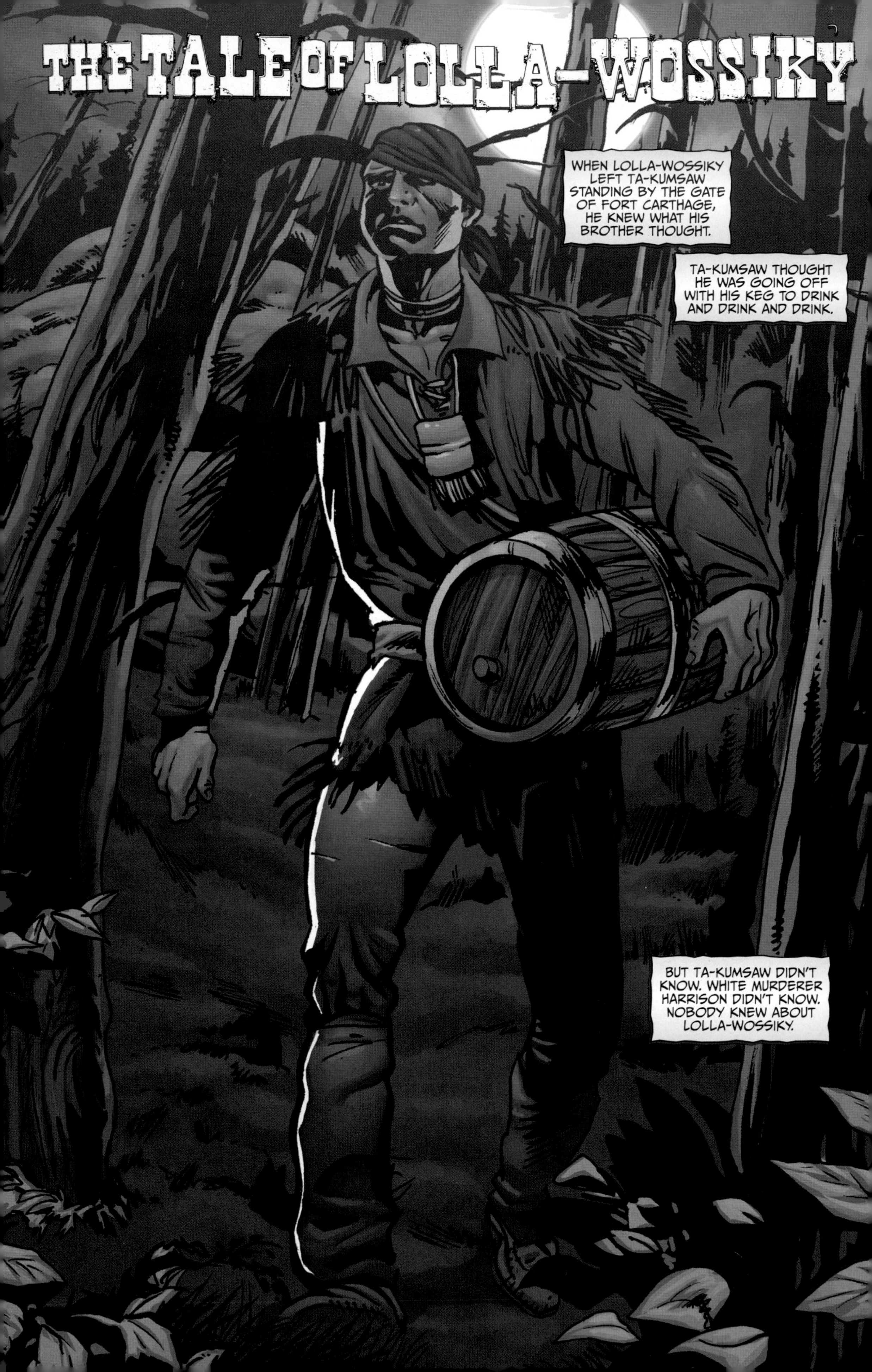
THE TALE OF LOLLA-WOSSIKY
WHEN LOLLA-WOSSIKY LEFT TA-KUMSAW STANDING BY THE GATE OF FORT CARTHAGE, HE KNEW WHAT HIS BROTHER THOUGHT.
TA-KUMSAW THOUGHT HE WAS GOING OFF WITH HIS KEG TO DRINK AND DRINK AND DRINK.
BUT TA-KUMSAW DIDN'T KNOW. WHITE MURDERER HARRISON DIDN'T KNOW. NOBODY KNEW ABOUT LOLLA-WOSSIKY.

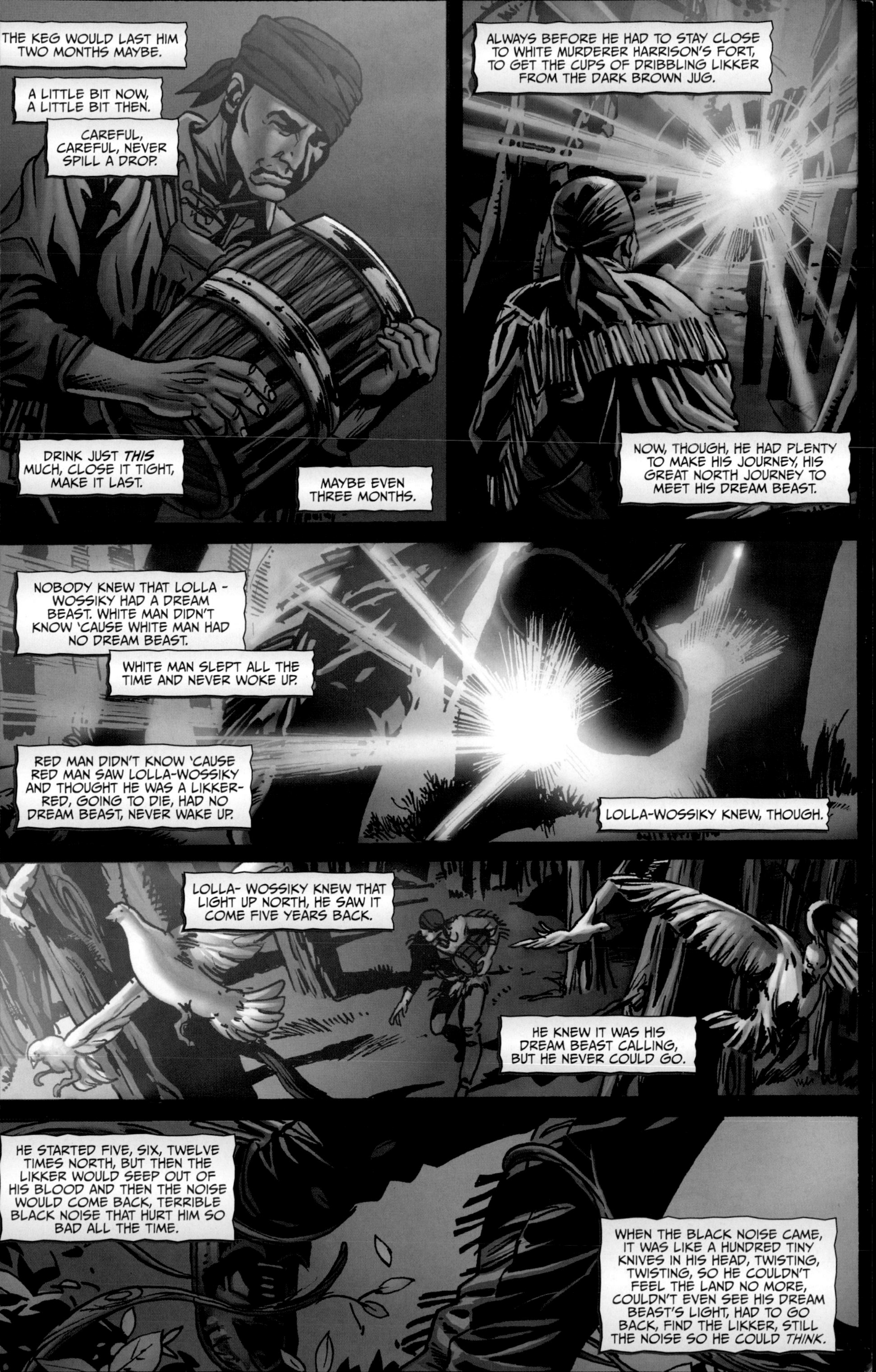

THE KEG WOULD LAST HIM TWO MONTHS MAYBE.
A LITTLE BIT NOW, A LITTLE BIT THEN.
CAREFUL, CAREFUL, NEVER SPILL A DROP.
DRINK JUST *THIS* MUCH, CLOSE IT TIGHT, MAKE IT LAST.
MAYBE EVEN THREE MONTHS.
ALWAYS BEFORE HE HAD TO STAY CLOSE TO WHITE MURDERER HARRISON'S FORT, TO GET THE CUPS OF DRIBBLING LIKKER FROM THE DARK BROWN JUG.
NOW, THOUGH, HE HAD PLENTY TO MAKE HIS JOURNEY, HIS GREAT NORTH JOURNEY TO MEET HIS DREAM BEAST.
NOBODY KNEW THAT LOLLA-WOSSIKY HAD A DREAM BEAST. WHITE MAN DIDN'T KNOW 'CAUSE WHITE MAN HAD NO DREAM BEAST.
WHITE MAN SLEPT ALL THE TIME AND NEVER WOKE UP.
RED MAN DIDN'T KNOW 'CAUSE RED MAN SAW LOLLA-WOSSIKY AND THOUGHT HE WAS A LIKKER-RED, GOING TO DIE, HAD NO DREAM BEAST, NEVER WAKE UP.
LOLLA-WOSSIKY KNEW, THOUGH.
LOLLA- WOSSIKY KNEW THAT LIGHT UP NORTH, HE SAW IT COME FIVE YEARS BACK.
HE KNEW IT WAS HIS DREAM BEAST CALLING, BUT HE NEVER COULD GO.
HE STARTED FIVE, SIX, TWELVE TIMES NORTH, BUT THEN THE LIKKER WOULD SEEP OUT OF HIS BLOOD AND THEN THE NOISE WOULD COME BACK, TERRIBLE BLACK NOISE THAT HURT HIM SO BAD ALL THE TIME.
WHEN THE BLACK NOISE CAME, IT WAS LIKE A HUNDRED TINY KNIVES IN HIS HEAD, TWISTING, TWISTING, SO HE COULDN'T FEEL THE LAND NO MORE, COULDN'T EVEN SEE HIS DREAM BEAST'S LIGHT, HAD TO GO BACK, FIND THE LIKKER, STILL THE NOISE SO HE COULD *THINK*.

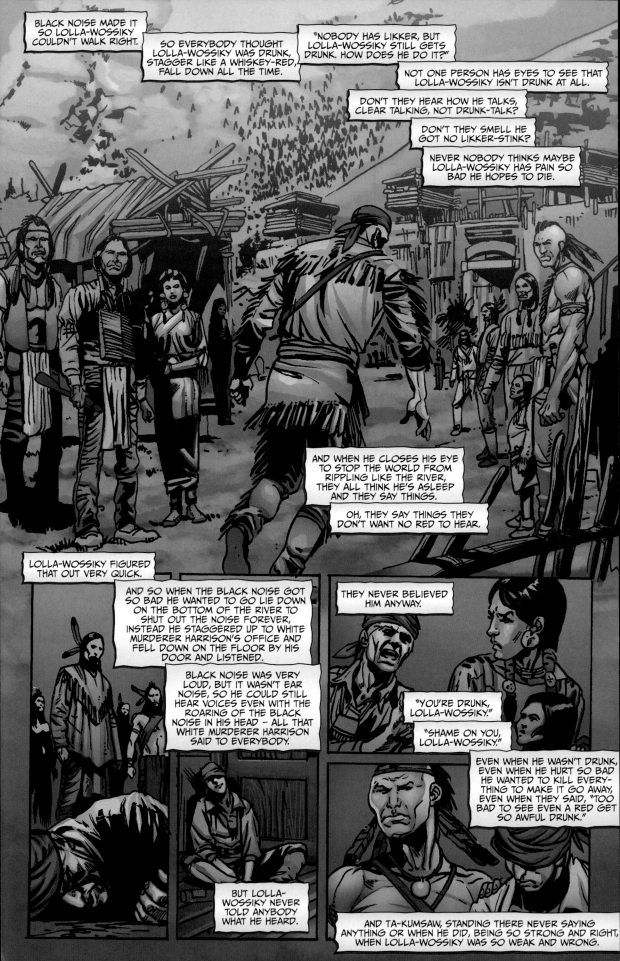

BLACK NOISE MADE IT SO LOLLA-WOSSIKY COULDN'T WALK RIGHT.

SO EVERYBODY THOUGHT LOLLA-WOSSIKY WAS DRUNK, STAGGER LIKE A WHISKEY-RED, FALL DOWN ALL THE TIME.

"NOBODY HAS LIKKER, BUT LOLLA-WOSSIKY STILL GETS DRUNK. HOW DOES HE DO IT?"

NOT ONE PERSON HAS EYES TO SEE THAT LOLLA-WOSSIKY ISN'T DRUNK AT ALL.

DON'T THEY HEAR HOW HE TALKS, CLEAR TALKING, NOT DRUNK-TALK?

DON'T THEY SMELL HE GOT NO LIKKER-STINK?

NEVER NOBODY THINKS MAYBE LOLLA-WOSSIKY HAS PAIN SO BAD HE HOPES TO DIE.

AND WHEN HE CLOSES HIS EYE TO STOP THE WORLD FROM RIPPLING LIKE THE RIVER, THEY ALL THINK HE'S ASLEEP AND THEY SAY THINGS.

OH, THEY SAY THINGS THEY DON'T WANT NO RED TO HEAR.

LOLLA-WOSSIKY FIGURED THAT OUT VERY QUICK.

AND SO WHEN THE BLACK NOISE GOT SO BAD HE WANTED TO GO LIE DOWN ON THE BOTTOM OF THE RIVER TO SHUT OUT THE NOISE FOREVER, INSTEAD HE STAGGERED UP TO WHITE MURDERER HARRISON'S OFFICE AND FELL DOWN ON THE FLOOR BY HIS DOOR AND LISTENED.

BLACK NOISE WAS VERY LOUD, BUT IT WASN'T EAR NOISE, SO HE COULD STILL HEAR VOICES EVEN WITH THE ROARING OF THE BLACK NOISE IN HIS HEAD — ALL THAT WHITE MURDERER HARRISON SAID TO EVERYBODY.

THEY NEVER BELIEVED HIM ANYWAY.

"YOU'RE DRUNK, LOLLA-WOSSIKY."

"SHAME ON YOU, LOLLA-WOSSIKY."

EVEN WHEN HE WASN'T DRUNK, EVEN WHEN HE HURT SO BAD HE WANTED TO KILL EVERY-THING TO MAKE IT GO AWAY, EVEN WHEN THEY SAID, "TOO BAD TO SEE EVEN A RED GET SO AWFUL DRUNK."

BUT LOLLA-WOSSIKY NEVER TOLD ANYBODY WHAT HE HEARD.

AND TA-KUMSAW, STANDING THERE NEVER SAYING ANYTHING OR WHEN HE DID, BEING SO STRONG AND RIGHT, WHEN LOLLA-WOSSIKY WAS SO WEAK AND WRONG.

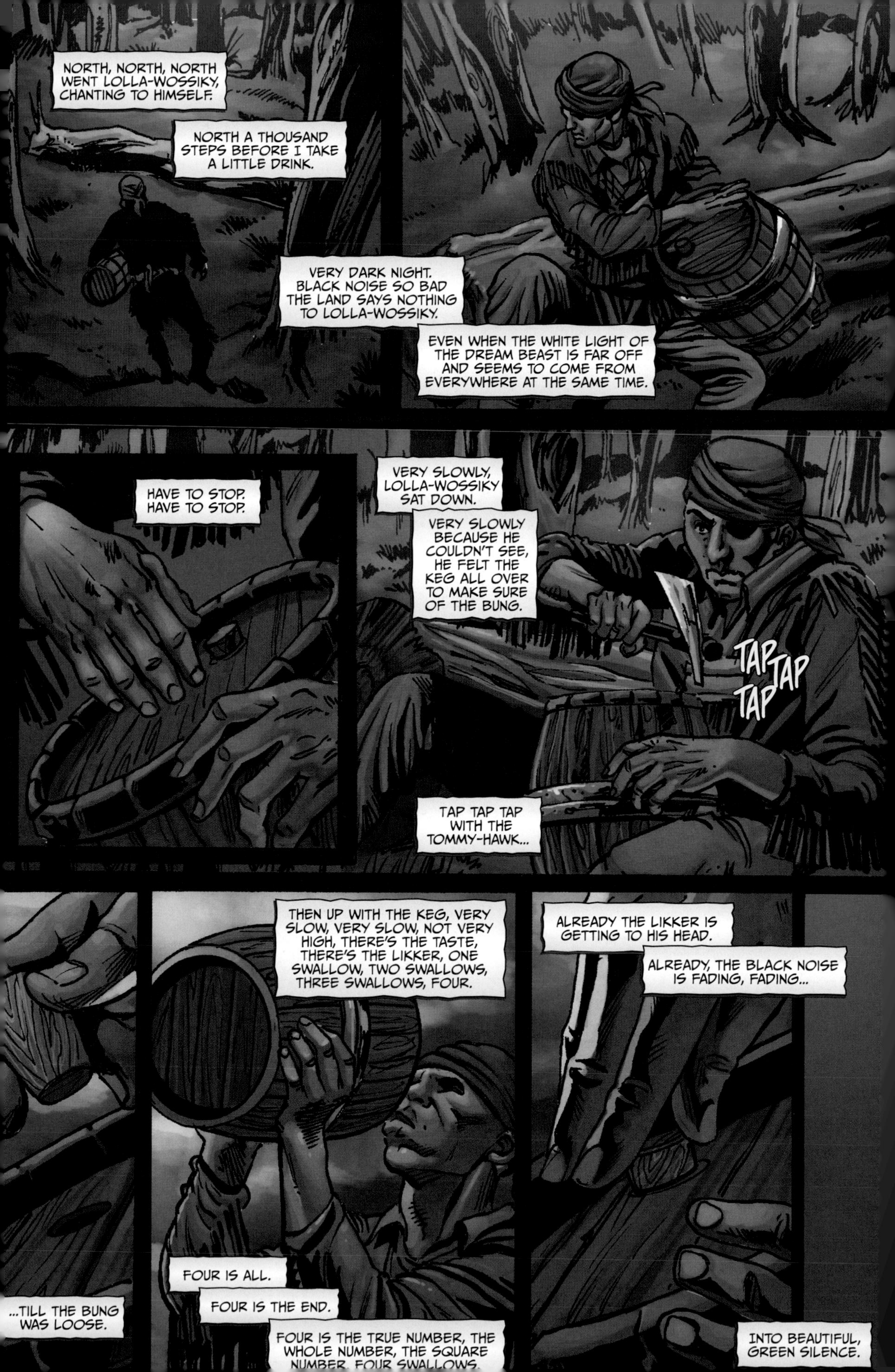
NORTH, NORTH, NORTH WENT LOLLA-WOSSIKY, CHANTING TO HIMSELF.
NORTH A THOUSAND STEPS BEFORE I TAKE A LITTLE DRINK.
VERY DARK NIGHT. BLACK NOISE SO BAD THE LAND SAYS NOTHING TO LOLLA-WOSSIKY.
EVEN WHEN THE WHITE LIGHT OF THE DREAM BEAST IS FAR OFF AND SEEMS TO COME FROM EVERYWHERE AT THE SAME TIME.
HAVE TO STOP. HAVE TO STOP.
VERY SLOWLY, LOLLA-WOSSIKY SAT DOWN.
VERY SLOWLY BECAUSE HE COULDN'T SEE, HE FELT THE KEG ALL OVER TO MAKE SURE OF THE BUNG.
TAP TAP TAP
TAP TAP TAP WITH THE TOMMY-HAWK...
...TILL THE BUNG WAS LOOSE.
THEN UP WITH THE KEG, VERY SLOW, VERY SLOW, NOT VERY HIGH, THERE'S THE TASTE, THERE'S THE LIKKER, ONE SWALLOW, TWO SWALLOWS, THREE SWALLOWS, FOUR.
FOUR IS ALL.
FOUR IS THE END.
FOUR IS THE TRUE NUMBER, THE WHOLE NUMBER, THE SQUARE NUMBER. FOUR SWALLOWS.
ALREADY THE LIKKER IS GETTING TO HIS HEAD.
ALREADY, THE BLACK NOISE IS FADING, FADING...
INTO BEAUTIFUL, GREEN SILENCE.

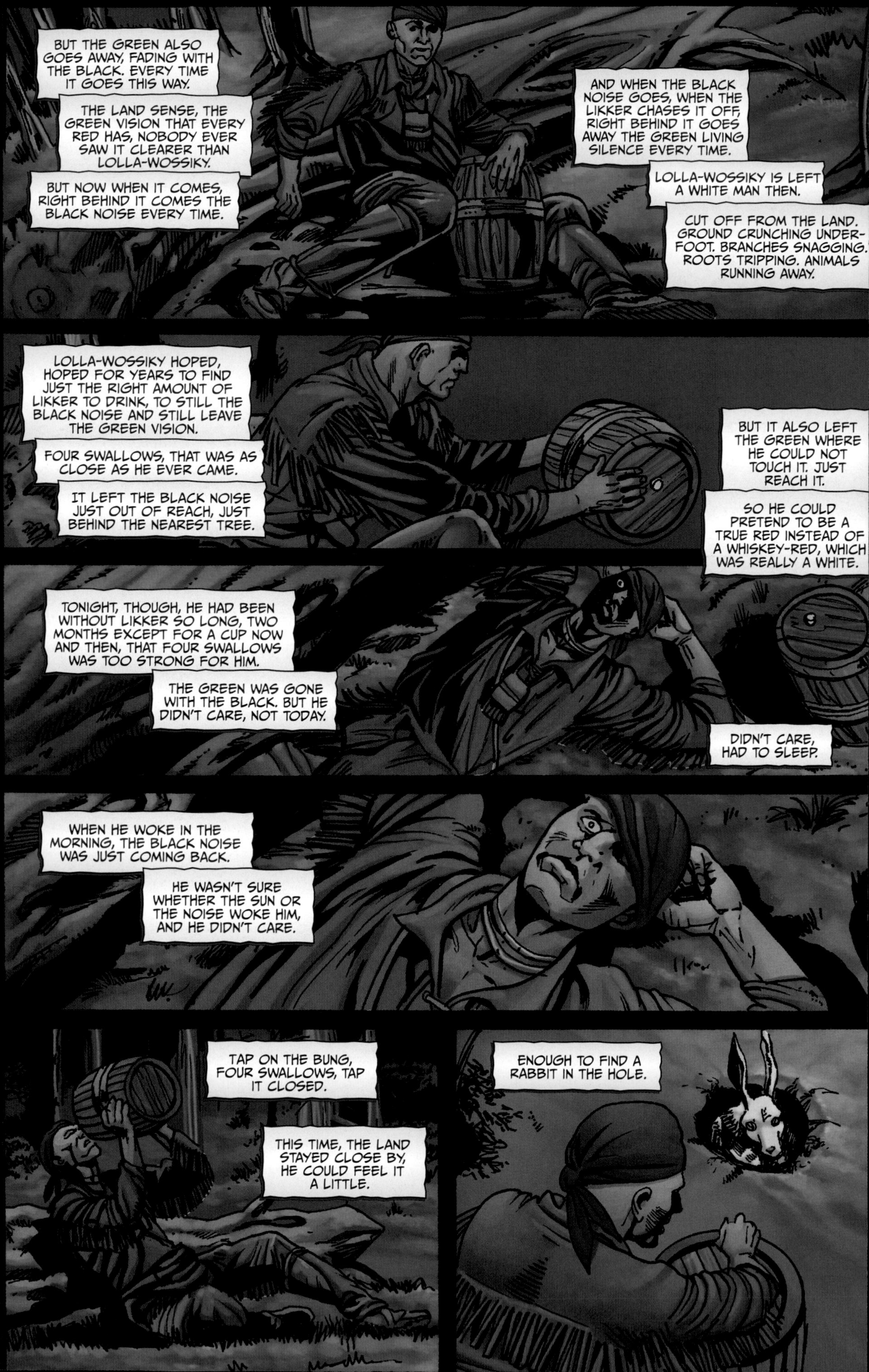
BUT THE GREEN ALSO GOES AWAY, FADING WITH THE BLACK. EVERY TIME IT GOES THIS WAY.
THE LAND SENSE, THE GREEN VISION THAT EVERY RED HAS, NOBODY EVER SAW IT CLEARER THAN LOLLA-WOSSIKY.
BUT NOW WHEN IT COMES, RIGHT BEHIND IT COMES THE BLACK NOISE EVERY TIME.
AND WHEN THE BLACK NOISE GOES, WHEN THE LIKKER CHASES IT OFF, RIGHT BEHIND IT GOES AWAY THE GREEN LIVING SILENCE EVERY TIME.
LOLLA-WOSSIKY IS LEFT A WHITE MAN THEN.
CUT OFF FROM THE LAND. GROUND CRUNCHING UNDER-FOOT. BRANCHES SNAGGING. ROOTS TRIPPING. ANIMALS RUNNING AWAY.
LOLLA-WOSSIKY HOPED, HOPED FOR YEARS TO FIND JUST THE RIGHT AMOUNT OF LIKKER TO DRINK, TO STILL THE BLACK NOISE AND STILL LEAVE THE GREEN VISION.
FOUR SWALLOWS, THAT WAS AS CLOSE AS HE EVER CAME.
IT LEFT THE BLACK NOISE JUST OUT OF REACH, JUST BEHIND THE NEAREST TREE.
BUT IT ALSO LEFT THE GREEN WHERE HE COULD NOT TOUCH IT. JUST REACH IT.
SO HE COULD PRETEND TO BE A TRUE RED INSTEAD OF A WHISKEY-RED, WHICH WAS REALLY A WHITE.
TONIGHT, THOUGH, HE HAD BEEN WITHOUT LIKKER SO LONG, TWO MONTHS EXCEPT FOR A CUP NOW AND THEN, THAT FOUR SWALLOWS WAS TOO STRONG FOR HIM.
THE GREEN WAS GONE WITH THE BLACK. BUT HE DIDN'T CARE, NOT TODAY.
DIDN'T CARE, HAD TO SLEEP.
WHEN HE WOKE IN THE MORNING, THE BLACK NOISE WAS JUST COMING BACK.
HE WASN'T SURE WHETHER THE SUN OR THE NOISE WOKE HIM, AND HE DIDN'T CARE.
TAP ON THE BUNG, FOUR SWALLOWS, TAP IT CLOSED.
THIS TIME, THE LAND STAYED CLOSE BY, HE COULD FEEL IT A LITTLE.
ENOUGH TO FIND A RABBIT IN THE HOLE.

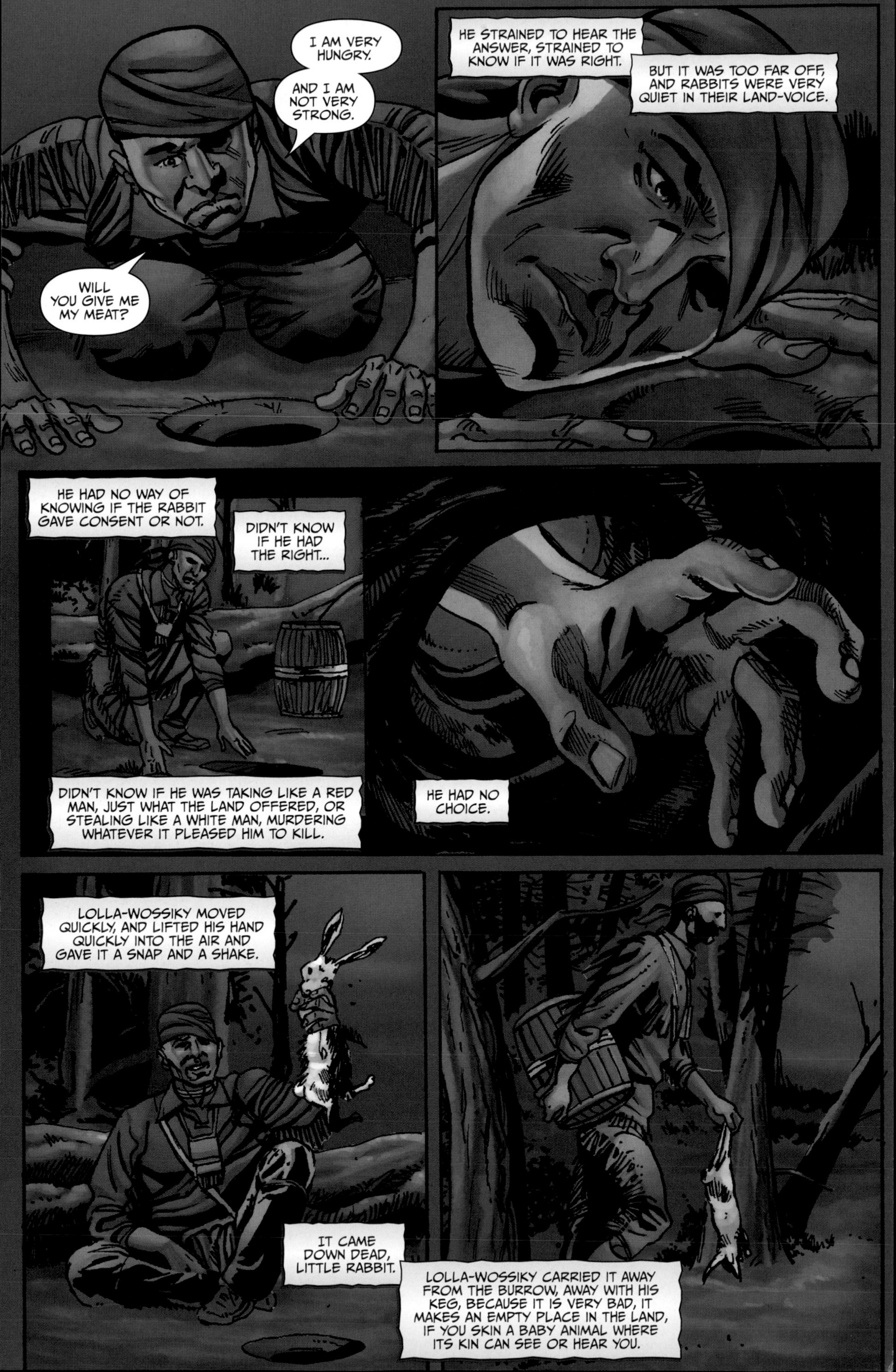

I AM VERY HUNGRY.
AND I AM NOT VERY STRONG.
WILL YOU GIVE ME MY MEAT?
HE STRAINED TO HEAR THE ANSWER, STRAINED TO KNOW IF IT WAS RIGHT.
BUT IT WAS TOO FAR OFF, AND RABBITS WERE VERY QUIET IN THEIR LAND-VOICE.
HE HAD NO WAY OF KNOWING IF THE RABBIT GAVE CONSENT OR NOT.
DIDN'T KNOW IF HE HAD THE RIGHT...
DIDN'T KNOW IF HE WAS TAKING LIKE A RED MAN, JUST WHAT THE LAND OFFERED, OR STEALING LIKE A WHITE MAN, MURDERING WHATEVER IT PLEASED HIM TO KILL.
HE HAD NO CHOICE.
LOLLA-WOSSIKY MOVED QUICKLY, AND LIFTED HIS HAND QUICKLY INTO THE AIR AND GAVE IT A SNAP AND A SHAKE.
IT CAME DOWN DEAD, LITTLE RABBIT.
LOLLA-WOSSIKY CARRIED IT AWAY FROM THE BURROW, AWAY WITH HIS KEG, BECAUSE IT IS VERY BAD, IT MAKES AN EMPTY PLACE IN THE LAND, IF YOU SKIN A BABY ANIMAL WHERE ITS KIN CAN SEE OR HEAR YOU.

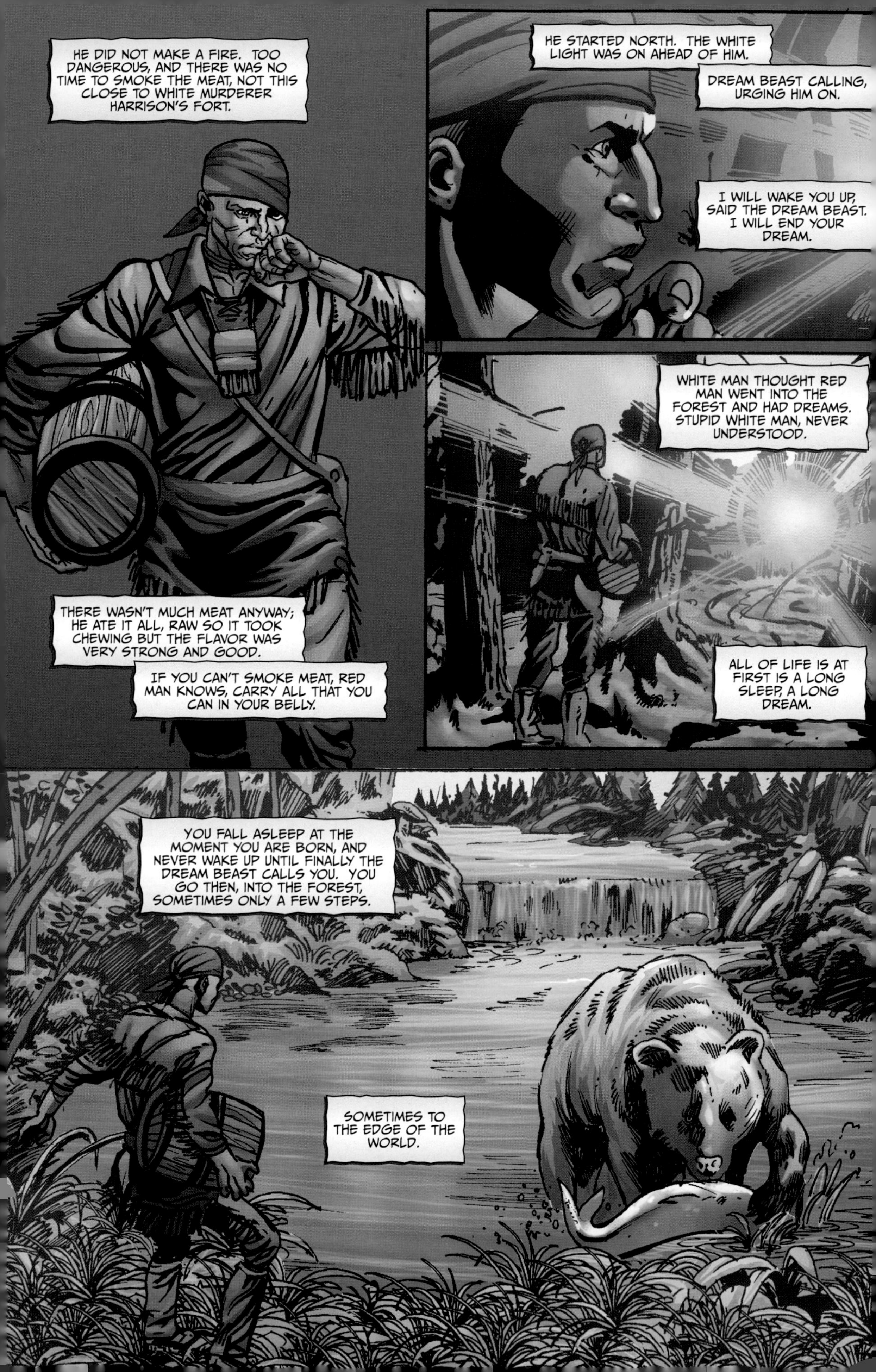
HE DID NOT MAKE A FIRE. TOO DANGEROUS, AND THERE WAS NO TIME TO SMOKE THE MEAT, NOT THIS CLOSE TO WHITE MURDERER HARRISON'S FORT.
THERE WASN'T MUCH MEAT ANYWAY; HE ATE IT ALL, RAW SO IT TOOK CHEWING BUT THE FLAVOR WAS VERY STRONG AND GOOD.
IF YOU CAN'T SMOKE MEAT, RED MAN KNOWS, CARRY ALL THAT YOU CAN IN YOUR BELLY.
HE STARTED NORTH. THE WHITE LIGHT WAS ON AHEAD OF HIM.
DREAM BEAST CALLING, URGING HIM ON.
I WILL WAKE YOU UP, SAID THE DREAM BEAST. I WILL END YOUR DREAM.
WHITE MAN THOUGHT RED MAN WENT INTO THE FOREST AND HAD DREAMS. STUPID WHITE MAN, NEVER UNDERSTOOD.
ALL OF LIFE IS AT FIRST IS A LONG SLEEP, A LONG DREAM.
YOU FALL ASLEEP AT THE MOMENT YOU ARE BORN, AND NEVER WAKE UP UNTIL FINALLY THE DREAM BEAST CALLS YOU. YOU GO THEN, INTO THE FOREST, SOMETIMES ONLY A FEW STEPS.
SOMETIMES TO THE EDGE OF THE WORLD.

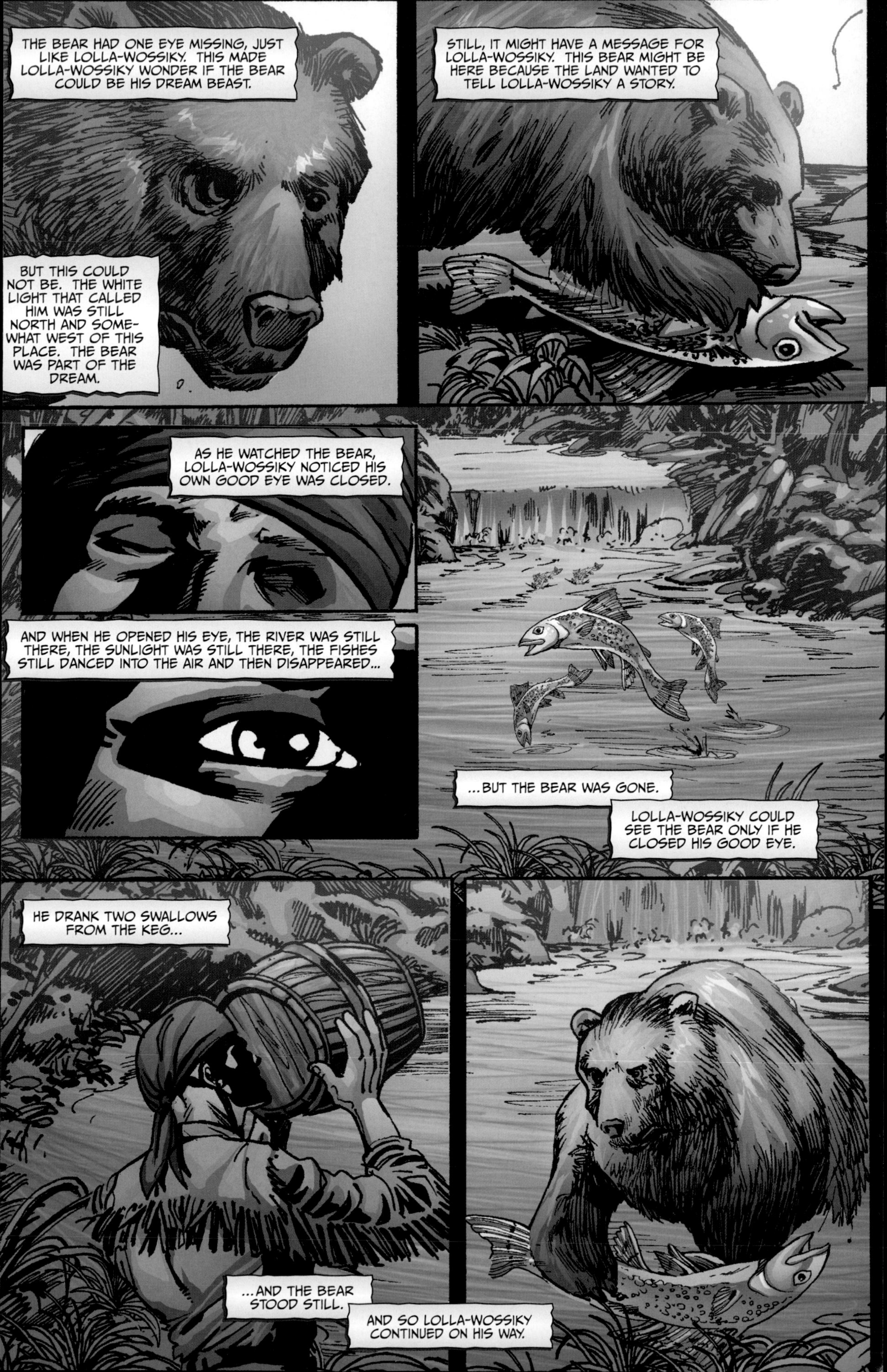
THE BEAR HAD ONE EYE MISSING, JUST LIKE LOLLA-WOSSIKY. THIS MADE LOLLA-WOSSIKY WONDER IF THE BEAR COULD BE HIS DREAM BEAST.
BUT THIS COULD NOT BE. THE WHITE LIGHT THAT CALLED HIM WAS STILL NORTH AND SOME-WHAT WEST OF THIS PLACE. THE BEAR WAS PART OF THE DREAM.
STILL, IT MIGHT HAVE A MESSAGE FOR LOLLA-WOSSIKY. THIS BEAR MIGHT BE HERE BECAUSE THE LAND WANTED TO TELL LOLLA-WOSSIKY A STORY.
AS HE WATCHED THE BEAR, LOLLA-WOSSIKY NOTICED HIS OWN GOOD EYE WAS CLOSED.
AND WHEN HE OPENED HIS EYE, THE RIVER WAS STILL THERE, THE SUNLIGHT WAS STILL THERE, THE FISHES STILL DANCED INTO THE AIR AND THEN DISAPPEARED...
...BUT THE BEAR WAS GONE.
LOLLA-WOSSIKY COULD SEE THE BEAR ONLY IF HE CLOSED HIS GOOD EYE.
HE DRANK TWO SWALLOWS FROM THE KEG...
...AND THE BEAR STOOD STILL.
AND SO LOLLA-WOSSIKY CONTINUED ON HIS WAY.

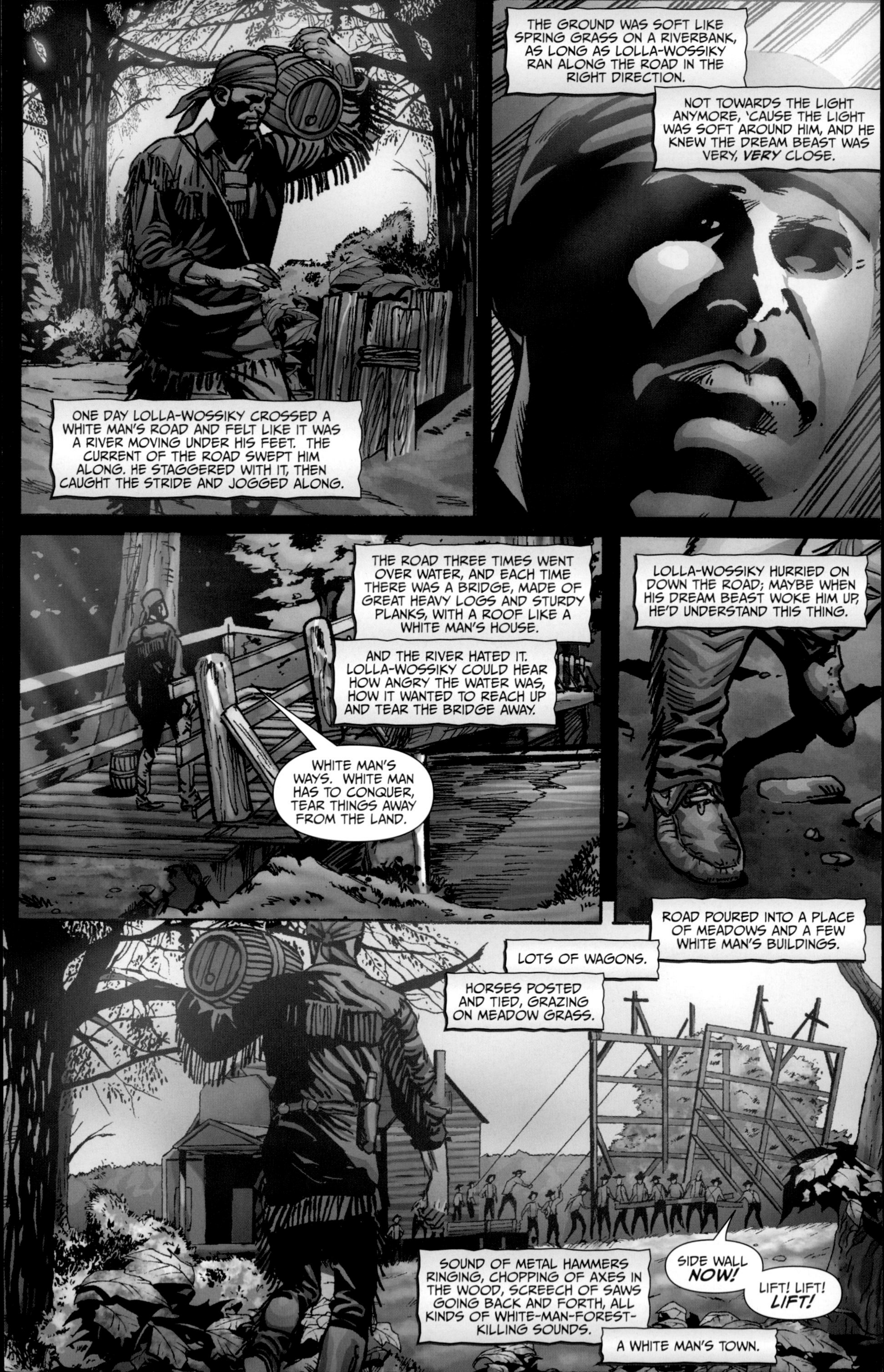
ONE DAY LOLLA-WOSSIKY CROSSED A WHITE MAN'S ROAD AND FELT LIKE IT WAS A RIVER MOVING UNDER HIS FEET. THE CURRENT OF THE ROAD SWEPT HIM ALONG. HE STAGGERED WITH IT, THEN CAUGHT THE STRIDE AND JOGGED ALONG.
THE GROUND WAS SOFT LIKE SPRING GRASS ON A RIVERBANK, AS LONG AS LOLLA-WOSSIKY RAN ALONG THE ROAD IN THE RIGHT DIRECTION.
NOT TOWARDS THE LIGHT ANYMORE, 'CAUSE THE LIGHT WAS SOFT AROUND HIM, AND HE KNEW THE DREAM BEAST WAS VERY, *VERY* CLOSE.
THE ROAD THREE TIMES WENT OVER WATER, AND EACH TIME THERE WAS A BRIDGE, MADE OF GREAT HEAVY LOGS AND STURDY PLANKS, WITH A ROOF LIKE A WHITE MAN'S HOUSE.
AND THE RIVER HATED IT. LOLLA-WOSSIKY COULD HEAR HOW ANGRY THE WATER WAS, HOW IT WANTED TO REACH UP AND TEAR THE BRIDGE AWAY.
WHITE MAN'S WAYS. WHITE MAN HAS TO CONQUER, TEAR THINGS AWAY FROM THE LAND.
LOLLA-WOSSIKY HURRIED ON DOWN THE ROAD; MAYBE WHEN HIS DREAM BEAST WOKE HIM UP, HE'D UNDERSTAND THIS THING.
ROAD POURED INTO A PLACE OF MEADOWS AND A FEW WHITE MAN'S BUILDINGS.
LOTS OF WAGONS.
HORSES POSTED AND TIED, GRAZING ON MEADOW GRASS.
SOUND OF METAL HAMMERS RINGING, CHOPPING OF AXES IN THE WOOD, SCREECH OF SAWS GOING BACK AND FORTH, ALL KINDS OF WHITE-MAN-FOREST-KILLING SOUNDS.
SIDE WALL **NOW!**
LIFT! LIFT! ***LIFT!***
A WHITE MAN'S TOWN.

LOLLA-WOSSIKY MELTED BACK INTO THE WOODS.

HE DRANK FOUR SWALLOWS FROM THE KEG, THEN FOUND A TREE AND SETTLED THE KEG INTO PLACE WHERE THREE THICK TRUNKS SPREAD APART.

LOLLA-WOSSIKY TOOK THE LONG WAY ROUND, BUT PRETTY SOON THERE HE WAS ON THE HILL WHERE THE NEW WALLS STOOD.

LOLLA-WOSSIKY LOOKED A LONG TIME, BUT HE COULDN'T UNDERSTAND WHAT THIS BUILDING WAS GOING TO BE.

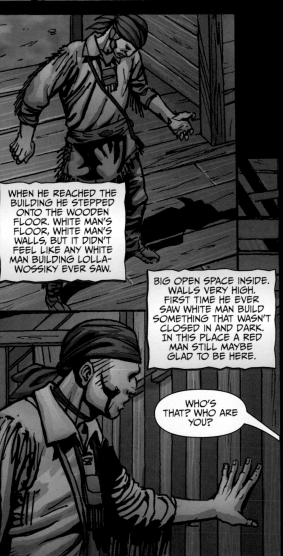

WHEN HE REACHED THE BUILDING HE STEPPED ONTO THE WOODEN FLOOR. WHITE MAN'S FLOOR, WHITE MAN'S WALLS, BUT IT DIDN'T FEEL LIKE ANY WHITE MAN BUILDING LOLLA-WOSSIKY EVER SAW.

BIG OPEN SPACE INSIDE. WALLS VERY HIGH. FIRST TIME HE EVER SAW WHITE MAN BUILD SOMETHING THAT WASN'T CLOSED IN AND DARK. IN THIS PLACE A RED MAN STILL MAYBE GLAD TO BE HERE.

WHO'S THAT? WHO ARE YOU?

LOLLA-WOSSIKY TURNED AROUND SO FAST HE ALMOST FELL. THE MAN HE SAW WASN'T DRESSED IN THE BUCKSKIN OF A HUNTER, OR IN THE UNIFORM OF A SOLDIER. HE WAS DRESSED LIKE A FARMER MAYBE, ONLY HE WAS CLEAN.

IN FACT LOLLA-WOSSIKY NEVER SAW SUCH A MAN IN CARTHAGE CITY.

WELL? WHO ARE YOU?

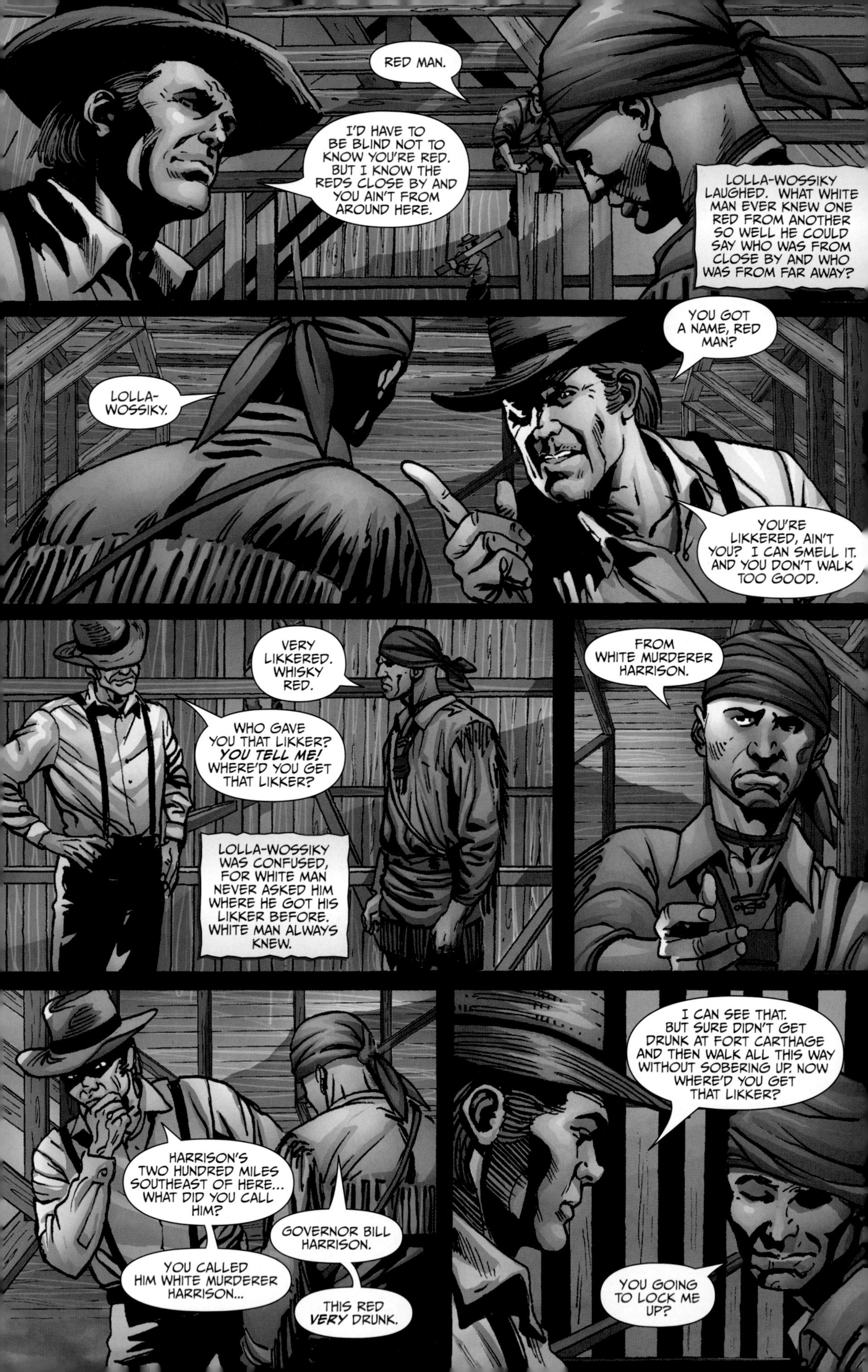
RED MAN.
I'D HAVE TO BE BLIND NOT TO KNOW YOU'RE RED. BUT I KNOW THE REDS CLOSE BY AND YOU AIN'T FROM AROUND HERE.
LOLLA-WOSSIKY LAUGHED. WHAT WHITE MAN EVER KNEW ONE RED FROM ANOTHER SO WELL HE COULD SAY WHO WAS FROM CLOSE BY AND WHO WAS FROM FAR AWAY?
YOU GOT A NAME, RED MAN?
LOLLA-WOSSIKY.
YOU'RE LIKKERED, AIN'T YOU? I CAN SMELL IT. AND YOU DON'T WALK TOO GOOD.
VERY LIKKERED. WHISKY RED.
WHO GAVE YOU THAT LIKKER? *YOU TELL ME!* WHERE'D YOU GET THAT LIKKER?
LOLLA-WOSSIKY WAS CONFUSED, FOR WHITE MAN NEVER ASKED HIM WHERE HE GOT HIS LIKKER BEFORE. WHITE MAN ALWAYS KNEW.
FROM WHITE MURDERER HARRISON.
HARRISON'S TWO HUNDRED MILES SOUTHEAST OF HERE... WHAT DID YOU CALL HIM?
GOVERNOR BILL HARRISON.
YOU CALLED HIM WHITE MURDERER HARRISON...
THIS RED *VERY* DRUNK.
I CAN SEE THAT. BUT SURE DIDN'T GET DRUNK AT FORT CARTHAGE AND THEN WALK ALL THIS WAY WITHOUT SOBERING UP. NOW WHERE'D YOU GET THAT LIKKER?
YOU GOING TO LOCK ME UP?

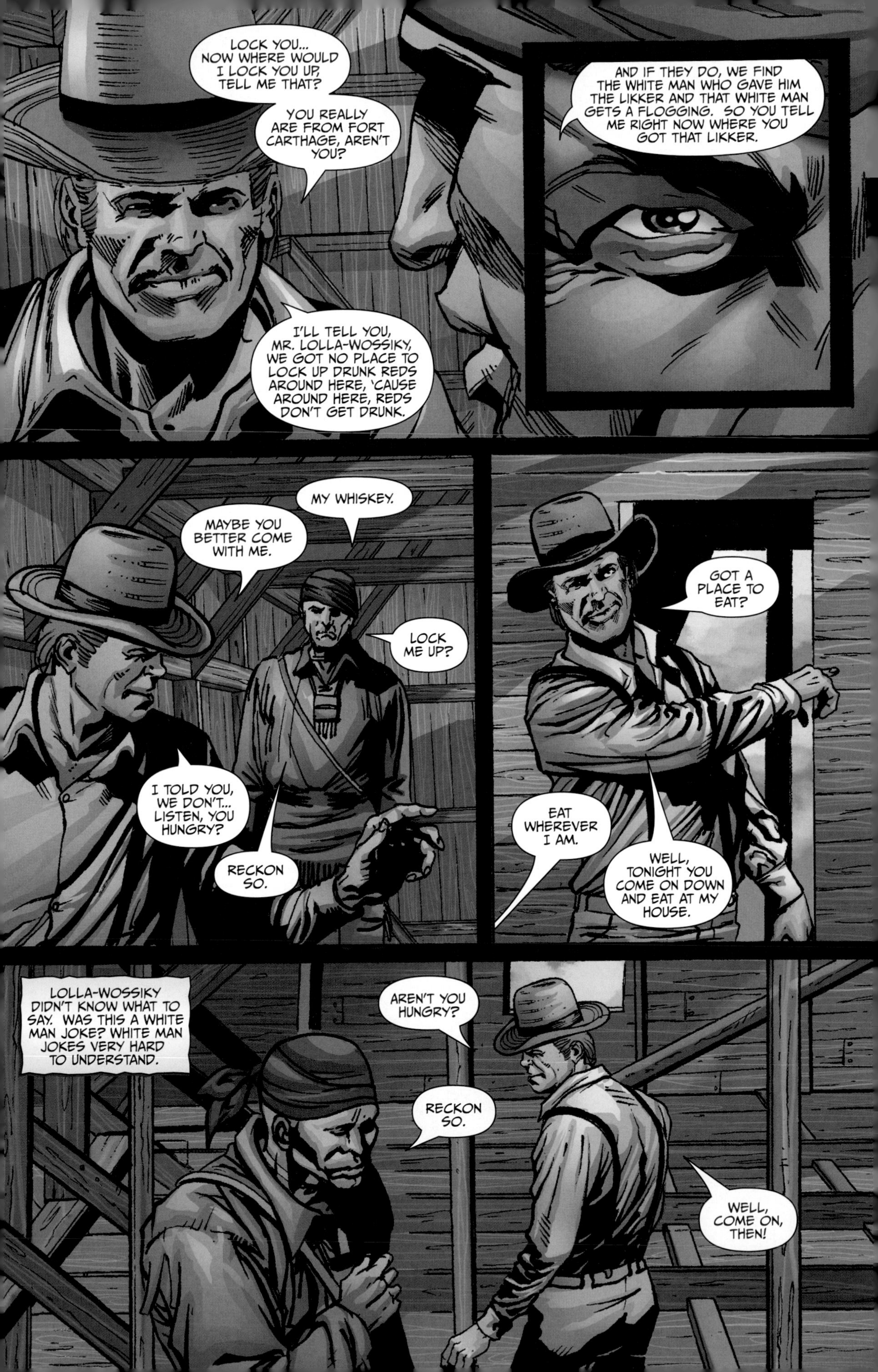
LOCK YOU... NOW WHERE WOULD I LOCK YOU UP, TELL ME THAT?
YOU REALLY ARE FROM FORT CARTHAGE, AREN'T YOU?
I'LL TELL YOU, MR. LOLLA-WOSSIKY, WE GOT NO PLACE TO LOCK UP DRUNK REDS AROUND HERE, 'CAUSE AROUND HERE, REDS DON'T GET DRUNK.
AND IF THEY DO, WE FIND THE WHITE MAN WHO GAVE HIM THE LIKKER AND THAT WHITE MAN GETS A FLOGGING. SO YOU TELL ME RIGHT NOW WHERE YOU GOT THAT LIKKER.
MY WHISKEY.
MAYBE YOU BETTER COME WITH ME.
LOCK ME UP?
I TOLD YOU, WE DON'T... LISTEN, YOU HUNGRY?
RECKON SO.
GOT A PLACE TO EAT?
EAT WHEREVER I AM.
WELL, TONIGHT YOU COME ON DOWN AND EAT AT MY HOUSE.
LOLLA-WOSSIKY DIDN'T KNOW WHAT TO SAY. WAS THIS A WHITE MAN JOKE? WHITE MAN JOKES VERY HARD TO UNDERSTAND.
AREN'T YOU HUNGRY?
RECKON SO.
WELL, COME ON, THEN!

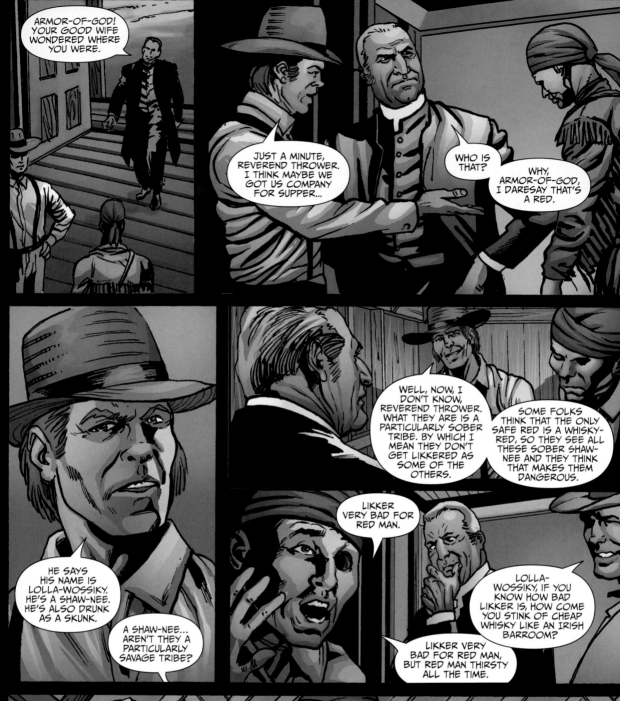

ARMOR-OF-GOD! YOUR GOOD WIFE WONDERED WHERE YOU WERE.

JUST A MINUTE, REVEREND THROWER. I THINK MAYBE WE GOT US COMPANY FOR SUPPER...

WHO IS THAT?

WHY, ARMOR-OF-GOD, I DARESAY THAT'S A RED.

WELL, NOW, I DON'T KNOW, REVEREND THROWER. WHAT THEY ARE IS A PARTICULARLY SOBER TRIBE. BY WHICH I MEAN THEY DON'T GET LIKKERED AS SOME OF THE OTHERS.

SOME FOLKS THINK THAT THE ONLY SAFE RED IS A WHISKY-RED, SO THEY SEE ALL THESE SOBER SHAW-NEE AND THEY THINK THAT MAKES THEM DANGEROUS.

HE SAYS HIS NAME IS LOLLA-WOSSIKY. HE'S A SHAW-NEE. HE'S ALSO DRUNK AS A SKUNK.

A SHAW-NEE... AREN'T THEY A PARTICULARLY SAVAGE TRIBE?

LIKKER VERY BAD FOR RED MAN.

LOLLA-WOSSIKY, IF YOU KNOW HOW BAD LIKKER IS, HOW COME YOU STINK OF CHEAP WHISKY LIKE AN IRISH BARROOM?

LIKKER VERY BAD FOR RED MAN, BUT RED MAN THIRSTY ALL THE TIME.

THERE'S A SIMPLE SCIENTIFIC EXPLANATION FOR THAT.

EUROPEANS HAVE HAD ALCOHOLIC BEVERAGES FOR SO LONG THAT THEY'VE BUILT UP A TOLERANCE.

BUT YOU REDS HAVE NEVER BUILT UP THAT TOLERANCE.

VERY DAMN RIGHT. TRUE-TALKING WHITE MAN—

— HOW COME WHITE MURDERER HARRISON NOT KILL YOU YET?

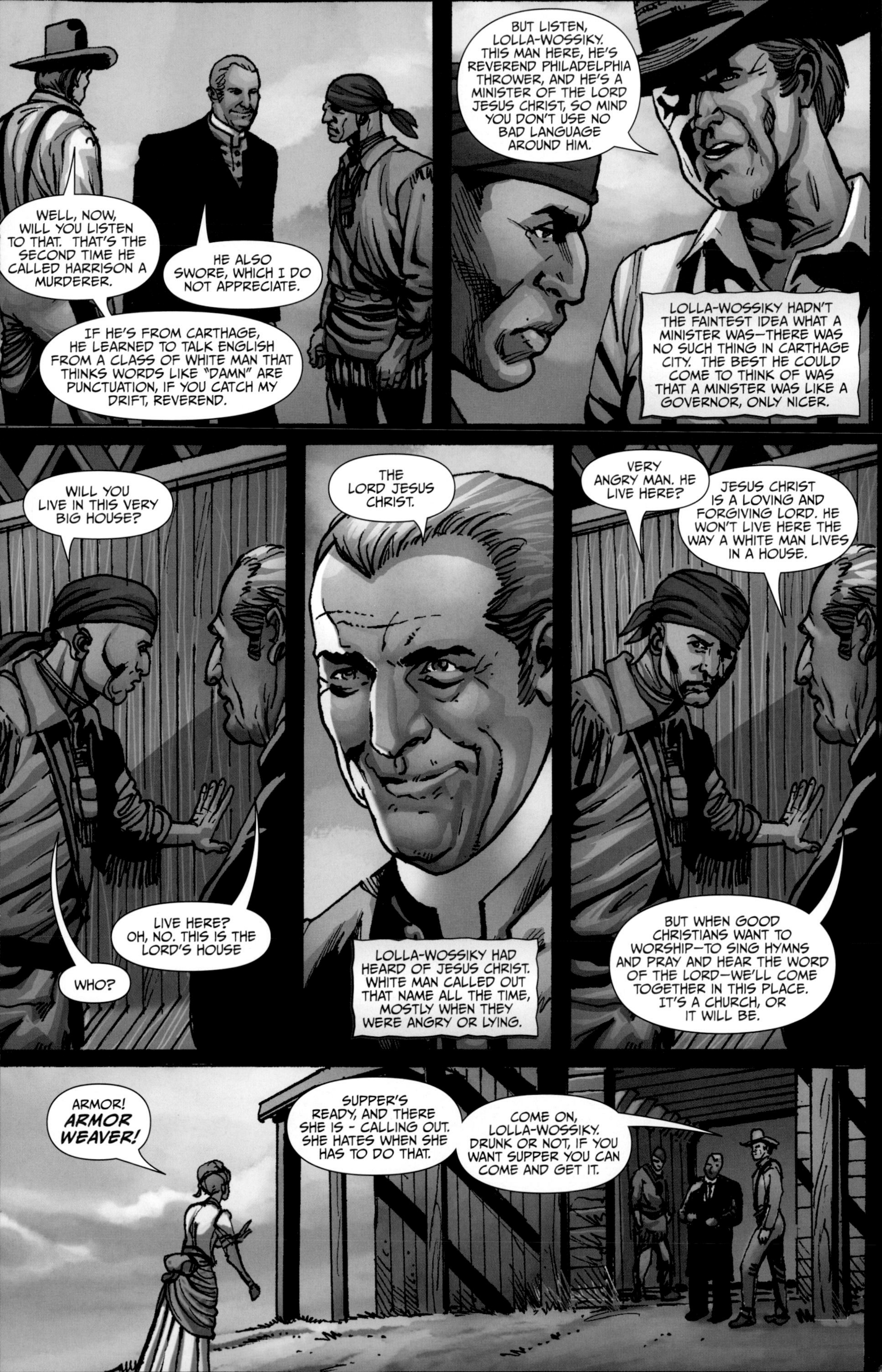
WELL, NOW, WILL YOU LISTEN TO THAT. THAT'S THE SECOND TIME HE CALLED HARRISON A MURDERER.
HE ALSO SWORE, WHICH I DO NOT APPRECIATE.
IF HE'S FROM CARTHAGE, HE LEARNED TO TALK ENGLISH FROM A CLASS OF WHITE MAN THAT THINKS WORDS LIKE "DAMN" ARE PUNCTUATION, IF YOU CATCH MY DRIFT, REVEREND.
BUT LISTEN, LOLLA-WOSSIKY. THIS MAN HERE, HE'S REVEREND PHILADELPHIA THROWER, AND HE'S A MINISTER OF THE LORD JESUS CHRIST, SO MIND YOU DON'T USE NO BAD LANGUAGE AROUND HIM.
LOLLA-WOSSIKY HADN'T THE FAINTEST IDEA WHAT A MINISTER WAS—THERE WAS NO SUCH THING IN CARTHAGE CITY. THE BEST HE COULD COME TO THINK OF WAS THAT A MINISTER WAS LIKE A GOVERNOR, ONLY NICER.
WILL YOU LIVE IN THIS VERY BIG HOUSE?
LIVE HERE? OH, NO. THIS IS THE LORD'S HOUSE
WHO?
THE LORD JESUS CHRIST.
LOLLA-WOSSIKY HAD HEARD OF JESUS CHRIST. WHITE MAN CALLED OUT THAT NAME ALL THE TIME, MOSTLY WHEN THEY WERE ANGRY OR LYING.
VERY ANGRY MAN. HE LIVE HERE?
JESUS CHRIST IS A LOVING AND FORGIVING LORD. HE WON'T LIVE HERE THE WAY A WHITE MAN LIVES IN A HOUSE.
BUT WHEN GOOD CHRISTIANS WANT TO WORSHIP—TO SING HYMNS AND PRAY AND HEAR THE WORD OF THE LORD—WE'LL COME TOGETHER IN THIS PLACE. IT'S A CHURCH, OR IT WILL BE.
ARMOR! ***ARMOR WEAVER!***
SUPPER'S READY, AND THERE SHE IS - CALLING OUT. SHE HATES WHEN SHE HAS TO DO THAT.
COME ON, LOLLA-WOSSIKY. DRUNK OR NOT, IF YOU WANT SUPPER YOU CAN COME AND GET IT.

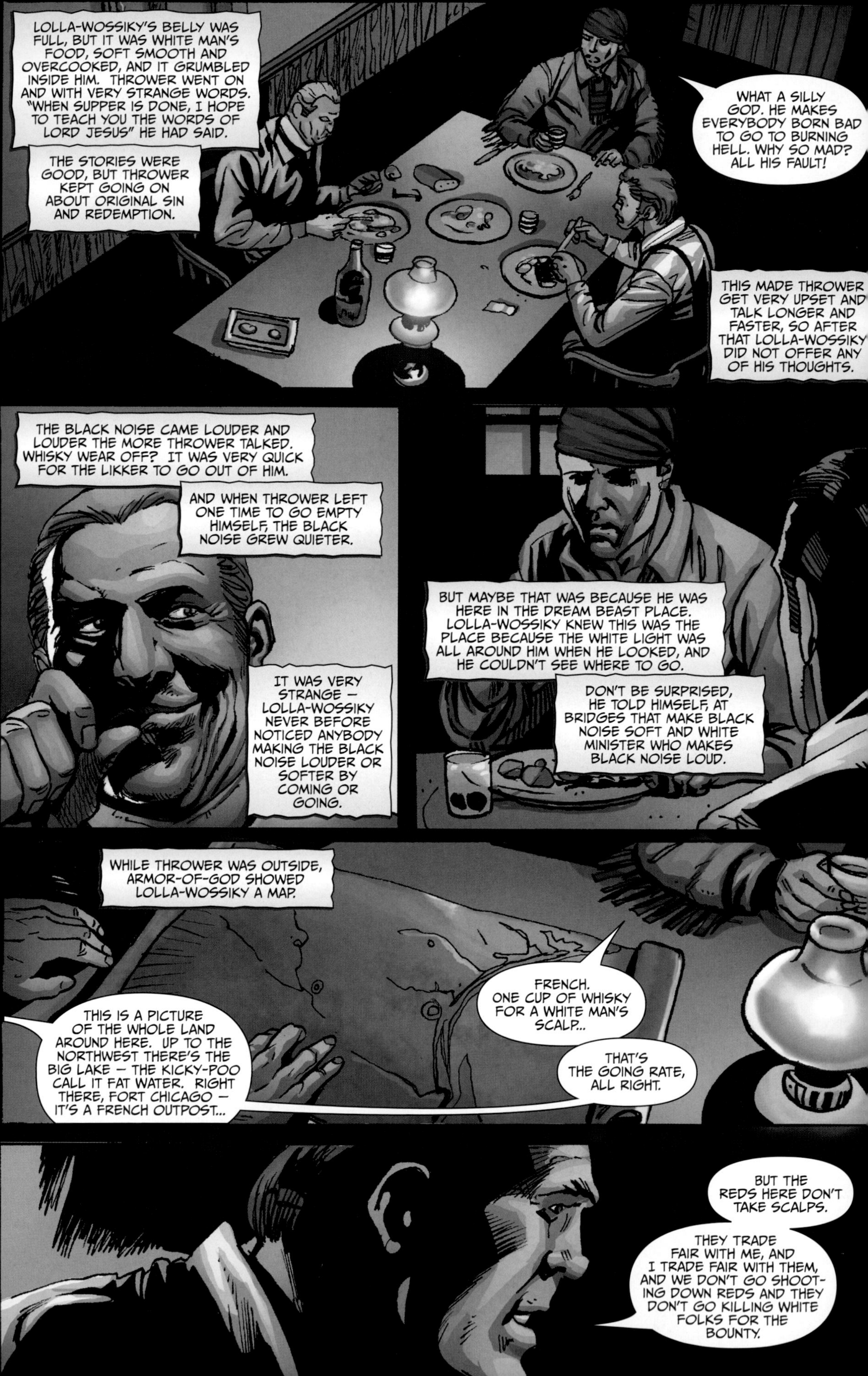

LOLLA-WOSSIKY'S BELLY WAS FULL, BUT IT WAS WHITE MAN'S FOOD, SOFT SMOOTH AND OVERCOOKED, AND IT GRUMBLED INSIDE HIM. THROWER WENT ON AND WITH VERY STRANGE WORDS. "WHEN SUPPER IS DONE, I HOPE TO TEACH YOU THE WORDS OF LORD JESUS" HE HAD SAID.
THE STORIES WERE GOOD, BUT THROWER KEPT GOING ON ABOUT ORIGINAL SIN AND REDEMPTION.
WHAT A SILLY GOD. HE MAKES EVERYBODY BORN BAD TO GO TO BURNING HELL. WHY SO MAD? ALL HIS FAULT!
THIS MADE THROWER GET VERY UPSET AND TALK LONGER AND FASTER, SO AFTER THAT LOLLA-WOSSIKY DID NOT OFFER ANY OF HIS THOUGHTS.
THE BLACK NOISE CAME LOUDER AND LOUDER THE MORE THROWER TALKED. WHISKY WEAR OFF? IT WAS VERY QUICK FOR THE LIKKER TO GO OUT OF HIM.
AND WHEN THROWER LEFT ONE TIME TO GO EMPTY HIMSELF, THE BLACK NOISE GREW QUIETER.
IT WAS VERY STRANGE — LOLLA-WOSSIKY NEVER BEFORE NOTICED ANYBODY MAKING THE BLACK NOISE LOUDER OR SOFTER BY COMING OR GOING.
BUT MAYBE THAT WAS BECAUSE HE WAS HERE IN THE DREAM BEAST PLACE. LOLLA-WOSSIKY KNEW THIS WAS THE PLACE BECAUSE THE WHITE LIGHT WAS ALL AROUND HIM WHEN HE LOOKED, AND HE COULDN'T SEE WHERE TO GO.
DON'T BE SURPRISED, HE TOLD HIMSELF, AT BRIDGES THAT MAKE BLACK NOISE SOFT AND WHITE MINISTER WHO MAKES BLACK NOISE LOUD.
WHILE THROWER WAS OUTSIDE, ARMOR-OF-GOD SHOWED LOLLA-WOSSIKY A MAP.
THIS IS A PICTURE OF THE WHOLE LAND AROUND HERE. UP TO THE NORTHWEST THERE'S THE BIG LAKE — THE KICKY-POO CALL IT FAT WATER. RIGHT THERE, FORT CHICAGO — IT'S A FRENCH OUTPOST...
FRENCH. ONE CUP OF WHISKY FOR A WHITE MAN'S SCALP...
THAT'S THE GOING RATE, ALL RIGHT.
BUT THE REDS HERE DON'T TAKE SCALPS.
THEY TRADE FAIR WITH ME, AND I TRADE FAIR WITH THEM, AND WE DON'T GO SHOOTING DOWN REDS AND THEY DON'T GO KILLING WHITE FOLKS FOR THE BOUNTY.

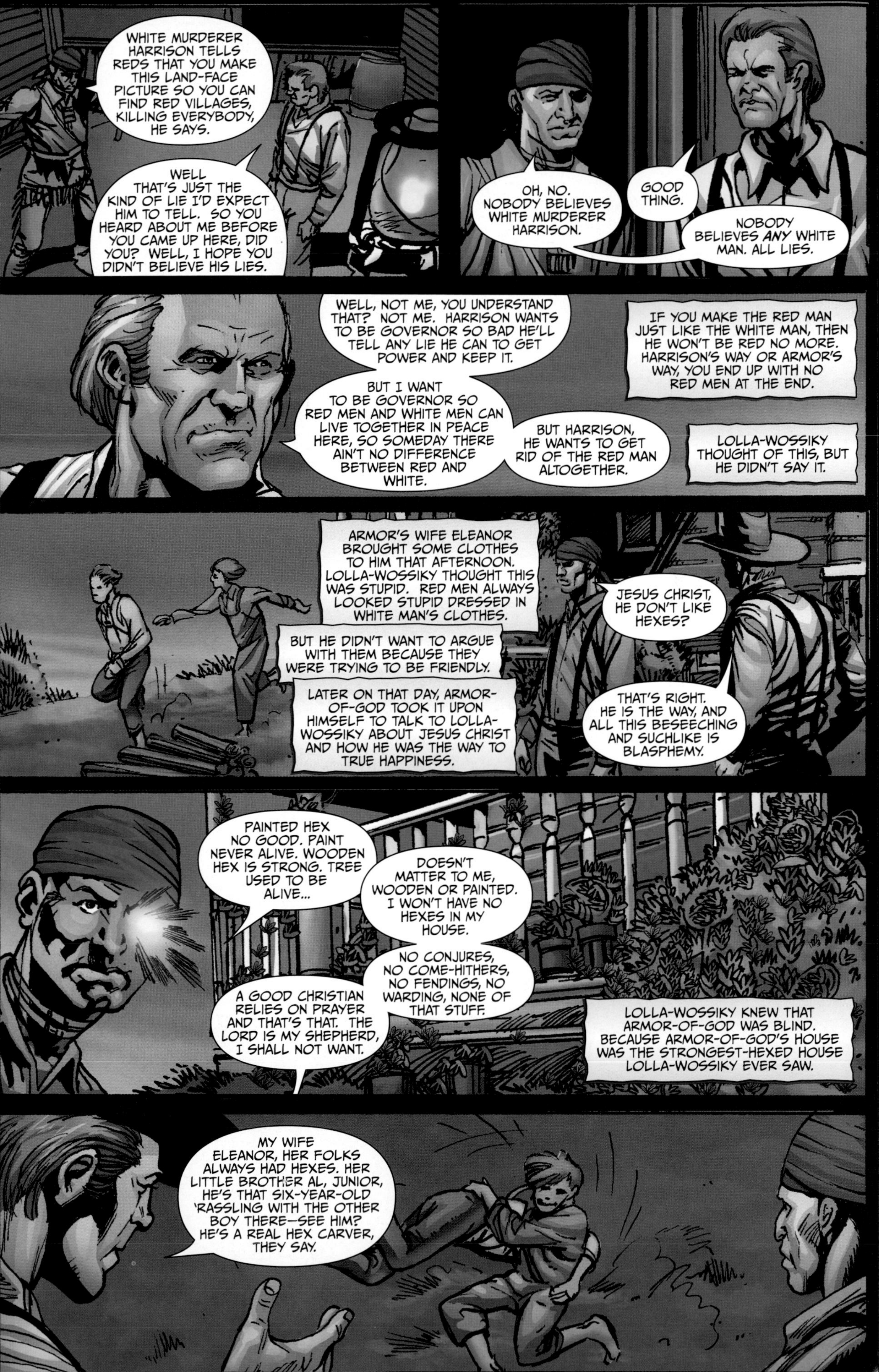

WHITE MURDERER HARRISON TELLS REDS THAT YOU MAKE THIS LAND-FACE PICTURE SO YOU CAN FIND RED VILLAGES, KILLING EVERYBODY, HE SAYS.
WELL THAT'S JUST THE KIND OF LIE I'D EXPECT HIM TO TELL. SO YOU HEARD ABOUT ME BEFORE YOU CAME UP HERE, DID YOU? WELL, I HOPE YOU DIDN'T BELIEVE HIS LIES.
OH, NO. NOBODY BELIEVES WHITE MURDERER HARRISON.
GOOD THING.
NOBODY BELIEVES *ANY* WHITE MAN. ALL LIES.
WELL, NOT ME, YOU UNDERSTAND THAT? NOT ME. HARRISON WANTS TO BE GOVERNOR SO BAD HE'LL TELL ANY LIE HE CAN TO GET POWER AND KEEP IT.
BUT I WANT TO BE GOVERNOR SO RED MEN AND WHITE MEN CAN LIVE TOGETHER IN PEACE HERE, SO SOMEDAY THERE AIN'T NO DIFFERENCE BETWEEN RED AND WHITE.
BUT HARRISON, HE WANTS TO GET RID OF THE RED MAN ALTOGETHER.
IF YOU MAKE THE RED MAN JUST LIKE THE WHITE MAN, THEN HE WON'T BE RED NO MORE. HARRISON'S WAY OR ARMOR'S WAY, YOU END UP WITH NO RED MEN AT THE END.
LOLLA-WOSSIKY THOUGHT OF THIS, BUT HE DIDN'T SAY IT.
ARMOR'S WIFE ELEANOR BROUGHT SOME CLOTHES TO HIM THAT AFTERNOON. LOLLA-WOSSIKY THOUGHT THIS WAS STUPID. RED MEN ALWAYS LOOKED STUPID DRESSED IN WHITE MAN'S CLOTHES.
BUT HE DIDN'T WANT TO ARGUE WITH THEM BECAUSE THEY WERE TRYING TO BE FRIENDLY.
LATER ON THAT DAY, ARMOR-OF-GOD TOOK IT UPON HIMSELF TO TALK TO LOLLA-WOSSIKY ABOUT JESUS CHRIST AND HOW HE WAS THE WAY TO TRUE HAPPINESS.
JESUS CHRIST, HE DON'T LIKE HEXES?
THAT'S RIGHT. HE IS THE WAY, AND ALL THIS BESEECHING AND SUCHLIKE IS BLASPHEMY.
PAINTED HEX NO GOOD. PAINT NEVER ALIVE. WOODEN HEX IS STRONG. TREE USED TO BE ALIVE...
DOESN'T MATTER TO ME, WOODEN OR PAINTED. I WON'T HAVE NO HEXES IN MY HOUSE.
NO CONJURES, NO COME-HITHERS, NO FENDINGS, NO WARDING, NONE OF THAT STUFF.
A GOOD CHRISTIAN RELIES ON PRAYER AND THAT'S THAT. THE LORD IS MY SHEPHERD, I SHALL NOT WANT.
LOLLA-WOSSIKY KNEW THAT ARMOR-OF-GOD WAS BLIND. BECAUSE ARMOR-OF-GOD'S HOUSE WAS THE STRONGEST-HEXED HOUSE LOLLA-WOSSIKY EVER SAW.
MY WIFE ELEANOR, HER FOLKS ALWAYS HAD HEXES. HER LITTLE BROTHER AL, JUNIOR, HE'S THAT SIX-YEAR-OLD 'RASSLING WITH THE OTHER BOY THERE—SEE HIM? HE'S A REAL HEX CARVER, THEY SAY.

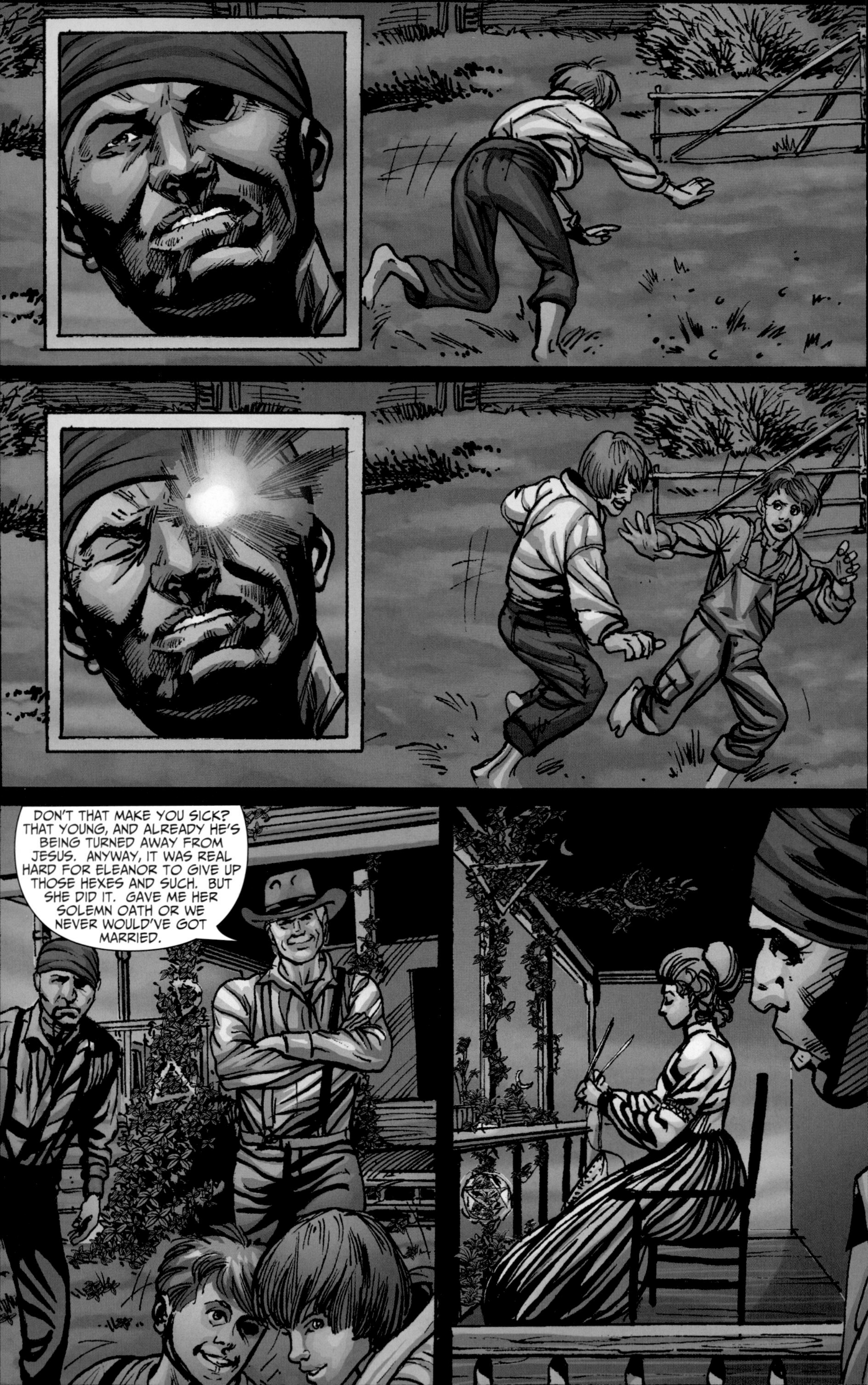
DON'T THAT MAKE YOU SICK? THAT YOUNG, AND ALREADY HE'S BEING TURNED AWAY FROM JESUS. ANYWAY, IT WAS REAL HARD FOR ELEANOR TO GIVE UP THOSE HEXES AND SUCH. BUT SHE DID IT. GAVE ME HER SOLEMN OATH OR WE NEVER WOULD'VE GOT MARRIED.

LOLLA-WOSSIKY WAS NOT AT THE CHURCH THE DAY THE ROOF-BEAM FELL.

≥SNORE≥

CRASH

HE WAS SLEEPING ON THE GRASS OF THE COMMONS, NEAR THE PORCH OF ARMOR'S HOUSE, WHEN HE HEARD THE CRASH...

WHAT HAPPENED? WAS A MAN KILLED? DID WHITE MURDERER HARRISON SHOOT SOMEBODY?

HE HAD TO KNOW, BECAUSE WHATEVER IT WAS, IT HAD MADE THE BLACK NOISE WORSE THAN IT HAD BEEN IN YEARS.

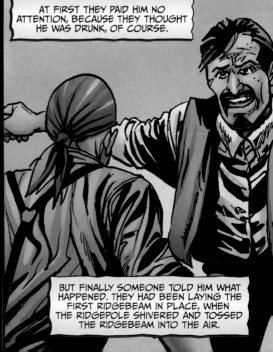

AT FIRST THEY PAID HIM NO ATTENTION, BECAUSE THEY THOUGHT HE WAS DRUNK, OF COURSE.

BUT FINALLY SOMEONE TOLD HIM WHAT HAPPENED. THEY HAD BEEN LAYING THE FIRST RIDGEBEAM IN PLACE, WHEN THE RIDGEPOLE SHIVERED AND TOSSED THE RIDGEBEAM INTO THE AIR.

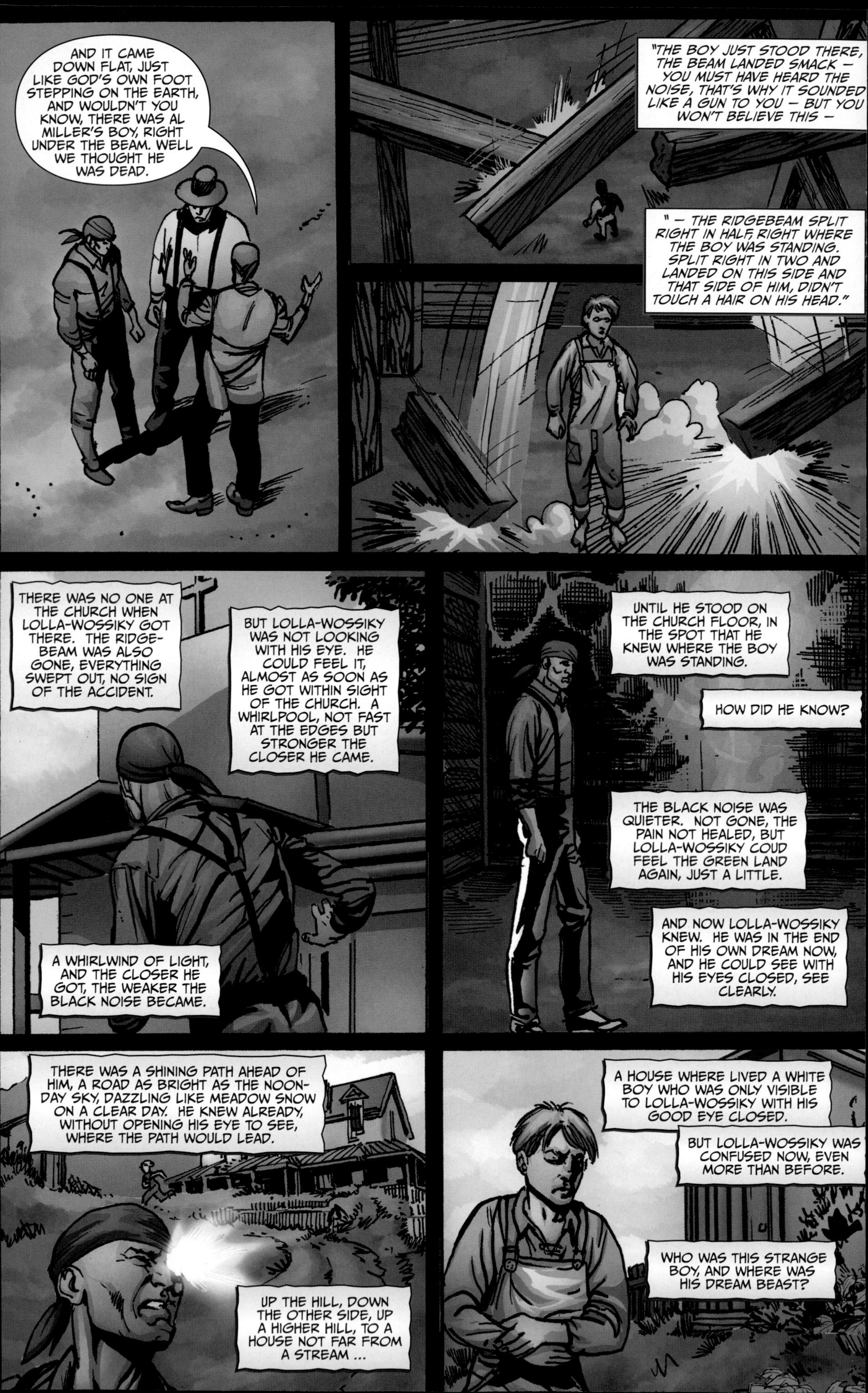
AND IT CAME DOWN FLAT, JUST LIKE GOD'S OWN FOOT STEPPING ON THE EARTH, AND WOULDN'T YOU KNOW, THERE WAS AL MILLER'S BOY, RIGHT UNDER THE BEAM. WELL WE THOUGHT HE WAS DEAD.
"THE BOY JUST STOOD THERE, THE BEAM LANDED SMACK — YOU MUST HAVE HEARD THE NOISE, THAT'S WHY IT SOUNDED LIKE A GUN TO YOU — BUT YOU WON'T BELIEVE THIS —
" — THE RIDGEBEAM SPLIT RIGHT IN HALF, RIGHT WHERE THE BOY WAS STANDING. SPLIT RIGHT IN TWO AND LANDED ON THIS SIDE AND THAT SIDE OF HIM, DIDN'T TOUCH A HAIR ON HIS HEAD."
THERE WAS NO ONE AT THE CHURCH WHEN LOLLA-WOSSIKY GOT THERE. THE RIDGE-BEAM WAS ALSO GONE, EVERYTHING SWEPT OUT, NO SIGN OF THE ACCIDENT.
BUT LOLLA-WOSSIKY WAS NOT LOOKING WITH HIS EYE. HE COULD FEEL IT, ALMOST AS SOON AS HE GOT WITHIN SIGHT OF THE CHURCH. A WHIRLPOOL, NOT FAST AT THE EDGES BUT STRONGER THE CLOSER HE CAME.
A WHIRLWIND OF LIGHT, AND THE CLOSER HE GOT, THE WEAKER THE BLACK NOISE BECAME.
UNTIL HE STOOD ON THE CHURCH FLOOR, IN THE SPOT THAT HE KNEW WHERE THE BOY WAS STANDING.
HOW DID HE KNOW?
THE BLACK NOISE WAS QUIETER. NOT GONE, THE PAIN NOT HEALED, BUT LOLLA-WOSSIKY COUD FEEL THE GREEN LAND AGAIN, JUST A LITTLE.
AND NOW LOLLA-WOSSIKY KNEW. HE WAS IN THE END OF HIS OWN DREAM NOW, AND HE COULD SEE WITH HIS EYES CLOSED, SEE CLEARLY.
THERE WAS A SHINING PATH AHEAD OF HIM, A ROAD AS BRIGHT AS THE NOON-DAY SKY, DAZZLING LIKE MEADOW SNOW ON A CLEAR DAY. HE KNEW ALREADY, WITHOUT OPENING HIS EYE TO SEE, WHERE THE PATH WOULD LEAD.
UP THE HILL, DOWN THE OTHER SIDE, UP A HIGHER HILL, TO A HOUSE NOT FAR FROM A STREAM ...
A HOUSE WHERE LIVED A WHITE BOY WHO WAS ONLY VISIBLE TO LOLLA-WOSSIKY WITH HIS GOOD EYE CLOSED.
BUT LOLLA-WOSSIKY WAS CONFUSED NOW, EVEN MORE THAN BEFORE.
WHO WAS THIS STRANGE BOY, AND WHERE WAS HIS DREAM BEAST?

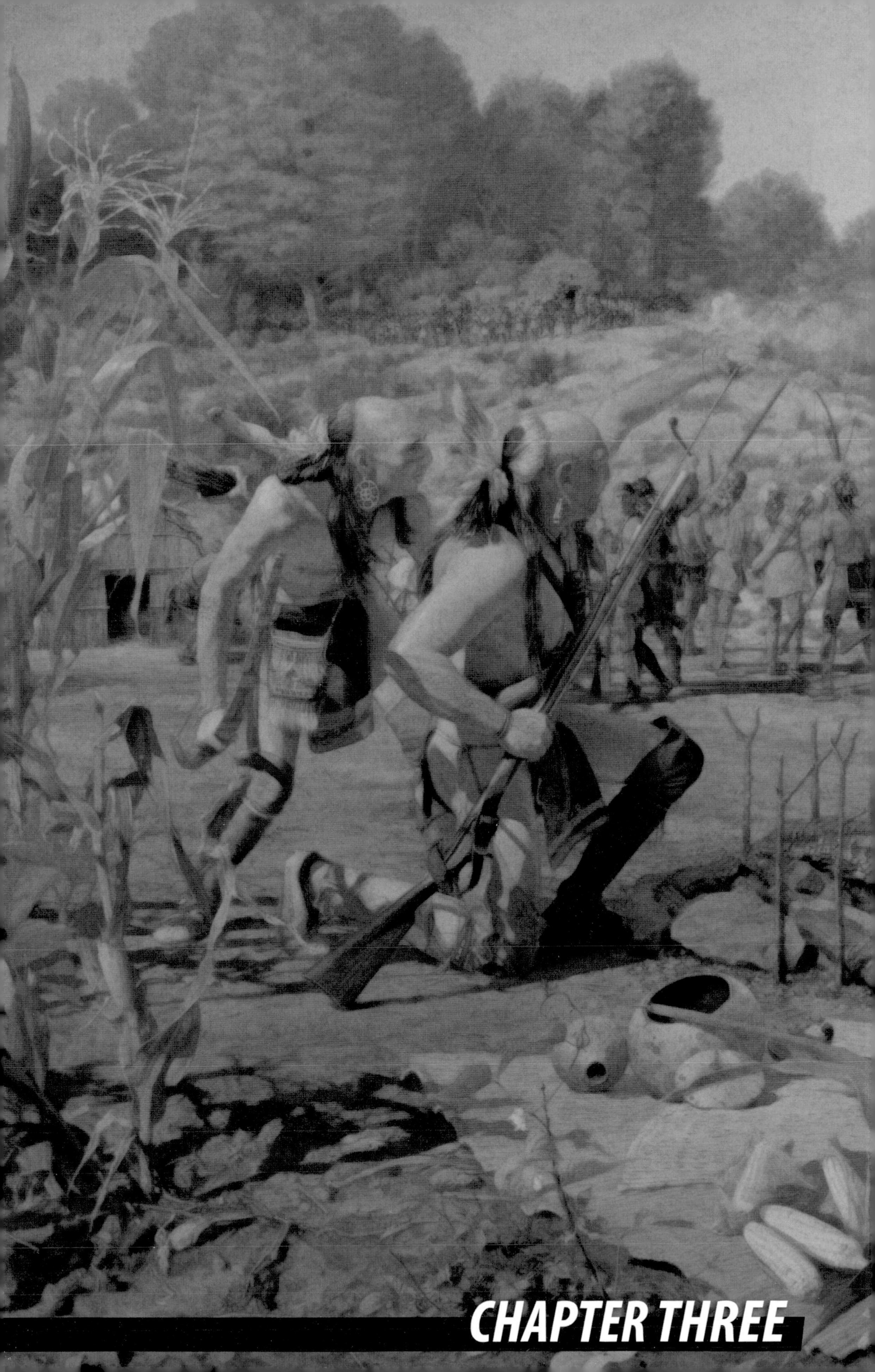

CHAPTER THREE

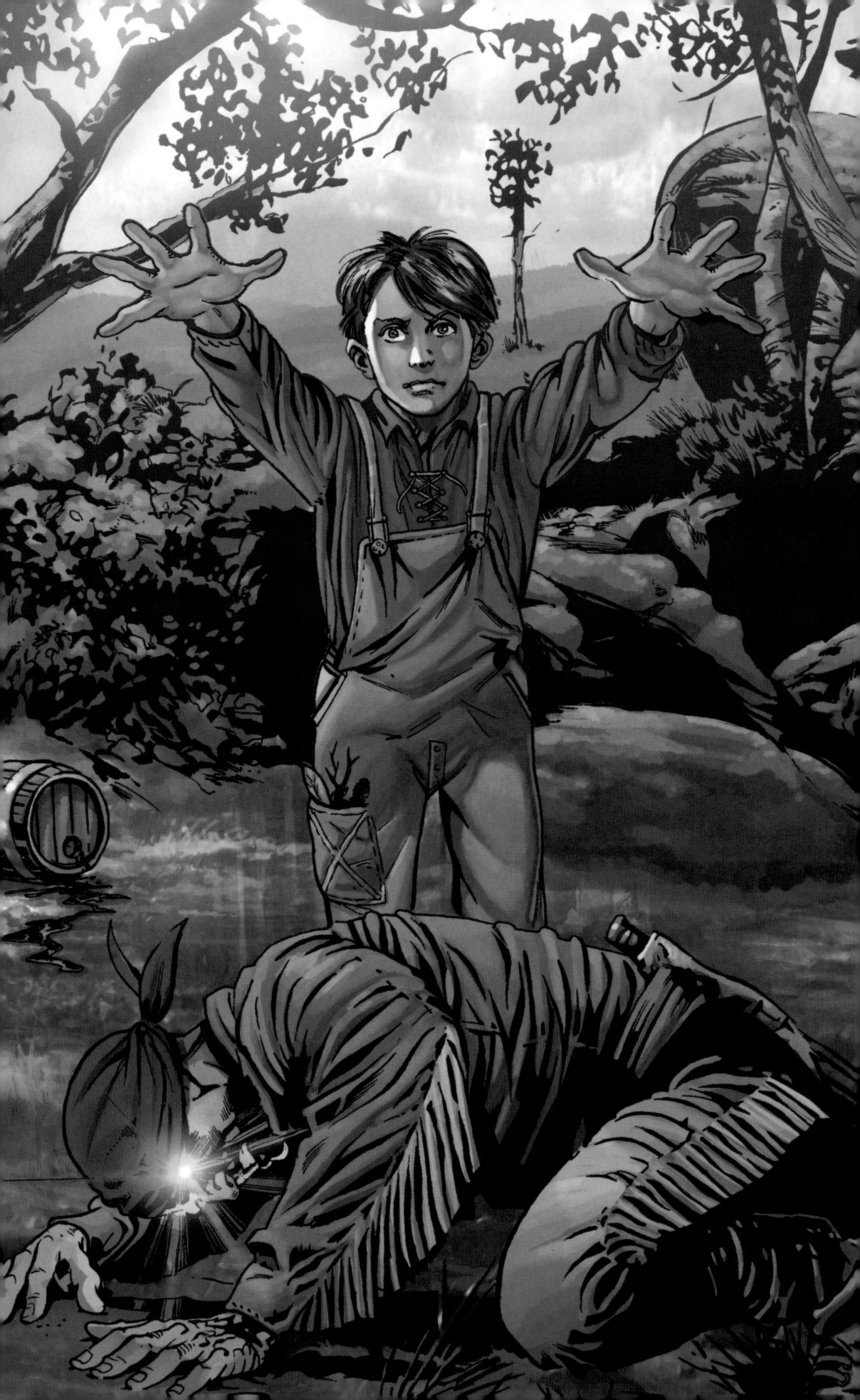

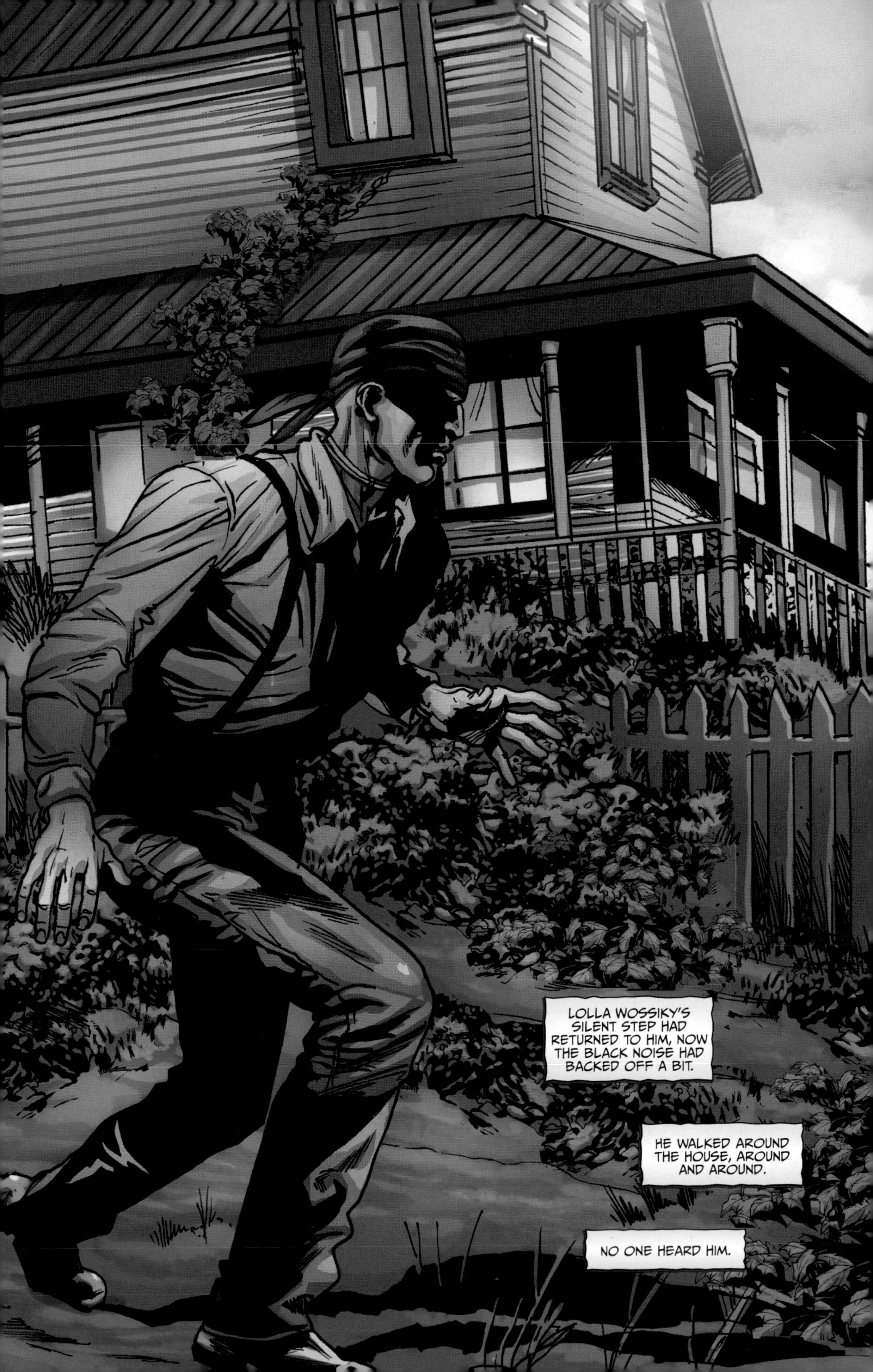
LOLLA WOSSIKY'S SILENT STEP HAD RETURNED TO HIM, NOW THE BLACK NOISE HAD BACKED OFF A BIT.
HE WALKED AROUND THE HOUSE, AROUND AND AROUND.
NO ONE HEARD HIM.

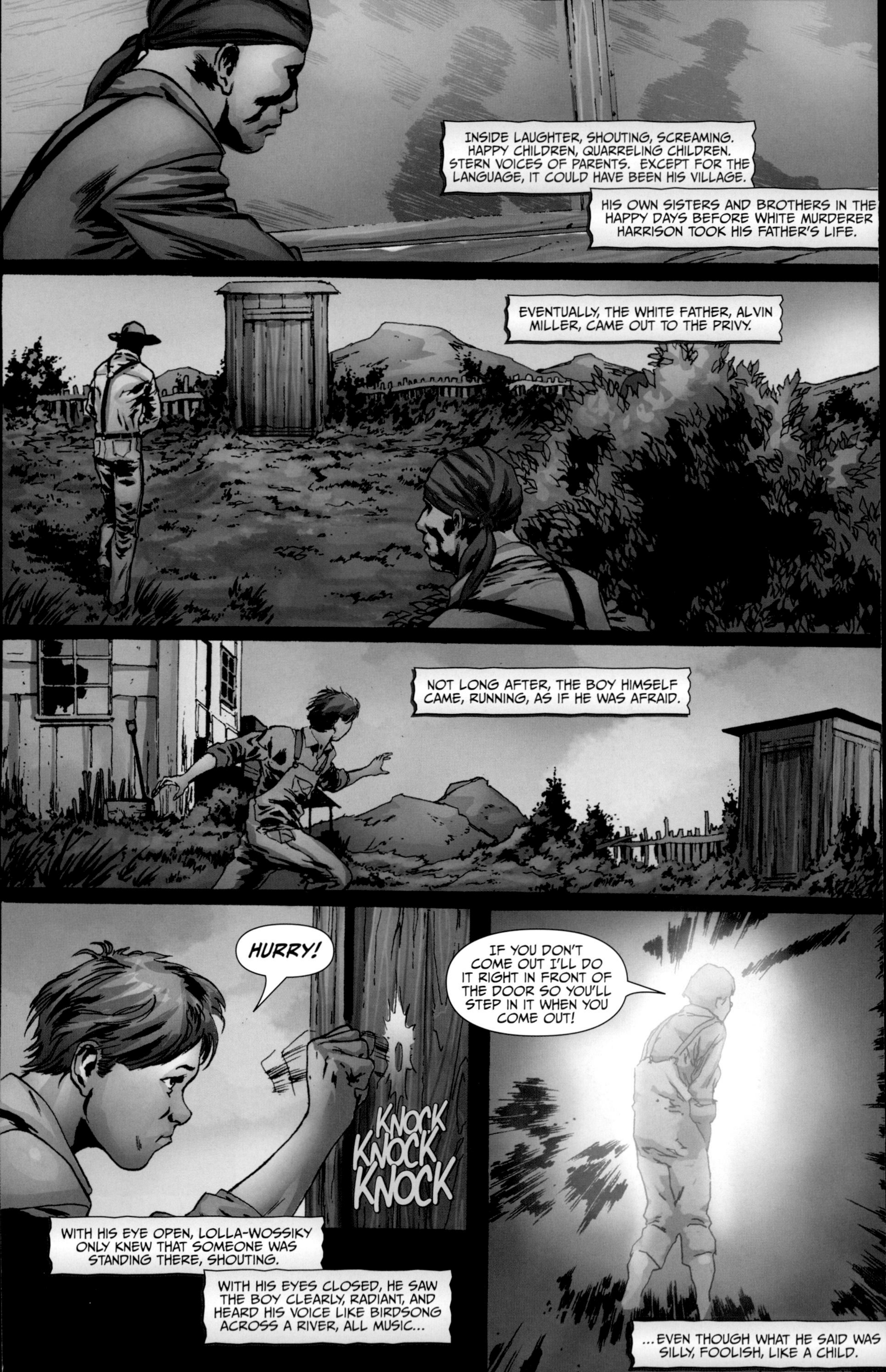

INSIDE LAUGHTER, SHOUTING, SCREAMING. HAPPY CHILDREN, QUARRELING CHILDREN. STERN VOICES OF PARENTS. EXCEPT FOR THE LANGUAGE, IT COULD HAVE BEEN HIS VILLAGE.
HIS OWN SISTERS AND BROTHERS IN THE HAPPY DAYS BEFORE WHITE MURDERER HARRISON TOOK HIS FATHER'S LIFE.
EVENTUALLY, THE WHITE FATHER, ALVIN MILLER, CAME OUT TO THE PRIVY.
NOT LONG AFTER, THE BOY HIMSELF CAME, RUNNING, AS IF HE WAS AFRAID.
HURRY!
KNOCK KNOCK KNOCK
WITH HIS EYE OPEN, LOLLA-WOSSIKY ONLY KNEW THAT SOMEONE WAS STANDING THERE, SHOUTING.
WITH HIS EYES CLOSED, HE SAW THE BOY CLEARLY, RADIANT, AND HEARD HIS VOICE LIKE BIRDSONG ACROSS A RIVER, ALL MUSIC...
IF YOU DON'T COME OUT I'LL DO IT RIGHT IN FRONT OF THE DOOR SO YOU'LL STEP IN IT WHEN YOU COME OUT!
...EVEN THOUGH WHAT HE SAID WAS SILLY, FOOLISH, LIKE A CHILD.

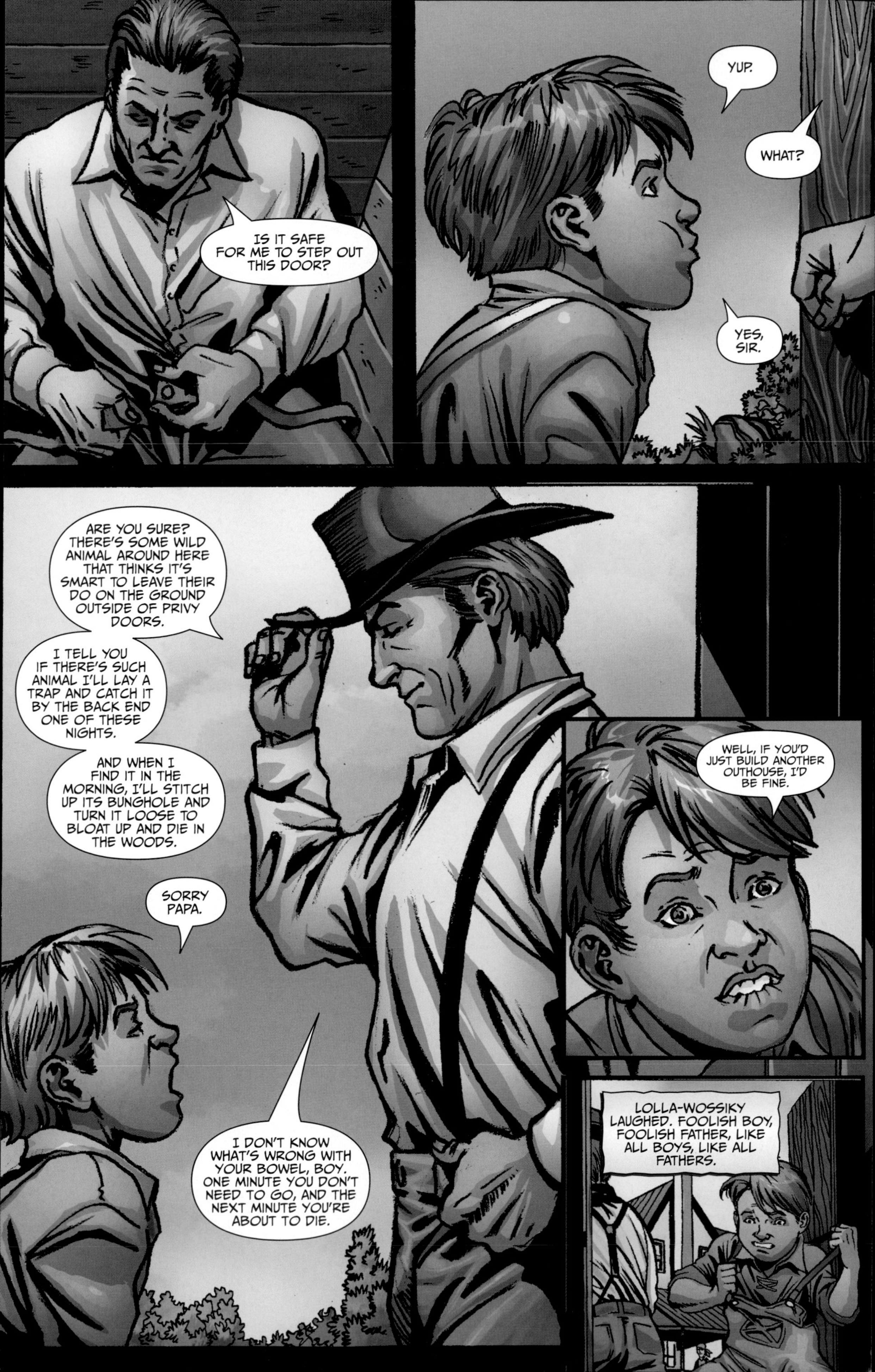
IS IT SAFE FOR ME TO STEP OUT THIS DOOR?
YUP.
WHAT?
YES, SIR.
ARE YOU SURE? THERE'S SOME WILD ANIMAL AROUND HERE THAT THINKS IT'S SMART TO LEAVE THEIR DO ON THE GROUND OUTSIDE OF PRIVY DOORS.
I TELL YOU IF THERE'S SUCH ANIMAL I'LL LAY A TRAP AND CATCH IT BY THE BACK END ONE OF THESE NIGHTS.
AND WHEN I FIND IT IN THE MORNING, I'LL STITCH UP ITS BUNGHOLE AND TURN IT LOOSE TO BLOAT UP AND DIE IN THE WOODS.
SORRY PAPA.
I DON'T KNOW WHAT'S WRONG WITH YOUR BOWEL, BOY. ONE MINUTE YOU DON'T NEED TO GO, AND THE NEXT MINUTE YOU'RE ABOUT TO DIE.
WELL, IF YOU'D JUST BUILD ANOTHER OUTHOUSE, I'D BE FINE.
LOLLA-WOSSIKY LAUGHED. FOOLISH BOY, FOOLISH FATHER, LIKE ALL BOYS, LIKE ALL FATHERS.

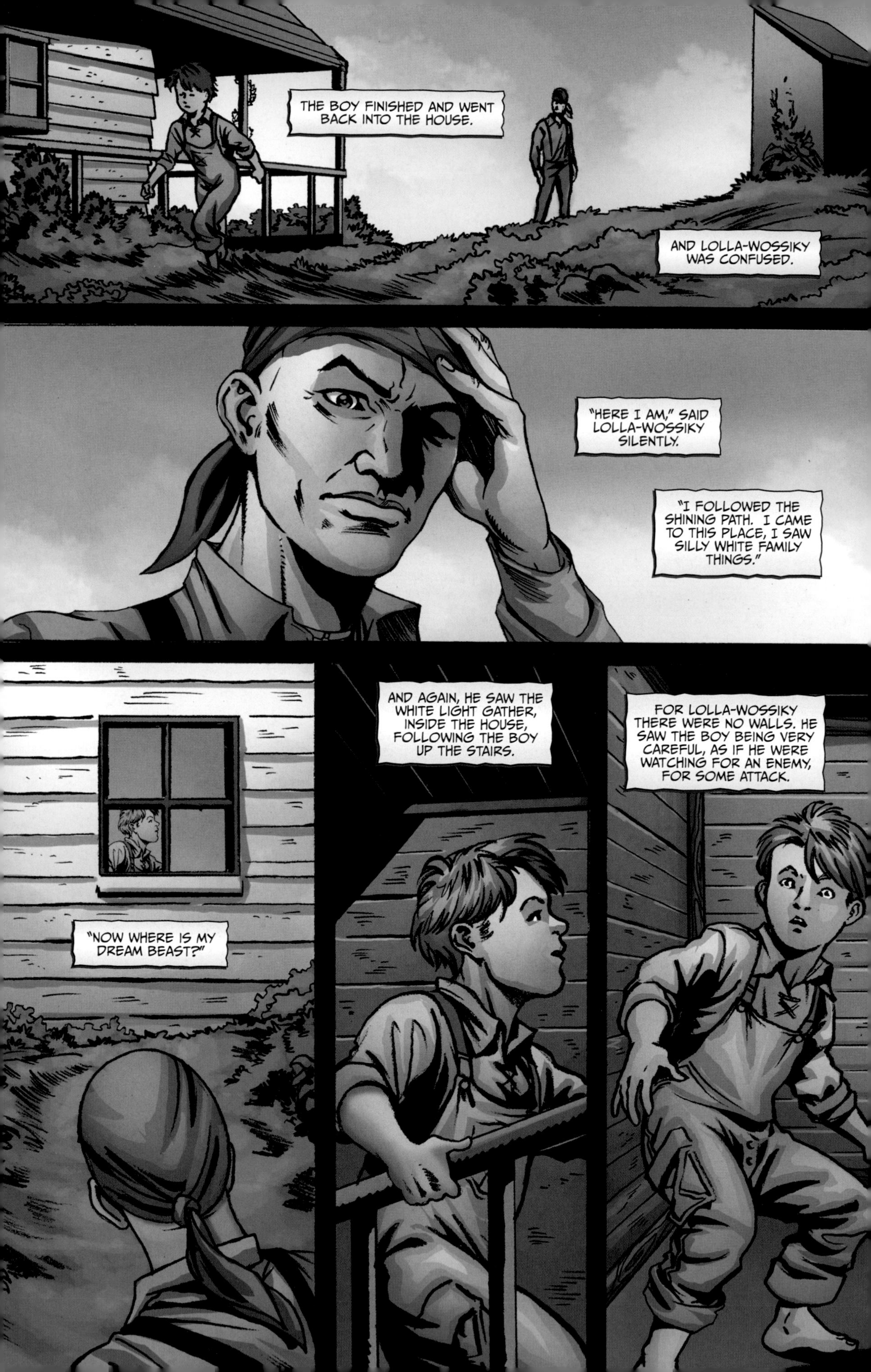
THE BOY FINISHED AND WENT BACK INTO THE HOUSE.
AND LOLLA-WOSSIKY WAS CONFUSED.
"HERE I AM," SAID LOLLA-WOSSIKY SILENTLY.
"I FOLLOWED THE SHINING PATH. I CAME TO THIS PLACE, I SAW SILLY WHITE FAMILY THINGS."
"NOW WHERE IS MY DREAM BEAST?"
AND AGAIN, HE SAW THE WHITE LIGHT GATHER, INSIDE THE HOUSE, FOLLOWING THE BOY UP THE STAIRS.
FOR LOLLA-WOSSIKY THERE WERE NO WALLS. HE SAW THE BOY BEING VERY CAREFUL, AS IF HE WERE WATCHING FOR AN ENEMY, FOR SOME ATTACK.

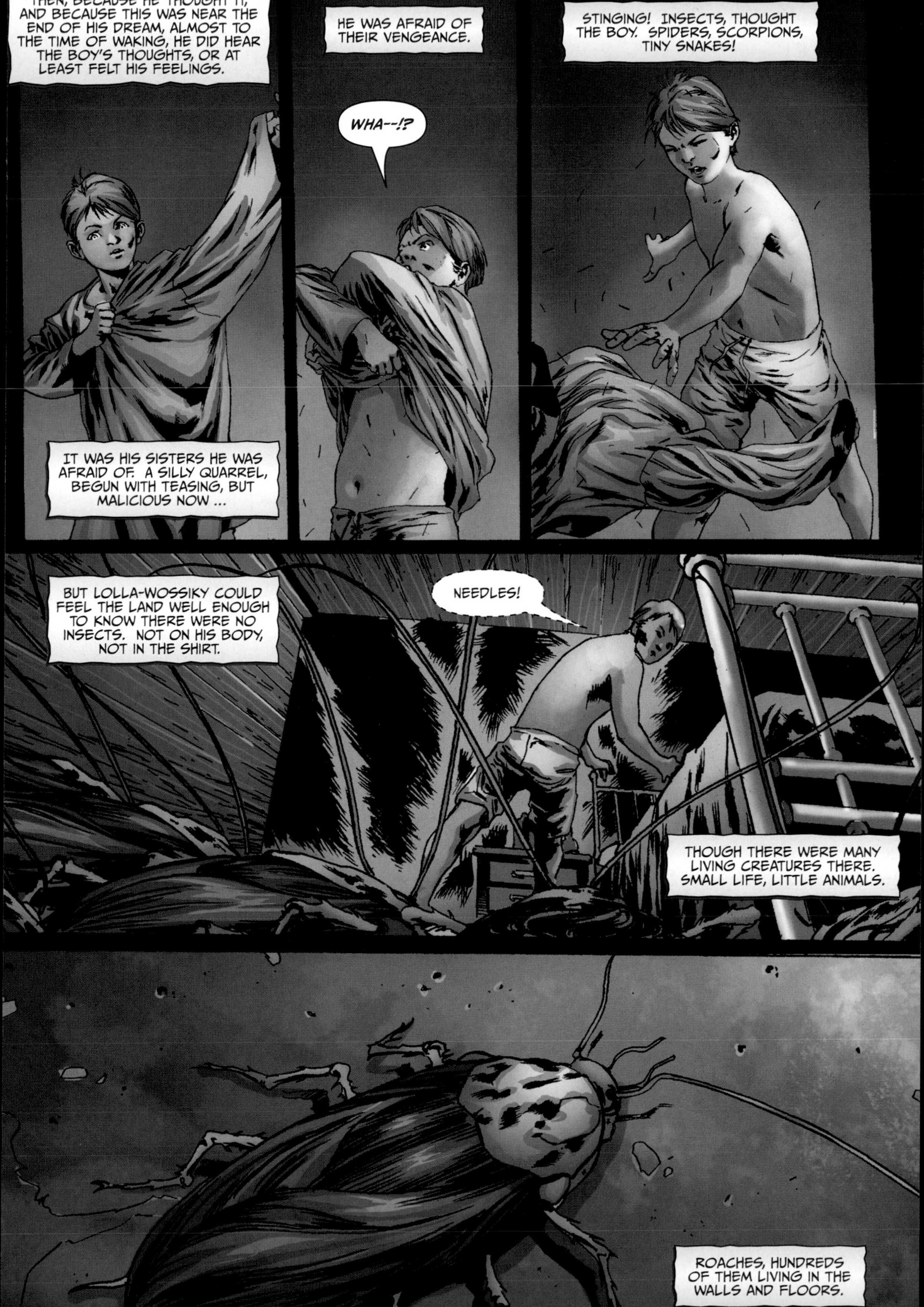
THEN, BECAUSE HE THOUGHT IT, AND BECAUSE THIS WAS NEAR THE END OF HIS DREAM, ALMOST TO THE TIME OF WAKING, HE DID HEAR THE BOY'S THOUGHTS, OR AT LEAST FELT HIS FEELINGS.
IT WAS HIS SISTERS HE WAS AFRAID OF. A SILLY QUARREL, BEGUN WITH TEASING, BUT MALICIOUS NOW ...
HE WAS AFRAID OF THEIR VENGEANCE.
WHA--!?
STINGING! INSECTS, THOUGHT THE BOY. SPIDERS, SCORPIONS, TINY SNAKES!
BUT LOLLA-WOSSIKY COULD FEEL THE LAND WELL ENOUGH TO KNOW THERE WERE NO INSECTS. NOT ON HIS BODY, NOT IN THE SHIRT.
NEEDLES!
THOUGH THERE WERE MANY LIVING CREATURES THERE. SMALL LIFE, LITTLE ANIMALS.
ROACHES, HUNDREDS OF THEM LIVING IN THE WALLS AND FLOORS.

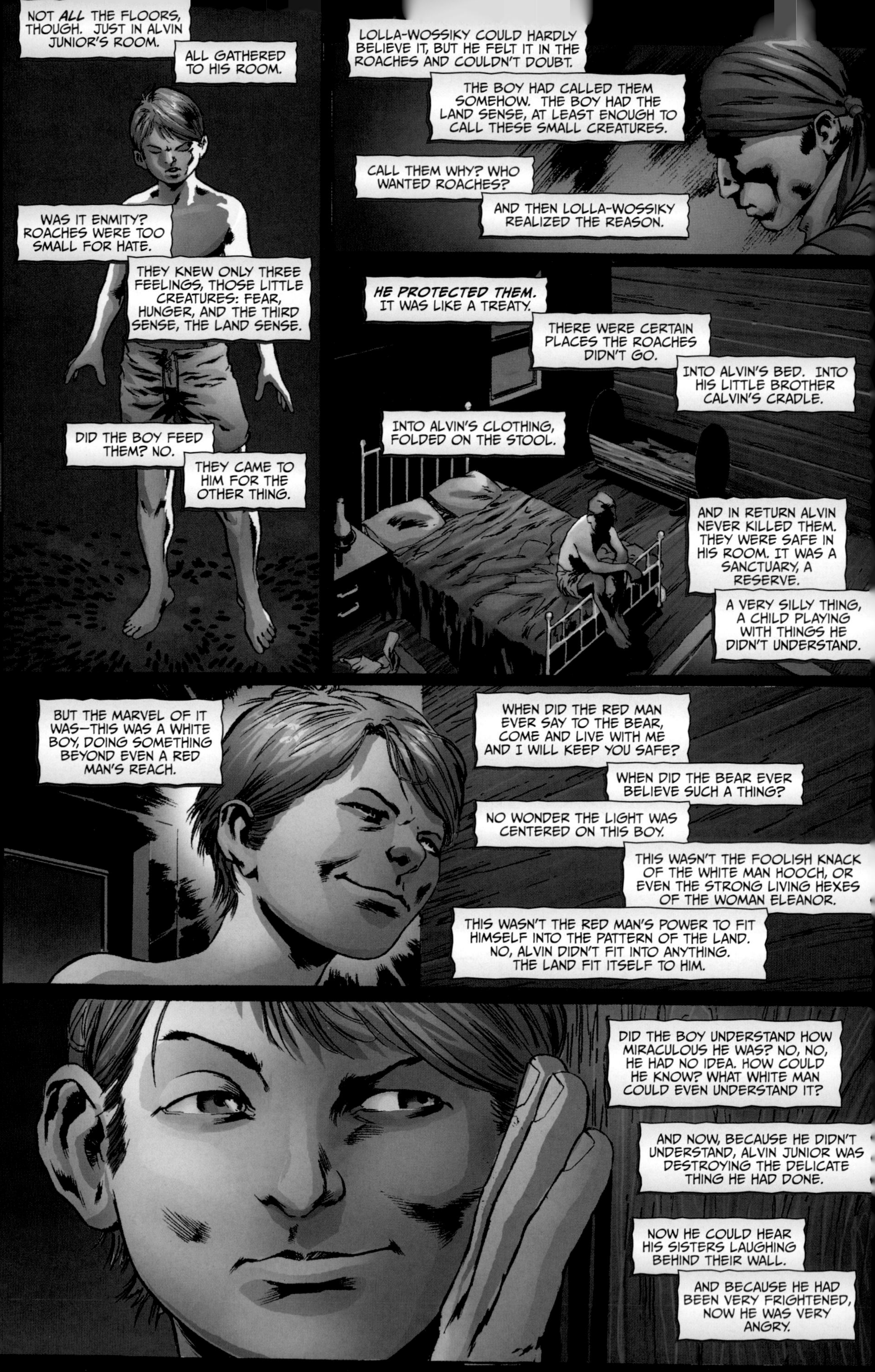
NOT *ALL* THE FLOORS, THOUGH. JUST IN ALVIN JUNIOR'S ROOM.
ALL GATHERED TO HIS ROOM.
WAS IT ENMITY? ROACHES WERE TOO SMALL FOR HATE.
THEY KNEW ONLY THREE FEELINGS, THOSE LITTLE CREATURES: FEAR, HUNGER, AND THE THIRD SENSE, THE LAND SENSE.
DID THE BOY FEED THEM? NO.
THEY CAME TO HIM FOR THE OTHER THING.
LOLLA-WOSSIKY COULD HARDLY BELIEVE IT, BUT HE FELT IT IN THE ROACHES AND COULDN'T DOUBT.
THE BOY HAD CALLED THEM SOMEHOW. THE BOY HAD THE LAND SENSE, AT LEAST ENOUGH TO CALL THESE SMALL CREATURES.
CALL THEM WHY? WHO WANTED ROACHES?
AND THEN LOLLA-WOSSIKY REALIZED THE REASON.
HE PROTECTED THEM. IT WAS LIKE A TREATY.
THERE WERE CERTAIN PLACES THE ROACHES DIDN'T GO.
INTO ALVIN'S BED. INTO HIS LITTLE BROTHER CALVIN'S CRADLE.
INTO ALVIN'S CLOTHING, FOLDED ON THE STOOL.
AND IN RETURN ALVIN NEVER KILLED THEM. THEY WERE SAFE IN HIS ROOM. IT WAS A SANCTUARY, A RESERVE.
A VERY SILLY THING, A CHILD PLAYING WITH THINGS HE DIDN'T UNDERSTAND.
BUT THE MARVEL OF IT WAS—THIS WAS A WHITE BOY, DOING SOMETHING BEYOND EVEN A RED MAN'S REACH.
WHEN DID THE RED MAN EVER SAY TO THE BEAR, COME AND LIVE WITH ME AND I WILL KEEP YOU SAFE?
WHEN DID THE BEAR EVER BELIEVE SUCH A THING?
NO WONDER THE LIGHT WAS CENTERED ON THIS BOY.
THIS WASN'T THE FOOLISH KNACK OF THE WHITE MAN HOOCH, OR EVEN THE STRONG LIVING HEXES OF THE WOMAN ELEANOR.
THIS WASN'T THE RED MAN'S POWER TO FIT HIMSELF INTO THE PATTERN OF THE LAND. NO, ALVIN DIDN'T FIT INTO ANYTHING. THE LAND FIT ITSELF TO HIM.
DID THE BOY UNDERSTAND HOW MIRACULOUS HE WAS? NO, NO, HE HAD NO IDEA. HOW COULD HE KNOW? WHAT WHITE MAN COULD EVEN UNDERSTAND IT?
AND NOW, BECAUSE HE DIDN'T UNDERSTAND, ALVIN JUNIOR WAS DESTROYING THE DELICATE THING HE HAD DONE.
NOW HE COULD HEAR HIS SISTERS LAUGHING BEHIND THEIR WALL.
AND BECAUSE HE HAD BEEN VERY FRIGHTENED, NOW HE WAS VERY ANGRY.

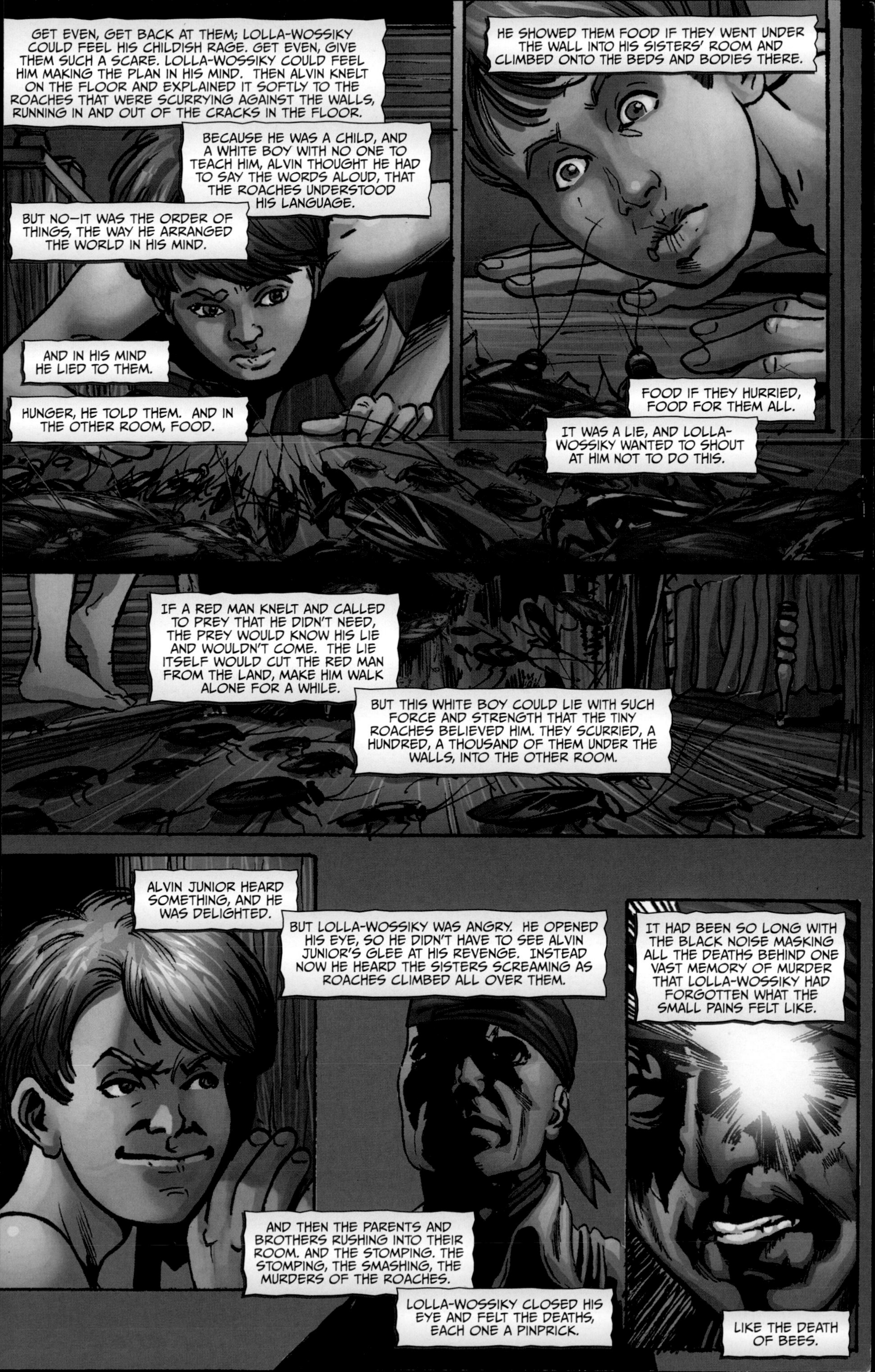
GET EVEN, GET BACK AT THEM; LOLLA-WOSSIKY COULD FEEL HIS CHILDISH RAGE. GET EVEN, GIVE THEM SUCH A SCARE. LOLLA-WOSSIKY COULD FEEL HIM MAKING THE PLAN IN HIS MIND. THEN ALVIN KNELT ON THE FLOOR AND EXPLAINED IT SOFTLY TO THE ROACHES THAT WERE SCURRYING AGAINST THE WALLS, RUNNING IN AND OUT OF THE CRACKS IN THE FLOOR.
BECAUSE HE WAS A CHILD, AND A WHITE BOY WITH NO ONE TO TEACH HIM, ALVIN THOUGHT HE HAD TO SAY THE WORDS ALOUD, THAT THE ROACHES UNDERSTOOD HIS LANGUAGE.
BUT NO—IT WAS THE ORDER OF THINGS, THE WAY HE ARRANGED THE WORLD IN HIS MIND.
AND IN HIS MIND HE LIED TO THEM.
HUNGER, HE TOLD THEM. AND IN THE OTHER ROOM, FOOD.
HE SHOWED THEM FOOD IF THEY WENT UNDER THE WALL INTO HIS SISTERS' ROOM AND CLIMBED ONTO THE BEDS AND BODIES THERE.
FOOD IF THEY HURRIED, FOOD FOR THEM ALL.
IT WAS A LIE, AND LOLLA-WOSSIKY WANTED TO SHOUT AT HIM NOT TO DO THIS.
IF A RED MAN KNELT AND CALLED TO PREY THAT HE DIDN'T NEED, THE PREY WOULD KNOW HIS LIE AND WOULDN'T COME. THE LIE ITSELF WOULD CUT THE RED MAN FROM THE LAND, MAKE HIM WALK ALONE FOR A WHILE.
BUT THIS WHITE BOY COULD LIE WITH SUCH FORCE AND STRENGTH THAT THE TINY ROACHES BELIEVED HIM. THEY SCURRIED, A HUNDRED, A THOUSAND OF THEM UNDER THE WALLS, INTO THE OTHER ROOM.
ALVIN JUNIOR HEARD SOMETHING, AND HE WAS DELIGHTED.
BUT LOLLA-WOSSIKY WAS ANGRY. HE OPENED HIS EYE, SO HE DIDN'T HAVE TO SEE ALVIN JUNIOR'S GLEE AT HIS REVENGE. INSTEAD NOW HE HEARD THE SISTERS SCREAMING AS ROACHES CLIMBED ALL OVER THEM.
AND THEN THE PARENTS AND BROTHERS RUSHING INTO THEIR ROOM. AND THE STOMPING. THE STOMPING, THE SMASHING, THE MURDERS OF THE ROACHES.
LOLLA-WOSSIKY CLOSED HIS EYE AND FELT THE DEATHS, EACH ONE A PINPRICK.
IT HAD BEEN SO LONG WITH THE BLACK NOISE MASKING ALL THE DEATHS BEHIND ONE VAST MEMORY OF MURDER THAT LOLLA-WOSSIKY HAD FORGOTTEN WHAT THE SMALL PAINS FELT LIKE.
LIKE THE DEATH OF BEES.

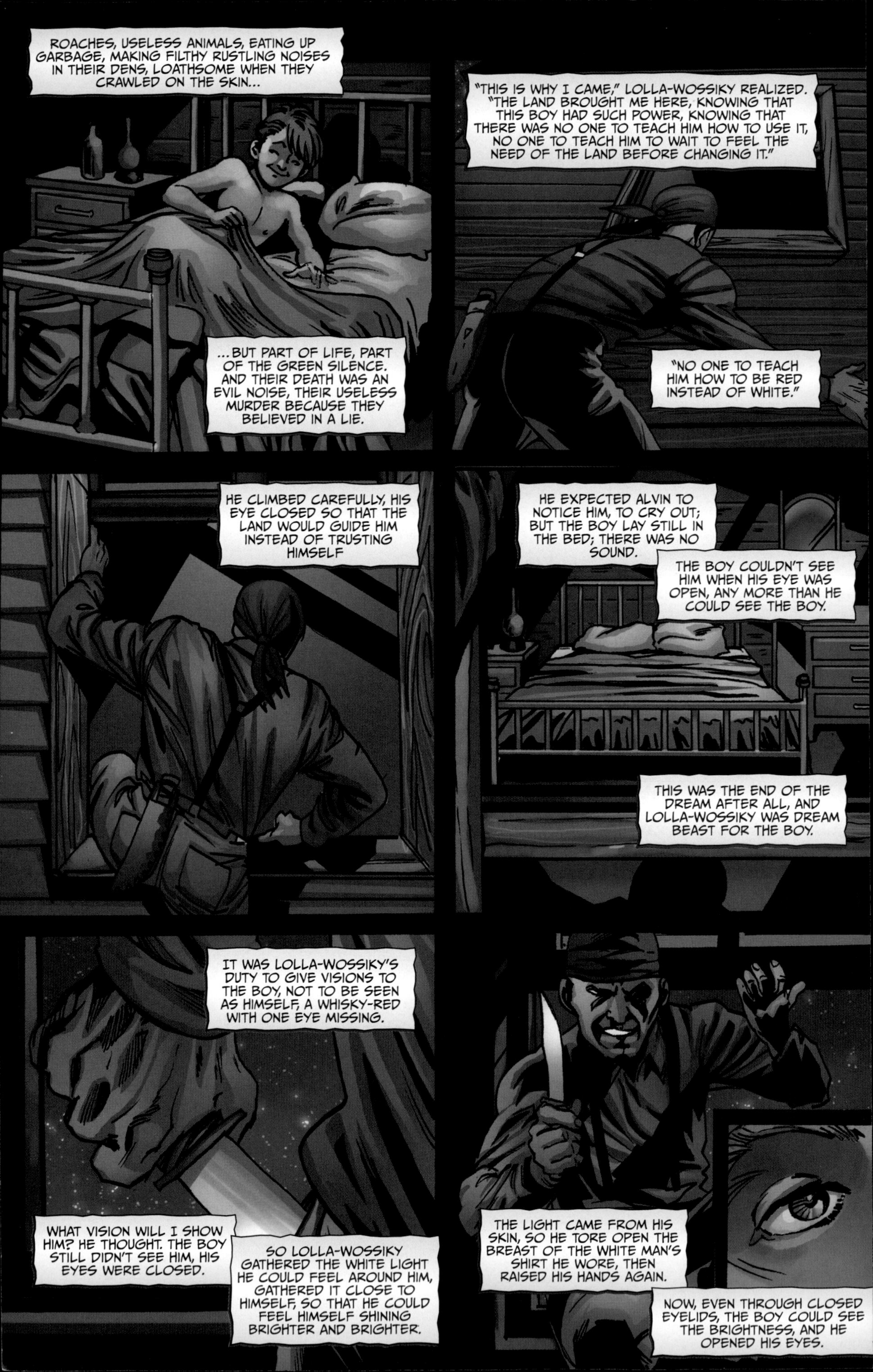
ROACHES, USELESS ANIMALS, EATING UP GARBAGE, MAKING FILTHY RUSTLING NOISES IN THEIR DENS, LOATHSOME WHEN THEY CRAWLED ON THE SKIN...
...BUT PART OF LIFE, PART OF THE GREEN SILENCE. AND THEIR DEATH WAS AN EVIL NOISE, THEIR USELESS MURDER BECAUSE THEY BELIEVED IN A LIE.
"THIS IS WHY I CAME," LOLLA-WOSSIKY REALIZED. "THE LAND BROUGHT ME HERE, KNOWING THAT THIS BOY HAD SUCH POWER, KNOWING THAT THERE WAS NO ONE TO TEACH HIM HOW TO USE IT, NO ONE TO TEACH HIM TO WAIT TO FEEL THE NEED OF THE LAND BEFORE CHANGING IT."
"NO ONE TO TEACH HIM HOW TO BE RED INSTEAD OF WHITE."
HE CLIMBED CAREFULLY, HIS EYE CLOSED SO THAT THE LAND WOULD GUIDE HIM INSTEAD OF TRUSTING HIMSELF
HE EXPECTED ALVIN TO NOTICE HIM, TO CRY OUT; BUT THE BOY LAY STILL IN THE BED; THERE WAS NO SOUND.
THE BOY COULDN'T SEE HIM WHEN HIS EYE WAS OPEN, ANY MORE THAN HE COULD SEE THE BOY.
THIS WAS THE END OF THE DREAM AFTER ALL, AND LOLLA-WOSSIKY WAS DREAM BEAST FOR THE BOY.
IT WAS LOLLA-WOSSIKY'S DUTY TO GIVE VISIONS TO THE BOY, NOT TO BE SEEN AS HIMSELF, A WHISKY-RED WITH ONE EYE MISSING.
WHAT VISION WILL I SHOW HIM? HE THOUGHT. THE BOY STILL DIDN'T SEE HIM, HIS EYES WERE CLOSED.
SO LOLLA-WOSSIKY GATHERED THE WHITE LIGHT HE COULD FEEL AROUND HIM, GATHERED IT CLOSE TO HIMSELF, SO THAT HE COULD FEEL HIMSELF SHINING BRIGHTER AND BRIGHTER.
THE LIGHT CAME FROM HIS SKIN, SO HE TORE OPEN THE BREAST OF THE WHITE MAN'S SHIRT HE WORE, THEN RAISED HIS HANDS AGAIN.
NOW, EVEN THROUGH CLOSED EYELIDS, THE BOY COULD SEE THE BRIGHTNESS, AND HE OPENED HIS EYES.

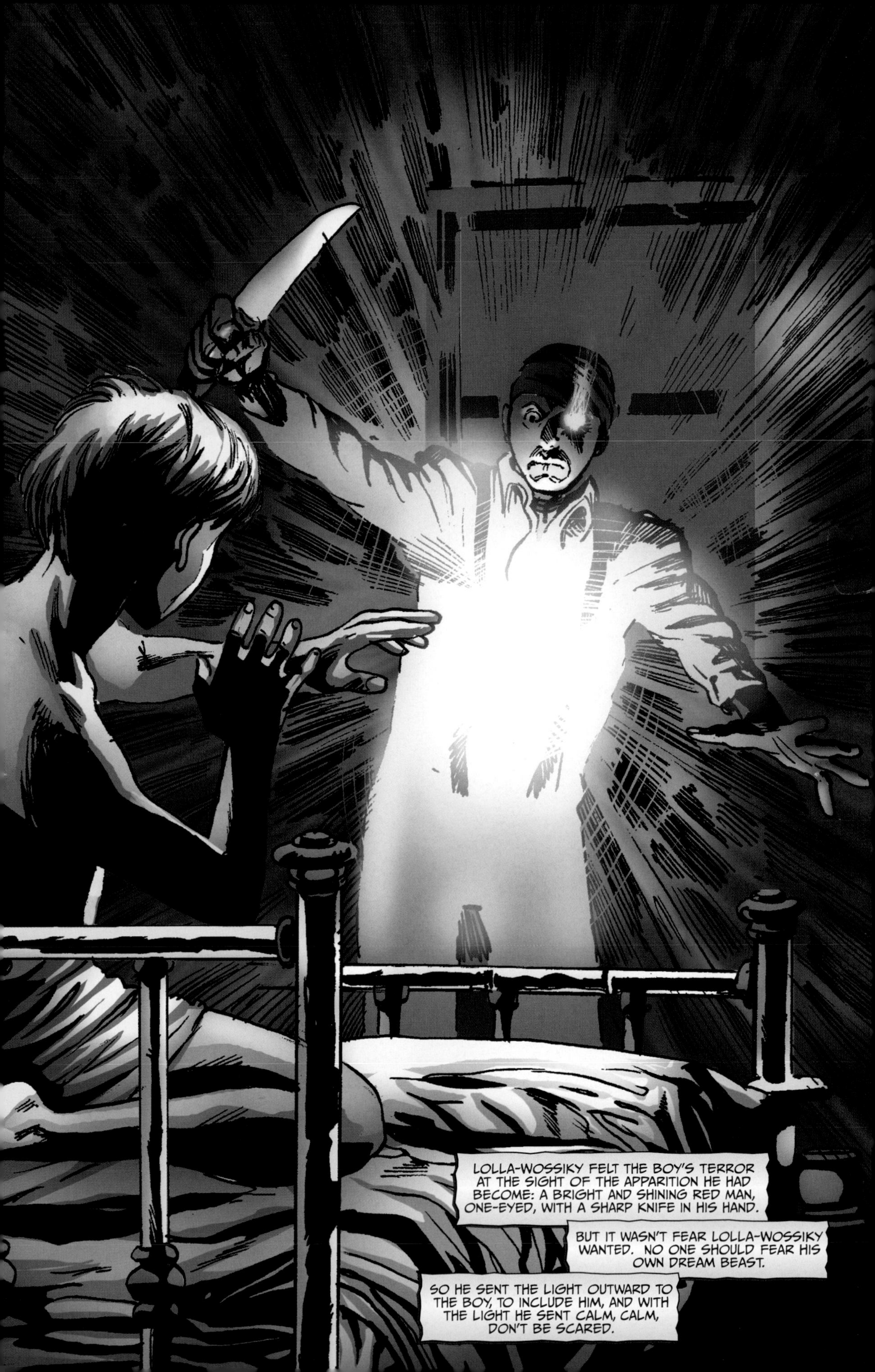
LOLLA-WOSSIKY FELT THE BOY'S TERROR AT THE SIGHT OF THE APPARITION HE HAD BECOME: A BRIGHT AND SHINING RED MAN, ONE-EYED, WITH A SHARP KNIFE IN HIS HAND.
BUT IT WASN'T FEAR LOLLA-WOSSIKY WANTED. NO ONE SHOULD FEAR HIS OWN DREAM BEAST.
SO HE SENT THE LIGHT OUTWARD TO THE BOY, TO INCLUDE HIM, AND WITH THE LIGHT HE SENT CALM, CALM, DON'T BE SCARED.

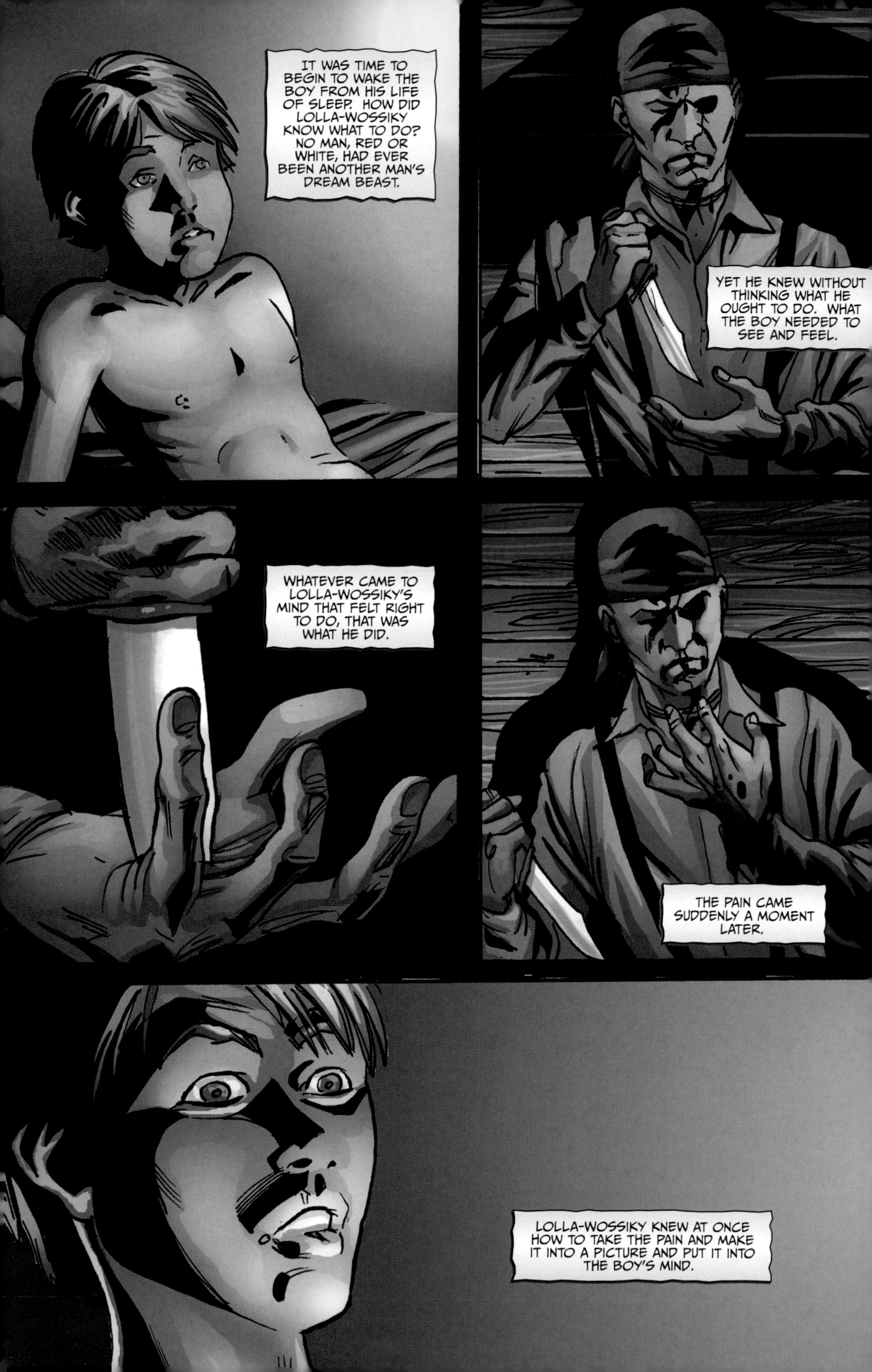
IT WAS TIME TO BEGIN TO WAKE THE BOY FROM HIS LIFE OF SLEEP. HOW DID LOLLA-WOSSIKY KNOW WHAT TO DO? NO MAN, RED OR WHITE, HAD EVER BEEN ANOTHER MAN'S DREAM BEAST.
YET HE KNEW WITHOUT THINKING WHAT HE OUGHT TO DO. WHAT THE BOY NEEDED TO SEE AND FEEL.
WHATEVER CAME TO LOLLA-WOSSIKY'S MIND THAT FELT RIGHT TO DO, THAT WAS WHAT HE DID.
THE PAIN CAME SUDDENLY A MOMENT LATER.
LOLLA-WOSSIKY KNEW AT ONCE HOW TO TAKE THE PAIN AND MAKE IT INTO A PICTURE AND PUT IT INTO THE BOY'S MIND.

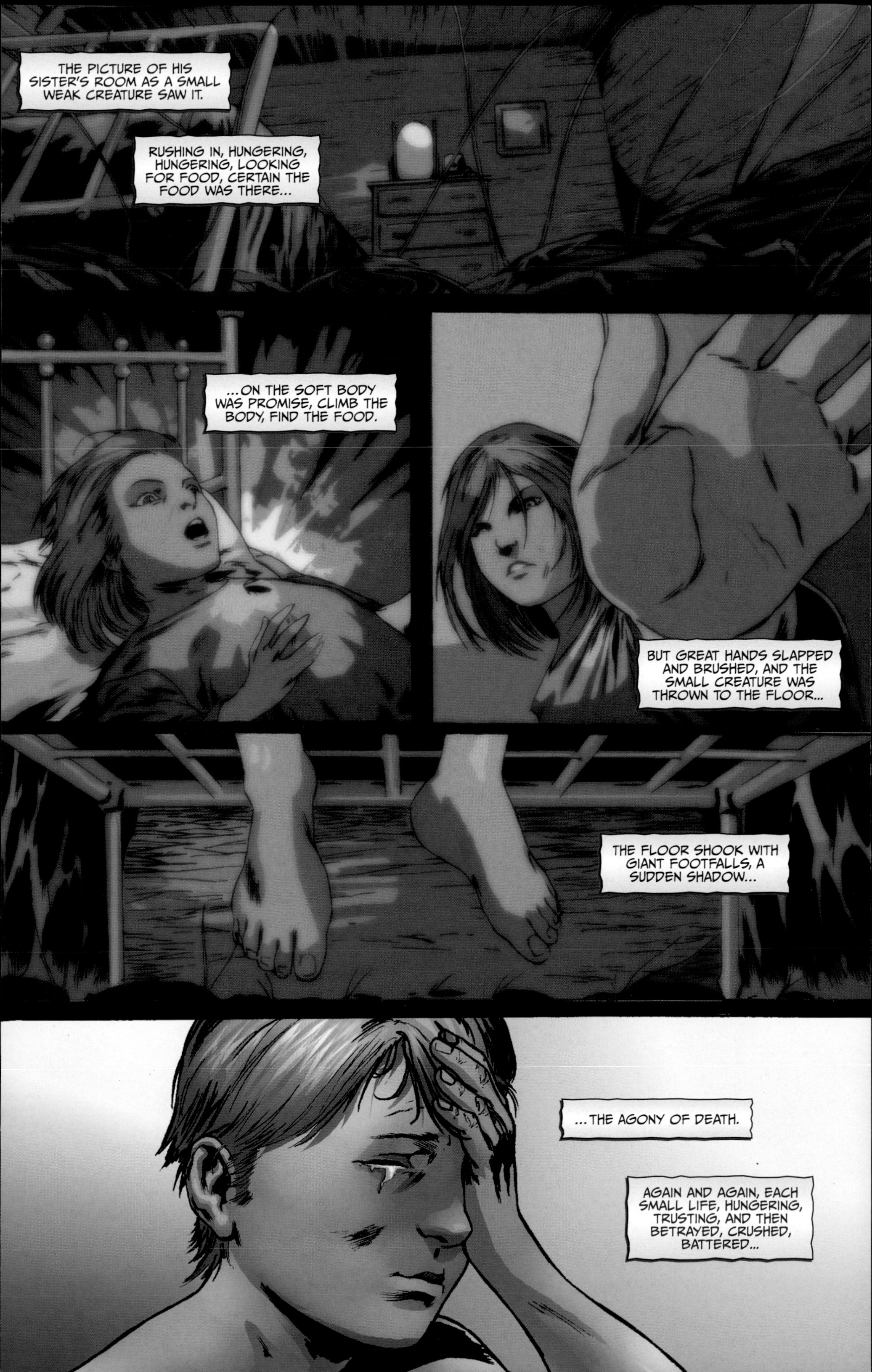
THE PICTURE OF HIS SISTER'S ROOM AS A SMALL WEAK CREATURE SAW IT.
RUSHING IN, HUNGERING, HUNGERING, LOOKING FOR FOOD, CERTAIN THE FOOD WAS THERE...
...ON THE SOFT BODY WAS PROMISE, CLIMB THE BODY, FIND THE FOOD.
BUT GREAT HANDS SLAPPED AND BRUSHED, AND THE SMALL CREATURE WAS THROWN TO THE FLOOR...
THE FLOOR SHOOK WITH GIANT FOOTFALLS, A SUDDEN SHADOW...
...THE AGONY OF DEATH.
AGAIN AND AGAIN, EACH SMALL LIFE, HUNGERING, TRUSTING, AND THEN BETRAYED, CRUSHED, BATTERED...

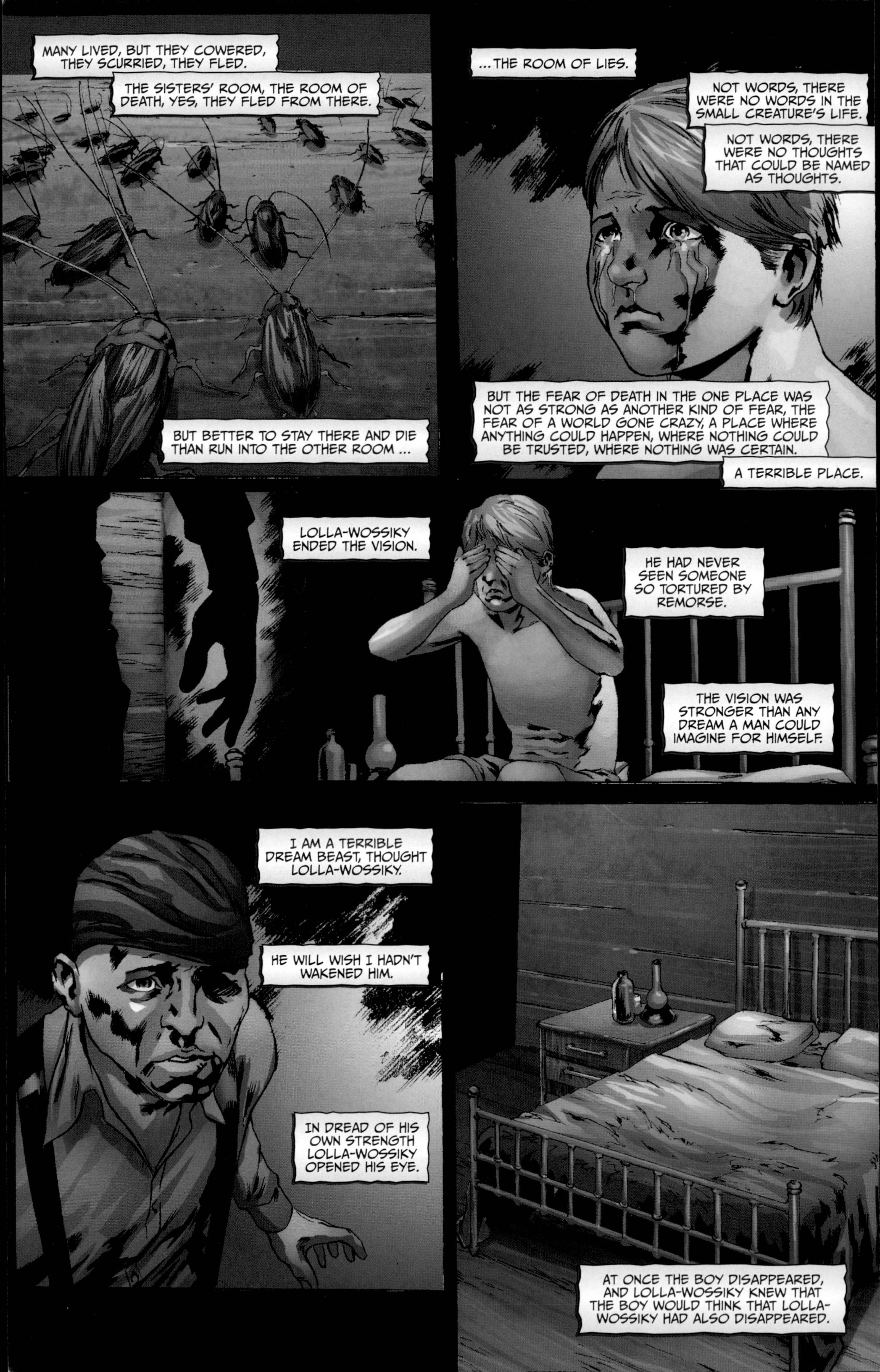
MANY LIVED, BUT THEY COWERED, THEY SCURRIED, THEY FLED.
THE SISTERS' ROOM, THE ROOM OF DEATH, YES, THEY FLED FROM THERE.
BUT BETTER TO STAY THERE AND DIE THAN RUN INTO THE OTHER ROOM ...
...THE ROOM OF LIES.
NOT WORDS, THERE WERE NO WORDS IN THE SMALL CREATURE'S LIFE.
NOT WORDS, THERE WERE NO THOUGHTS THAT COULD BE NAMED AS THOUGHTS.
BUT THE FEAR OF DEATH IN THE ONE PLACE WAS NOT AS STRONG AS ANOTHER KIND OF FEAR, THE FEAR OF A WORLD GONE CRAZY, A PLACE WHERE ANYTHING COULD HAPPEN, WHERE NOTHING COULD BE TRUSTED, WHERE NOTHING WAS CERTAIN.
A TERRIBLE PLACE.
LOLLA-WOSSIKY ENDED THE VISION.
HE HAD NEVER SEEN SOMEONE SO TORTURED BY REMORSE.
THE VISION WAS STRONGER THAN ANY DREAM A MAN COULD IMAGINE FOR HIMSELF.
I AM A TERRIBLE DREAM BEAST, THOUGHT LOLLA-WOSSIKY.
HE WILL WISH I HADN'T WAKENED HIM.
IN DREAD OF HIS OWN STRENGTH LOLLA-WOSSIKY OPENED HIS EYE.
AT ONCE THE BOY DISAPPEARED, AND LOLLA-WOSSIKY KNEW THAT THE BOY WOULD THINK THAT LOLLA-WOSSIKY HAD ALSO DISAPPEARED.

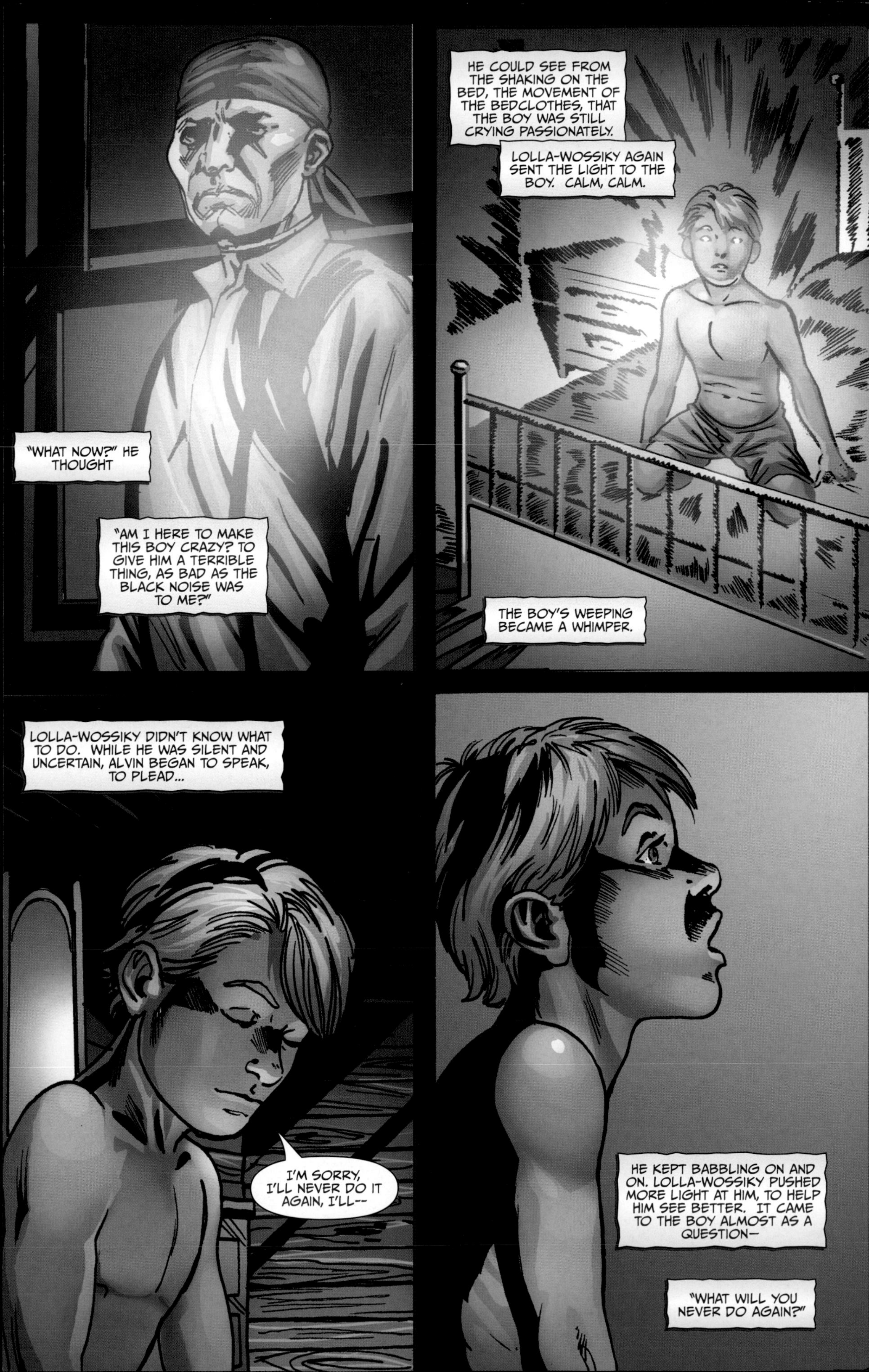
"WHAT NOW?" HE THOUGHT
"AM I HERE TO MAKE THIS BOY CRAZY? TO GIVE HIM A TERRIBLE THING, AS BAD AS THE BLACK NOISE WAS TO ME?"
HE COULD SEE FROM THE SHAKING ON THE BED, THE MOVEMENT OF THE BEDCLOTHES, THAT THE BOY WAS STILL CRYING PASSIONATELY.
LOLLA-WOSSIKY AGAIN SENT THE LIGHT TO THE BOY. CALM, CALM.
THE BOY'S WEEPING BECAME A WHIMPER.
LOLLA-WOSSIKY DIDN'T KNOW WHAT TO DO. WHILE HE WAS SILENT AND UNCERTAIN, ALVIN BEGAN TO SPEAK, TO PLEAD...
I'M SORRY, I'LL NEVER DO IT AGAIN, I'LL--
HE KEPT BABBLING ON AND ON. LOLLA-WOSSIKY PUSHED MORE LIGHT AT HIM, TO HELP HIM SEE BETTER. IT CAME TO THE BOY ALMOST AS A QUESTION—
"WHAT WILL YOU NEVER DO AGAIN?"

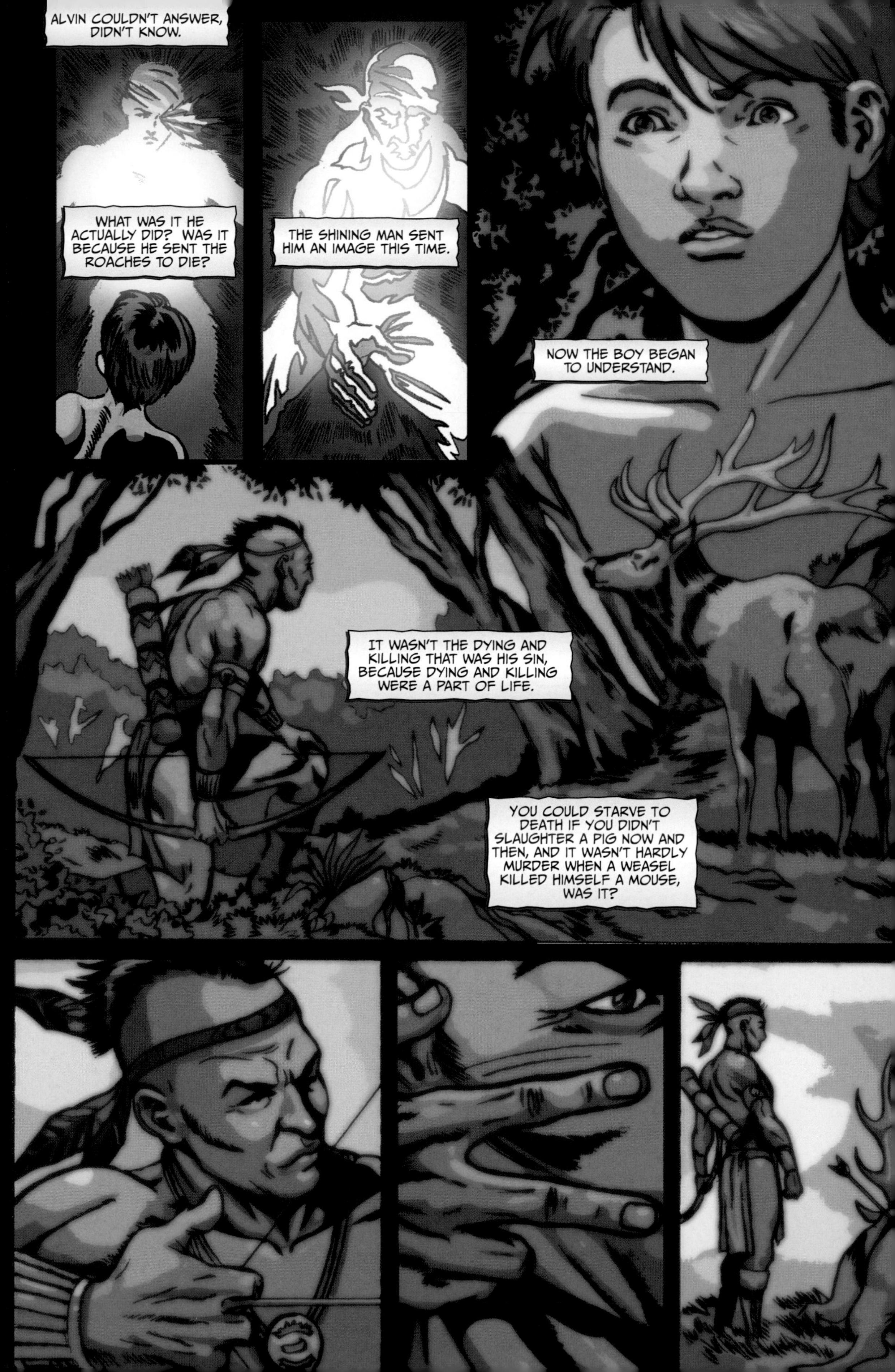
ALVIN COULDN'T ANSWER, DIDN'T KNOW.
WHAT WAS IT HE ACTUALLY DID? WAS IT BECAUSE HE SENT THE ROACHES TO DIE?
THE SHINING MAN SENT HIM AN IMAGE THIS TIME.
NOW THE BOY BEGAN TO UNDERSTAND.
IT WASN'T THE DYING AND KILLING THAT WAS HIS SIN, BECAUSE DYING AND KILLING WERE A PART OF LIFE.
YOU COULD STARVE TO DEATH IF YOU DIDN'T SLAUGHTER A PIG NOW AND THEN, AND IT WASN'T HARDLY MURDER WHEN A WEASEL KILLED HIMSELF A MOUSE, WAS IT?

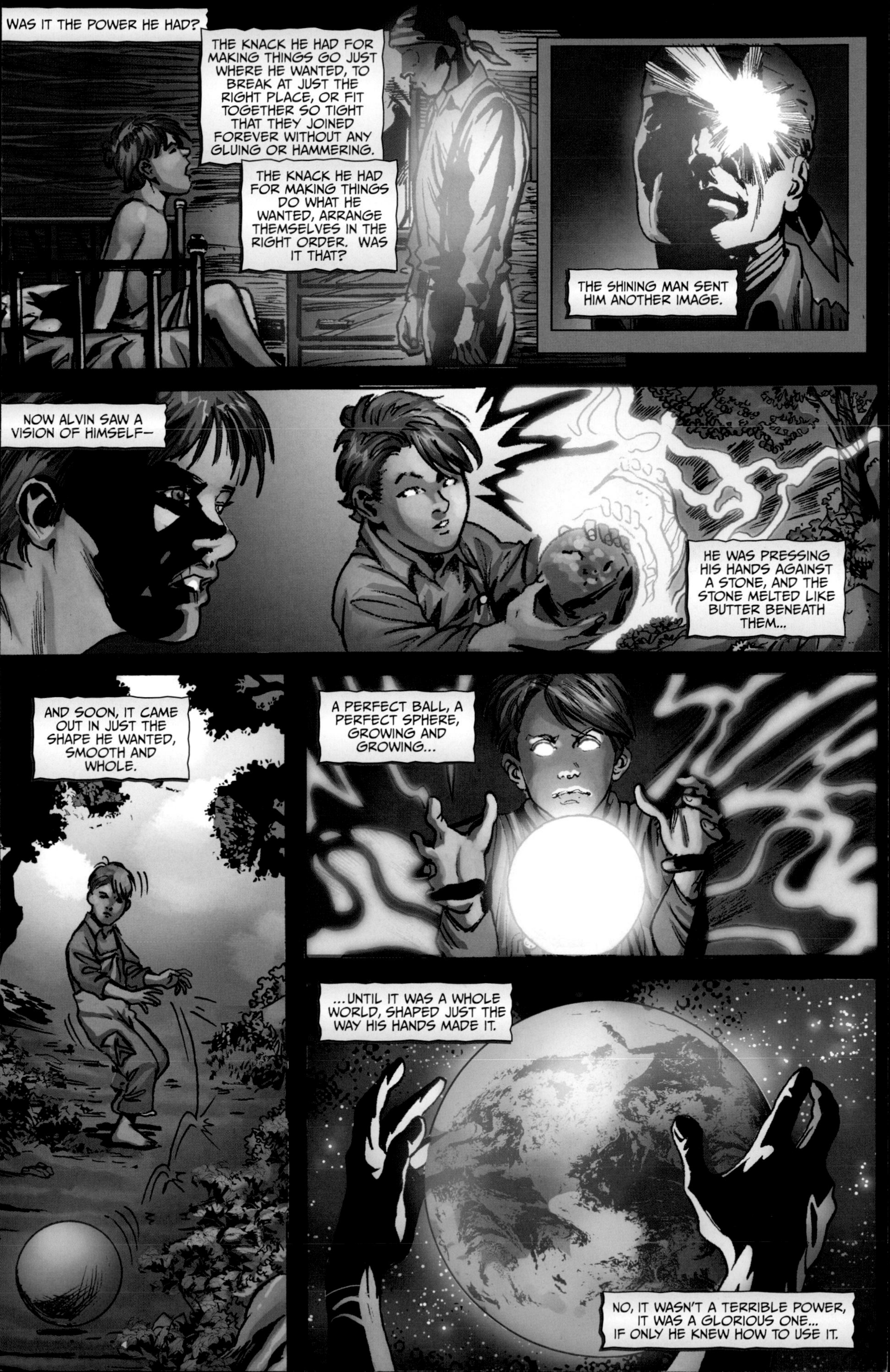
WAS IT THE POWER HE HAD?
THE KNACK HE HAD FOR MAKING THINGS GO JUST WHERE HE WANTED, TO BREAK AT JUST THE RIGHT PLACE, OR FIT TOGETHER SO TIGHT THAT THEY JOINED FOREVER WITHOUT ANY GLUING OR HAMMERING.
THE KNACK HE HAD FOR MAKING THINGS DO WHAT HE WANTED, ARRANGE THEMSELVES IN THE RIGHT ORDER. WAS IT THAT?
THE SHINING MAN SENT HIM ANOTHER IMAGE.
NOW ALVIN SAW A VISION OF HIMSELF—
HE WAS PRESSING HIS HANDS AGAINST A STONE, AND THE STONE MELTED LIKE BUTTER BENEATH THEM...
AND SOON, IT CAME OUT IN JUST THE SHAPE HE WANTED, SMOOTH AND WHOLE.
A PERFECT BALL, A PERFECT SPHERE, GROWING AND GROWING...
...UNTIL IT WAS A WHOLE WORLD, SHAPED JUST THE WAY HIS HANDS MADE IT.
NO, IT WASN'T A TERRIBLE POWER, IT WAS A GLORIOUS ONE... IF ONLY HE KNEW HOW TO USE IT.

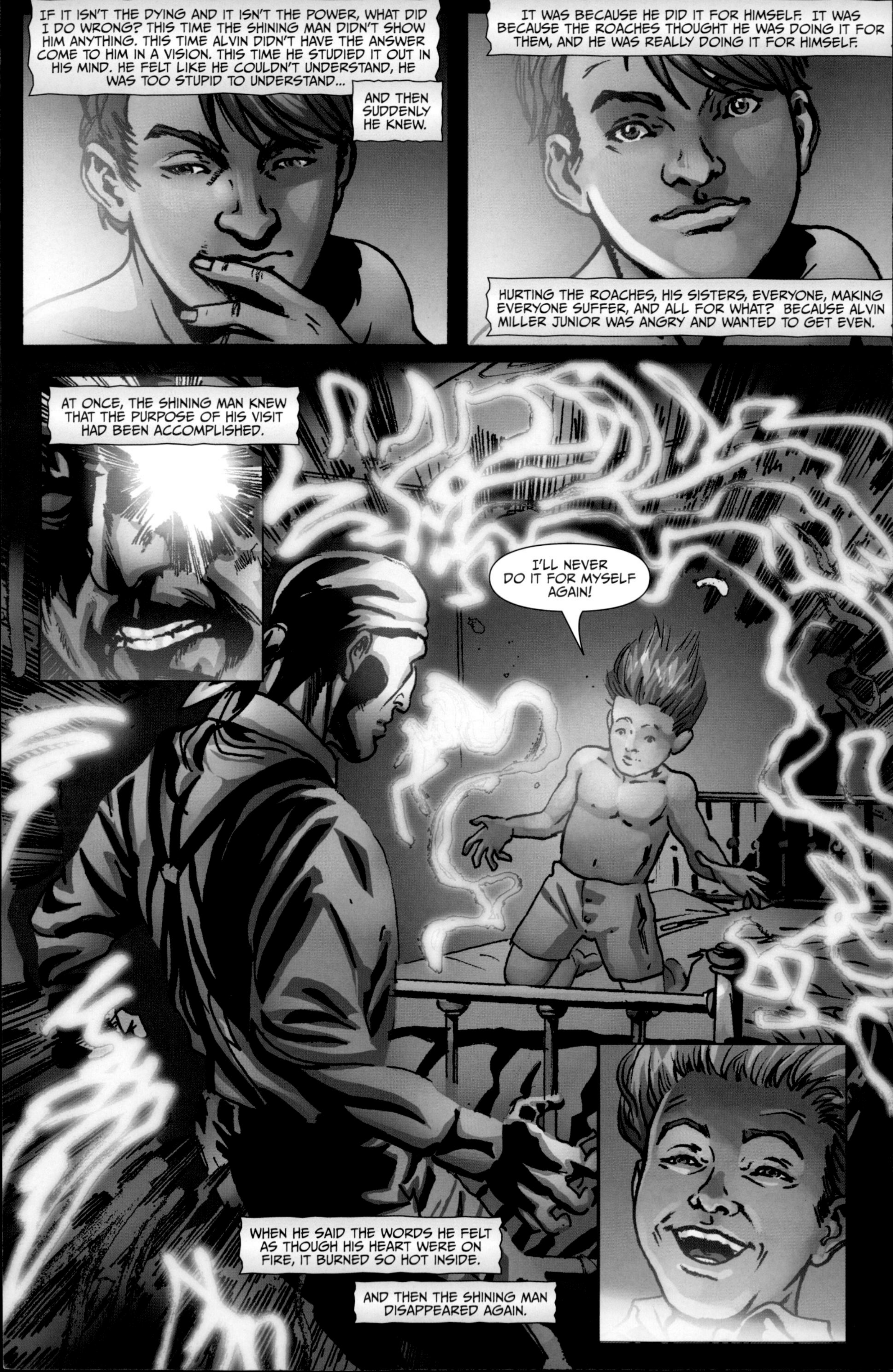
IF IT ISN'T THE DYING AND IT ISN'T THE POWER, WHAT DID I DO WRONG? THIS TIME THE SHINING MAN DIDN'T SHOW HIM ANYTHING. THIS TIME ALVIN DIDN'T HAVE THE ANSWER COME TO HIM IN A VISION. THIS TIME HE STUDIED IT OUT IN HIS MIND. HE FELT LIKE HE COULDN'T UNDERSTAND, HE WAS TOO STUPID TO UNDERSTAND...
AND THEN SUDDENLY HE KNEW.
IT WAS BECAUSE HE DID IT FOR HIMSELF. IT WAS BECAUSE THE ROACHES THOUGHT HE WAS DOING IT FOR THEM, AND HE WAS REALLY DOING IT FOR HIMSELF.
HURTING THE ROACHES, HIS SISTERS, EVERYONE, MAKING EVERYONE SUFFER, AND ALL FOR WHAT? BECAUSE ALVIN MILLER JUNIOR WAS ANGRY AND WANTED TO GET EVEN.
AT ONCE, THE SHINING MAN KNEW THAT THE PURPOSE OF HIS VISIT HAD BEEN ACCOMPLISHED.
I'LL NEVER DO IT FOR MYSELF AGAIN!
WHEN HE SAID THE WORDS HE FELT AS THOUGH HIS HEART WERE ON FIRE, IT BURNED SO HOT INSIDE.
AND THEN THE SHINING MAN DISAPPEARED AGAIN.

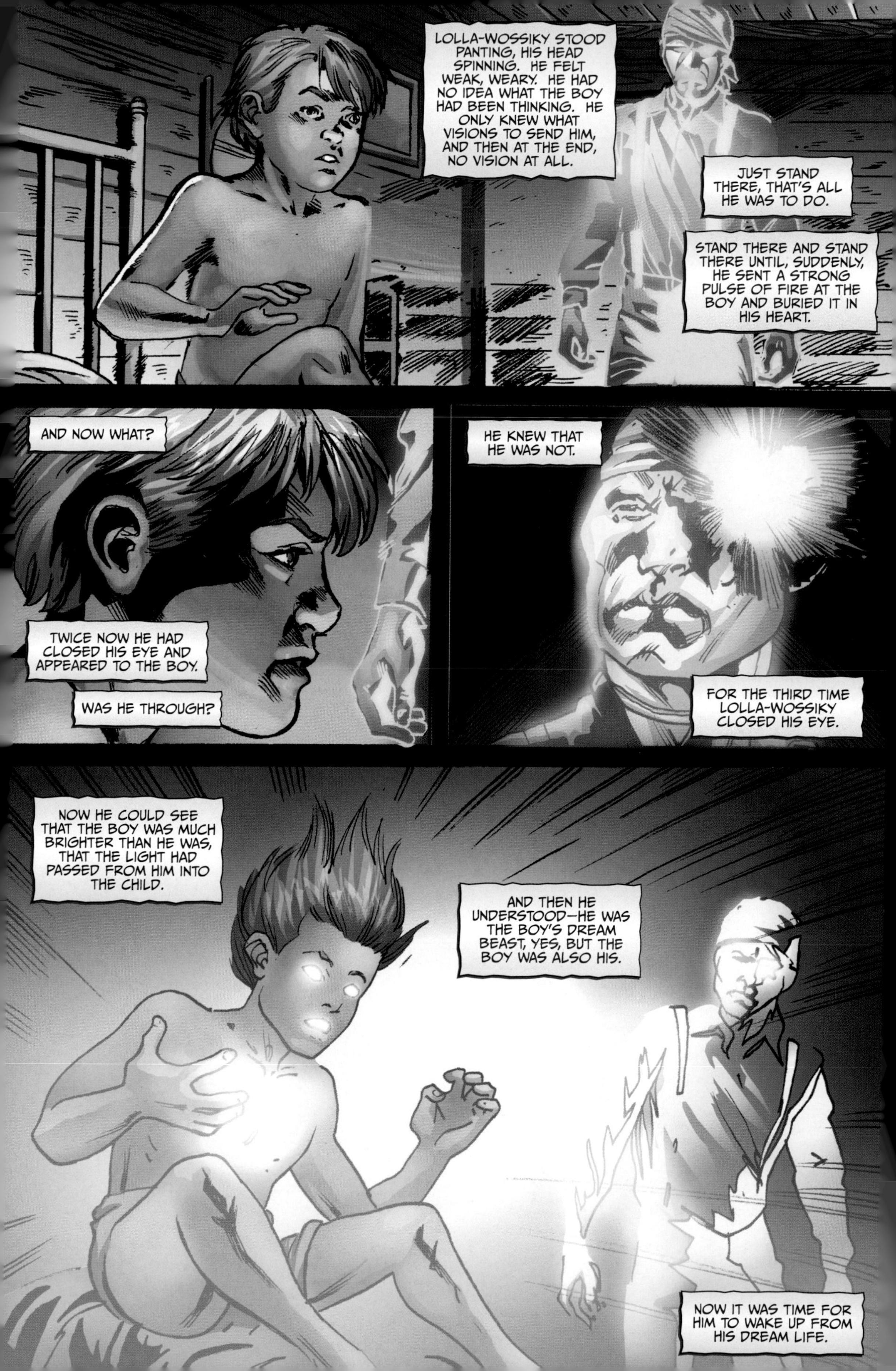
LOLLA-WOSSIKY STOOD PANTING, HIS HEAD SPINNING. HE FELT WEAK, WEARY. HE HAD NO IDEA WHAT THE BOY HAD BEEN THINKING. HE ONLY KNEW WHAT VISIONS TO SEND HIM, AND THEN AT THE END, NO VISION AT ALL.
JUST STAND THERE, THAT'S ALL HE WAS TO DO.
STAND THERE AND STAND THERE UNTIL, SUDDENLY, HE SENT A STRONG PULSE OF FIRE AT THE BOY AND BURIED IT IN HIS HEART.
AND NOW WHAT?
TWICE NOW HE HAD CLOSED HIS EYE AND APPEARED TO THE BOY.
WAS HE THROUGH?
HE KNEW THAT HE WAS NOT.
FOR THE THIRD TIME LOLLA-WOSSIKY CLOSED HIS EYE.
NOW HE COULD SEE THAT THE BOY WAS MUCH BRIGHTER THAN HE WAS, THAT THE LIGHT HAD PASSED FROM HIM INTO THE CHILD.
AND THEN HE UNDERSTOOD—HE WAS THE BOY'S DREAM BEAST, YES, BUT THE BOY WAS ALSO HIS.
NOW IT WAS TIME FOR HIM TO WAKE UP FROM HIS DREAM LIFE.

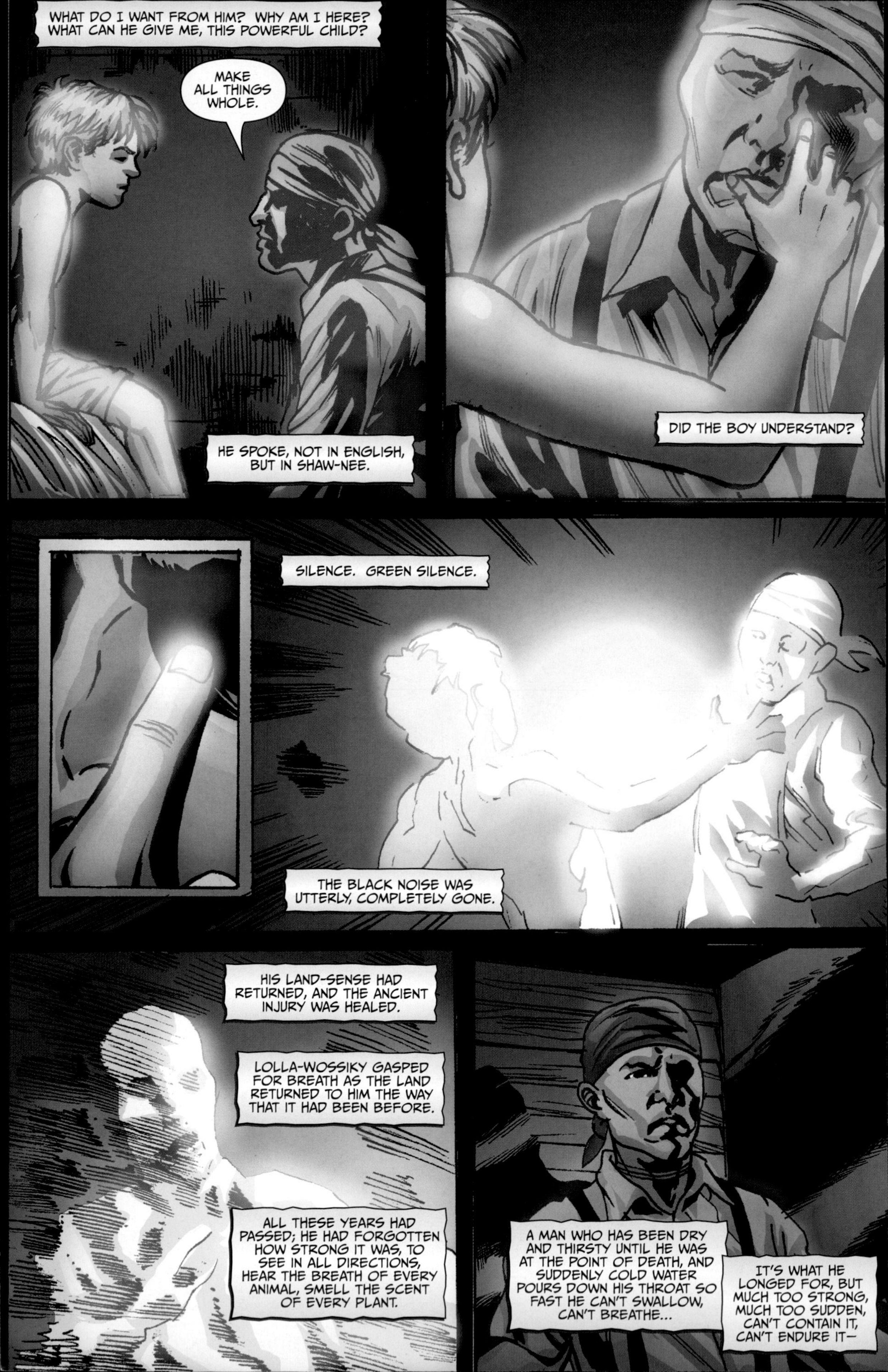

WHAT DO I WANT FROM HIM? WHY AM I HERE? WHAT CAN HE GIVE ME, THIS POWERFUL CHILD?
MAKE ALL THINGS WHOLE.
HE SPOKE, NOT IN ENGLISH, BUT IN SHAW-NEE.
DID THE BOY UNDERSTAND?
SILENCE. GREEN SILENCE.
THE BLACK NOISE WAS UTTERLY, COMPLETELY GONE.
HIS LAND-SENSE HAD RETURNED, AND THE ANCIENT INJURY WAS HEALED.
LOLLA-WOSSIKY GASPED FOR BREATH AS THE LAND RETURNED TO HIM THE WAY THAT IT HAD BEEN BEFORE.
ALL THESE YEARS HAD PASSED; HE HAD FORGOTTEN HOW STRONG IT WAS, TO SEE IN ALL DIRECTIONS, HEAR THE BREATH OF EVERY ANIMAL, SMELL THE SCENT OF EVERY PLANT.
A MAN WHO HAS BEEN DRY AND THIRSTY UNTIL HE WAS AT THE POINT OF DEATH, AND SUDDENLY COLD WATER POURS DOWN HIS THROAT SO FAST HE CAN'T SWALLOW, CAN'T BREATHE...
IT'S WHAT HE LONGED FOR, BUT MUCH TOO STRONG, MUCH TOO SUDDEN, CAN'T CONTAIN IT, CAN'T ENDURE IT—

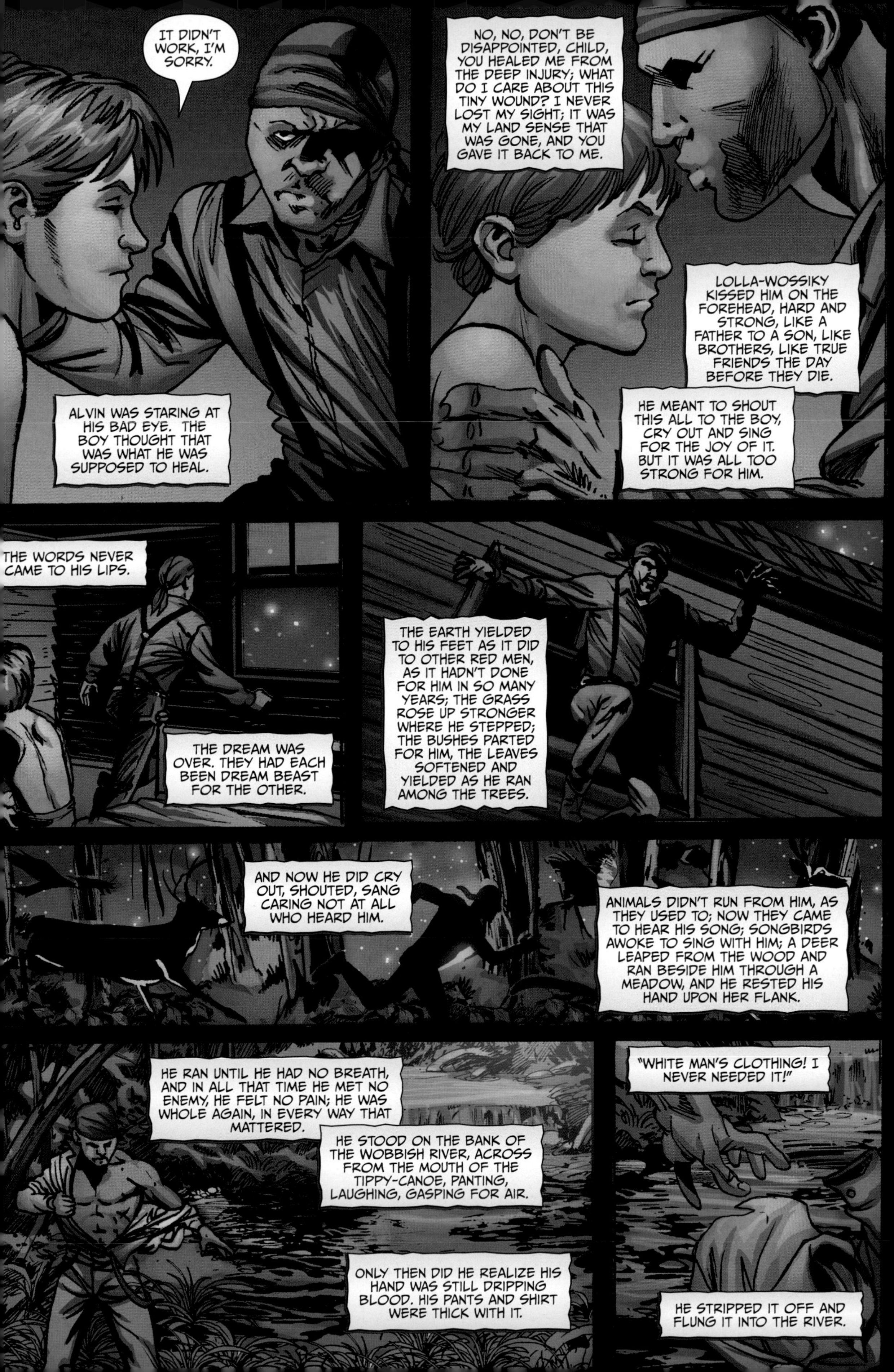
IT DIDN'T WORK, I'M SORRY.
ALVIN WAS STARING AT HIS BAD EYE. THE BOY THOUGHT THAT WAS WHAT HE WAS SUPPOSED TO HEAL.
NO, NO, DON'T BE DISAPPOINTED, CHILD, YOU HEALED ME FROM THE DEEP INJURY; WHAT DO I CARE ABOUT THIS TINY WOUND? I NEVER LOST MY SIGHT; IT WAS MY LAND SENSE THAT WAS GONE, AND YOU GAVE IT BACK TO ME.
LOLLA-WOSSIKY KISSED HIM ON THE FOREHEAD, HARD AND STRONG, LIKE A FATHER TO A SON, LIKE BROTHERS, LIKE TRUE FRIENDS THE DAY BEFORE THEY DIE.
HE MEANT TO SHOUT THIS ALL TO THE BOY, CRY OUT AND SING FOR THE JOY OF IT. BUT IT WAS ALL TOO STRONG FOR HIM.
THE WORDS NEVER CAME TO HIS LIPS.
THE DREAM WAS OVER. THEY HAD EACH BEEN DREAM BEAST FOR THE OTHER.
THE EARTH YIELDED TO HIS FEET AS IT DID TO OTHER RED MEN, AS IT HADN'T DONE FOR HIM IN SO MANY YEARS; THE GRASS ROSE UP STRONGER WHERE HE STEPPED; THE BUSHES PARTED FOR HIM, THE LEAVES SOFTENED AND YIELDED AS HE RAN AMONG THE TREES.
AND NOW HE DID CRY OUT, SHOUTED, SANG CARING NOT AT ALL WHO HEARD HIM.
ANIMALS DIDN'T RUN FROM HIM, AS THEY USED TO; NOW THEY CAME TO HEAR HIS SONG; SONGBIRDS AWOKE TO SING WITH HIM; A DEER LEAPED FROM THE WOOD AND RAN BESIDE HIM THROUGH A MEADOW, AND HE RESTED HIS HAND UPON HER FLANK.
HE RAN UNTIL HE HAD NO BREATH, AND IN ALL THAT TIME HE MET NO ENEMY, HE FELT NO PAIN; HE WAS WHOLE AGAIN, IN EVERY WAY THAT MATTERED.
HE STOOD ON THE BANK OF THE WOBBISH RIVER, ACROSS FROM THE MOUTH OF THE TIPPY-CANOE, PANTING, LAUGHING, GASPING FOR AIR.
ONLY THEN DID HE REALIZE HIS HAND WAS STILL DRIPPING BLOOD. HIS PANTS AND SHIRT WERE THICK WITH IT.
"WHITE MAN'S CLOTHING! I NEVER NEEDED IT!"
HE STRIPPED IT OFF AND FLUNG IT INTO THE RIVER.

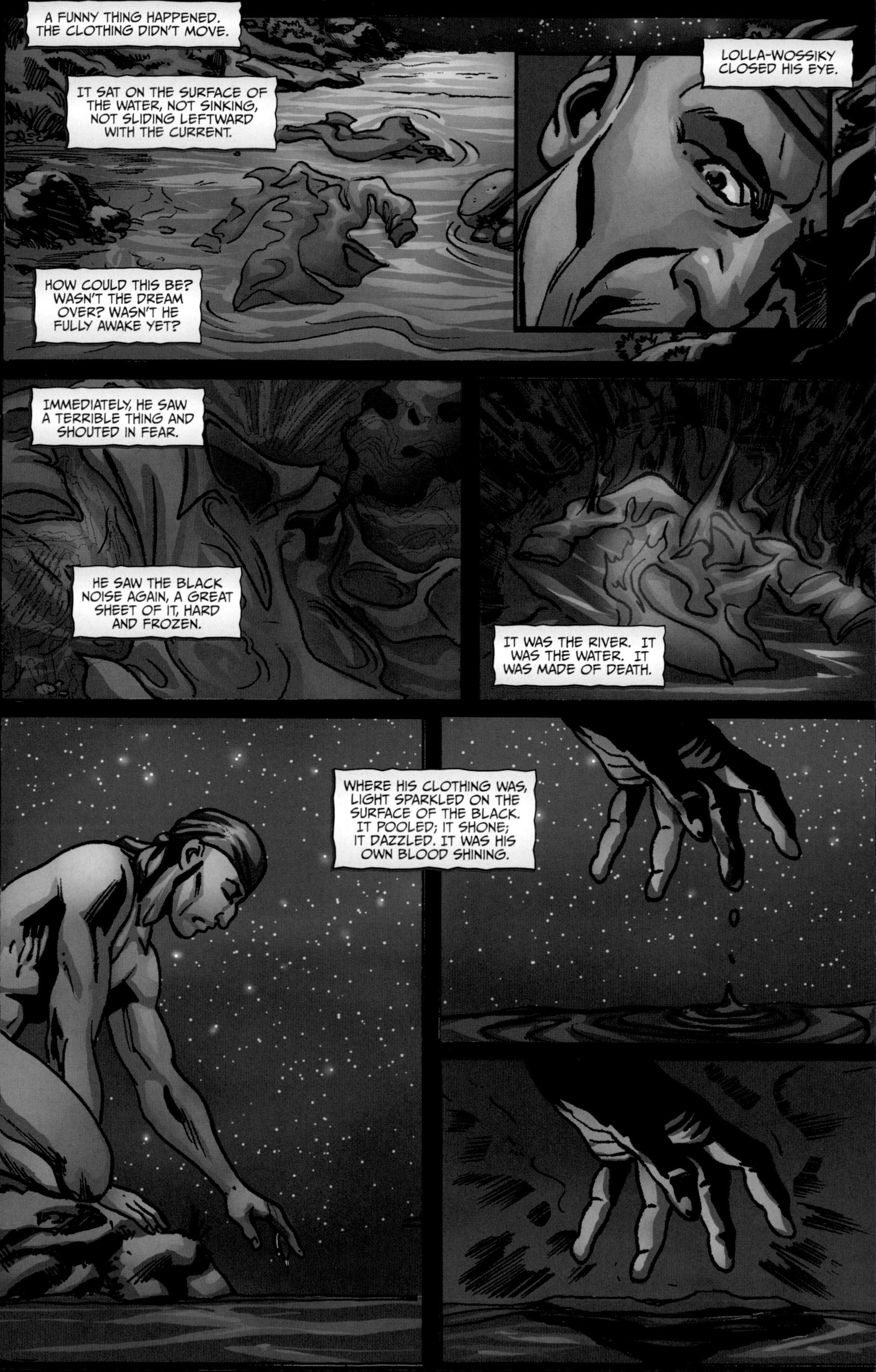
A FUNNY THING HAPPENED. THE CLOTHING DIDN'T MOVE.
IT SAT ON THE SURFACE OF THE WATER, NOT SINKING, NOT SLIDING LEFTWARD WITH THE CURRENT.
HOW COULD THIS BE? WASN'T THE DREAM OVER? WASN'T HE FULLY AWAKE YET?
LOLLA-WOSSIKY CLOSED HIS EYE.
IMMEDIATELY, HE SAW A TERRIBLE THING AND SHOUTED IN FEAR.
HE SAW THE BLACK NOISE AGAIN, A GREAT SHEET OF IT, HARD AND FROZEN.
IT WAS THE RIVER. IT WAS THE WATER. IT WAS MADE OF DEATH.
WHERE HIS CLOTHING WAS, LIGHT SPARKLED ON THE SURFACE OF THE BLACK. IT POOLED; IT SHONE; IT DAZZLED. IT WAS HIS OWN BLOOD SHINING.

IT WAS SOLID, WARM, AND SOLID. HE SMEARED HIS BLOOD ACROSS THE SURFACE AND IT MADE A PLATFORM.

HE CRAWLED OUT ONTO THE PLATFORM. IT WAS SMOOTH AND AS HARD AS ICE, ONLY WARM, WELCOMING.

WHAT HE WAS DOING WAS IMPOSSIBLE. THE BOY HAD DONE MUCH MORE THAN HEAL HIM. HE HAD CHANGED THE ORDER OF THINGS. IT WAS FRIGHTENING AND WONDERFUL.

THEN HE CLOSED HIS EYE, AND A WHOLE NEW VISION LEAPED TO VIEW.

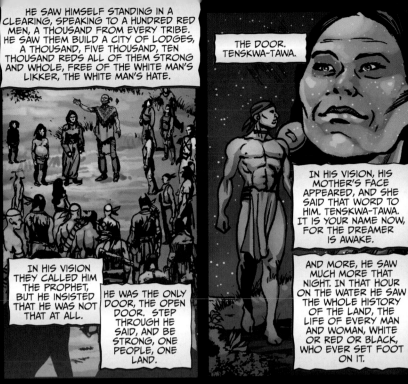

HE SAW HIMSELF STANDING IN A CLEARING, SPEAKING TO A HUNDRED RED MEN, A THOUSAND FROM EVERY TRIBE. HE SAW THEM BUILD A CITY OF LODGES, A THOUSAND, FIVE THOUSAND, TEN THOUSAND REDS ALL OF THEM STRONG AND WHOLE, FREE OF THE WHITE MAN'S LIKKER, THE WHITE MAN'S HATE.

IN HIS VISION THEY CALLED HIM THE PROPHET, BUT HE INSISTED THAT HE WAS NOT THAT AT ALL.

HE WAS THE ONLY DOOR, THE OPEN DOOR. STEP THROUGH HE SAID, AND BE STRONG, ONE PEOPLE, ONE LAND.

THE DOOR. TENSKWA-TAWA.

IN HIS VISION, HIS MOTHER'S FACE APPEARED, AND SHE SAID THAT WORD TO HIM. TENSKWA-TAWA. IT IS YOUR NAME NOW, FOR THE DREAMER IS AWAKE.

AND MORE, HE SAW MUCH MORE THAT NIGHT. IN THAT HOUR ON THE WATER HE SAW THE WHOLE HISTORY OF THE LAND, THE LIFE OF EVERY MAN AND WOMAN, WHITE OR RED OR BLACK, WHO EVER SET FOOT ON IT.

HE SAW THE BEGINNING AND HE SAW THE END. GREAT WARS AND PETTY CRUELTIES, ALL THE MURDERINGS OF MEN, ALL THE SIN; BUT ALSO ALL THE GOODNESS, ALL THE BEAUTY.

AND ABOVE ALL, A VISION OF THE CRYSTAL CITY.

THE CITY MADE OF WATER AS SOLID AND AS CLEAR AS GLASS, WATER THAT WOULD NEVER MELT, FORMED INTO CRYSTAL TOWERS SO HIGH THAT THEY SHOULD HAVE CAST SHADOWS SEVEN MILES ACROSS THE LAND. BUT BECAUSE THEY WERE SO PURE THEY CAST NO SHADOW AT ALL.

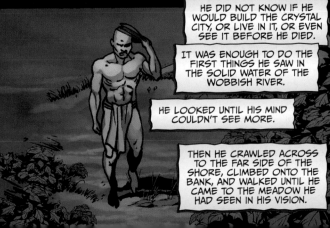

HE DID NOT KNOW IF HE WOULD BUILD THE CRYSTAL CITY, OR LIVE IN IT, OR EVEN SEE IT BEFORE HE DIED.

IT WAS ENOUGH TO DO THE FIRST THINGS HE SAW IN THE SOLID WATER OF THE WOBBISH RIVER.

HE LOOKED UNTIL HIS MIND COULDN'T SEE MORE.

THEN HE CRAWLED ACROSS TO THE FAR SIDE OF THE SHORE, CLIMBED ONTO THE BANK, AND WALKED UNTIL HE CAME TO THE MEADOW HE HAD SEEN IN HIS VISION.

THIS WAS WHERE HE WOULD CALL THE REDS TOGETHER, TEACH THEM WHAT HE SAW IN HIS VISION, AND HELP THEM TO BE, NOT THE STRONGEST, BUT STRONG; NOT THE LARGEST, BUT LARGE; NOT THE FREEST, BUT FREE.

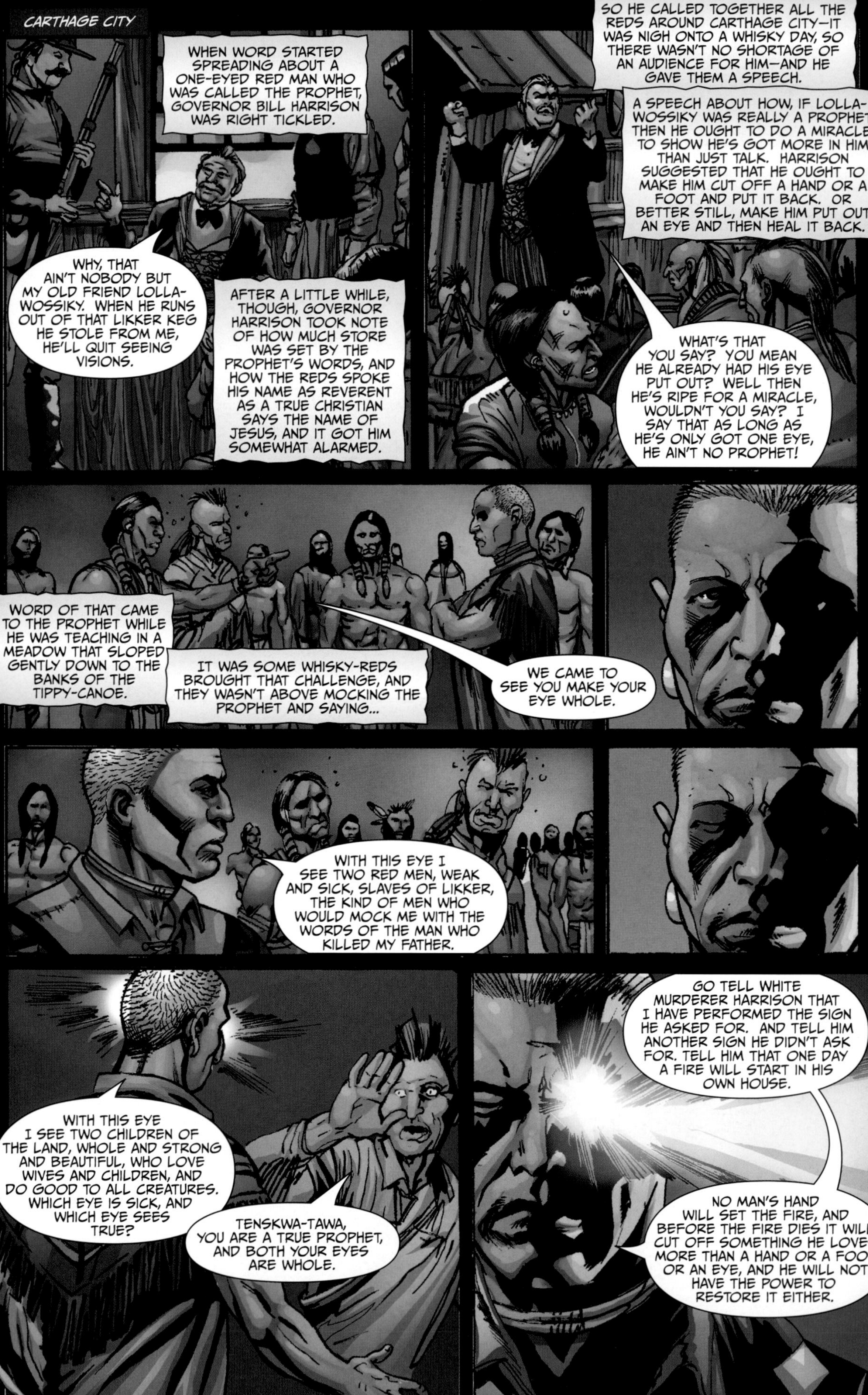
CARTHAGE CITY
WHEN WORD STARTED SPREADING ABOUT A ONE-EYED RED MAN WHO WAS CALLED THE PROPHET, GOVERNOR BILL HARRISON WAS RIGHT TICKLED.
WHY, THAT AIN'T NOBODY BUT MY OLD FRIEND LOLLA-WOSSIKY. WHEN HE RUNS OUT OF THAT LIKKER KEG HE STOLE FROM ME, HE'LL QUIT SEEING VISIONS.
AFTER A LITTLE WHILE, THOUGH, GOVERNOR HARRISON TOOK NOTE OF HOW MUCH STORE WAS SET BY THE PROPHET'S WORDS, AND HOW THE REDS SPOKE HIS NAME AS REVERENT AS A TRUE CHRISTIAN SAYS THE NAME OF JESUS, AND IT GOT HIM SOMEWHAT ALARMED.
SO HE CALLED TOGETHER ALL THE REDS AROUND CARTHAGE CITY—IT WAS NIGH ONTO A WHISKY DAY, SO THERE WASN'T NO SHORTAGE OF AN AUDIENCE FOR HIM—AND HE GAVE THEM A SPEECH.
A SPEECH ABOUT HOW, IF LOLLA-WOSSIKY WAS REALLY A PROPHET, THEN HE OUGHT TO DO A MIRACLE, TO SHOW HE'S GOT MORE IN HIM THAN JUST TALK. HARRISON SUGGESTED THAT HE OUGHT TO MAKE HIM CUT OFF A HAND OR A FOOT AND PUT IT BACK. OR BETTER STILL, MAKE HIM PUT OUT AN EYE AND THEN HEAL IT BACK.
WHAT'S THAT YOU SAY? YOU MEAN HE ALREADY HAD HIS EYE PUT OUT? WELL THEN HE'S RIPE FOR A MIRACLE, WOULDN'T YOU SAY? I SAY THAT AS LONG AS HE'S ONLY GOT ONE EYE, HE AIN'T NO PROPHET!
WORD OF THAT CAME TO THE PROPHET WHILE HE WAS TEACHING IN A MEADOW THAT SLOPED GENTLY DOWN TO THE BANKS OF THE TIPPY-CANOE.
IT WAS SOME WHISKY-REDS BROUGHT THAT CHALLENGE, AND THEY WASN'T ABOVE MOCKING THE PROPHET AND SAYING...
WE CAME TO SEE YOU MAKE YOUR EYE WHOLE.
WITH THIS EYE I SEE TWO RED MEN, WEAK AND SICK, SLAVES OF LIKKER, THE KIND OF MEN WHO WOULD MOCK ME WITH THE WORDS OF THE MAN WHO KILLED MY FATHER.
WITH THIS EYE I SEE TWO CHILDREN OF THE LAND, WHOLE AND STRONG AND BEAUTIFUL, WHO LOVE WIVES AND CHILDREN, AND DO GOOD TO ALL CREATURES. WHICH EYE IS SICK, AND WHICH EYE SEES TRUE?
TENSKWA-TAWA, YOU ARE A TRUE PROPHET, AND BOTH YOUR EYES ARE WHOLE.
GO TELL WHITE MURDERER HARRISON THAT I HAVE PERFORMED THE SIGN HE ASKED FOR. AND TELL HIM ANOTHER SIGN HE DIDN'T ASK FOR. TELL HIM THAT ONE DAY A FIRE WILL START IN HIS OWN HOUSE.
NO MAN'S HAND WILL SET THE FIRE, AND BEFORE THE FIRE DIES IT WILL CUT OFF SOMETHING HE LOVES MORE THAN A HAND OR A FOOT OR AN EYE, AND HE WILL NOT HAVE THE POWER TO RESTORE IT EITHER.

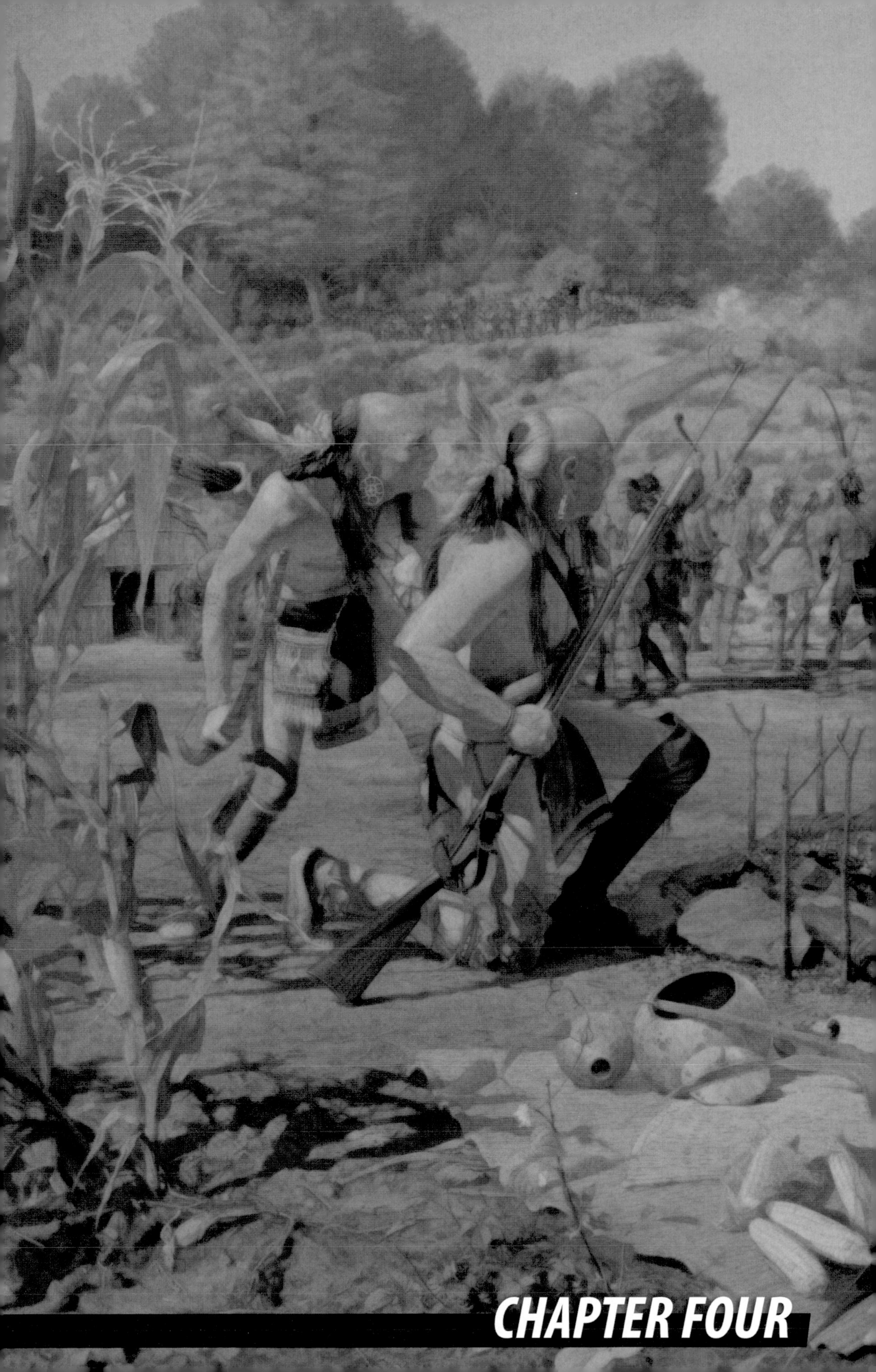

CHAPTER FOUR

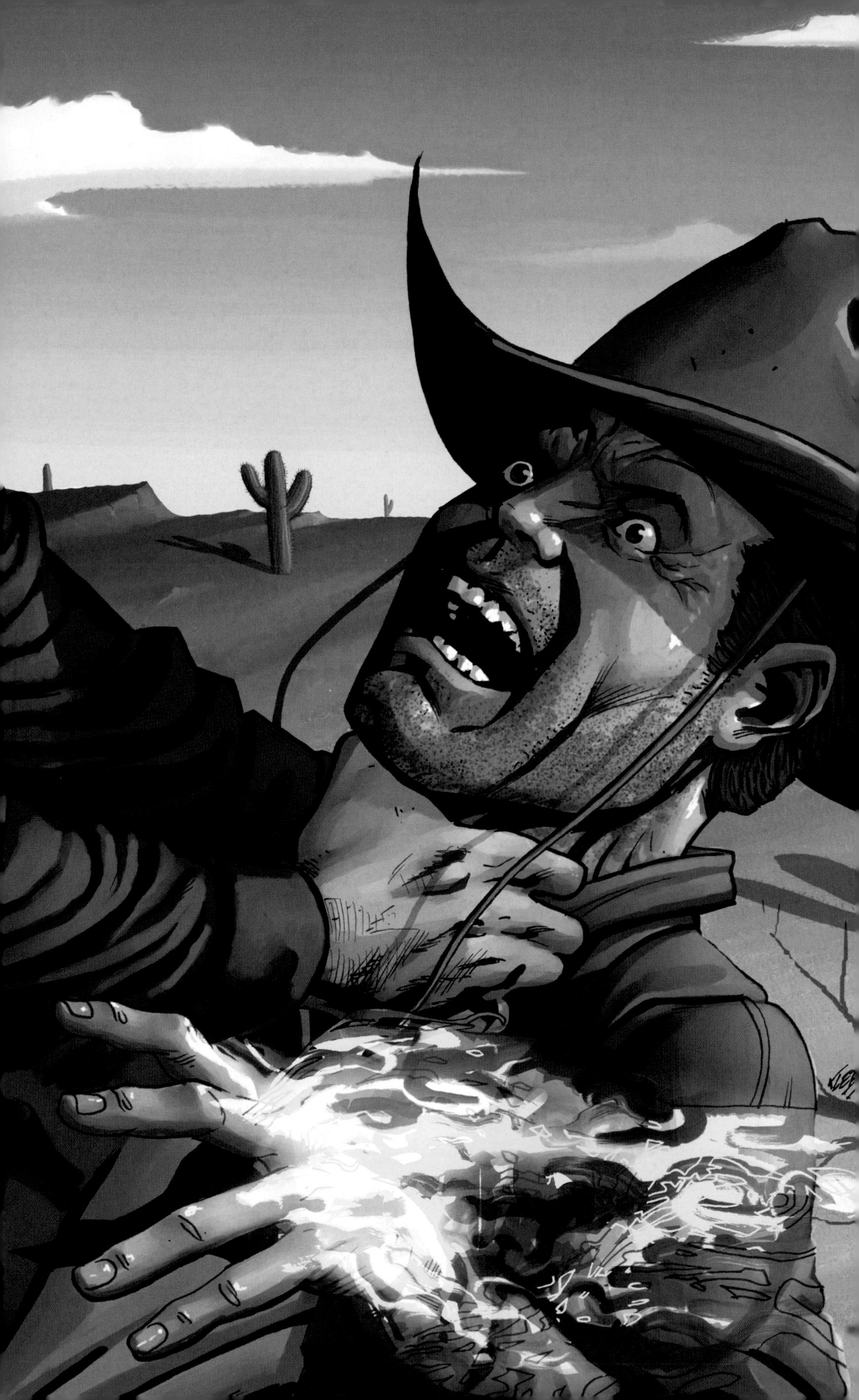

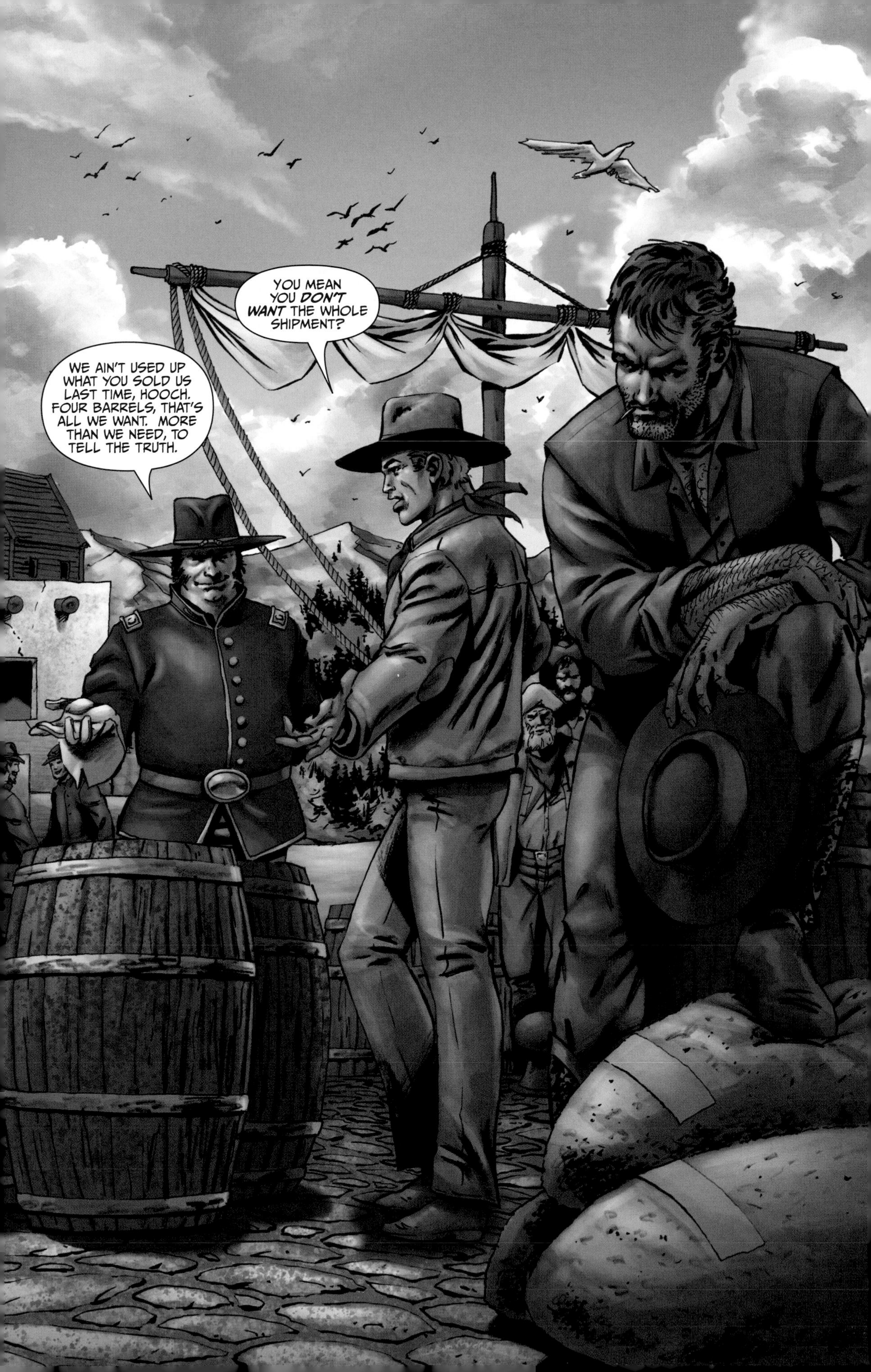
YOU MEAN YOU *DON'T WANT* THE WHOLE SHIPMENT?
WE AIN'T USED UP WHAT YOU SOLD US LAST TIME, HOOCH. FOUR BARRELS, THAT'S ALL WE WANT. MORE THAN WE NEED, TO TELL THE TRUTH.

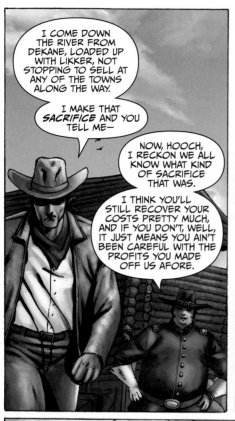

I COME DOWN THE RIVER FROM DEKANE, LOADED UP WITH LIKKER, NOT STOPPING TO SELL AT ANY OF THE TOWNS ALONG THE WAY.

I MAKE THAT *SACRIFICE* AND YOU TELL ME—

NOW, HOOCH, I RECKON WE ALL KNOW WHAT KIND OF SACRIFICE THAT WAS.

I THINK YOU'LL STILL RECOVER YOUR COSTS PRETTY MUCH, AND IF YOU DON'T, WELL, IT JUST MEANS YOU AIN'T BEEN CAREFUL WITH THE PROFITS YOU MADE OFF US AFORE.

WHO ELSE IS SELLING TO YOU?

NOBODY.

I BEEN COMING TO CARTHAGE CITY FOR NIGH ON SEVEN YEARS NOW, AND THE LAST FOUR YEARS I'VE HAD A MONOPOLY—

AND IF YOU'LL PAY HEED, YOU'LL REMEMBER THAT IN THE OLD DAYS IT USED TO BE REDS WHAT BOUGHT MOST OF YOUR LIKKER.

HOOCH LOOKED AROUND, WALKED AWAY FROM THE QUARTERMASTER, STOOD ON THE MOIST GRASSY GROUND OF THE RIVERBANK.

THERE WASN'T A RED TO BE SEEN, NOT A ONE, AND THAT WAS A FACT.

REDS HAD BEEN SLACKING OFF THE LAST FEW TIMES HE CAME.

ALWAYS THERE USED TO BE A FEW DRUNKS, THOUGH.

YOU TELLING ME THERE AIN'T NO WHISKY-REDS LEFT!

SURE THERE'S WHISKY-REDS. BUT WE AIN'T RUN OUT OF WHISKY YET. SO THEY'RE ALL OFF SOMEWHERE LYING AROUND BEING DRUNK.

HOOCH CUSSED A LITTLE.

I'M GOING TO SEE THE *GOV* ABOUT THIS.

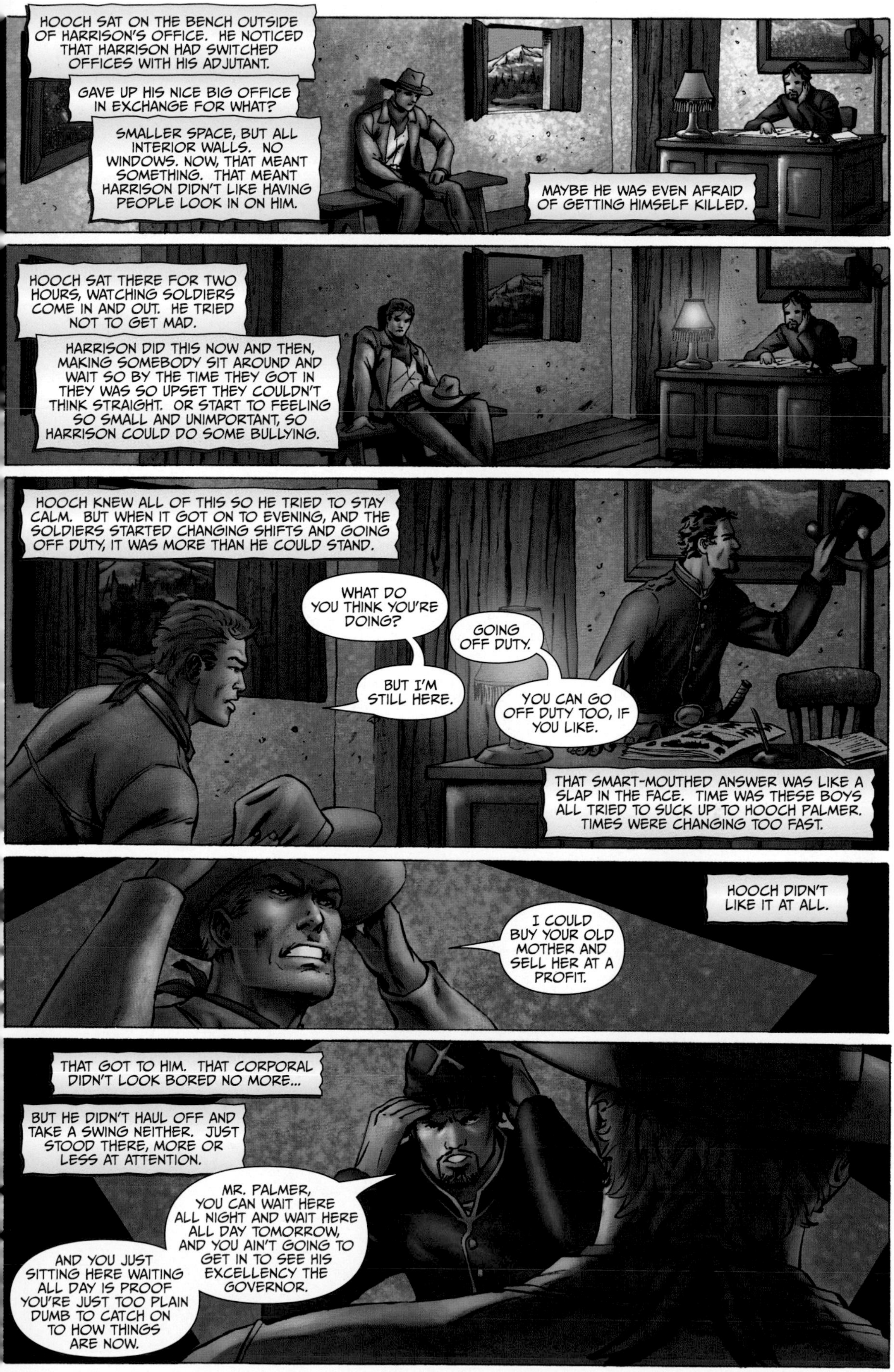
HOOCH SAT ON THE BENCH OUTSIDE OF HARRISON'S OFFICE. HE NOTICED THAT HARRISON HAD SWITCHED OFFICES WITH HIS ADJUTANT.
GAVE UP HIS NICE BIG OFFICE IN EXCHANGE FOR WHAT?
SMALLER SPACE, BUT ALL INTERIOR WALLS. NO WINDOWS. NOW, THAT MEANT SOMETHING. THAT MEANT HARRISON DIDN'T LIKE HAVING PEOPLE LOOK IN ON HIM.
MAYBE HE WAS EVEN AFRAID OF GETTING HIMSELF KILLED.
HOOCH SAT THERE FOR TWO HOURS, WATCHING SOLDIERS COME IN AND OUT. HE TRIED NOT TO GET MAD.
HARRISON DID THIS NOW AND THEN, MAKING SOMEBODY SIT AROUND AND WAIT SO BY THE TIME THEY GOT IN THEY WAS SO UPSET THEY COULDN'T THINK STRAIGHT. OR START TO FEELING SO SMALL AND UNIMPORTANT, SO HARRISON COULD DO SOME BULLYING.
HOOCH KNEW ALL OF THIS SO HE TRIED TO STAY CALM. BUT WHEN IT GOT ON TO EVENING, AND THE SOLDIERS STARTED CHANGING SHIFTS AND GOING OFF DUTY, IT WAS MORE THAN HE COULD STAND.
WHAT DO YOU THINK YOU'RE DOING?
GOING OFF DUTY.
BUT I'M STILL HERE.
YOU CAN GO OFF DUTY TOO, IF YOU LIKE.
THAT SMART-MOUTHED ANSWER WAS LIKE A SLAP IN THE FACE. TIME WAS THESE BOYS ALL TRIED TO SUCK UP TO HOOCH PALMER. TIMES WERE CHANGING TOO FAST.
HOOCH DIDN'T LIKE IT AT ALL.
I COULD BUY YOUR OLD MOTHER AND SELL HER AT A PROFIT.
THAT GOT TO HIM. THAT CORPORAL DIDN'T LOOK BORED NO MORE...
BUT HE DIDN'T HAUL OFF AND TAKE A SWING NEITHER. JUST STOOD THERE, MORE OR LESS AT ATTENTION.
MR. PALMER, YOU CAN WAIT HERE ALL NIGHT AND WAIT HERE ALL DAY TOMORROW, AND YOU AIN'T GOING TO GET IN TO SEE HIS EXCELLENCY THE GOVERNOR.
AND YOU JUST SITTING HERE WAITING ALL DAY IS PROOF YOU'RE JUST TOO PLAIN DUMB TO CATCH ON TO HOW THINGS ARE NOW.

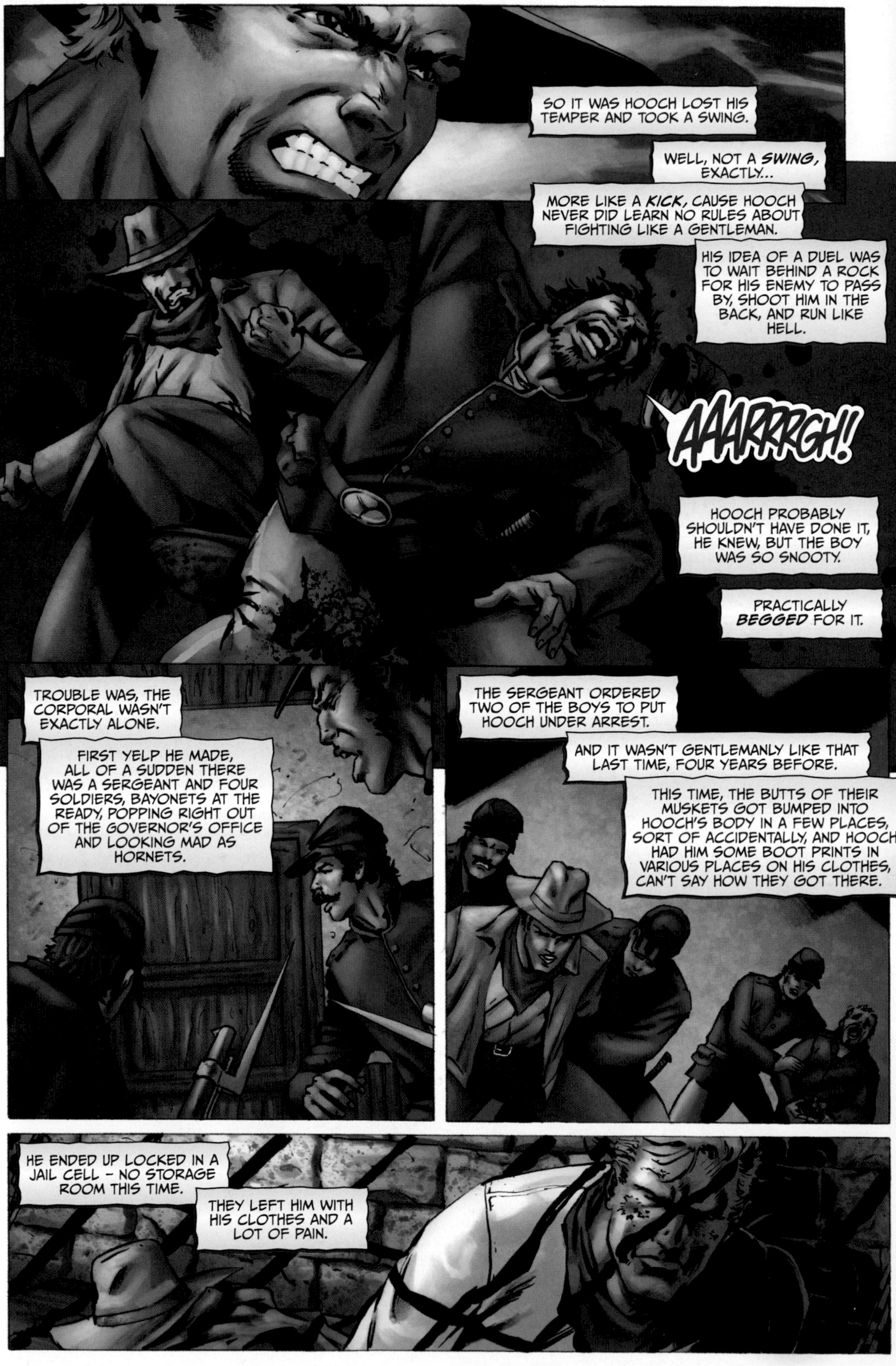
SO IT WAS HOOCH LOST HIS TEMPER AND TOOK A SWING.
WELL, NOT A *SWING,* EXACTLY...
MORE LIKE A *KICK,* CAUSE HOOCH NEVER DID LEARN NO RULES ABOUT FIGHTING LIKE A GENTLEMAN.
HIS IDEA OF A DUEL WAS TO WAIT BEHIND A ROCK FOR HIS ENEMY TO PASS BY, SHOOT HIM IN THE BACK, AND RUN LIKE HELL.
AAARRRGH!
HOOCH PROBABLY SHOULDN'T HAVE DONE IT, HE KNEW, BUT THE BOY WAS SO SNOOTY.
PRACTICALLY ***BEGGED*** FOR IT.
TROUBLE WAS, THE CORPORAL WASN'T EXACTLY ALONE.
FIRST YELP HE MADE, ALL OF A SUDDEN THERE WAS A SERGEANT AND FOUR SOLDIERS, BAYONETS AT THE READY, POPPING RIGHT OUT OF THE GOVERNOR'S OFFICE AND LOOKING MAD AS HORNETS.
THE SERGEANT ORDERED TWO OF THE BOYS TO PUT HOOCH UNDER ARREST.
AND IT WASN'T GENTLEMANLY LIKE THAT LAST TIME, FOUR YEARS BEFORE.
THIS TIME, THE BUTTS OF THEIR MUSKETS GOT BUMPED INTO HOOCH'S BODY IN A FEW PLACES, SORT OF ACCIDENTALLY, AND HOOCH HAD HIM SOME BOOT PRINTS IN VARIOUS PLACES ON HIS CLOTHES, CAN'T SAY HOW THEY GOT THERE.
HE ENDED UP LOCKED IN A JAIL CELL – NO STORAGE ROOM THIS TIME.
THEY LEFT HIM WITH HIS CLOTHES AND A LOT OF PAIN.

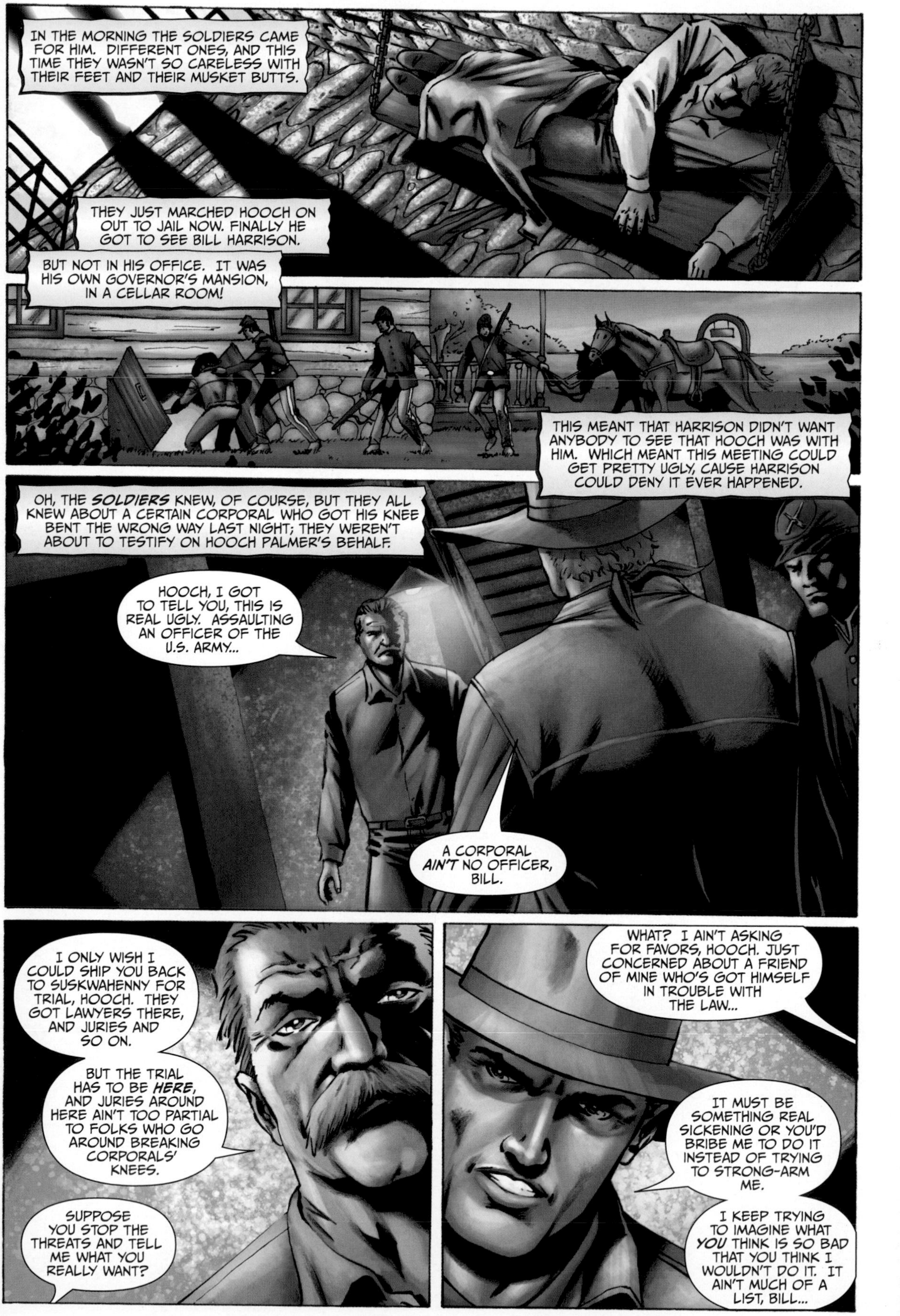
IN THE MORNING THE SOLDIERS CAME FOR HIM. DIFFERENT ONES, AND THIS TIME THEY WASN'T SO CARELESS WITH THEIR FEET AND THEIR MUSKET BUTTS.
THEY JUST MARCHED HOOCH ON OUT TO JAIL NOW. FINALLY HE GOT TO SEE BILL HARRISON.
BUT NOT IN HIS OFFICE. IT WAS HIS OWN GOVERNOR'S MANSION, IN A CELLAR ROOM!
THIS MEANT THAT HARRISON DIDN'T WANT ANYBODY TO SEE THAT HOOCH WAS WITH HIM. WHICH MEANT THIS MEETING COULD GET PRETTY UGLY, CAUSE HARRISON COULD DENY IT EVER HAPPENED.
OH, THE *SOLDIERS* KNEW, OF COURSE, BUT THEY ALL KNEW ABOUT A CERTAIN CORPORAL WHO GOT HIS KNEE BENT THE WRONG WAY LAST NIGHT; THEY WEREN'T ABOUT TO TESTIFY ON HOOCH PALMER'S BEHALF.
HOOCH, I GOT TO TELL YOU, THIS IS REAL UGLY. ASSAULTING AN OFFICER OF THE U.S. ARMY...
A CORPORAL *AIN'T* NO OFFICER, BILL.
I ONLY WISH I COULD SHIP YOU BACK TO SUSKWAHENNY FOR TRIAL, HOOCH. THEY GOT LAWYERS THERE, AND JURIES AND SO ON.
BUT THE TRIAL HAS TO BE *HERE*, AND JURIES AROUND HERE AIN'T TOO PARTIAL TO FOLKS WHO GO AROUND BREAKING CORPORALS' KNEES.
SUPPOSE YOU STOP THE THREATS AND TELL ME WHAT YOU REALLY WANT?
WHAT? I AIN'T ASKING FOR FAVORS, HOOCH. JUST CONCERNED ABOUT A FRIEND OF MINE WHO'S GOT HIMSELF IN TROUBLE WITH THE LAW...
IT MUST BE SOMETHING REAL SICKENING OR YOU'D BRIBE ME TO DO IT INSTEAD OF TRYING TO STRONG-ARM ME.
I KEEP TRYING TO IMAGINE WHAT *YOU* THINK IS SO BAD THAT YOU THINK I WOULDN'T DO IT. IT AIN'T MUCH OF A LIST, BILL...

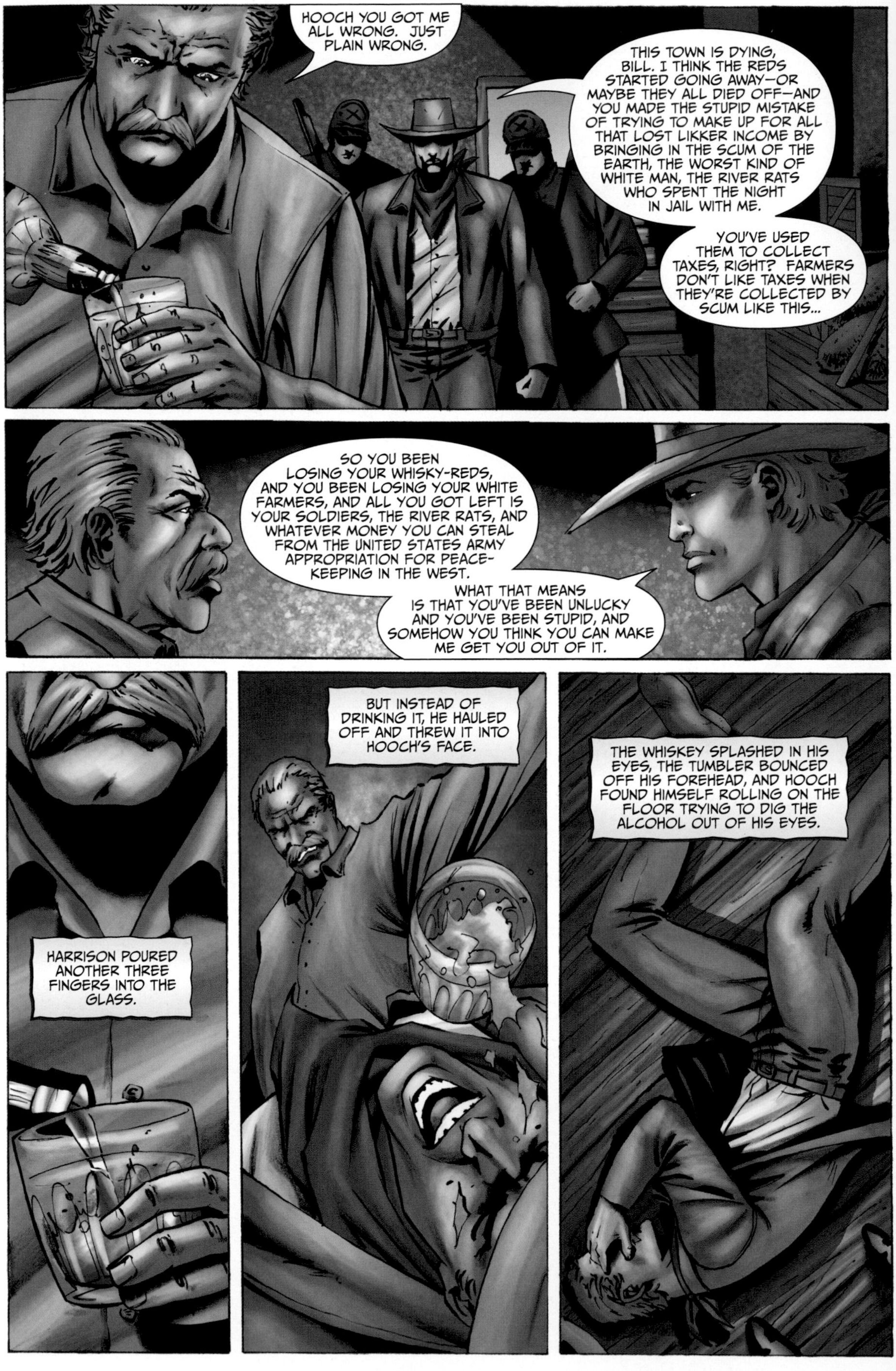
HOOCH YOU GOT ME ALL WRONG. JUST PLAIN WRONG.
THIS TOWN IS DYING, BILL. I THINK THE REDS STARTED GOING AWAY—OR MAYBE THEY ALL DIED OFF—AND YOU MADE THE STUPID MISTAKE OF TRYING TO MAKE UP FOR ALL THAT LOST LIKKER INCOME BY BRINGING IN THE SCUM OF THE EARTH, THE WORST KIND OF WHITE MAN, THE RIVER RATS WHO SPENT THE NIGHT IN JAIL WITH ME.
YOU'VE USED THEM TO COLLECT TAXES, RIGHT? FARMERS DON'T LIKE TAXES WHEN THEY'RE COLLECTED BY SCUM LIKE THIS...
SO YOU BEEN LOSING YOUR WHISKY-REDS, AND YOU BEEN LOSING YOUR WHITE FARMERS, AND ALL YOU GOT LEFT IS YOUR SOLDIERS, THE RIVER RATS, AND WHATEVER MONEY YOU CAN STEAL FROM THE UNITED STATES ARMY APPROPRIATION FOR PEACE-KEEPING IN THE WEST.
WHAT THAT MEANS IS THAT YOU'VE BEEN UNLUCKY AND YOU'VE BEEN STUPID, AND SOMEHOW YOU THINK YOU CAN MAKE ME GET YOU OUT OF IT.
HARRISON POURED ANOTHER THREE FINGERS INTO THE GLASS.
BUT INSTEAD OF DRINKING IT, HE HAULED OFF AND THREW IT INTO HOOCH'S FACE.
THE WHISKEY SPLASHED IN HIS EYES, THE TUMBLER BOUNCED OFF HIS FOREHEAD, AND HOOCH FOUND HIMSELF ROLLING ON THE FLOOR TRYING TO DIG THE ALCOHOL OUT OF HIS EYES.

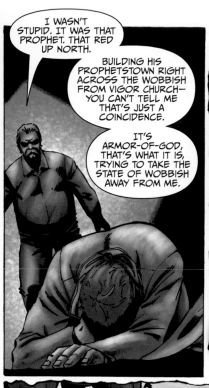

I WASN'T STUPID. IT WAS THAT PROPHET. THAT RED UP NORTH.

BUILDING HIS PROPHETSTOWN RIGHT ACROSS THE WOBBISH FROM VIGOR CHURCH—YOU CAN'T TELL ME THAT'S JUST A COINCIDENCE.

IT'S ARMOR-OF-GOD, THAT'S WHAT IT IS, TRYING TO TAKE THE STATE OF WOBBISH AWAY FROM ME.

"I KNEW THAT A LOT OF REDS WERE GOING NORTH, EVERYBODY KNEW THAT, BUT I STILL HAD MY WHISKY-REDS, THEM AS HADN'T DIED OFF.

"AND WITH FEWER REDS AROUND HERE—ESPECIALLY THE SHAW-NEE, WHEN THEY LEFT—WELL, I THOUGHT I'D GET MORE WHITE SETTLERS.

"AND YOU'RE WRONG ABOUT MY TAX COLLECTORS. THEY DIDN'T RUN THE WHITE SETTLERS OFF.

"IT WAS TA-KUMSAW.

"HE'S BEEN REAL SMART. HE DOESN'T KILL WHITE FOLKS. HE JUST SHOWS UP AT THEIR FARMS WITH FIFTY SHAW-NEE.

"DOESN'T SHOOT ANYBODY, BUT WHEN YOU GOT FIFTY PAINTED-UP WARRIORS ALL AROUND YOUR HOUSE, THESE WHITE FOLKS DIDN'T EXACTLY FIGURE IT WAS SMART TO START SHOOTING.

"SO THE WHITE FARMERS WATCHED WHILE THE SHAW-NEE OPENED EVERY GATE, EVERY STABLE, EVERY COOP. LET THEM ANIMALS GO ON OUT.

"HORSES, PIGS, MILK COWS, CHICKENS. JUST LIKE NOAH BRINGING BEASTS INTO THE ARK, THE SHAW-NEE WALK INTO THE WOODS AND THE ANIMALS TROT ON RIGHT BEHIND. JUST LIKE THAT. NEVER SEE THEM AGAIN."

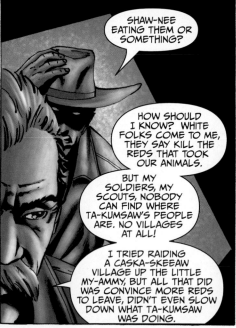

SHAW-NEE EATING THEM OR SOMETHING?

HOW SHOULD I KNOW? WHITE FOLKS COME TO ME, THEY SAY KILL THE REDS THAT TOOK OUR ANIMALS.

BUT MY SOLDIERS, MY SCOUTS, NOBODY CAN FIND WHERE TA-KUMSAW'S PEOPLE ARE. NO VILLAGES AT ALL!

I TRIED RAIDING A CASKA-SKEEAW VILLAGE UP THE LITTLE MY-AMMY, BUT ALL THAT DID WAS CONVINCE MORE REDS TO LEAVE, DIDN'T EVEN SLOW DOWN WHAT TA-KUMSAW WAS DOING.

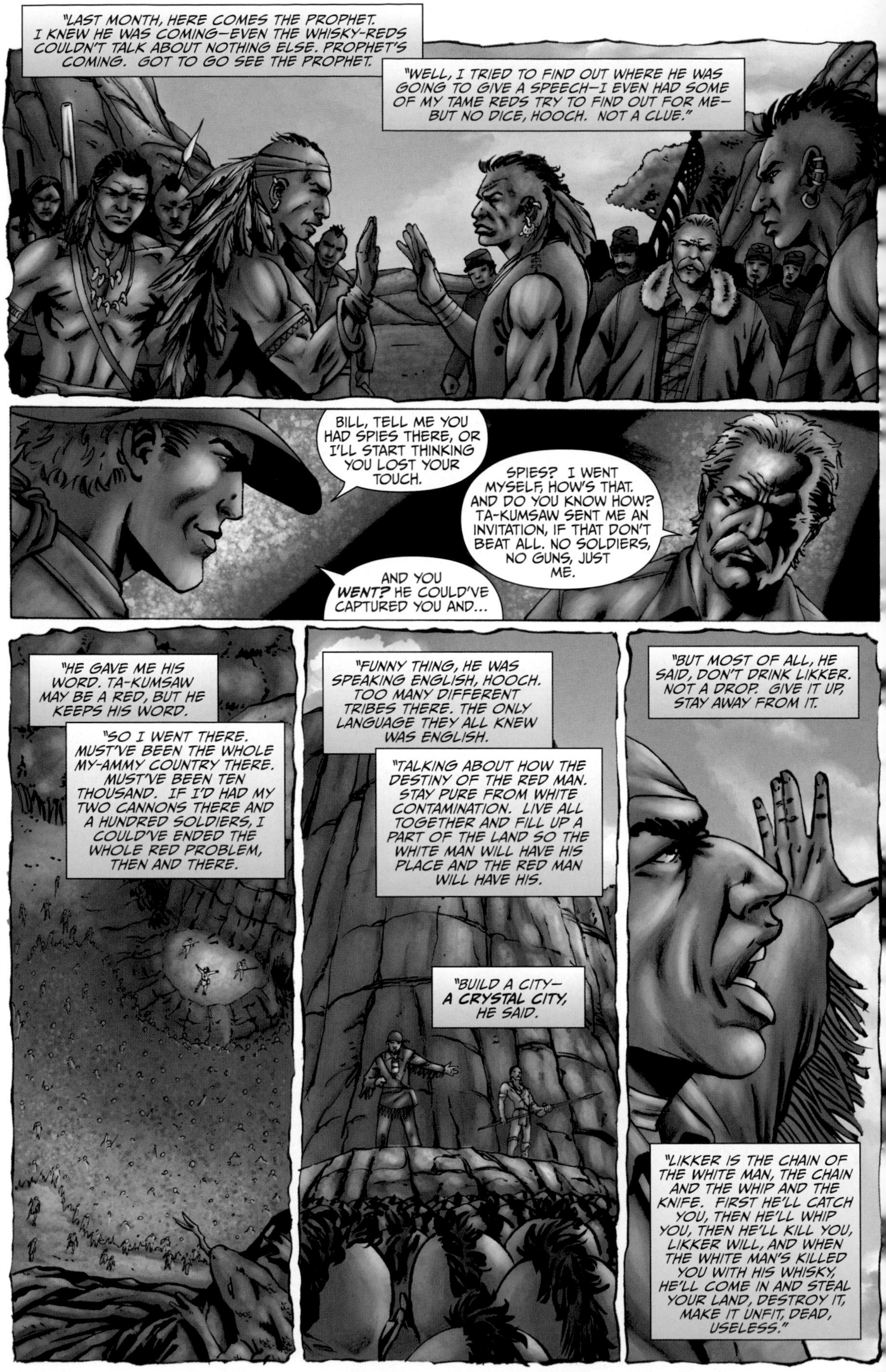
"LAST MONTH, HERE COMES THE PROPHET. I KNEW HE WAS COMING—EVEN THE WHISKY-REDS COULDN'T TALK ABOUT NOTHING ELSE. PROPHET'S COMING. GOT TO GO SEE THE PROPHET.
"WELL, I TRIED TO FIND OUT WHERE HE WAS GOING TO GIVE A SPEECH—I EVEN HAD SOME OF MY TAME REDS TRY TO FIND OUT FOR ME—BUT NO DICE, HOOCH. NOT A CLUE."
BILL, TELL ME YOU HAD SPIES THERE, OR I'LL START THINKING YOU LOST YOUR TOUCH.
SPIES? I WENT MYSELF, HOW'S THAT. AND DO YOU KNOW HOW? TA-KUMSAW SENT ME AN INVITATION, IF THAT DON'T BEAT ALL. NO SOLDIERS, NO GUNS, JUST ME.
AND YOU WENT? HE COULD'VE CAPTURED YOU AND...
"HE GAVE ME HIS WORD. TA-KUMSAW MAY BE A RED, BUT HE KEEPS HIS WORD.
"SO I WENT THERE. MUST'VE BEEN THE WHOLE MY-AMMY COUNTRY THERE. MUST'VE BEEN TEN THOUSAND. IF I'D HAD MY TWO CANNONS THERE AND A HUNDRED SOLDIERS, I COULD'VE ENDED THE WHOLE RED PROBLEM, THEN AND THERE.
"FUNNY THING, HE WAS SPEAKING ENGLISH, HOOCH. TOO MANY DIFFERENT TRIBES THERE. THE ONLY LANGUAGE THEY ALL KNEW WAS ENGLISH.
"TALKING ABOUT HOW THE DESTINY OF THE RED MAN. STAY PURE FROM WHITE CONTAMINATION. LIVE ALL TOGETHER AND FILL UP A PART OF THE LAND SO THE WHITE MAN WILL HAVE HIS PLACE AND THE RED MAN WILL HAVE HIS.
"BUILD A CITY—A CRYSTAL CITY, HE SAID.
"BUT MOST OF ALL, HE SAID, DON'T DRINK LIKKER. NOT A DROP. GIVE IT UP, STAY AWAY FROM IT.
"LIKKER IS THE CHAIN OF THE WHITE MAN, THE CHAIN AND THE WHIP AND THE KNIFE. FIRST HE'LL CATCH YOU, THEN HE'LL WHIP YOU, THEN HE'LL KILL YOU, LIKKER WILL, AND WHEN THE WHITE MAN'S KILLED YOU WITH HIS WHISKY, HE'LL COME IN AND STEAL YOUR LAND, DESTROY IT, MAKE IT UNFIT, DEAD, USELESS."

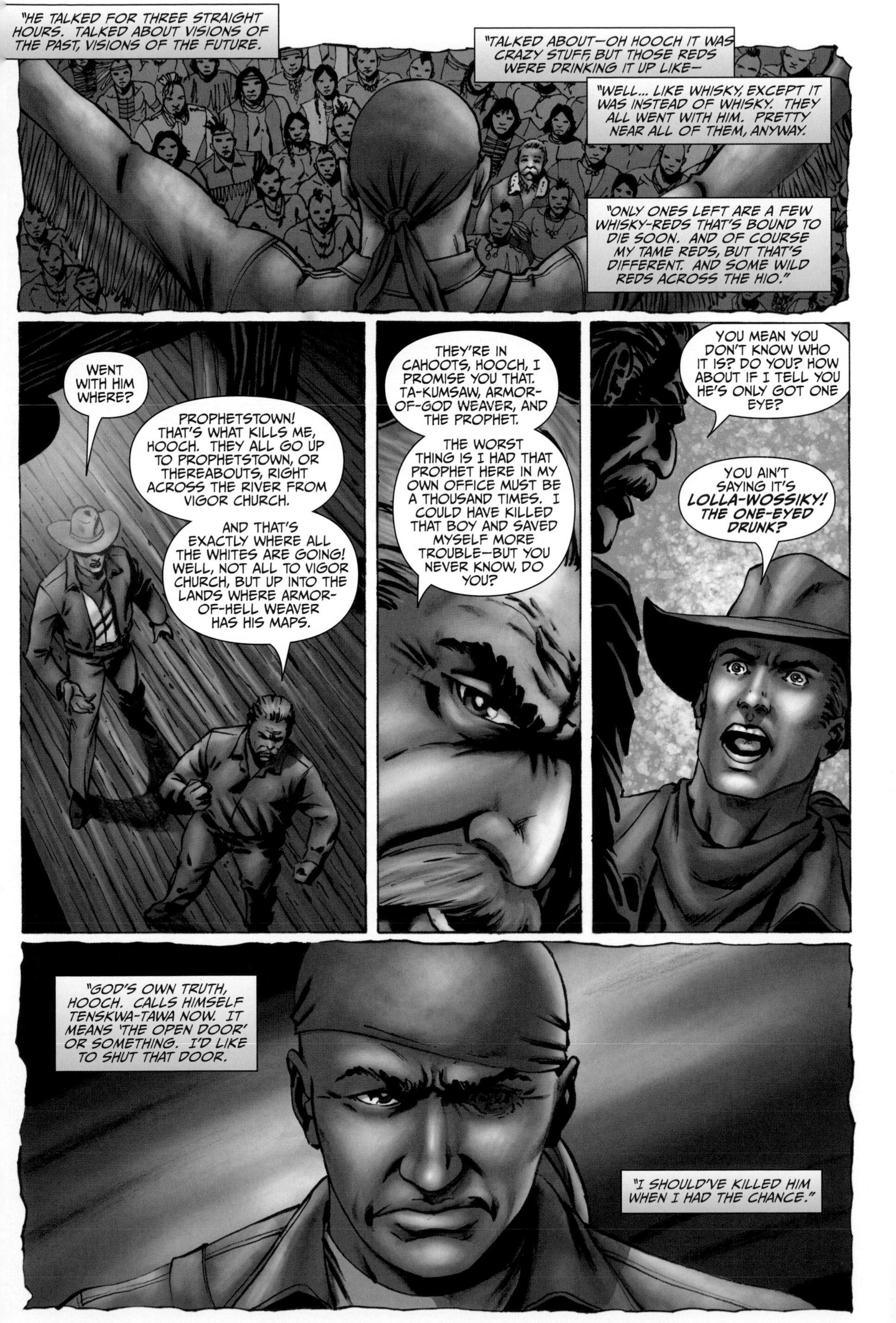
"HE TALKED FOR THREE STRAIGHT HOURS. TALKED ABOUT VISIONS OF THE PAST, VISIONS OF THE FUTURE.
"TALKED ABOUT—OH HOOCH IT WAS CRAZY STUFF, BUT THOSE REDS WERE DRINKING IT UP LIKE—
"WELL... LIKE WHISKY, EXCEPT IT WAS INSTEAD OF WHISKY. THEY ALL WENT WITH HIM. PRETTY NEAR ALL OF THEM, ANYWAY.
"ONLY ONES LEFT ARE A FEW WHISKY-REDS THAT'S BOUND TO DIE SOON. AND OF COURSE MY TAME REDS, BUT THAT'S DIFFERENT. AND SOME WILD REDS ACROSS THE HIO."
WENT WITH HIM WHERE?
PROPHETSTOWN! THAT'S WHAT KILLS ME, HOOCH. THEY ALL GO UP TO PROPHETSTOWN, OR THEREABOUTS, RIGHT ACROSS THE RIVER FROM VIGOR CHURCH.
AND THAT'S EXACTLY WHERE ALL THE WHITES ARE GOING! WELL, NOT ALL TO VIGOR CHURCH, BUT UP INTO THE LANDS WHERE ARMOR-OF-HELL WEAVER HAS HIS MAPS.
THEY'RE IN CAHOOTS, HOOCH, I PROMISE YOU THAT. TA-KUMSAW, ARMOR-OF-GOD WEAVER, AND THE PROPHET.
THE WORST THING IS I HAD THAT PROPHET HERE IN MY OWN OFFICE MUST BE A THOUSAND TIMES. I COULD HAVE KILLED THAT BOY AND SAVED MYSELF MORE TROUBLE—BUT YOU NEVER KNOW, DO YOU?
YOU MEAN YOU DON'T KNOW WHO IT IS? DO YOU? HOW ABOUT IF I TELL YOU HE'S ONLY GOT ONE EYE?
YOU AIN'T SAYING IT'S **LOLLA-WOSSIKY! THE ONE-EYED DRUNK?**
"GOD'S OWN TRUTH, HOOCH. CALLS HIMSELF TENSKWA-TAWA NOW. IT MEANS 'THE OPEN DOOR' OR SOMETHING. I'D LIKE TO SHUT THAT DOOR.
"I SHOULD'VE KILLED HIM WHEN I HAD THE CHANCE."

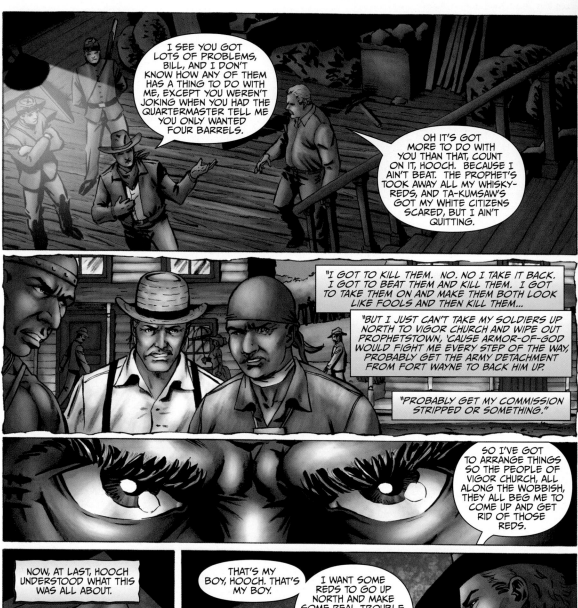

I SEE YOU GOT LOTS OF PROBLEMS, BILL, AND I DON'T KNOW HOW ANY OF THEM HAS A THING TO DO WITH ME, EXCEPT YOU WEREN'T JOKING WHEN YOU HAD THE QUARTERMASTER TELL ME YOU ONLY WANTED FOUR BARRELS.

OH IT'S GOT MORE TO DO WITH YOU THAN THAT, COUNT ON IT, HOOCH. BECAUSE I AIN'T BEAT. THE PROPHET'S TOOK AWAY ALL MY WHISKY-REDS, AND TA-KUMSAW'S GOT MY WHITE CITIZENS SCARED, BUT I AIN'T QUITTING.

"I GOT TO KILL THEM. NO. NO I TAKE IT BACK. I GOT TO BEAT THEM AND KILL THEM. I GOT TO TAKE THEM ON AND MAKE THEM BOTH LOOK LIKE FOOLS AND THEN KILL THEM...

"BUT I JUST CAN'T TAKE MY SOLDIERS UP NORTH TO VIGOR CHURCH AND WIPE OUT PROPHETSTOWN, 'CAUSE ARMOR-OF-GOD WOULD FIGHT ME EVERY STEP OF THE WAY, PROBABLY GET THE ARMY DETACHMENT FROM FORT WAYNE TO BACK HIM UP.

"PROBABLY GET MY COMMISSION STRIPPED OR SOMETHING."

SO I'VE GOT TO ARRANGE THINGS SO THE PEOPLE OF VIGOR CHURCH, ALL ALONG THE WOBBISH, THEY ALL BEG ME TO COME UP AND GET RID OF THOSE REDS.

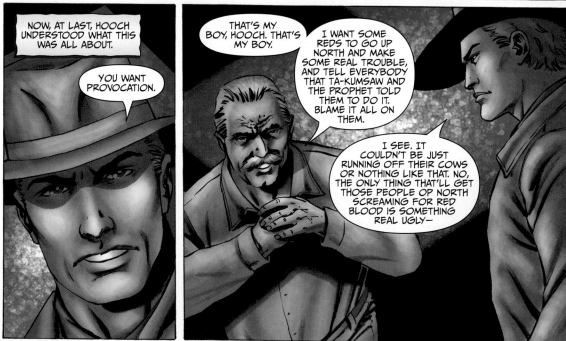

NOW, AT LAST, HOOCH UNDERSTOOD WHAT THIS WAS ALL ABOUT.

YOU WANT PROVOCATION.

THAT'S MY BOY, HOOCH. THAT'S MY BOY.

I WANT SOME REDS TO GO UP NORTH AND MAKE SOME REAL TROUBLE, AND TELL EVERYBODY THAT TA-KUMSAW AND THE PROPHET TOLD THEM TO DO IT. BLAME IT ALL ON THEM.

I SEE. IT COULDN'T BE JUST RUNNING OFF THEIR COWS OR NOTHING LIKE THAT. NO, THE ONLY THING THAT'LL GET THOSE PEOPLE UP NORTH SCREAMING FOR RED BLOOD IS SOMETHING REAL UGLY—

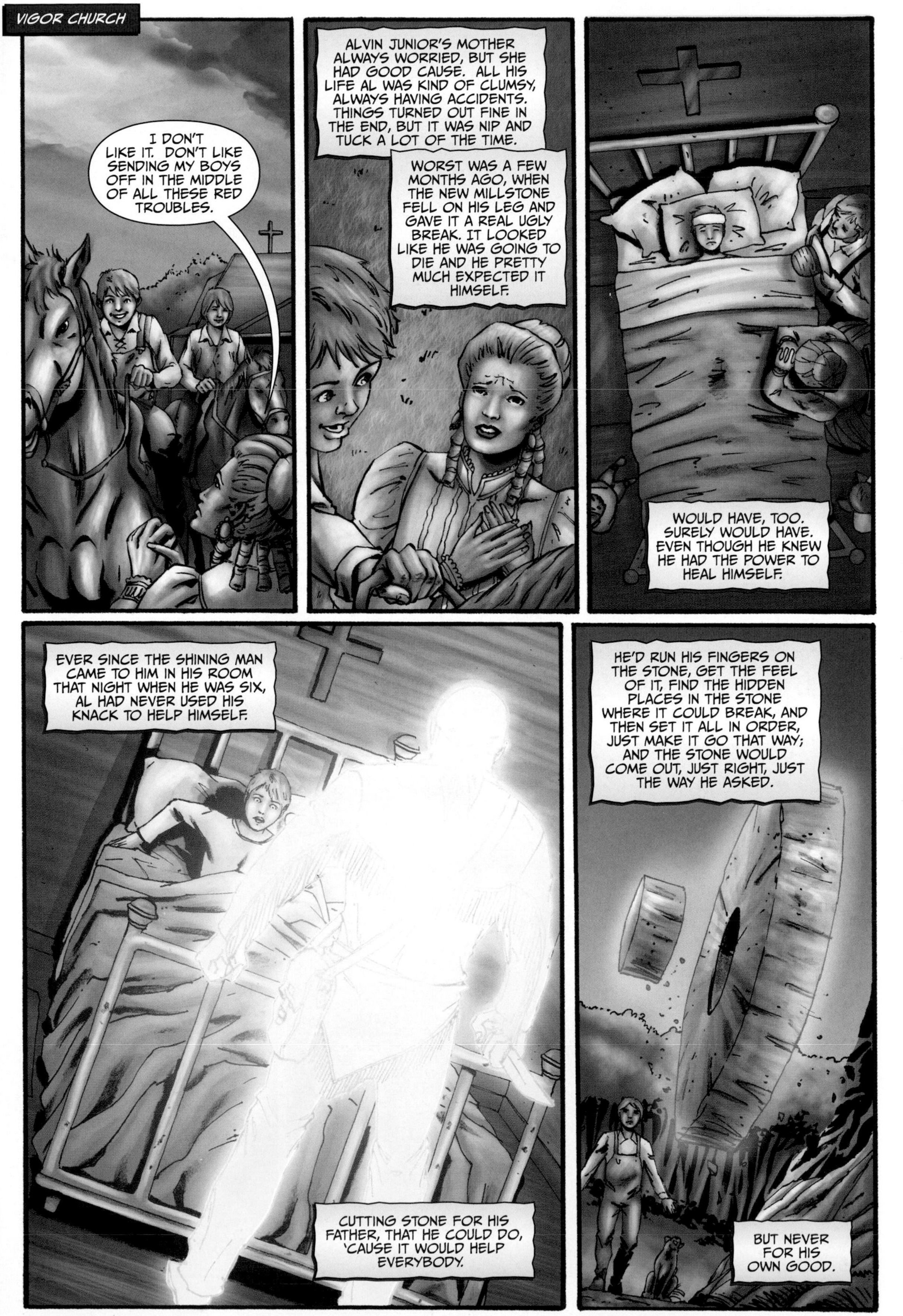
VIGOR CHURCH
I DON'T LIKE IT. DON'T LIKE SENDING MY BOYS OFF IN THE MIDDLE OF ALL THESE RED TROUBLES.
ALVIN JUNIOR'S MOTHER ALWAYS WORRIED, BUT SHE HAD GOOD CAUSE. ALL HIS LIFE AL WAS KIND OF CLUMSY, ALWAYS HAVING ACCIDENTS. THINGS TURNED OUT FINE IN THE END, BUT IT WAS NIP AND TUCK A LOT OF THE TIME.
WORST WAS A FEW MONTHS AGO, WHEN THE NEW MILLSTONE FELL ON HIS LEG AND GAVE IT A REAL UGLY BREAK. IT LOOKED LIKE HE WAS GOING TO DIE AND HE PRETTY MUCH EXPECTED IT HIMSELF.
WOULD HAVE, TOO. SURELY WOULD HAVE. EVEN THOUGH HE KNEW HE HAD THE POWER TO HEAL HIMSELF.
EVER SINCE THE SHINING MAN CAME TO HIM IN HIS ROOM THAT NIGHT WHEN HE WAS SIX, AL HAD NEVER USED HIS KNACK TO HELP HIMSELF.
CUTTING STONE FOR HIS FATHER, THAT HE COULD DO, 'CAUSE IT WOULD HELP EVERYBODY.
HE'D RUN HIS FINGERS ON THE STONE, GET THE FEEL OF IT, FIND THE HIDDEN PLACES IN THE STONE WHERE IT COULD BREAK, AND THEN SET IT ALL IN ORDER, JUST MAKE IT GO THAT WAY; AND THE STONE WOULD COME OUT, JUST RIGHT, JUST THE WAY HE ASKED.
BUT NEVER FOR HIS OWN GOOD.

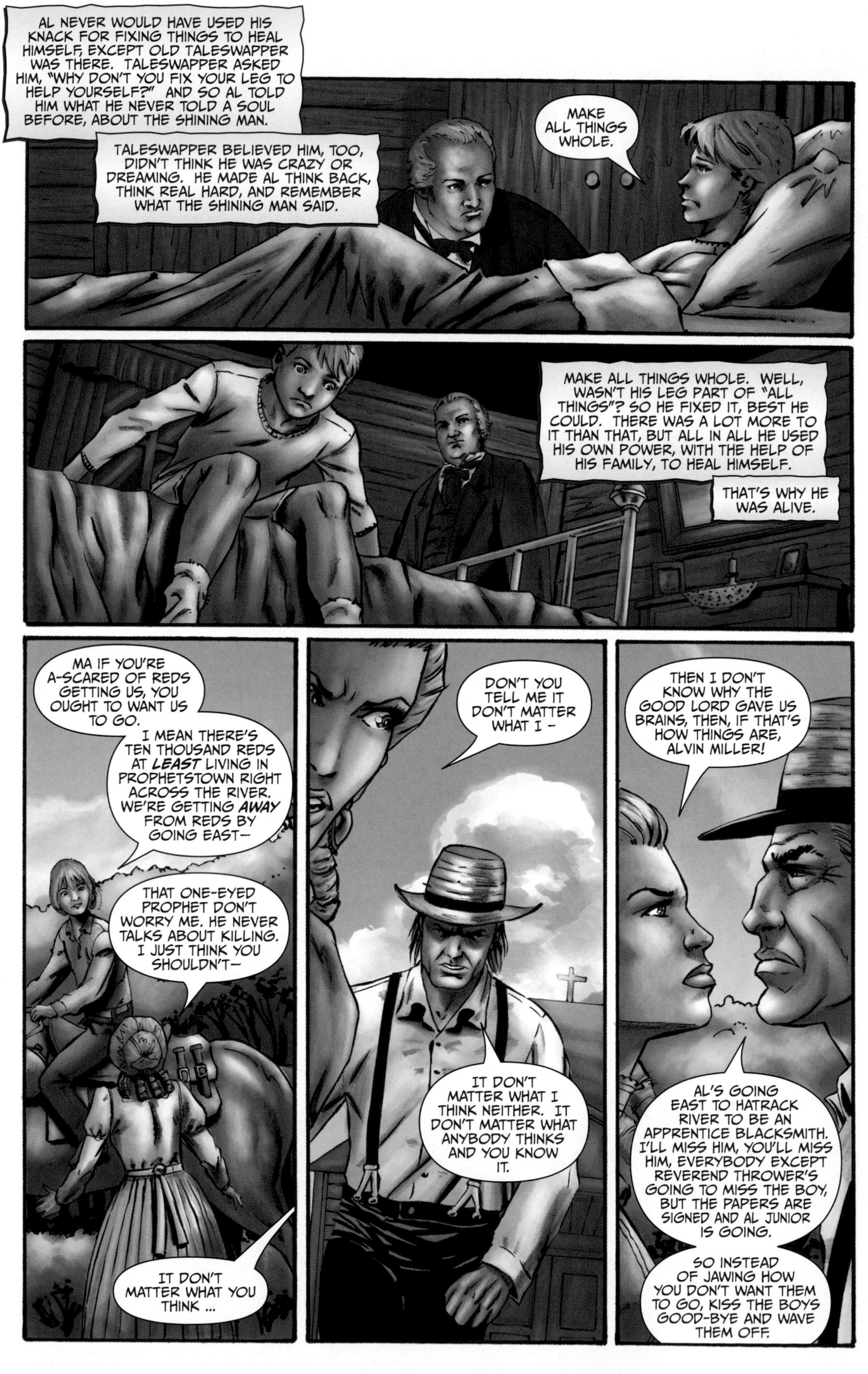
AL NEVER WOULD HAVE USED HIS KNACK FOR FIXING THINGS TO HEAL HIMSELF, EXCEPT OLD TALESWAPPER WAS THERE. TALESWAPPER ASKED HIM, "WHY DON'T YOU FIX YOUR LEG TO HELP YOURSELF?" AND SO AL TOLD HIM WHAT HE NEVER TOLD A SOUL BEFORE, ABOUT THE SHINING MAN.
TALESWAPPER BELIEVED HIM, TOO, DIDN'T THINK HE WAS CRAZY OR DREAMING. HE MADE AL THINK BACK, THINK REAL HARD, AND REMEMBER WHAT THE SHINING MAN SAID.
MAKE ALL THINGS WHOLE.
MAKE ALL THINGS WHOLE. WELL, WASN'T HIS LEG PART OF "ALL THINGS"? SO HE FIXED IT, BEST HE COULD. THERE WAS A LOT MORE TO IT THAN THAT, BUT ALL IN ALL HE USED HIS OWN POWER, WITH THE HELP OF HIS FAMILY, TO HEAL HIMSELF.
THAT'S WHY HE WAS ALIVE.
MA IF YOU'RE A-SCARED OF REDS GETTING US, YOU OUGHT TO WANT US TO GO.
I MEAN THERE'S TEN THOUSAND REDS AT *LEAST* LIVING IN PROPHETSTOWN RIGHT ACROSS THE RIVER. WE'RE GETTING *AWAY* FROM REDS BY GOING EAST–
THAT ONE-EYED PROPHET DON'T WORRY ME. HE NEVER TALKS ABOUT KILLING. I JUST THINK YOU SHOULDN'T–
IT DON'T MATTER WHAT YOU THINK ...
DON'T YOU TELL ME IT DON'T MATTER WHAT I –
IT DON'T MATTER WHAT I THINK NEITHER. IT DON'T MATTER WHAT ANYBODY THINKS AND YOU KNOW IT.
THEN I DON'T KNOW WHY THE GOOD LORD GAVE US BRAINS, THEN, IF THAT'S HOW THINGS ARE, ALVIN MILLER!
AL'S GOING EAST TO HATRACK RIVER TO BE AN APPRENTICE BLACKSMITH. I'LL MISS HIM, YOU'LL MISS HIM, EVERYBODY EXCEPT REVEREND THROWER'S GOING TO MISS THE BOY, BUT THE PAPERS ARE SIGNED AND AL JUNIOR IS GOING.
SO INSTEAD OF JAWING HOW YOU DON'T WANT THEM TO GO, KISS THE BOYS GOOD-BYE AND WAVE THEM OFF.

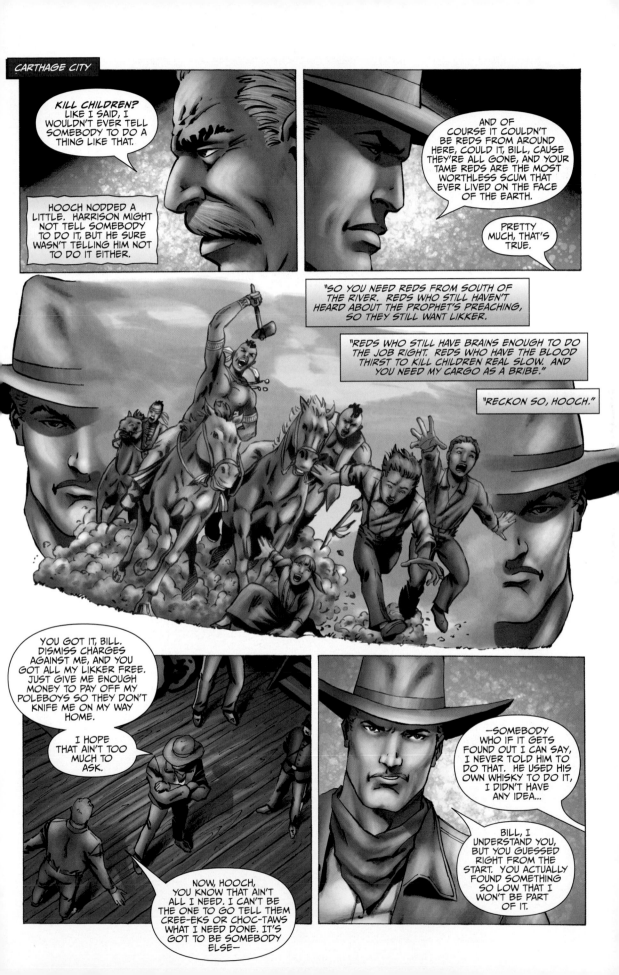

KILL CHILDREN? LIKE I SAID, I WOULDN'T EVER TELL SOMEBODY TO DO A THING LIKE THAT.

HOOCH NODDED A LITTLE. HARRISON MIGHT NOT TELL SOMEBODY TO DO IT, BUT HE SURE WASN'T TELLING HIM NOT TO DO IT EITHER.

AND OF COURSE IT COULDN'T BE REDS FROM AROUND HERE, COULD IT, BILL, CAUSE THEY'RE ALL GONE, AND YOUR TAME REDS ARE THE MOST WORTHLESS SCUM THAT EVER LIVED ON THE FACE OF THE EARTH.

PRETTY MUCH, THAT'S TRUE.

"SO YOU NEED REDS FROM SOUTH OF THE RIVER. REDS WHO STILL HAVEN'T HEARD ABOUT THE PROPHET'S PREACHING, SO THEY STILL WANT LIKKER.

"REDS WHO STILL HAVE BRAINS ENOUGH TO DO THE JOB RIGHT. REDS WHO HAVE THE BLOOD THIRST TO KILL CHILDREN REAL SLOW. AND YOU NEED MY CARGO AS A BRIBE."

"RECKON SO, HOOCH."

YOU GOT IT, BILL. DISMISS CHARGES AGAINST ME, AND YOU GOT ALL MY LIKKER FREE. JUST GIVE ME ENOUGH MONEY TO PAY OFF MY POLEBOYS SO THEY DON'T KNIFE ME ON MY WAY HOME.

I HOPE THAT AIN'T TOO MUCH TO ASK.

NOW, HOOCH, YOU KNOW THAT AIN'T ALL I NEED. I CAN'T BE THE ONE TO GO TELL THEM CREE-EKS OR CHOC-TAWS WHAT I NEED DONE. IT'S GOT TO BE SOMEBODY ELSE—

—SOMEBODY WHO IF IT GETS FOUND OUT I CAN SAY, I NEVER TOLD HIM TO DO THAT. HE USED HIS OWN WHISKY TO DO IT, I DIDN'T HAVE ANY IDEA...

BILL, I UNDERSTAND YOU, BUT YOU GUESSED RIGHT FROM THE START. YOU ACTUALLY FOUND SOMETHING SO LOW THAT I WON'T BE PART OF IT.

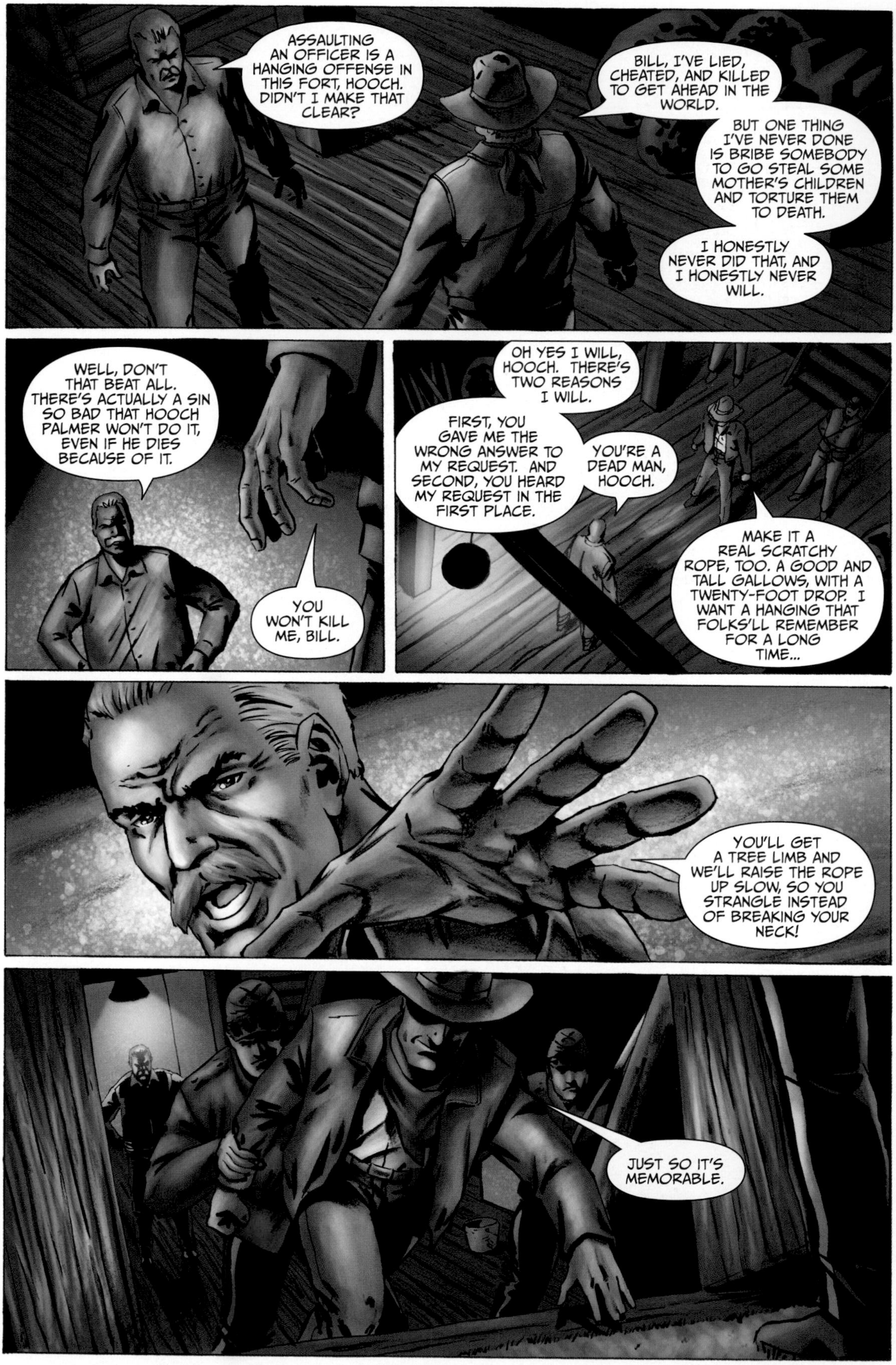
ASSAULTING AN OFFICER IS A HANGING OFFENSE IN THIS FORT, HOOCH. DIDN'T I MAKE THAT CLEAR?
BILL, I'VE LIED, CHEATED, AND KILLED TO GET AHEAD IN THE WORLD.
BUT ONE THING I'VE NEVER DONE IS BRIBE SOMEBODY TO GO STEAL SOME MOTHER'S CHILDREN AND TORTURE THEM TO DEATH.
I HONESTLY NEVER DID THAT, AND I HONESTLY NEVER WILL.
WELL, DON'T THAT BEAT ALL. THERE'S ACTUALLY A SIN SO BAD THAT HOOCH PALMER WON'T DO IT, EVEN IF HE DIES BECAUSE OF IT.
YOU WON'T KILL ME, BILL.
OH YES I WILL, HOOCH. THERE'S TWO REASONS I WILL.
FIRST, YOU GAVE ME THE WRONG ANSWER TO MY REQUEST. AND SECOND, YOU HEARD MY REQUEST IN THE FIRST PLACE.
YOU'RE A DEAD MAN, HOOCH.
MAKE IT A REAL SCRATCHY ROPE, TOO. A GOOD AND TALL GALLOWS, WITH A TWENTY-FOOT DROP. I WANT A HANGING THAT FOLKS'LL REMEMBER FOR A LONG TIME...
YOU'LL GET A TREE LIMB AND WE'LL RAISE THE ROPE UP SLOW, SO YOU STRANGLE INSTEAD OF BREAKING YOUR NECK!
JUST SO IT'S MEMORABLE.

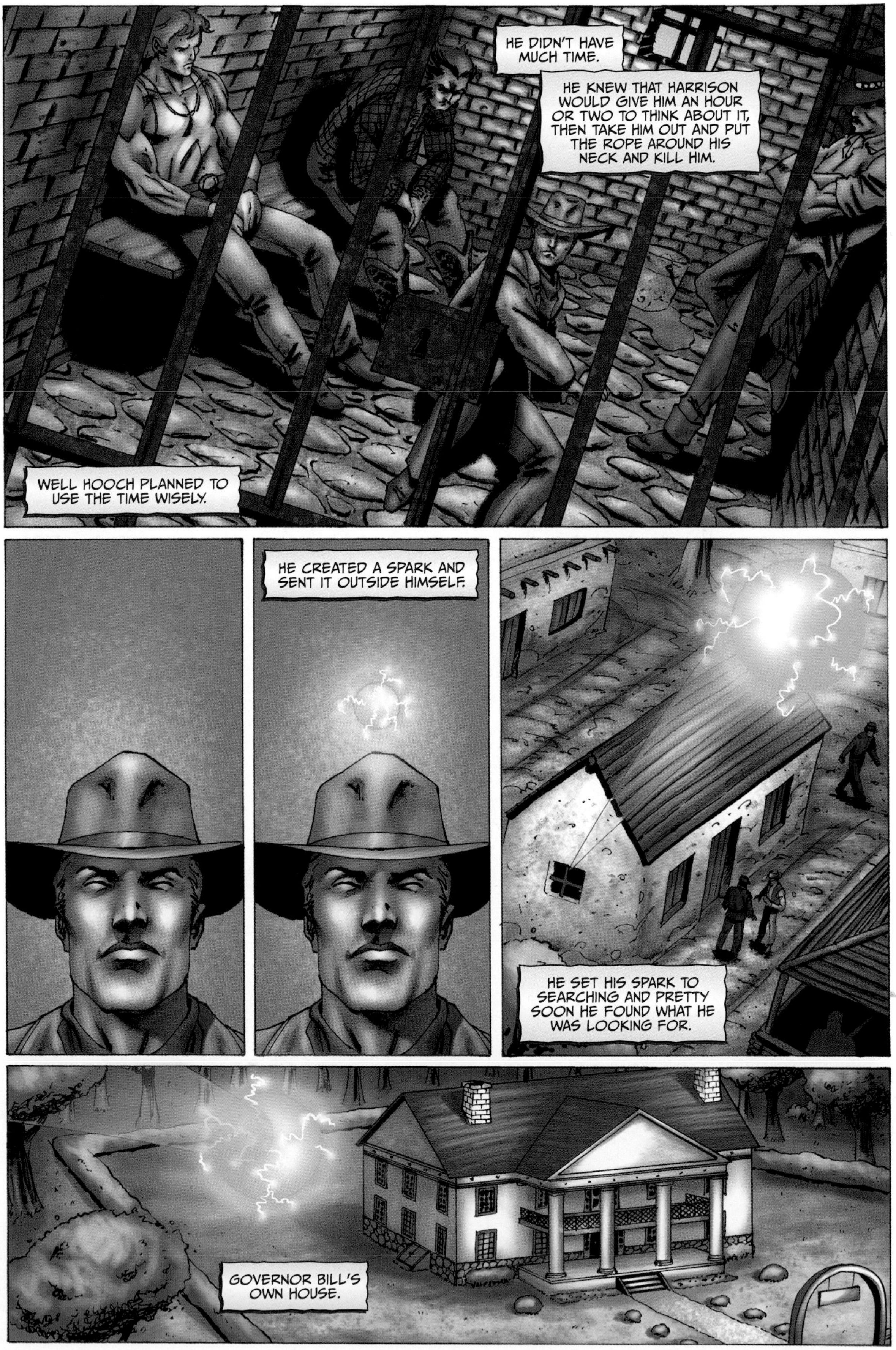
HE DIDN'T HAVE MUCH TIME.
HE KNEW THAT HARRISON WOULD GIVE HIM AN HOUR OR TWO TO THINK ABOUT IT, THEN TAKE HIM OUT AND PUT THE ROPE AROUND HIS NECK AND KILL HIM.
WELL HOOCH PLANNED TO USE THE TIME WISELY.
HE CREATED A SPARK AND SENT IT OUTSIDE HIMSELF.
HE SET HIS SPARK TO SEARCHING AND PRETTY SOON HE FOUND WHAT HE WAS LOOKING FOR.
GOVERNOR BILL'S OWN HOUSE.

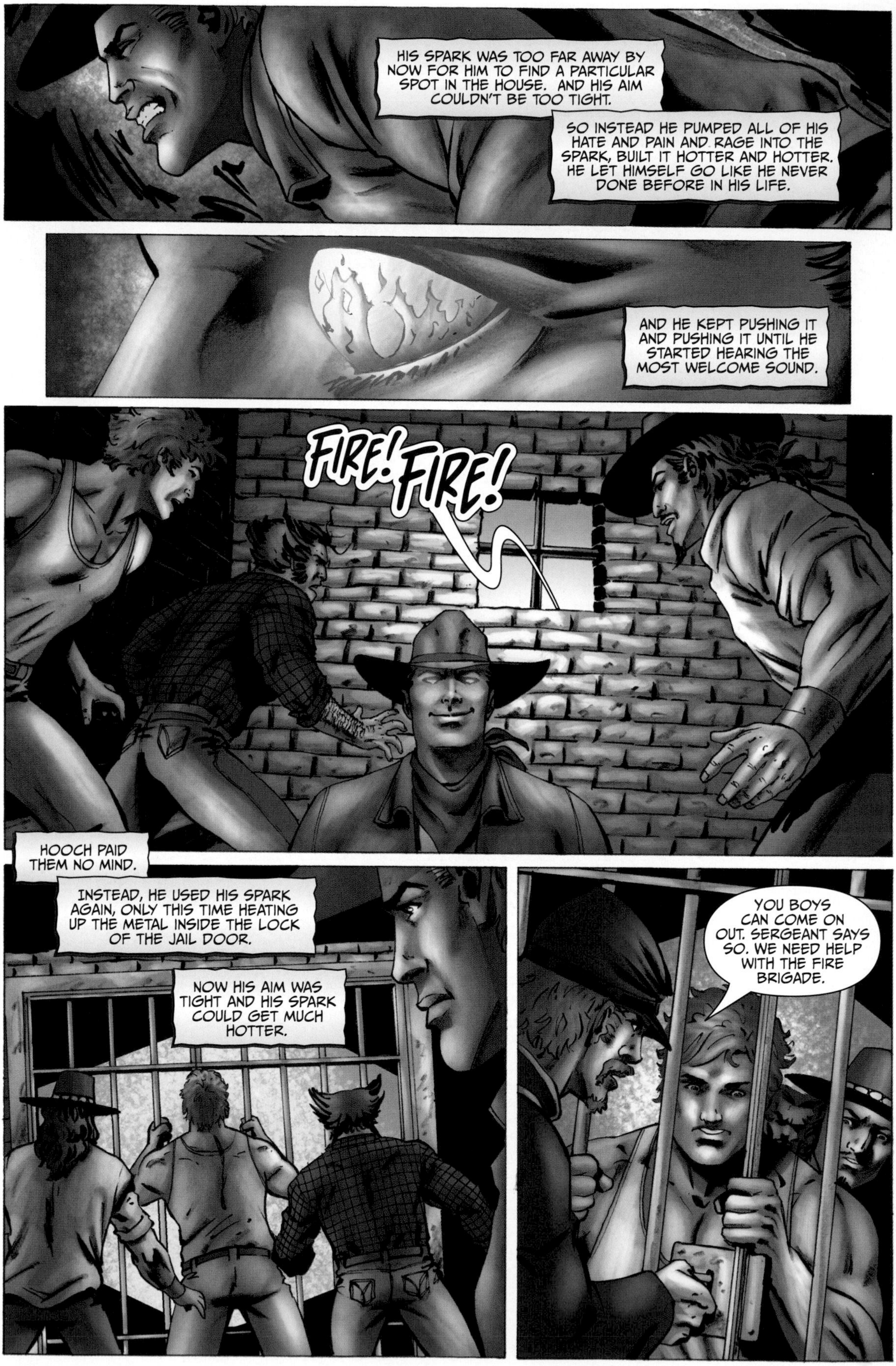
HIS SPARK WAS TOO FAR AWAY BY NOW FOR HIM TO FIND A PARTICULAR SPOT IN THE HOUSE. AND HIS AIM COULDN'T BE TOO TIGHT.
SO INSTEAD HE PUMPED ALL OF HIS HATE AND PAIN AND RAGE INTO THE SPARK, BUILT IT HOTTER AND HOTTER. HE LET HIMSELF GO LIKE HE NEVER DONE BEFORE IN HIS LIFE.
AND HE KEPT PUSHING IT AND PUSHING IT UNTIL HE STARTED HEARING THE MOST WELCOME SOUND.
FIRE! FIRE!
HOOCH PAID THEM NO MIND.
INSTEAD, HE USED HIS SPARK AGAIN, ONLY THIS TIME HEATING UP THE METAL INSIDE THE LOCK OF THE JAIL DOOR.
NOW HIS AIM WAS TIGHT AND HIS SPARK COULD GET MUCH HOTTER.
YOU BOYS CAN COME ON OUT. SERGEANT SAYS SO. WE NEED HELP WITH THE FIRE BRIGADE.

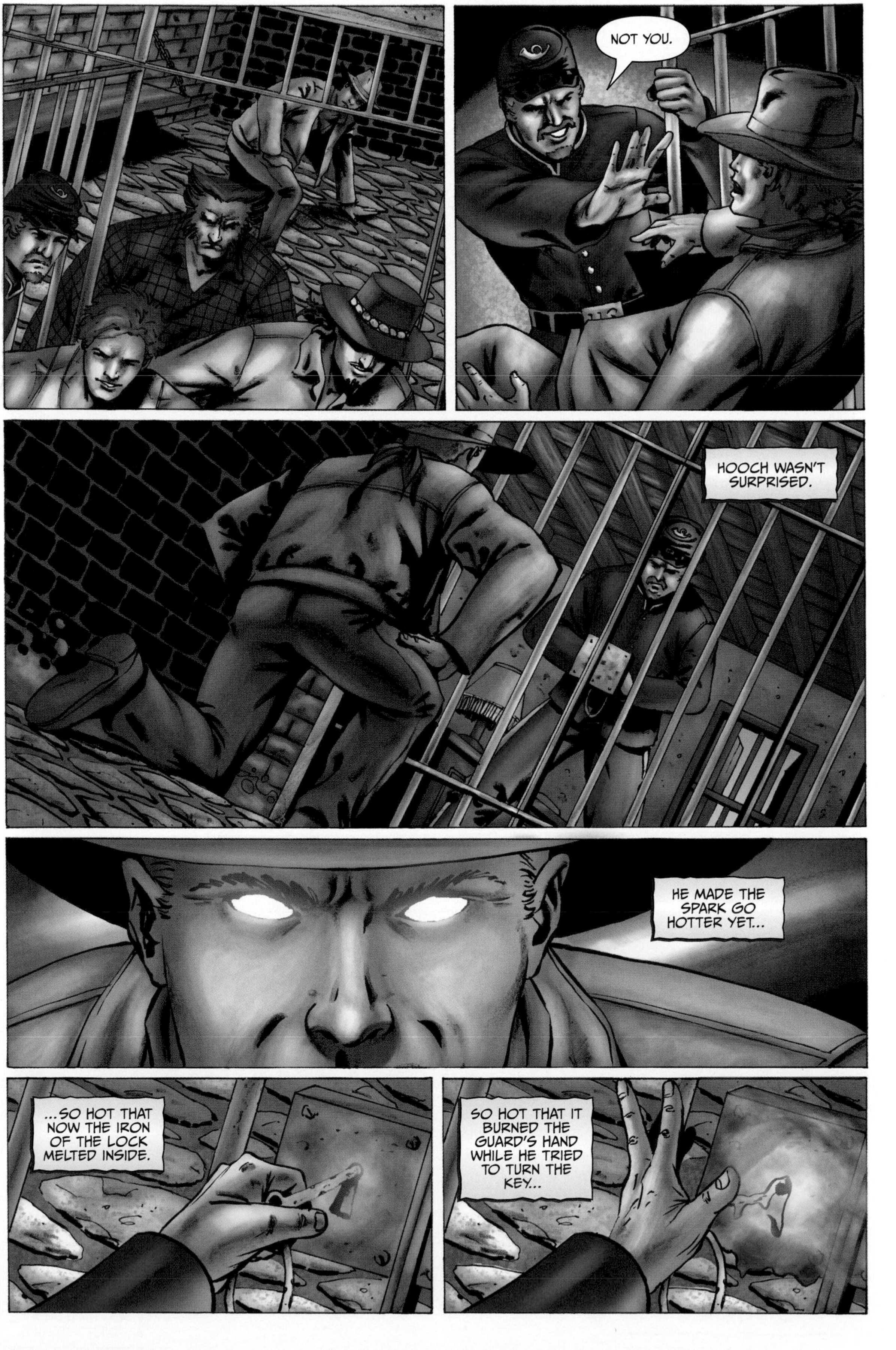
NOT YOU.
HOOCH WASN'T SURPRISED.
HE MADE THE SPARK GO HOTTER YET...
...SO HOT THAT NOW THE IRON OF THE LOCK MELTED INSIDE.
SO HOT THAT IT BURNED THE GUARD'S HAND WHILE HE TRIED TO TURN THE KEY...

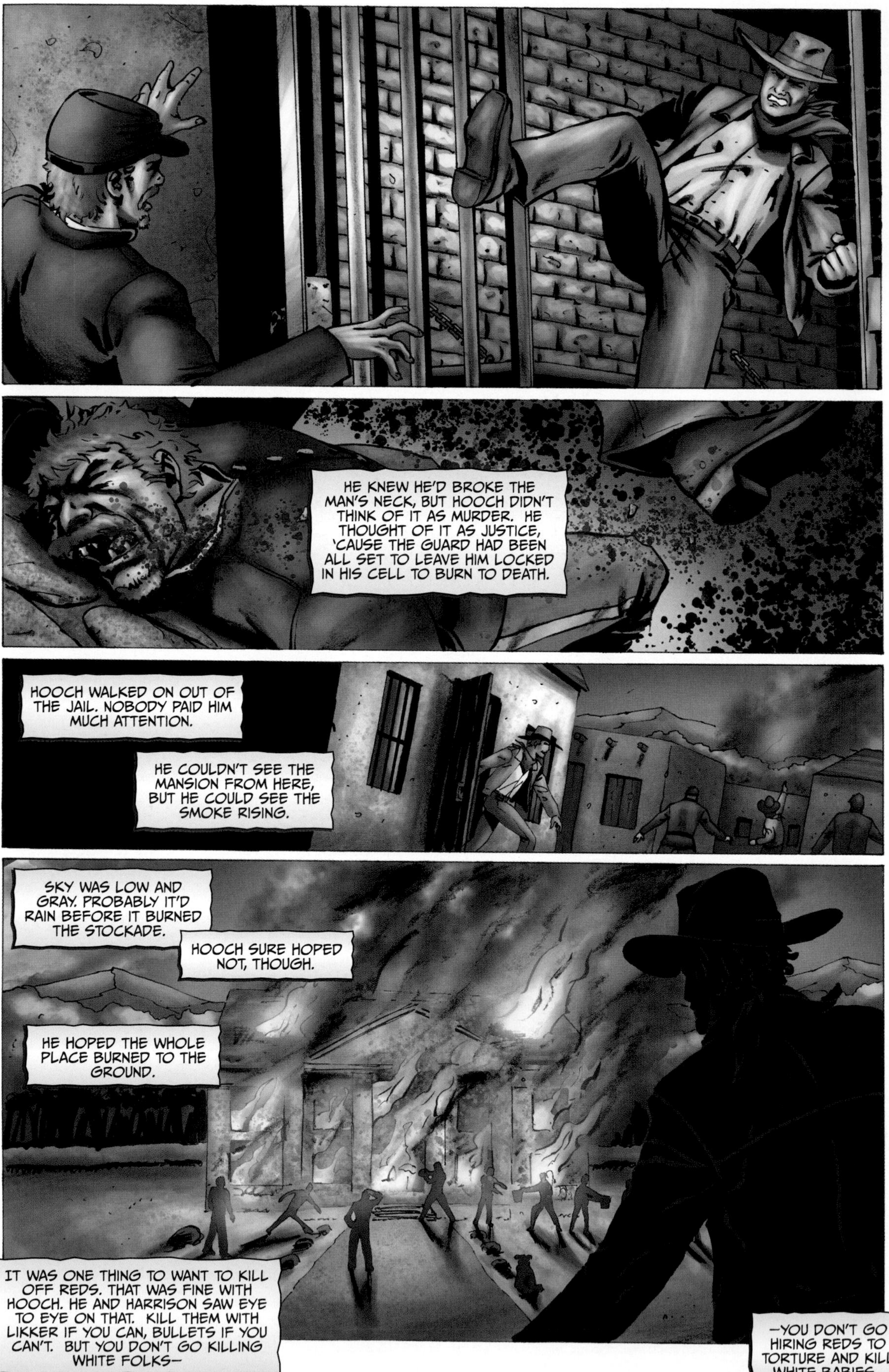
HE KNEW HE'D BROKE THE MAN'S NECK, BUT HOOCH DIDN'T THINK OF IT AS MURDER. HE THOUGHT OF IT AS JUSTICE, 'CAUSE THE GUARD HAD BEEN ALL SET TO LEAVE HIM LOCKED IN HIS CELL TO BURN TO DEATH.
HOOCH WALKED ON OUT OF THE JAIL. NOBODY PAID HIM MUCH ATTENTION.
HE COULDN'T SEE THE MANSION FROM HERE, BUT HE COULD SEE THE SMOKE RISING.
SKY WAS LOW AND GRAY. PROBABLY IT'D RAIN BEFORE IT BURNED THE STOCKADE.
HOOCH SURE HOPED NOT, THOUGH.
HE HOPED THE WHOLE PLACE BURNED TO THE GROUND.
IT WAS ONE THING TO WANT TO KILL OFF REDS. THAT WAS FINE WITH HOOCH. HE AND HARRISON SAW EYE TO EYE ON THAT. KILL THEM WITH LIKKER IF YOU CAN, BULLETS IF YOU CAN'T. BUT YOU DON'T GO KILLING WHITE FOLKS—
—YOU DON'T GO HIRING REDS TO TORTURE AND KILL WHITE BABIES.

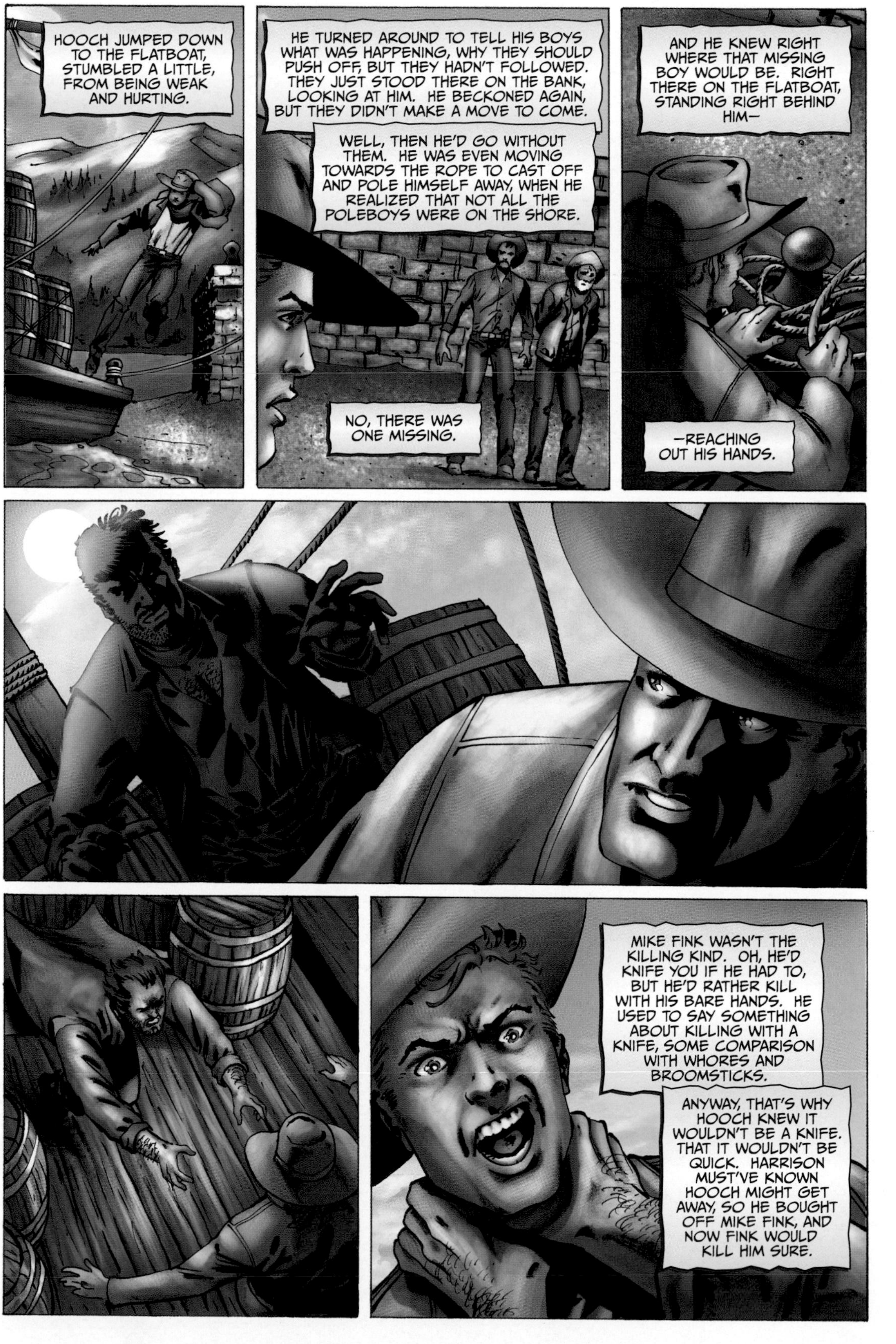
HOOCH JUMPED DOWN TO THE FLATBOAT, STUMBLED A LITTLE, FROM BEING WEAK AND HURTING.
HE TURNED AROUND TO TELL HIS BOYS WHAT WAS HAPPENING, WHY THEY SHOULD PUSH OFF, BUT THEY HADN'T FOLLOWED. THEY JUST STOOD THERE ON THE BANK, LOOKING AT HIM. HE BECKONED AGAIN, BUT THEY DIDN'T MAKE A MOVE TO COME.
WELL, THEN HE'D GO WITHOUT THEM. HE WAS EVEN MOVING TOWARDS THE ROPE TO CAST OFF AND POLE HIMSELF AWAY, WHEN HE REALIZED THAT NOT ALL THE POLEBOYS WERE ON THE SHORE.
NO, THERE WAS ONE MISSING.
AND HE KNEW RIGHT WHERE THAT MISSING BOY WOULD BE. RIGHT THERE ON THE FLATBOAT, STANDING RIGHT BEHIND HIM—
—REACHING OUT HIS HANDS.
MIKE FINK WASN'T THE KILLING KIND. OH, HE'D KNIFE YOU IF HE HAD TO, BUT HE'D RATHER KILL WITH HIS BARE HANDS. HE USED TO SAY SOMETHING ABOUT KILLING WITH A KNIFE, SOME COMPARISON WITH WHORES AND BROOMSTICKS.
ANYWAY, THAT'S WHY HOOCH KNEW IT WOULDN'T BE A KNIFE. THAT IT WOULDN'T BE QUICK. HARRISON MUST'VE KNOWN HOOCH MIGHT GET AWAY, SO HE BOUGHT OFF MIKE FINK, AND NOW FINK WOULD KILL HIM SURE.

SURE, BUT SLOW. AND SLOW GAVE HOOCH TIME. TIME TO MAKE SURE HE DIDN'T DIE ALONE.

SO AS THE FINGERS CLOSED AROUND HIS THROAT AND CINCHED TIGHT, MUCH TIGHTER THAN HOOCH EVER IMAGINED, CLAMPING HIM SO HE THOUGHT HIS HEAD WOULD GET WRUNG RIGHT OFF, HE FORCED HIMSELF TO MAKE HIS SPARK GO, TO FIND THAT KEG—

—THAT ONE PLACE, HE KNEW RIGHT WHERE THAT PLACE WAS ON THE FLAT-BOAT, TO HOT UP THAT KEG, AS HOT AS HE COULD, HOTTER, HOTTER—

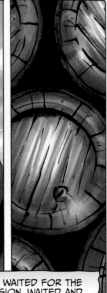

AND HE WAITED FOR THE EXPLOSION, WAITED AND WAITED, BUT IT NEVER CAME.

IT FELT LIKE FINK'S FINGERS HAD PRESSED THOUGH THE FRONT OF HIS THROAT CLEAR TO THE SPINE, AND HE FELT ALL HIS MUSCLES JUST GIVING WAY. HE FELT HIMSELF KICKING, HIS LUNGS HEAVING TO TRY TO SUCK IN AIR THAT JUST WOULDN'T COME.

HE KEPT HIS SPARK GOING TO THE LAST SECOND, WAITING FOR THE GUNPOWDER KEG TO BLOW.

THEN HE DIED.

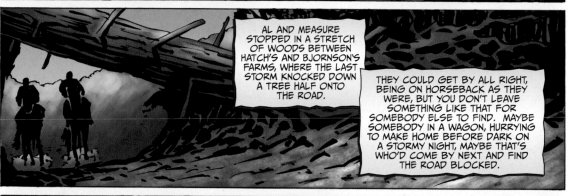

AL AND MEASURE STOPPED IN A STRETCH OF WOODS BETWEEN HATCH'S AND BJORNSON'S FARMS, WHERE THE LAST STORM KNOCKED DOWN A TREE HALF ONTO THE ROAD.

THEY COULD GET BY ALL RIGHT, BEING ON HORSEBACK AS THEY WERE, BUT YOU DON'T LEAVE SOMETHING LIKE THAT FOR SOMEBODY ELSE TO FIND. MAYBE SOMEBODY IN A WAGON, HURRYING TO MAKE HOME BEFORE DARK ON A STORMY NIGHT, MAYBE THAT'S WHO'D COME BY NEXT AND FIND THE ROAD BLOCKED.

SO THEY STOPPED AND ATE THE LUNCH MA PACKED FOR THEM, AND THEN SET TO WORK WITH THEIR HATCHETS, CUTTING IT FREE FROM THE FEW TAUT STRANDS OF WOOD THAT CLUNG TO THE RAGGED STUMP.

THEY WERE WISHING FOR A SAW LONG BEFORE THEY WERE DONE.

THEY TALKED SOMEWHAT DURING THE WORK, OF COURSE. SOME OF THE CONVERSATION TURNED ON THE STORIES ABOUT RED MASSACRES DOWN SOUTH.

OH, I HEAR THOSE STORIES, BUT THE BLOODY ONES ARE ALL THINGS SOMEBODY HEARD SOMEBODY HEARD FROM SOMEBODY ELSE.

THE FOLKS WHO ACTUALLY LIVE THERE AND GOT RUN OUT, ALL THEY EVER SAY IS TA-KUMSAW COME AND RUN OFF THEIR PIGS AND CHICKENS, THAT'S ALL.

NOT A ONE SAID NOTHING ABOUT NO ARROWS FLYING OR FOLKS GETTING KILLED.

AL, BEING TEN YEARS OLD, WAS MORE INCLINED TO BELIEVE THE STORIES, THE BLOODIER THE BETTER.

MAYBE WHEN THEY KILL SOMEBODY, THEY KILL THE WHOLE FAMILY SO NOBODY TALKS ABOUT IT...

SEEING HOW THEY WEREN'T MORE THAN A HALF MILE FROM TWO DIFFERENT FARMS, IN COUNTRY THEY VISITED FOUR OR FIVE TIMES A YEAR FOR TEN YEARS, IT NEVER CAME TO MEASURE OR AL'S MINDS THAT THEY OUGHT TO KEEP THEIR EYES OPEN FOR TROUBLE.

YOU JUST DON'T KEEP TOO WARY THAT CLOSE TO HOME, NOT EVEN WHEN YOU'RE TALKING ABOUT RED MASSACRES AND STORIES ABOUT MURDER AND TORTURE.

FACT IS, THOUGH, CAREFUL OR NOT THERE WASN'T MUCH THEY COULD'VE DONE.

AL WAS COILING ROPES AND MEASURE WAS CINCHING UP THE SADDLES WHEN ALL OF A SUDDEN ...

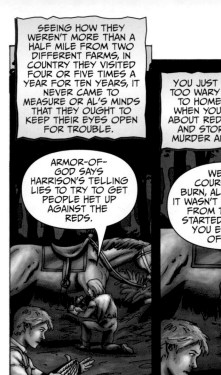

ARMOR-OF-GOD SAYS HARRISON'S TELLING LIES TO TRY TO GET PEOPLE HET UP AGAINST THE REDS.

WELL OF COURSE IT *DID* BURN, AL. BUT MAYBE IT WASN'T FIRE ARROWS FROM TA-KUMSAW STARTED THAT FIRE. YOU EVER THINK OF THAT?

WELL, HE COULDN'T VERY WELL LIE ABOUT THEM BURNING DOWN HIS HOUSE AND HIS STOCKADE. PEOPLE COULD PLAIN SEE IT GOT BURNT, COULDN'T THEY? AND HE COULDN'T VERY WELL LIE ABOUT IT KILLING HIS WIFE AND HIS LITTLE BOY, COULD HE?

GOVERNOR HARRISON ISN'T GOING TO BURN DOWN HIS OWN HOUSE AND KILL HIS OWN FAMILY JUST SO HE CAN GET PEOPLE HOT AGAINST THE REDS. THAT'S JUST PLAIN DUMB.

HOWDY!

THESE AIN'T NO HOWDY REDS. THEY GOT MUSKETS.

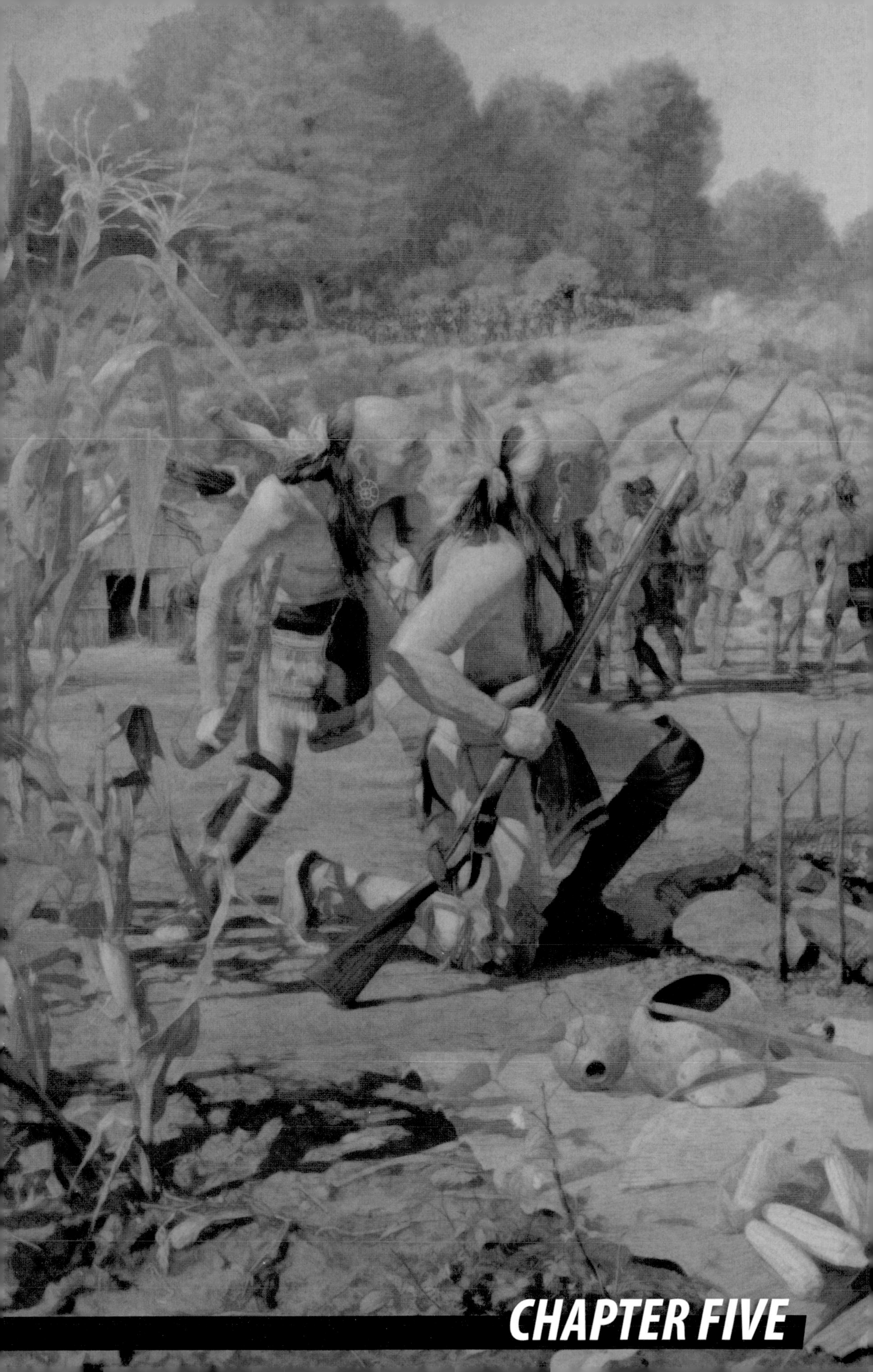

CHAPTER FIVE

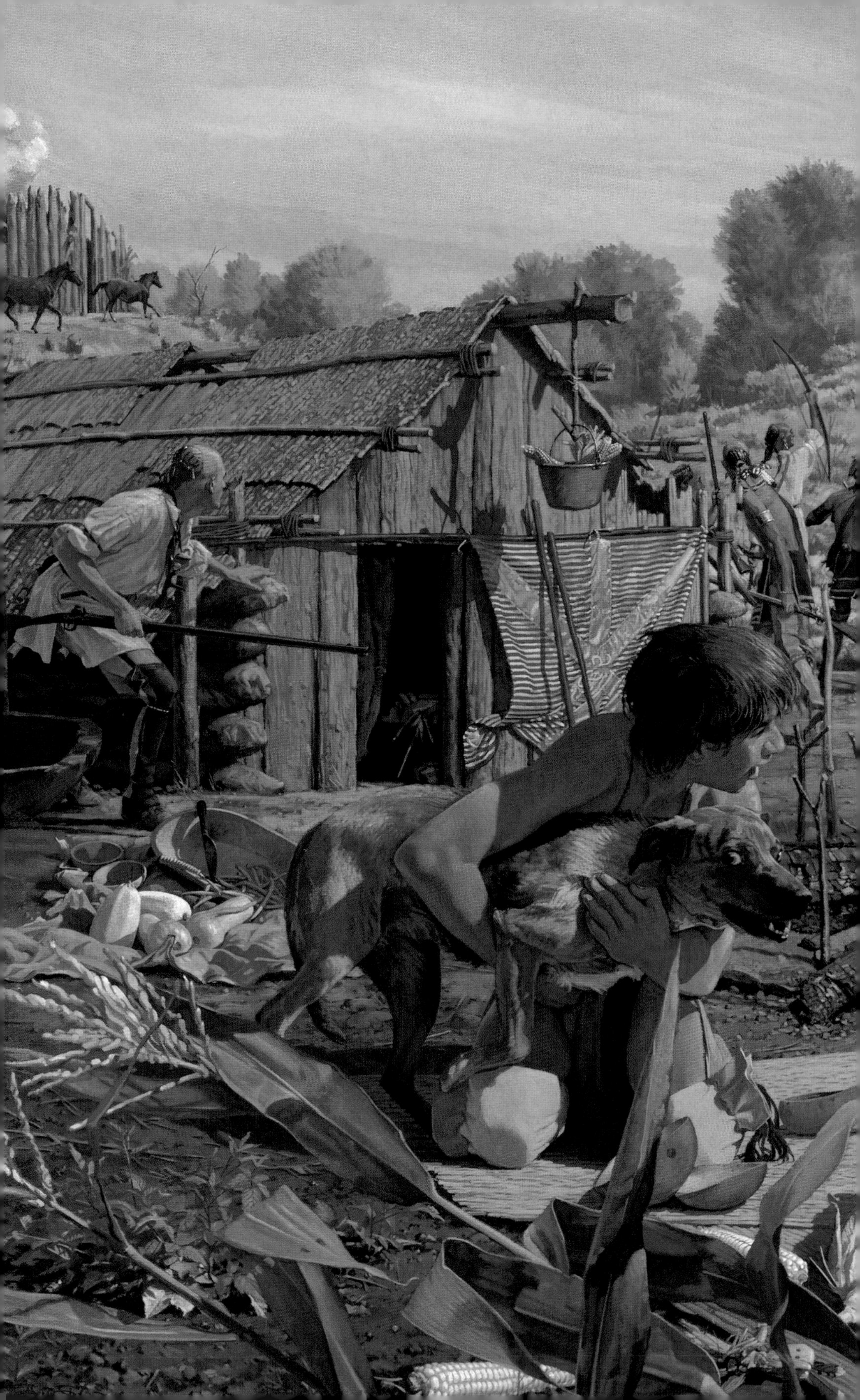

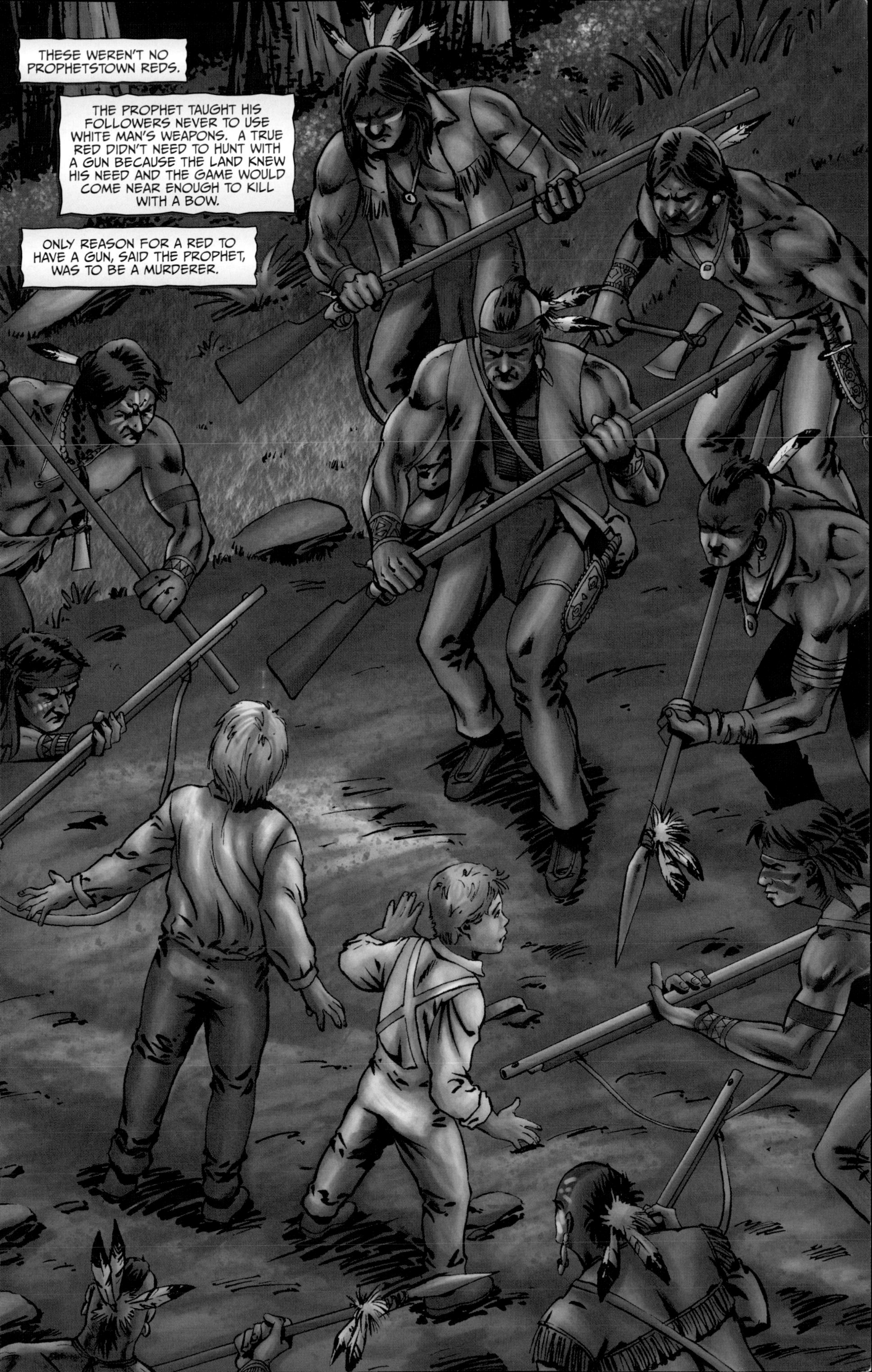
THESE WEREN'T NO PROPHETSTOWN REDS.
THE PROPHET TAUGHT HIS FOLLOWERS NEVER TO USE WHITE MAN'S WEAPONS. A TRUE RED DIDN'T NEED TO HUNT WITH A GUN BECAUSE THE LAND KNEW HIS NEED AND THE GAME WOULD COME NEAR ENOUGH TO KILL WITH A BOW.
ONLY REASON FOR A RED TO HAVE A GUN, SAID THE PROPHET, WAS TO BE A MURDERER.

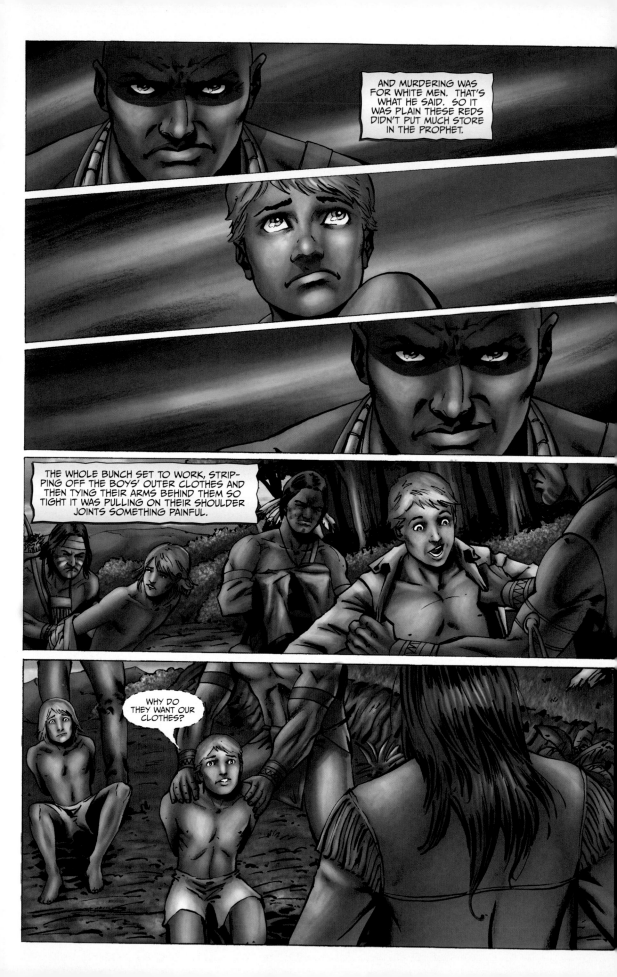

AND MURDERING WAS FOR WHITE MEN. THAT'S WHAT HE SAID. SO IT WAS PLAIN THESE REDS DIDN'T PUT MUCH STORE IN THE PROPHET.

THE WHOLE BUNCH SET TO WORK, STRIPPING OFF THE BOYS' OUTER CLOTHES AND THEN TYING THEIR ARMS BEHIND THEM SO TIGHT IT WAS PULLING ON THEIR SHOULDER JOINTS SOMETHING PAINFUL.

WHY DO THEY WANT OUR CLOTHES?

IN ANSWER, ONE OF THE REDS SLAPPED HIM HARD ACROSS THE FACE.

THWACK!

HE MUST'VE LIKED THE SOUND IT MADE, BECAUSE HE SLAPPED HIM AGAIN...

THE STING OF IT BROUGHT TEARS TO AL'S EYES, BUT HE DIDN'T CRY OUT, PARTLY 'CAUSE HE WAS SO SURPRISED, PARTLY CAUSE IT MADE HIM MAD AND HE DIDN'T WANT TO GIVE THEM 'THE SATISFACTION.

SLAPPING WAS AN IDEA THAT CAUGHT ON REAL GOOD WITH THE OTHER REDS, 'CAUSE THEY STARTED SLAPPING MEASURE, TOO, BOTH OF THE BOYS, AGAIN AND AGAIN, TILL THEY WERE HALF-DAZED AND THEIR CHEEKS WERE BLEEDING INSIDE AND OUT

ONE RED BABBLED SOMETHING, AND THEY GAVE HIM AL'S SHIRT. HE SLASHED IT WITH HIS KNIFE, AND THEN RUBBED IT ON AL'S BLEEDING FACE.

MUST NOT HAVE GOT ENOUGH BLOOD ON IT, BECAUSE HE TOOK HIS KNIFE AND SLASHED IT ACROSS AL'S FOREHEAD.

THE BLOOD JUST GUSHED OUT, AND A SECOND LATER THE PAIN HIT AL AND FOR THE FIRST TIME HE DID CRY OUT.

YAAAH!

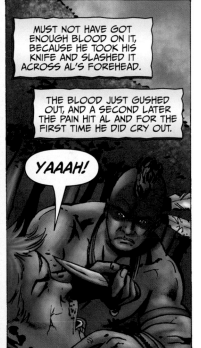

MEASURE YELLED FOR THEM TO LEAVE AL ALONE, BUT THERE WASN'T NO CHANCE OF THAT. EVERYBODY KNEW THAT ONCE A RED STARTED TO CUTTING YOU, YOU WERE BOUND TO END UP DEAD.

ONCE AL CRIED OUT AND THE BLOOD STARTED COMING, THEM REDS STARTED LAUGHING AND MAKING LITTLE HOOTING SOUNDS. THIS BUNCH WAS OUT FOR REAL TROUBLE, AND AL THOUGHT BACK TO ALL THE STORIES HE HAD HEARD...

MOST FAMOUS ONE WAS PROBABLY ABOUT DAN BOONE, A PENNSYLVANIA MAN WHO TRIED TO SETTLE IN THE CROWN COLONIES FOR A WHILE. THAT WAS BACK WHEN THE CHERRIKY WERE AGAINST THE WHITE MAN, AND ONE DAY DAN BOONE'S BOY GOT KIDNAPPED.

BOONE WASN'T A HALF HOUR BEHIND THE REDS. IT WAS LIKE THEY WERE PLAYING WITH HIM. THEY'D STOP AND CUT OFF PARTS OF THE BOY'S SKIN, OR POKE OUT AN EYE, SOMETHING TO CAUSE PAIN AND MAKE HIM SCREAM. BOONE HEARD HIS BOY SCREAMING, AND FOLLOWED, HIM AND HIS NEIGHBORS, ARMED WITH MUSKETS AND HALF-MAD WITH RAGE.

THEY'D REACH THE PLACE WHERE THE BOY'D BEEN TORTURED, AND THE REDS WERE GONE, NOT A TRACE OF A TRACK IN THE WOOD, AND THEN THERE'D COME ANOTHER SCREAM.

TWENTY MILES THEY WENT THAT DAY, AND FINALLY AT NIGHTFALL THEY FOUND THE BOY HANGING FROM THREE DIFFERENT TREES.

THEY SAY BOONE NEVER FORGOT THAT, HE COULD NEVER LOOK A RED IN THE EYE AFTER THAT WITHOUT THINKING OF THAT TWENTY-MILE DAY.

AL HAD THAT TWENTY-MILE DAY ON HIS MIND NOW, TOO, HEARING THEM REDS LAUGH, FEELING THE PAIN, JUST THE START OF THE PAIN, KNOWING THAT WHATEVER THESE REDS WERE AFTER, THEY WANTED IT TO START WITH TWO DEAD WHITE BOYS, AND THEY WOULDN'T MIND A LITTLE NOISE ALONG THE WAY.

KEEP STILL, HE TOLD HIMSELF. KEEP STILL.

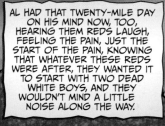

THEY RUBBED HIS SLASHED-UP SHIRT ON HIS FACE, AND MEASURE'S HACKED-UP CLOTHES, TOO. WHILE THEY WERE DOING THAT, AL KEPT HIS MIND ON OTHER THINGS.

ONLY TIME HE EVER TRIED TO HEAL HIMSELF WAS THAT BUSTED LEG OF HIS, AND THEN HE WAS LYING DOWN, RESTING, PLENTY OF TIME TO STUDY IT OUT, TO FIND ALL THOSE SMALL PLACES WHERE THERE WAS BROKEN VEINS AND HEAL THEM UP, KNIT TOGETHER THE SKIN AND BONE.

THIS TIME HE WAS A-SCARED AND GETTING PUSHED THIS WAY AND THAT, NOT CALM, NOT RESTING. BUT HE STILL MANAGED TO FIND THE BIGGEST VEINS AND ARTERIES.

MAKE THEM CLOSE UP.

THEY HADN'T CUT MEASURE YET. HE WAS LOOKING AT AL, AND THERE WAS A SICK LOOK ON MEASURE'S FACE. AL KNEW HIS BROTHER WELL ENOUGH TO GUESS WHAT HE WAS THINKING.

ABOUT HOW MA AND PA TRUSTED AL INTO MEASURE'S KEEPING, AND NOW LOOK HOW HE LET THEM DOWN.

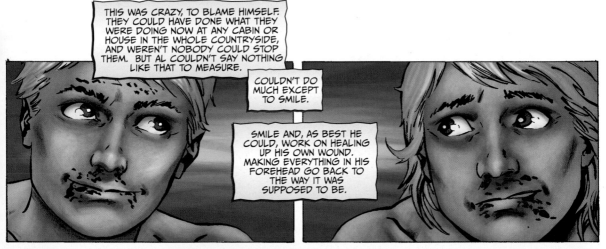

THIS WAS CRAZY, TO BLAME HIMSELF. THEY COULD HAVE DONE WHAT THEY WERE DOING NOW AT ANY CABIN OR HOUSE IN THE WHOLE COUNTRYSIDE, AND WEREN'T NOBODY COULD STOP THEM. BUT AL COULDN'T SAY NOTHING LIKE THAT TO MEASURE.

COULDN'T DO MUCH EXCEPT TO SMILE.

SMILE AND, AS BEST HE COULD, WORK ON HEALING UP HIS OWN WOUND. MAKING EVERYTHING IN HIS FOREHEAD GO BACK TO THE WAY IT WAS SUPPOSED TO BE.

HE KEPT AT IT, FINDING IT EASIER AND EASIER TO DO, WHILE HE WATCHED WHAT THE REDS WERE DOING.

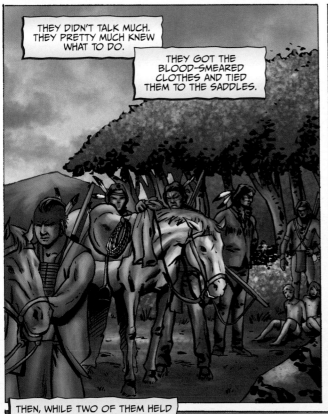

THEY DIDN'T TALK MUCH. THEY PRETTY MUCH KNEW WHAT TO DO.

THEY GOT THE BLOOD-SMEARED CLOTHES AND TIED THEM TO THE SADDLES.

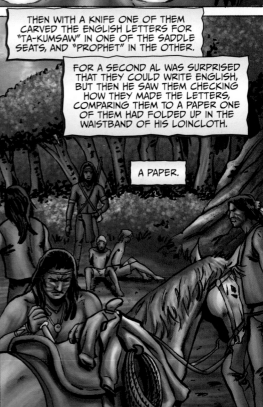

THEN WITH A KNIFE ONE OF THEM CARVED THE ENGLISH LETTERS FOR "TA-KUMSAW" IN ONE OF THE SADDLE SEATS, AND "PROPHET" IN THE OTHER.

FOR A SECOND AL WAS SURPRISED THAT THEY COULD WRITE ENGLISH, BUT THEN HE SAW THEM CHECKING HOW THEY MADE THE LETTERS, COMPARING THEM TO A PAPER ONE OF THEM HAD FOLDED UP IN THE WAISTBAND OF HIS LOINCLOTH.

A PAPER.

THEN, WHILE TWO OF THEM HELD EACH HORSE BY THE BRIDLE, ANOTHER RED JABBED THE HORSES' FLANKS WITH A KNIFE, LITTLE CUTS, NOT ALL THAT DEEP, BUT ENOUGH TO MAKE THEM CRAZY WITH PAIN, KICKING OUT, BUCKING, REARING UP.

THE HORSES KNOCKED DOWN THE REDS HOLDING THEM AND TOOK OFF, RAN AWAY, HEADING—AS THE REDS KNEW THEY WOULD—ON UP THE ROAD TOWARD HOME.

TA-KUMSAW

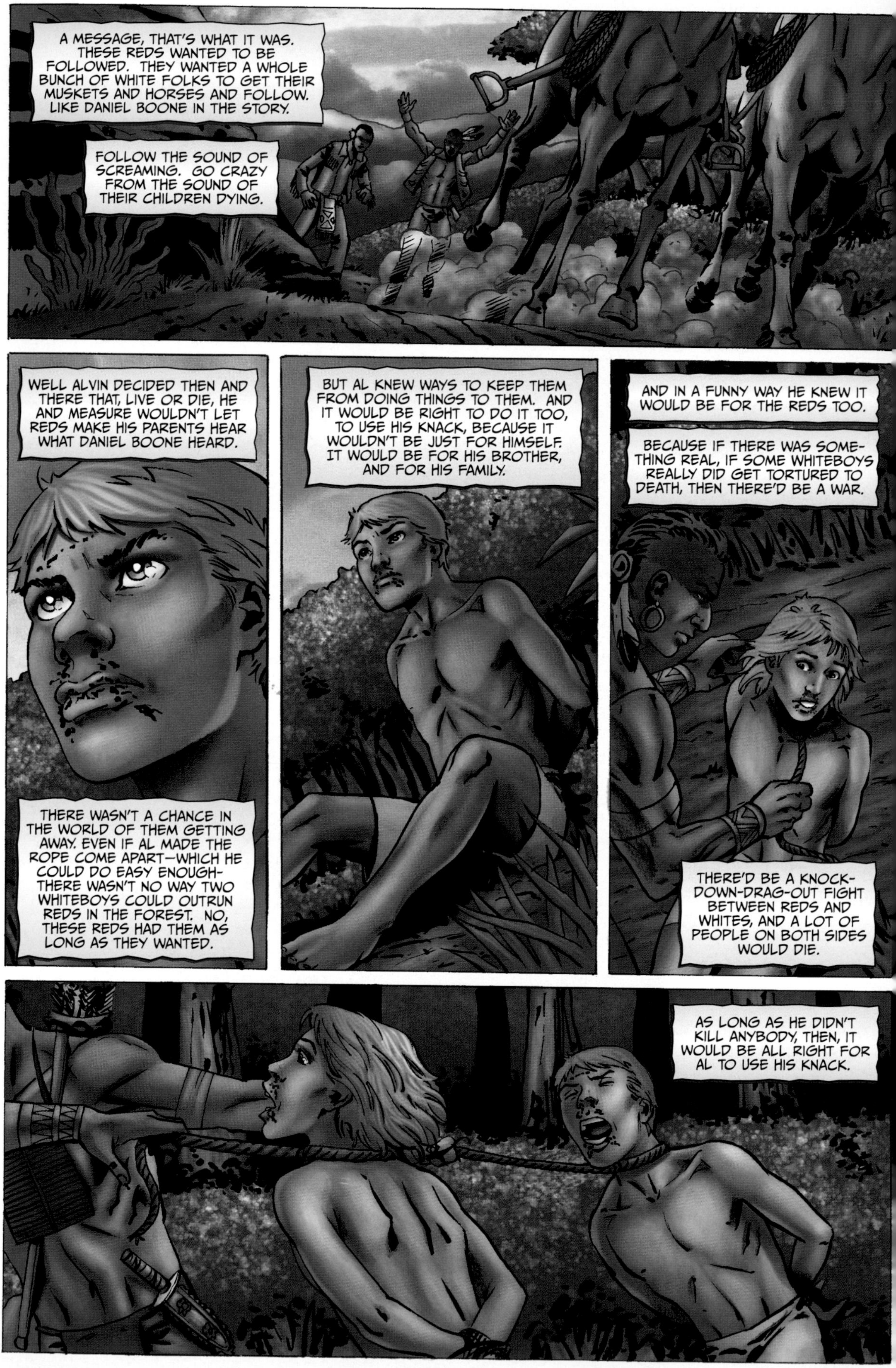
A MESSAGE, THAT'S WHAT IT WAS. THESE REDS WANTED TO BE FOLLOWED. THEY WANTED A WHOLE BUNCH OF WHITE FOLKS TO GET THEIR MUSKETS AND HORSES AND FOLLOW. LIKE DANIEL BOONE IN THE STORY.
FOLLOW THE SOUND OF SCREAMING. GO CRAZY FROM THE SOUND OF THEIR CHILDREN DYING.
WELL ALVIN DECIDED THEN AND THERE THAT, LIVE OR DIE, HE AND MEASURE WOULDN'T LET REDS MAKE HIS PARENTS HEAR WHAT DANIEL BOONE HEARD.
THERE WASN'T A CHANCE IN THE WORLD OF THEM GETTING AWAY. EVEN IF AL MADE THE ROPE COME APART—WHICH HE COULD DO EASY ENOUGH—THERE WASN'T NO WAY TWO WHITEBOYS COULD OUTRUN REDS IN THE FOREST. NO, THESE REDS HAD THEM AS LONG AS THEY WANTED.
BUT AL KNEW WAYS TO KEEP THEM FROM DOING THINGS TO THEM. AND IT WOULD BE RIGHT TO DO IT TOO, TO USE HIS KNACK, BECAUSE IT WOULDN'T BE JUST FOR HIMSELF. IT WOULD BE FOR HIS BROTHER, AND FOR HIS FAMILY.
AND IN A FUNNY WAY HE KNEW IT WOULD BE FOR THE REDS TOO.
BECAUSE IF THERE WAS SOMETHING REAL, IF SOME WHITEBOYS REALLY DID GET TORTURED TO DEATH, THEN THERE'D BE A WAR.
THERE'D BE A KNOCK-DOWN-DRAG-OUT FIGHT BETWEEN REDS AND WHITES, AND A LOT OF PEOPLE ON BOTH SIDES WOULD DIE.
AS LONG AS HE DIDN'T KILL ANYBODY, THEN, IT WOULD BE ALL RIGHT FOR AL TO USE HIS KNACK.

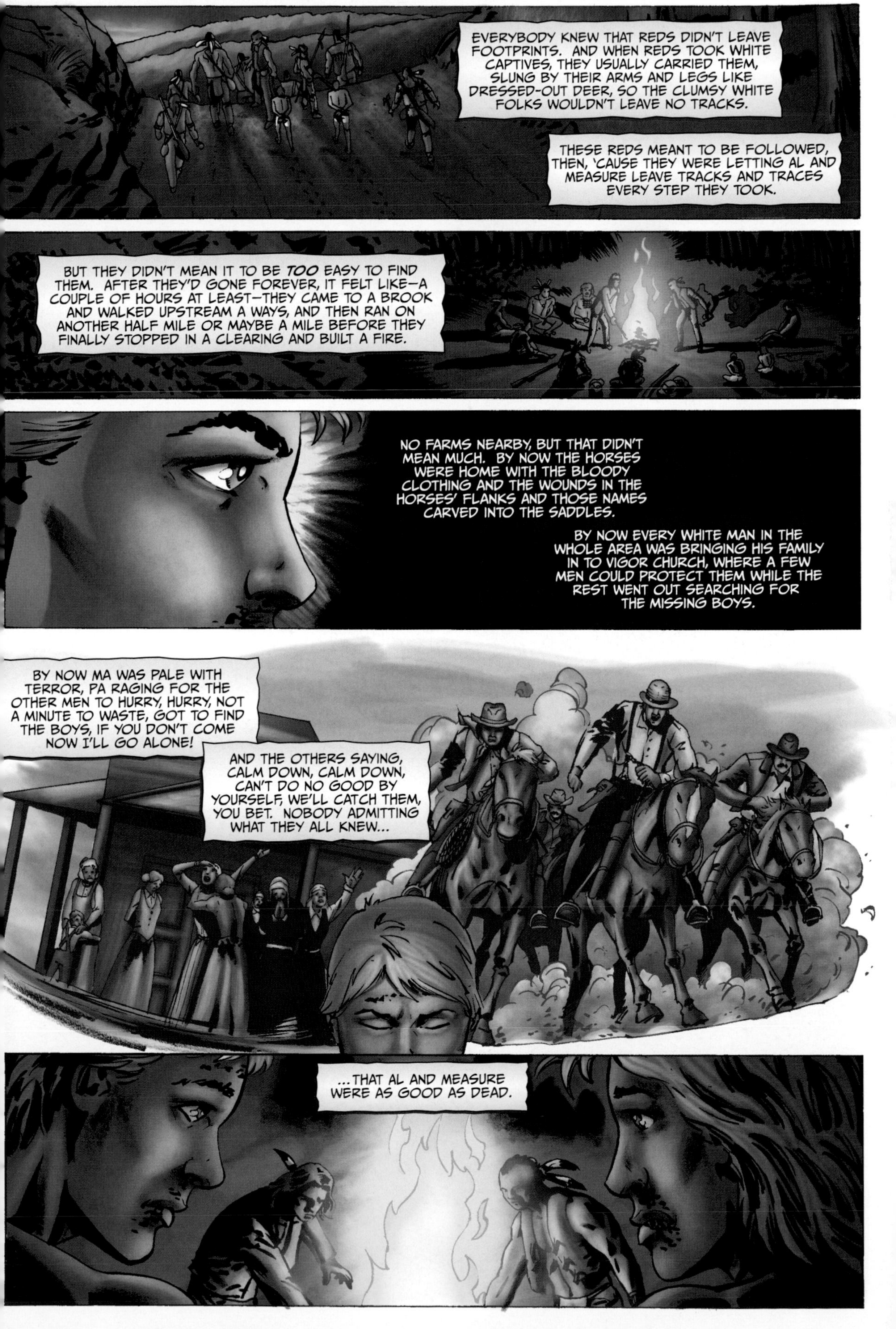
EVERYBODY KNEW THAT REDS DIDN'T LEAVE FOOTPRINTS. AND WHEN REDS TOOK WHITE CAPTIVES, THEY USUALLY CARRIED THEM, SLUNG BY THEIR ARMS AND LEGS LIKE DRESSED-OUT DEER, SO THE CLUMSY WHITE FOLKS WOULDN'T LEAVE NO TRACKS.
THESE REDS MEANT TO BE FOLLOWED, THEN, 'CAUSE THEY WERE LETTING AL AND MEASURE LEAVE TRACKS AND TRACES EVERY STEP THEY TOOK.
BUT THEY DIDN'T MEAN IT TO BE *TOO* EASY TO FIND THEM. AFTER THEY'D GONE FOREVER, IT FELT LIKE—A COUPLE OF HOURS AT LEAST—THEY CAME TO A BROOK AND WALKED UPSTREAM A WAYS, AND THEN RAN ON ANOTHER HALF MILE OR MAYBE A MILE BEFORE THEY FINALLY STOPPED IN A CLEARING AND BUILT A FIRE.
NO FARMS NEARBY, BUT THAT DIDN'T MEAN MUCH. BY NOW THE HORSES WERE HOME WITH THE BLOODY CLOTHING AND THE WOUNDS IN THE HORSES' FLANKS AND THOSE NAMES CARVED INTO THE SADDLES.
BY NOW EVERY WHITE MAN IN THE WHOLE AREA WAS BRINGING HIS FAMILY IN TO VIGOR CHURCH, WHERE A FEW MEN COULD PROTECT THEM WHILE THE REST WENT OUT SEARCHING FOR THE MISSING BOYS.
BY NOW MA WAS PALE WITH TERROR, PA RAGING FOR THE OTHER MEN TO HURRY, HURRY, NOT A MINUTE TO WASTE, GOT TO FIND THE BOYS, IF YOU DON'T COME NOW I'LL GO ALONE!
AND THE OTHERS SAYING, CALM DOWN, CALM DOWN, CAN'T DO NO GOOD BY YOURSELF, WE'LL CATCH THEM, YOU BET. NOBODY ADMITTING WHAT THEY ALL KNEW...
...THAT AL AND MEASURE WERE AS GOOD AS DEAD.

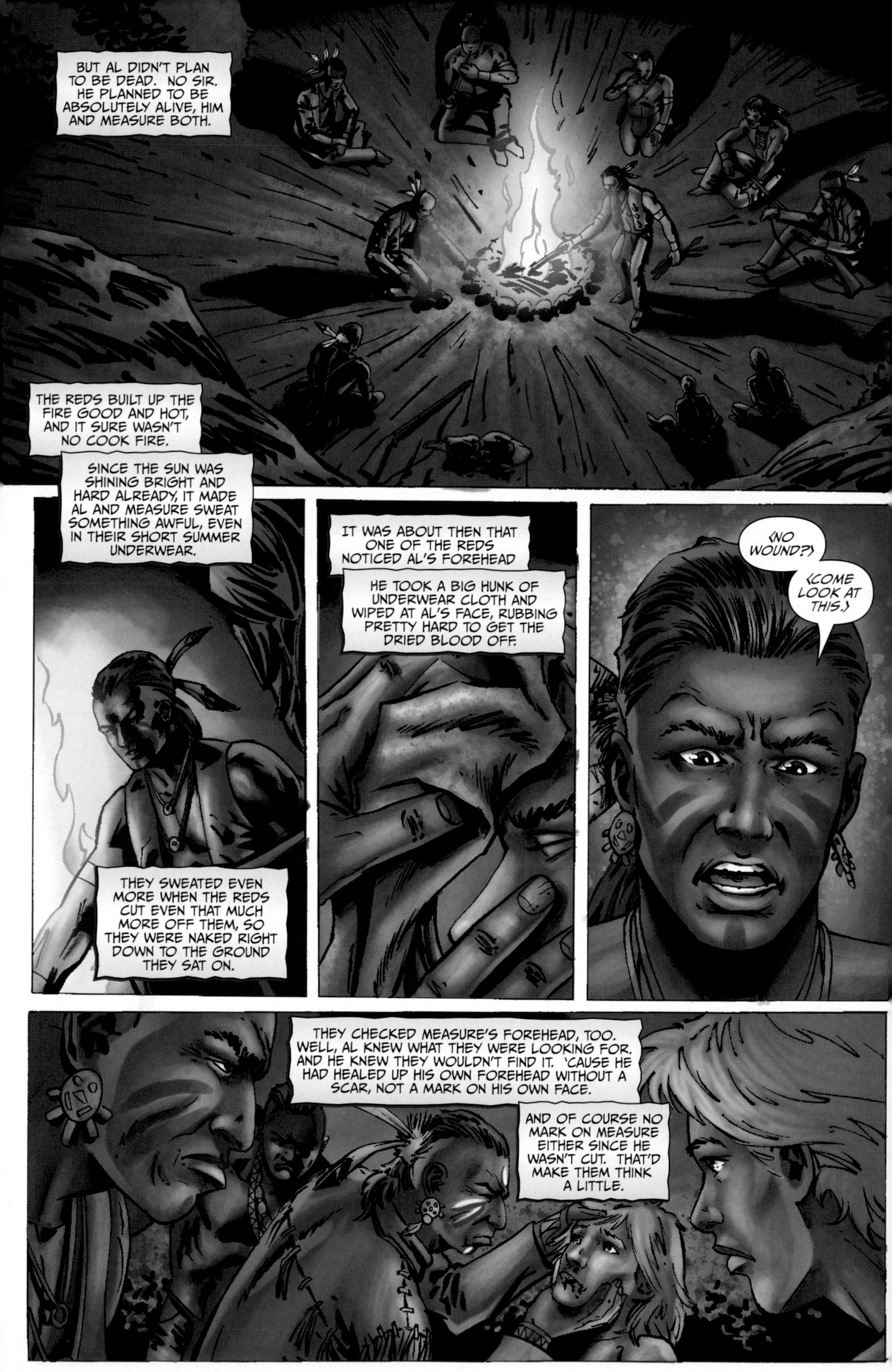

BUT AL DIDN'T PLAN TO BE DEAD. NO SIR. HE PLANNED TO BE ABSOLUTELY ALIVE, HIM AND MEASURE BOTH.
THE REDS BUILT UP THE FIRE GOOD AND HOT, AND IT SURE WASN'T NO COOK FIRE.
SINCE THE SUN WAS SHINING BRIGHT AND HARD ALREADY, IT MADE AL AND MEASURE SWEAT SOMETHING AWFUL, EVEN IN THEIR SHORT SUMMER UNDERWEAR.
THEY SWEATED EVEN MORE WHEN THE REDS CUT EVEN THAT MUCH MORE OFF THEM, SO THEY WERE NAKED RIGHT DOWN TO THE GROUND THEY SAT ON.
IT WAS ABOUT THEN THAT ONE OF THE REDS NOTICED AL'S FOREHEAD
HE TOOK A BIG HUNK OF UNDERWEAR CLOTH AND WIPED AT AL'S FACE, RUBBING PRETTY HARD TO GET THE DRIED BLOOD OFF.
‹NO WOUND?›
‹COME LOOK AT THIS.›
THEY CHECKED MEASURE'S FOREHEAD, TOO. WELL, AL KNEW WHAT THEY WERE LOOKING FOR. AND HE KNEW THEY WOULDN'T FIND IT. 'CAUSE HE HAD HEALED UP HIS OWN FOREHEAD WITHOUT A SCAR, NOT A MARK ON HIS OWN FACE.
AND OF COURSE NO MARK ON MEASURE EITHER SINCE HE WASN'T CUT. THAT'D MAKE THEM THINK A LITTLE.

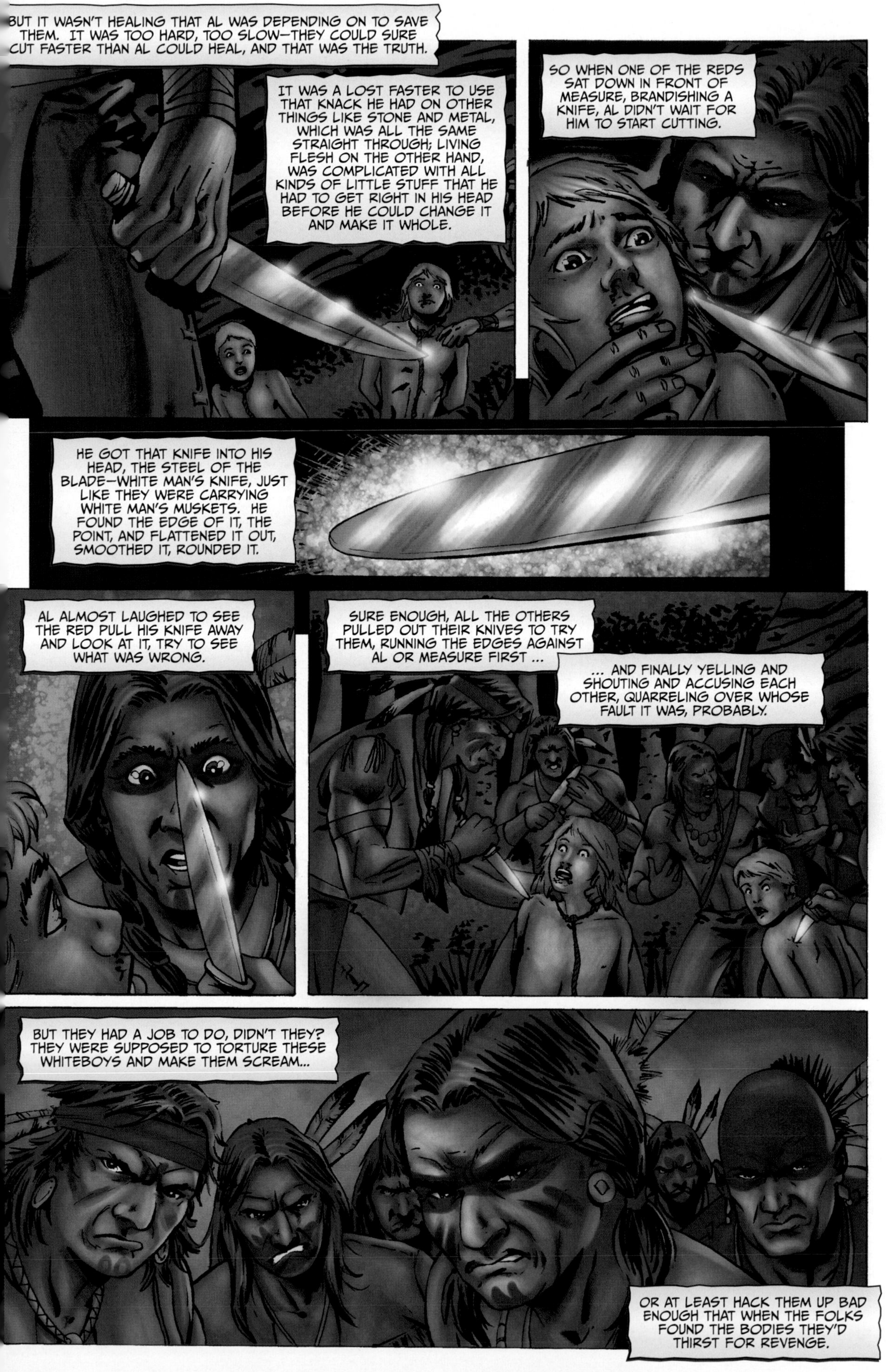
BUT IT WASN'T HEALING THAT AL WAS DEPENDING ON TO SAVE THEM. IT WAS TOO HARD, TOO SLOW—THEY COULD SURE CUT FASTER THAN AL COULD HEAL, AND THAT WAS THE TRUTH.
IT WAS A LOST FASTER TO USE THAT KNACK HE HAD ON OTHER THINGS LIKE STONE AND METAL, WHICH WAS ALL THE SAME STRAIGHT THROUGH; LIVING FLESH ON THE OTHER HAND, WAS COMPLICATED WITH ALL KINDS OF LITTLE STUFF THAT HE HAD TO GET RIGHT IN HIS HEAD BEFORE HE COULD CHANGE IT AND MAKE IT WHOLE.
SO WHEN ONE OF THE REDS SAT DOWN IN FRONT OF MEASURE, BRANDISHING A KNIFE, AL DIDN'T WAIT FOR HIM TO START CUTTING.
HE GOT THAT KNIFE INTO HIS HEAD, THE STEEL OF THE BLADE—WHITE MAN'S KNIFE, JUST LIKE THEY WERE CARRYING WHITE MAN'S MUSKETS. HE FOUND THE EDGE OF IT, THE POINT, AND FLATTENED IT OUT, SMOOTHED IT, ROUNDED IT.
AL ALMOST LAUGHED TO SEE THE RED PULL HIS KNIFE AWAY AND LOOK AT IT, TRY TO SEE WHAT WAS WRONG.
SURE ENOUGH, ALL THE OTHERS PULLED OUT THEIR KNIVES TO TRY THEM, RUNNING THE EDGES AGAINST AL OR MEASURE FIRST ...
... AND FINALLY YELLING AND SHOUTING AND ACCUSING EACH OTHER, QUARRELING OVER WHOSE FAULT IT WAS, PROBABLY.
BUT THEY HAD A JOB TO DO, DIDN'T THEY? THEY WERE SUPPOSED TO TORTURE THESE WHITEBOYS AND MAKE THEM SCREAM...
OR AT LEAST HACK THEM UP BAD ENOUGH THAT WHEN THE FOLKS FOUND THE BODIES THEY'D THIRST FOR REVENGE.

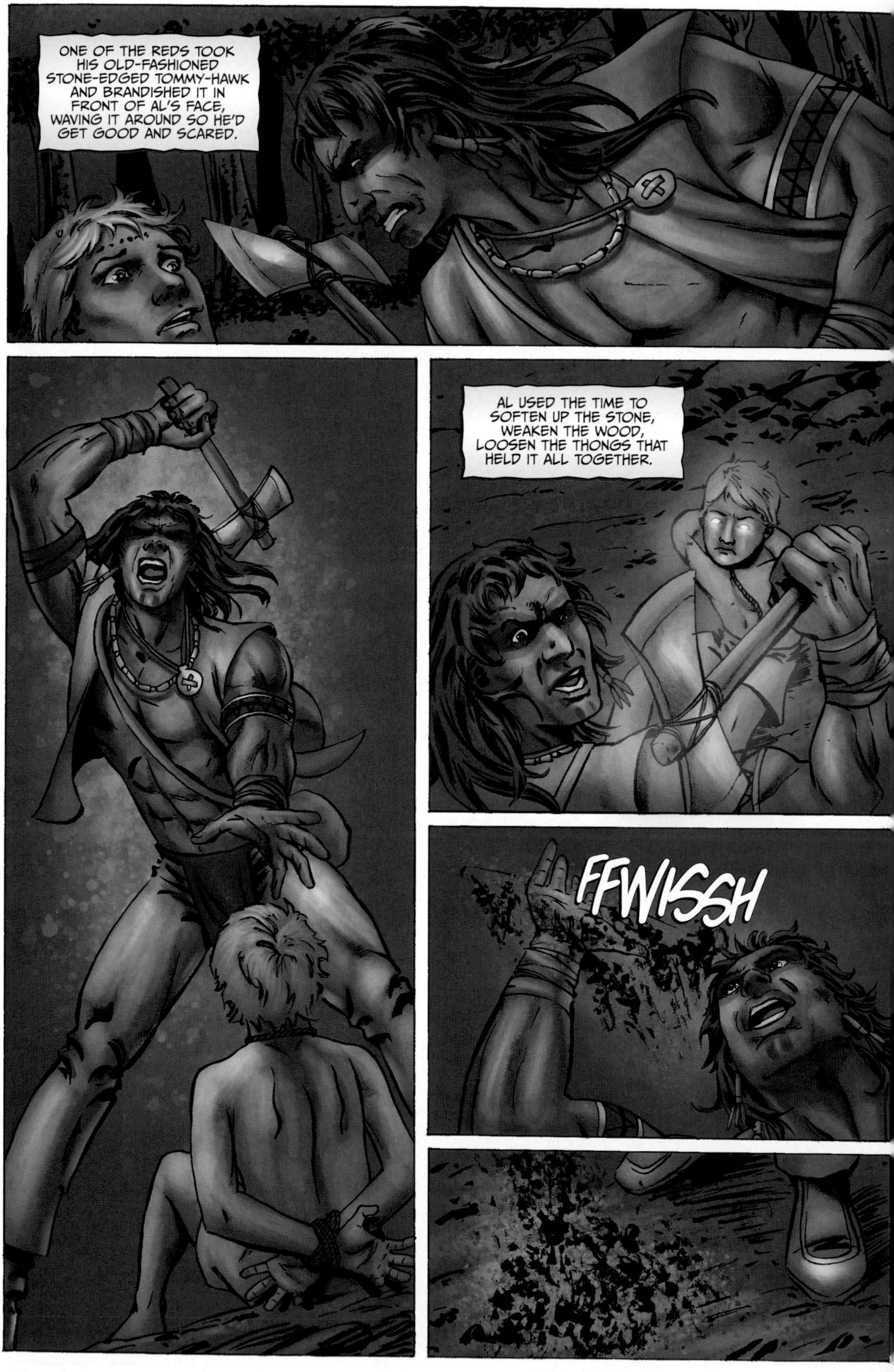
ONE OF THE REDS TOOK HIS OLD-FASHIONED STONE-EDGED TOMMY-HAWK AND BRANDISHED IT IN FRONT OF AL'S FACE, WAVING IT AROUND SO HE'D GET GOOD AND SCARED.
AL USED THE TIME TO SOFTEN UP THE STONE, WEAKEN THE WOOD, LOOSEN THE THONGS THAT HELD IT ALL TOGETHER.
FFWISSH

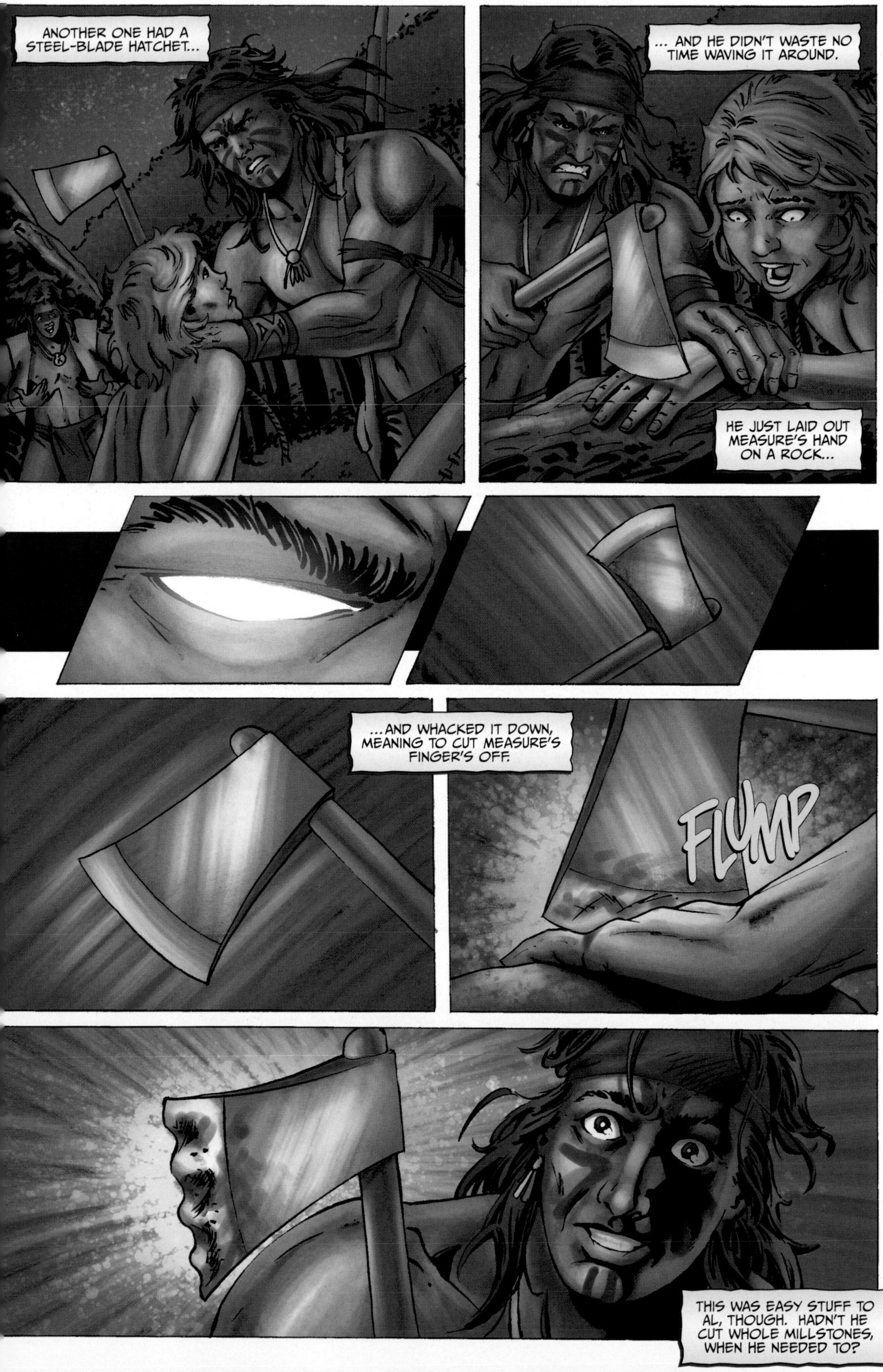
ANOTHER ONE HAD A STEEL-BLADE HATCHET...
... AND HE DIDN'T WASTE NO TIME WAVING IT AROUND.
HE JUST LAID OUT MEASURE'S HAND ON A ROCK...
...AND WHACKED IT DOWN, MEANING TO CUT MEASURE'S FINGER'S OFF.
FLUMP
THIS WAS EASY STUFF TO AL, THOUGH. HADN'T HE CUT WHOLE MILLSTONES, WHEN HE NEEDED TO?

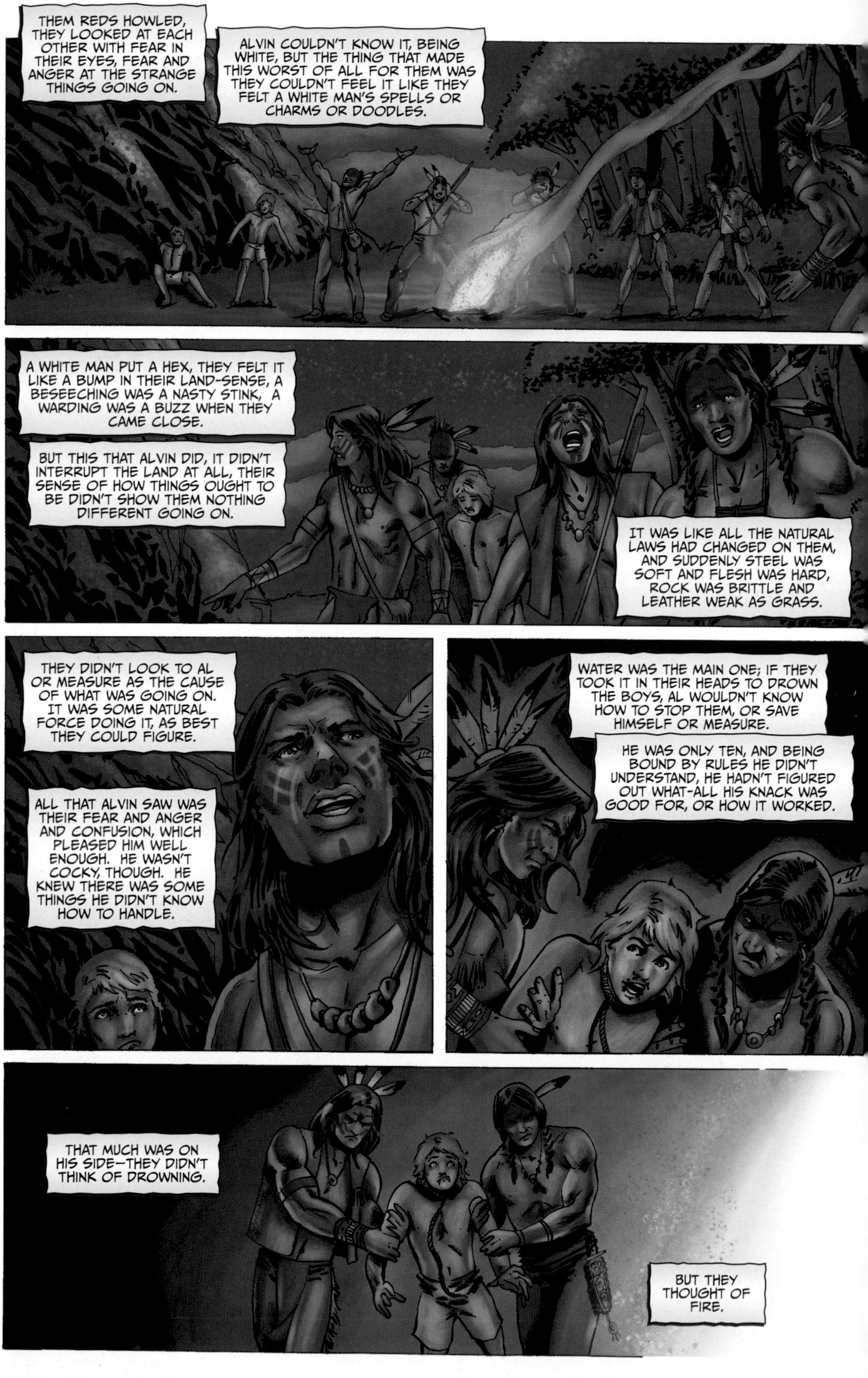
THEM REDS HOWLED, THEY LOOKED AT EACH OTHER WITH FEAR IN THEIR EYES, FEAR AND ANGER AT THE STRANGE THINGS GOING ON.
ALVIN COULDN'T KNOW IT, BEING WHITE, BUT THE THING THAT MADE THIS WORST OF ALL FOR THEM WAS THEY COULDN'T FEEL IT LIKE THEY FELT A WHITE MAN'S SPELLS OR CHARMS OR DOODLES.
A WHITE MAN PUT A HEX, THEY FELT IT LIKE A BUMP IN THEIR LAND-SENSE, A BESEECHING WAS A NASTY STINK, A WARDING WAS A BUZZ WHEN THEY CAME CLOSE.
BUT THIS THAT ALVIN DID, IT DIDN'T INTERRUPT THE LAND AT ALL, THEIR SENSE OF HOW THINGS OUGHT TO BE DIDN'T SHOW THEM NOTHING DIFFERENT GOING ON.
IT WAS LIKE ALL THE NATURAL LAWS HAD CHANGED ON THEM, AND SUDDENLY STEEL WAS SOFT AND FLESH WAS HARD, ROCK WAS BRITTLE AND LEATHER WEAK AS GRASS.
THEY DIDN'T LOOK TO AL OR MEASURE AS THE CAUSE OF WHAT WAS GOING ON. IT WAS SOME NATURAL FORCE DOING IT, AS BEST THEY COULD FIGURE.
ALL THAT ALVIN SAW WAS THEIR FEAR AND ANGER AND CONFUSION, WHICH PLEASED HIM WELL ENOUGH. HE WASN'T COCKY, THOUGH. HE KNEW THERE WAS SOME THINGS HE DIDN'T KNOW HOW TO HANDLE.
WATER WAS THE MAIN ONE; IF THEY TOOK IT IN THEIR HEADS TO DROWN THE BOYS, AL WOULDN'T KNOW HOW TO STOP THEM, OR SAVE HIMSELF OR MEASURE.
HE WAS ONLY TEN, AND BEING BOUND BY RULES HE DIDN'T UNDERSTAND, HE HADN'T FIGURED OUT WHAT-ALL HIS KNACK WAS GOOD FOR, OR HOW IT WORKED.
THAT MUCH WAS ON HIS SIDE—THEY DIDN'T THINK OF DROWNING.
BUT THEY THOUGHT OF FIRE.

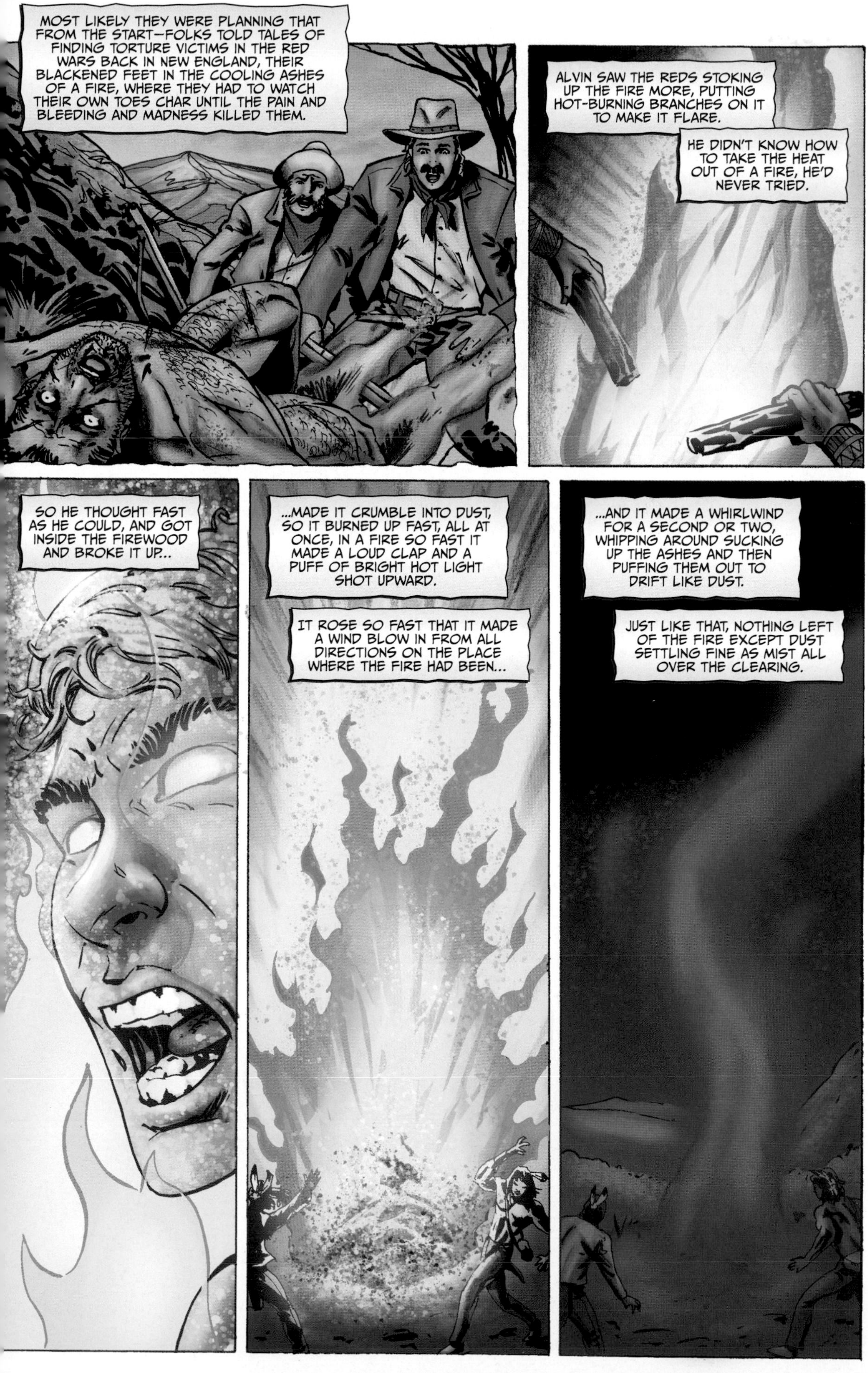
MOST LIKELY THEY WERE PLANNING THAT FROM THE START—FOLKS TOLD TALES OF FINDING TORTURE VICTIMS IN THE RED WARS BACK IN NEW ENGLAND, THEIR BLACKENED FEET IN THE COOLING ASHES OF A FIRE, WHERE THEY HAD TO WATCH THEIR OWN TOES CHAR UNTIL THE PAIN AND BLEEDING AND MADNESS KILLED THEM.
ALVIN SAW THE REDS STOKING UP THE FIRE MORE, PUTTING HOT-BURNING BRANCHES ON IT TO MAKE IT FLARE.
HE DIDN'T KNOW HOW TO TAKE THE HEAT OUT OF A FIRE, HE'D NEVER TRIED.
SO HE THOUGHT FAST AS HE COULD, AND GOT INSIDE THE FIREWOOD AND BROKE IT UP...
...MADE IT CRUMBLE INTO DUST, SO IT BURNED UP FAST, ALL AT ONCE, IN A FIRE SO FAST IT MADE A LOUD CLAP AND A PUFF OF BRIGHT HOT LIGHT SHOT UPWARD.
IT ROSE SO FAST THAT IT MADE A WIND BLOW IN FROM ALL DIRECTIONS ON THE PLACE WHERE THE FIRE HAD BEEN...
...AND IT MADE A WHIRLWIND FOR A SECOND OR TWO, WHIPPING AROUND SUCKING UP THE ASHES AND THEN PUFFING THEM OUT TO DRIFT LIKE DUST.
JUST LIKE THAT, NOTHING LEFT OF THE FIRE EXCEPT DUST SETTLING FINE AS MIST ALL OVER THE CLEARING.

OH, THEY HOWLED, THEY JUMPED AND DANCED AND BEAT ON THEIR OWN SHOULDERS AND CHESTS.

AND WHILE THEY WERE CARRYING ON LIKE AN IRISH FUNERAL, AL LOOSENED THE ROPES ON HIM AND MEASURE, HOPING AGAINST HOPE THAT THEY MIGHT GET AWAY AFTER ALL BEFORE THEIR FOLKS AND NEIGHBORS FOUND THEM AND STARTED IN WITH THE SHOOTING AND KILLING AND DYING.

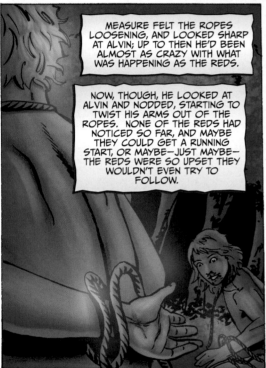

MEASURE FELT THE ROPES LOOSENING, AND LOOKED SHARP AT ALVIN; UP TO THEN HE'D BEEN ALMOST AS CRAZY WITH WHAT WAS HAPPENING AS THE REDS.

NOW, THOUGH, HE LOOKED AT ALVIN AND NODDED, STARTING TO TWIST HIS ARMS OUT OF THE ROPES. NONE OF THE REDS HAD NOTICED SO FAR, AND MAYBE THEY COULD GET A RUNNING START, OR MAYBE—JUST MAYBE—THE REDS WERE SO UPSET THEY WOULDN'T EVEN TRY TO FOLLOW.

RIGHT THEN, THOUGH, EVERYTHING CHANGED. THERE WAS A HOOTING SOUND FROM THE FOREST, AND THEN IT GOT PICKED UP BY WHAT SOUNDED LIKE THREE HUNDRED OWLS, ALL IN A CIRCLE.

MEASURE MUST HAVE THOUGHT FOR A SECOND THAT AL WAS CAUSING THAT TO HAPPEN, TOO, THE WAY HE LOOKED AT HIS LITTLE BROTHER—BUT THE REDS KNEW WHAT IT WAS, AND STOPPED THEIR CARRYING ON RIGHT AWAY.

FROM THE FEAR ON THEIR FACES, AL FIGURED IT MUST BE SOMETHING GOOD...

...MAYBE EVEN SOME-THING LIKE RESCUE.

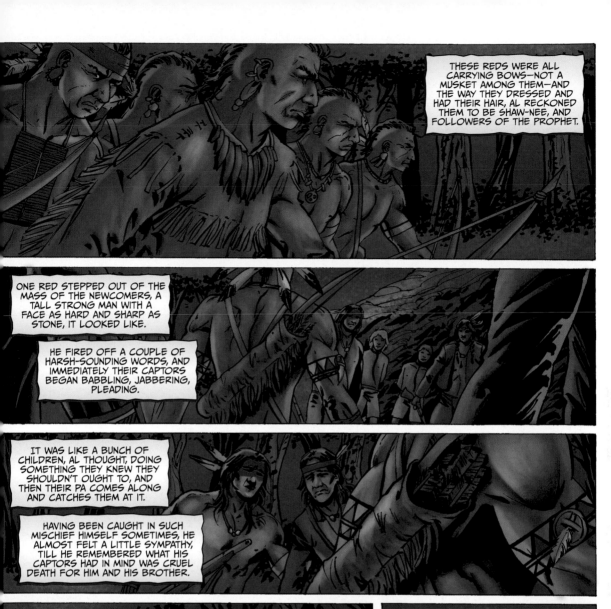

THESE REDS WERE ALL CARRYING BOWS—NOT A MUSKET AMONG THEM—AND THE WAY THEY DRESSED AND HAD THEIR HAIR, AL RECKONED THEM TO BE SHAW-NEE, AND FOLLOWERS OF THE PROPHET.

ONE RED STEPPED OUT OF THE MASS OF THE NEWCOMERS, A TALL STRONG MAN WITH A FACE AS HARD AND SHARP AS STONE, IT LOOKED LIKE.

HE FIRED OFF A COUPLE OF HARSH-SOUNDING WORDS, AND IMMEDIATELY THEIR CAPTORS BEGAN BABBLING, JABBERING, PLEADING.

IT WAS LIKE A BUNCH OF CHILDREN, AL THOUGHT, DOING SOMETHING THEY KNEW THEY SHOULDN'T OUGHT TO, AND THEN THEIR PA COMES ALONG AND CATCHES THEM AT IT.

HAVING BEEN CAUGHT IN SUCH MISCHIEF HIMSELF SOMETIMES, HE ALMOST FELT A LITTLE SYMPATHY, TILL HE REMEMBERED WHAT HIS CAPTORS HAD IN MIND WAS CRUEL DEATH FOR HIM AND HIS BROTHER.

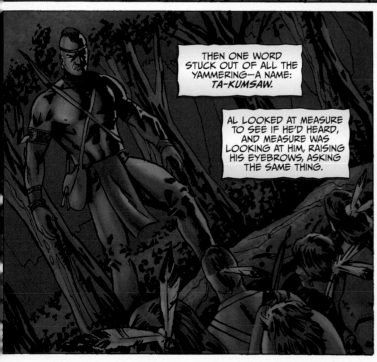

THEN ONE WORD STUCK OUT OF ALL THE YAMMERING—A NAME: *TA-KUMSAW.*

AL LOOKED AT MEASURE TO SEE IF HE'D HEARD, AND MEASURE WAS LOOKING AT HIM, RAISING HIS EYEBROWS, ASKING THE SAME THING.

THEY BOTH MOUTHED THE NAME AT THE SAME TIME... *TA-KUMSAW.*

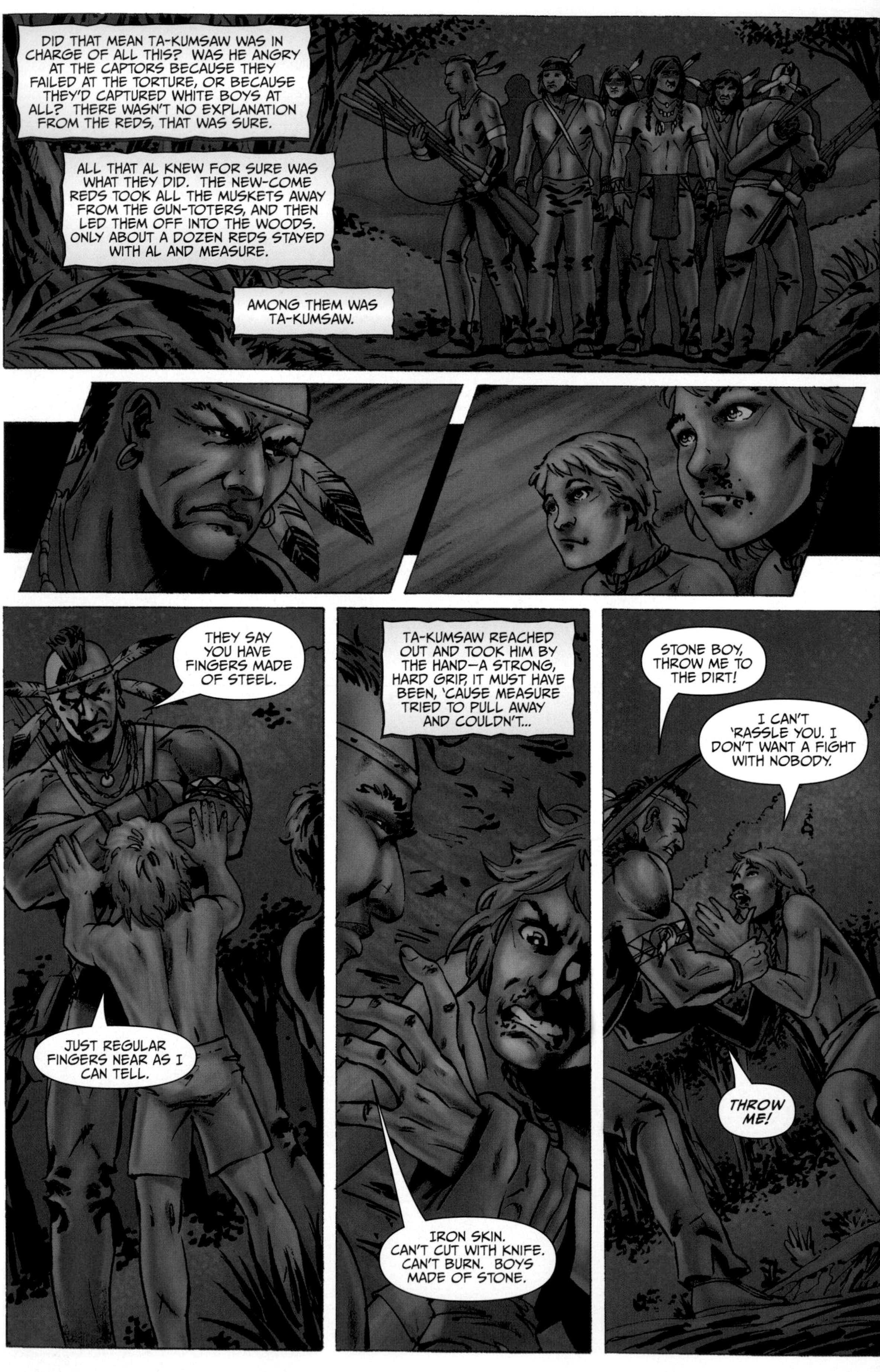
DID THAT MEAN TA-KUMSAW WAS IN CHARGE OF ALL THIS? WAS HE ANGRY AT THE CAPTORS BECAUSE THEY FAILED AT THE TORTURE, OR BECAUSE THEY'D CAPTURED WHITE BOYS AT ALL? THERE WASN'T NO EXPLANATION FROM THE REDS, THAT WAS SURE.
ALL THAT AL KNEW FOR SURE WAS WHAT THEY DID. THE NEW-COME REDS TOOK ALL THE MUSKETS AWAY FROM THE GUN-TOTERS, AND THEN LED THEM OFF INTO THE WOODS. ONLY ABOUT A DOZEN REDS STAYED WITH AL AND MEASURE.
AMONG THEM WAS TA-KUMSAW.
THEY SAY YOU HAVE FINGERS MADE OF STEEL.
JUST REGULAR FINGERS NEAR AS I CAN TELL.
TA-KUMSAW REACHED OUT AND TOOK HIM BY THE HAND—A STRONG, HARD GRIP, IT MUST HAVE BEEN, 'CAUSE MEASURE TRIED TO PULL AWAY AND COULDN'T...
IRON SKIN. CAN'T CUT WITH KNIFE. CAN'T BURN. BOYS MADE OF STONE.
STONE BOY, THROW ME TO THE DIRT!
I CAN'T 'RASSLE YOU. I DON'T WANT A FIGHT WITH NOBODY.
THROW ME!

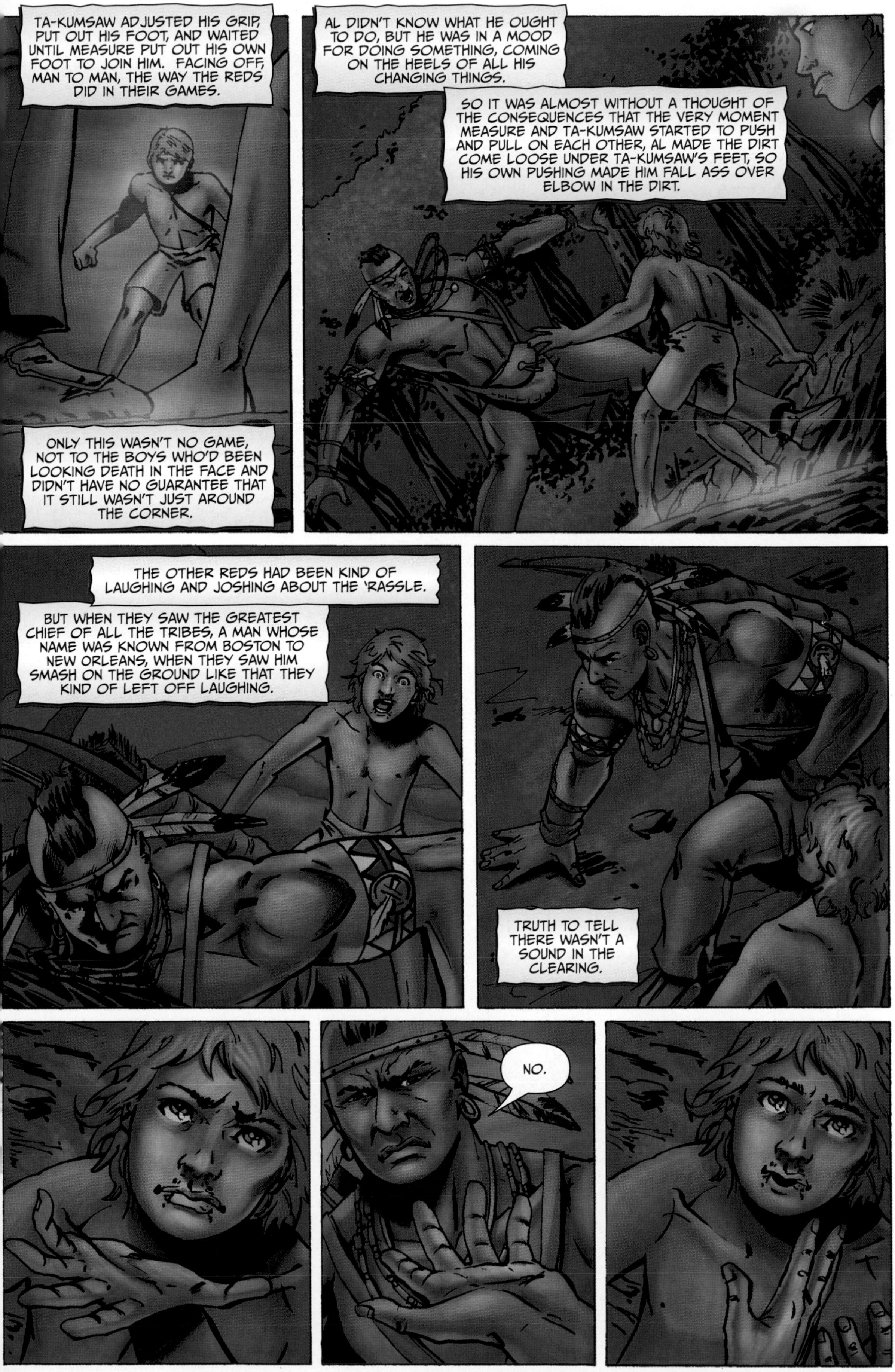
TA-KUMSAW ADJUSTED HIS GRIP, PUT OUT HIS FOOT, AND WAITED UNTIL MEASURE PUT OUT HIS OWN FOOT TO JOIN HIM. FACING OFF, MAN TO MAN, THE WAY THE REDS DID IN THEIR GAMES.
ONLY THIS WASN'T NO GAME, NOT TO THE BOYS WHO'D BEEN LOOKING DEATH IN THE FACE AND DIDN'T HAVE NO GUARANTEE THAT IT STILL WASN'T JUST AROUND THE CORNER.
AL DIDN'T KNOW WHAT HE OUGHT TO DO, BUT HE WAS IN A MOOD FOR DOING SOMETHING, COMING ON THE HEELS OF ALL HIS CHANGING THINGS.
SO IT WAS ALMOST WITHOUT A THOUGHT OF THE CONSEQUENCES THAT THE VERY MOMENT MEASURE AND TA-KUMSAW STARTED TO PUSH AND PULL ON EACH OTHER, AL MADE THE DIRT COME LOOSE UNDER TA-KUMSAW'S FEET, SO HIS OWN PUSHING MADE HIM FALL ASS OVER ELBOW IN THE DIRT.
THE OTHER REDS HAD BEEN KIND OF LAUGHING AND JOSHING ABOUT THE 'RASSLE.
BUT WHEN THEY SAW THE GREATEST CHIEF OF ALL THE TRIBES, A MAN WHOSE NAME WAS KNOWN FROM BOSTON TO NEW ORLEANS, WHEN THEY SAW HIM SMASH ON THE GROUND LIKE THAT THEY KIND OF LEFT OFF LAUGHING.
TRUTH TO TELL THERE WASN'T A SOUND IN THE CLEARING.
NO.

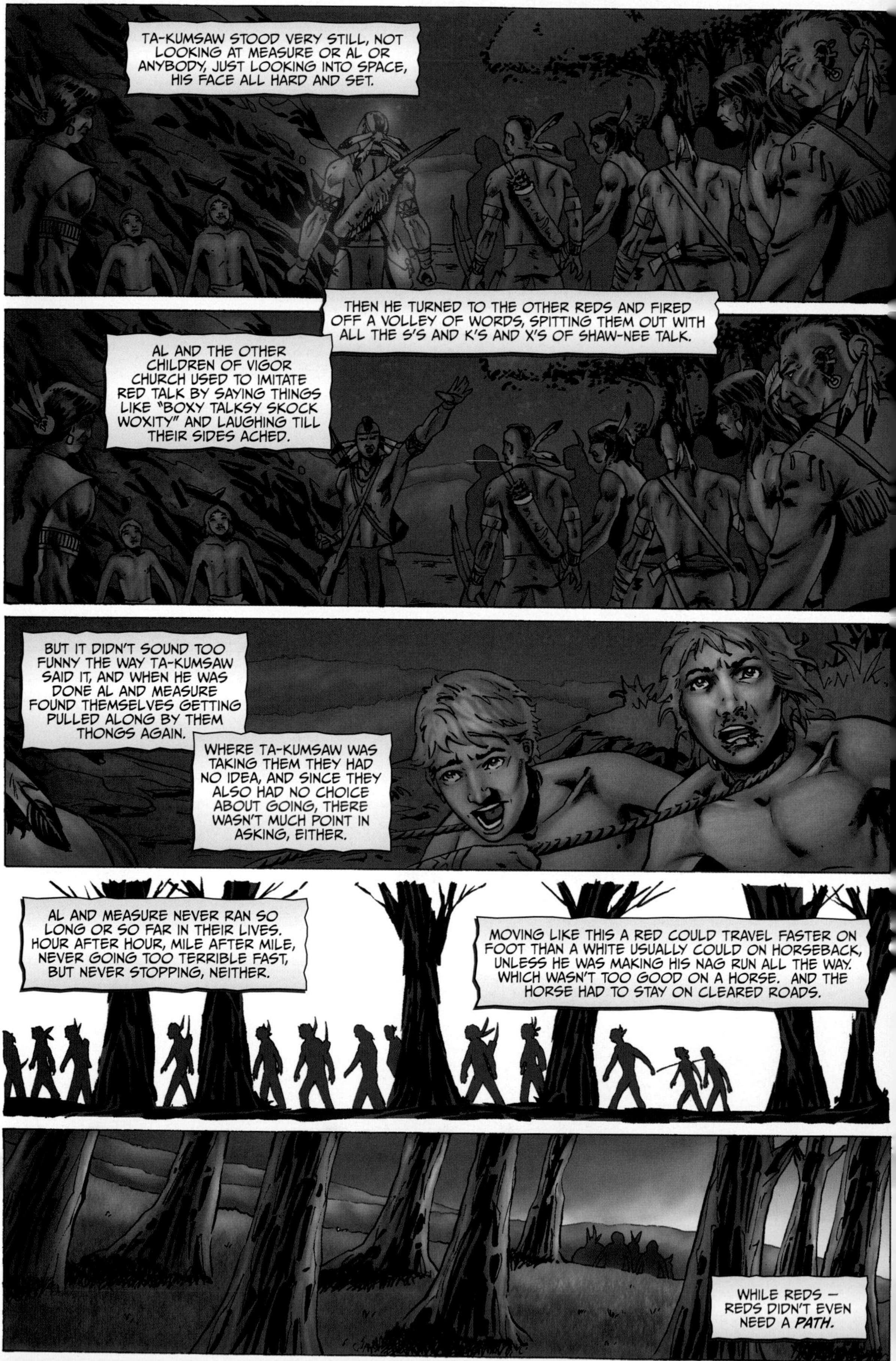
TA-KUMSAW STOOD VERY STILL, NOT LOOKING AT MEASURE OR AL OR ANYBODY, JUST LOOKING INTO SPACE, HIS FACE ALL HARD AND SET.
THEN HE TURNED TO THE OTHER REDS AND FIRED OFF A VOLLEY OF WORDS, SPITTING THEM OUT WITH ALL THE S'S AND K'S AND X'S OF SHAW-NEE TALK.
AL AND THE OTHER CHILDREN OF VIGOR CHURCH USED TO IMITATE RED TALK BY SAYING THINGS LIKE "BOXY TALKSY SKOCK WOXITY" AND LAUGHING TILL THEIR SIDES ACHED.
BUT IT DIDN'T SOUND TOO FUNNY THE WAY TA-KUMSAW SAID IT, AND WHEN HE WAS DONE AL AND MEASURE FOUND THEMSELVES GETTING PULLED ALONG BY THEM THONGS AGAIN.
WHERE TA-KUMSAW WAS TAKING THEM THEY HAD NO IDEA, AND SINCE THEY ALSO HAD NO CHOICE ABOUT GOING, THERE WASN'T MUCH POINT IN ASKING, EITHER.
AL AND MEASURE NEVER RAN SO LONG OR SO FAR IN THEIR LIVES. HOUR AFTER HOUR, MILE AFTER MILE, NEVER GOING TOO TERRIBLE FAST, BUT NEVER STOPPING, NEITHER.
MOVING LIKE THIS A RED COULD TRAVEL FASTER ON FOOT THAN A WHITE USUALLY COULD ON HORSEBACK, UNLESS HE WAS MAKING HIS NAG RUN ALL THE WAY. WHICH WASN'T TOO GOOD ON A HORSE. AND THE HORSE HAD TO STAY ON CLEARED ROADS.
WHILE REDS — REDS DIDN'T EVEN NEED A *PATH.*

COURSE, THERE WERE WHITES IN THE WOODS TOO THAT DAY, LOOKING FOR THOSE BOYS.

THEY GATHERED IN THE CLEARING, SOME THIRTY WHITE MEN, GRIM-FACED AND ANGRY AND TIRED FROM WALKING THROUGH THE WOODS. THE TRAIL WAS EASY ENOUGH TO FOLLOW, BUT IT SEEMED LIKE THE BRANCHES GRABBED AT THEM AND THE ROOTS TRIPPED THEM UP—THE FOREST WAS NEVER KIND TO A WHITE MAN.

THEN THERE WAS THE HOUR LOST WHEN THE TRAIL REACHED A STREAM AND THEY HAD TO GO UP AND DOWN THE STREAM TO FIND WHERE THE REDS TOOK THEM BOYS OUT THE WATER AND UP ONTO THE LAND AGAIN.

OLD ALVIN MILLER LIKE TO WENT CRAZY WHEN HE SAW THEY DRAGGED THE BOYS THROUGH WATER—IT TOOK HIS SON CALM ABOUT TEN MINUTES TO GET HIM QUIET AND ABLE TO GO ON. THE MAN WAS JUST MAD WITH FEAR.

SHOULDN'T'VE SENT HIM AWAY, I NEVER SHOULD'VE LET HIM GO...

COULD'VE HAPPENED ANYWHERE, DON'T BLAME YOURSELF, WE'LL FIND THEM ALL RIGHT, THEY'RE STILL WALKING AIN'T THEY?

WE'LL NEVER TRACK THEM FROM HERE, THE BOYS AREN'T LEAVING NO FOOTPRINTS NOW—

WHICH DON'T MEAN NOTHING, MR. MILLER, SO DON'T YOU FRET.

THEY MIGHT BE TOTING THE BOYS, OR THEY MIGHT BE STEPPING AFTER THEM, KIND OF WIPING OUT THEIR PRINTS.

WE ALL KNOW IF A RED DON'T WANT TO LEAVE A TRAIL, THERE AIN'T NO TRAIL.

ARMOR CALLED HIS FATHER-IN-LAW MR. MILLER EVER SINCE AL THREWED HIM OUT OF THE HOUSE INTO THE SNOW THAT TIME HE CAME TO SAY AL JUNIOR WAS DYING 'CAUSE THE FAMILY COMMITTED THE SIN OF USING HEXES AND BESEECHINGS.

IT JUST DON'T SEEM RIGHT TO CALL A MAN *PA* AFTER HE HEAVES YOU OFF HIS PORCH.

WE ALL KNOW ABOUT REDS AND WHAT THEY DO TO WHITE BOYS WHEN THEY—

SO FAR ALL WE KNOW IS THEY TRYING TO SCARE US...

DOING A GOOD JOB SO FAR. SCARED MOSTLY TO DEATH, MY FAMILY AND ME.

BESIDES, EVERYBODY KNOWS ARMOR-OF-GOD HERE IS A RED-LOVER!

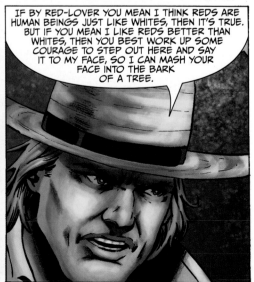

IF BY RED-LOVER YOU MEAN I THINK REDS ARE HUMAN BEINGS JUST LIKE WHITES, THEN IT'S TRUE. BUT IF YOU MEAN I LIKE REDS BETTER THAN WHITES, THEN YOU BEST WORK UP SOME COURAGE TO STEP OUT HERE AND SAY IT TO MY FACE, SO I CAN MASH YOUR FACE INTO THE BARK OF A TREE.

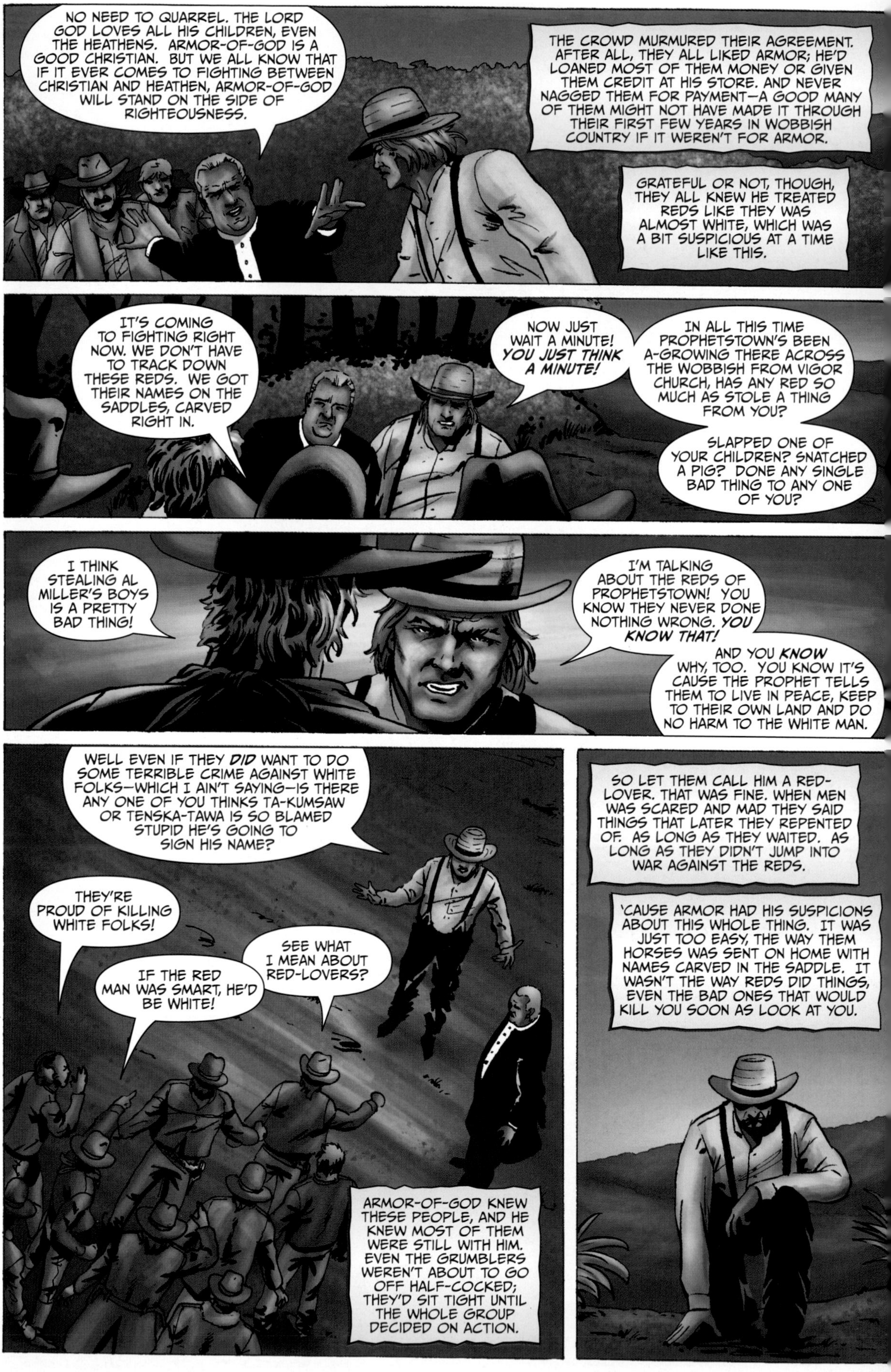
NO NEED TO QUARREL. THE LORD GOD LOVES ALL HIS CHILDREN, EVEN THE HEATHENS. ARMOR-OF-GOD IS A GOOD CHRISTIAN. BUT WE ALL KNOW THAT IF IT EVER COMES TO FIGHTING BETWEEN CHRISTIAN AND HEATHEN, ARMOR-OF-GOD WILL STAND ON THE SIDE OF RIGHTEOUSNESS.
THE CROWD MURMURED THEIR AGREEMENT. AFTER ALL, THEY ALL LIKED ARMOR; HE'D LOANED MOST OF THEM MONEY OR GIVEN THEM CREDIT AT HIS STORE. AND NEVER NAGGED THEM FOR PAYMENT—A GOOD MANY OF THEM MIGHT NOT HAVE MADE IT THROUGH THEIR FIRST FEW YEARS IN WOBBISH COUNTRY IF IT WEREN'T FOR ARMOR.
GRATEFUL OR NOT, THOUGH, THEY ALL KNEW HE TREATED REDS LIKE THEY WAS ALMOST WHITE, WHICH WAS A BIT SUSPICIOUS AT A TIME LIKE THIS.
IT'S COMING TO FIGHTING RIGHT NOW. WE DON'T HAVE TO TRACK DOWN THESE REDS. WE GOT THEIR NAMES ON THE SADDLES, CARVED RIGHT IN.
NOW JUST WAIT A MINUTE! *YOU JUST THINK A MINUTE!*
IN ALL THIS TIME PROPHETSTOWN'S BEEN A-GROWING THERE ACROSS THE WOBBISH FROM VIGOR CHURCH, HAS ANY RED SO MUCH AS STOLE A THING FROM YOU?
SLAPPED ONE OF YOUR CHILDREN? SNATCHED A PIG? DONE ANY SINGLE BAD THING TO ANY ONE OF YOU?
I THINK STEALING AL MILLER'S BOYS IS A PRETTY BAD THING!
I'M TALKING ABOUT THE REDS OF PROPHETSTOWN! YOU KNOW THEY NEVER DONE NOTHING WRONG. *YOU KNOW THAT!*
AND YOU *KNOW* WHY, TOO. YOU KNOW IT'S CAUSE THE PROPHET TELLS THEM TO LIVE IN PEACE, KEEP TO THEIR OWN LAND AND DO NO HARM TO THE WHITE MAN.
WELL EVEN IF THEY *DID* WANT TO DO SOME TERRIBLE CRIME AGAINST WHITE FOLKS—WHICH I AIN'T SAYING—IS THERE ANY ONE OF YOU THINKS TA-KUMSAW OR TENSKA-TAWA IS SO BLAMED STUPID HE'S GOING TO SIGN HIS NAME?
THEY'RE PROUD OF KILLING WHITE FOLKS!
SEE WHAT I MEAN ABOUT RED-LOVERS?
IF THE RED MAN WAS SMART, HE'D BE WHITE!
ARMOR-OF-GOD KNEW THESE PEOPLE, AND HE KNEW MOST OF THEM WERE STILL WITH HIM. EVEN THE GRUMBLERS WEREN'T ABOUT TO GO OFF HALF-COCKED; THEY'D SIT TIGHT UNTIL THE WHOLE GROUP DECIDED ON ACTION.
SO LET THEM CALL HIM A RED-LOVER. THAT WAS FINE. WHEN MEN WAS SCARED AND MAD THEY SAID THINGS THAT LATER THEY REPENTED OF. AS LONG AS THEY WAITED. AS LONG AS THEY DIDN'T JUMP INTO WAR AGAINST THE REDS.
'CAUSE ARMOR HAD HIS SUSPICIONS ABOUT THIS WHOLE THING. IT WAS JUST TOO EASY, THE WAY THEM HORSES WAS SENT ON HOME WITH NAMES CARVED IN THE SADDLE. IT WASN'T THE WAY REDS DID THINGS, EVEN THE BAD ONES THAT WOULD KILL YOU SOON AS LOOK AT YOU.

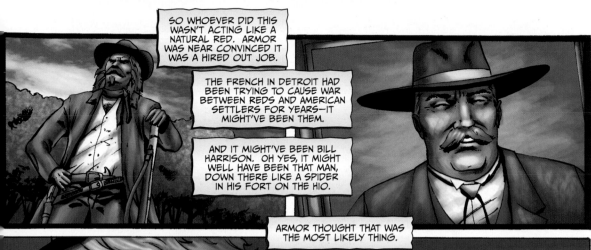

SO WHOEVER DID THIS WASN'T ACTING LIKE A NATURAL RED. ARMOR WAS NEAR CONVINCED IT WAS A HIRED OUT JOB.

THE FRENCH IN DETROIT HAD BEEN TRYING TO CAUSE WAR BETWEEN REDS AND AMERICAN SETTLERS FOR YEARS—IT MIGHT'VE BEEN THEM.

AND IT MIGHT'VE BEEN BILL HARRISON. OH YES, IT MIGHT WELL HAVE BEEN THAT MAN, DOWN THERE LIKE A SPIDER IN HIS FORT ON THE HIO.

ARMOR THOUGHT THAT WAS THE MOST LIKELY THING.

COURSE HE WOULDN'T DARE TO SAY IT OUT LOUD, 'CAUSE FOLKS WOULD THINK HE WAS JUST JEALOUS OF BILL HARRISON, WHICH WAS TRUE — HE *WAS* JEALOUS. BUT HE ALSO KNEW HARRISON WAS A WICKED MAN WHO'D DO ANYTHING TO GET HIS WAY.

MAYBE EVEN GET SOME WILD REDS TO COME UP AND KILL A FEW WHITE BOYS NEAR PROPHETSTOWN.

BUT HE COULDN'T SAY NONE OF THIS, 'CAUSE THERE WAS NO PROOF. HE JUST HAD TO TRY TO KEEP THINGS CALM, TILL SOME REAL EVIDENCE SHOWED UP.

WHICH MIGHT BE RIGHT NOW. THEY'D BROUGHT ALONG OLD TACK SWEEPER, WHEEZING HIS WAY WITH THE BEST OF THEM— IT WAS REMARKABLE HOW VIGOROUS HE WAS, FOR A MAN WHOSE LUNGS SOUNDED LIKE A BABY'S RATTLE WHEN HE BREATHED.

TACK SWEEPER HAD HIM A KNACK, WHICH WASN'T ALL THAT RELIABLE, HE WAS THE FIRST TO SAY. BUT SOMETIMES IT WORKED REMARKABLY WELL. WHAT HE DID WAS STAND AROUND IN A PLACE FOR A WHILE WITH HIS EYES CLOSED AND SORT OF SEE THINGS THAT HAPPENED THERE IN THE PAST.

JUST QUICK LITTLE VISIONS, A FEW FACES.

LIKE THAT TIME THEY WAS AFRAID JACK DE VRIES KILLED HISSELF ON PURPOSE, OR MAYBE WAS MURDERED, TACK WAS ABLE TO SEE HOW IT WAS AN ACCIDENT WHEN HIS GUN WENT OFF IN HIS OWN FACE, SO THEY COULD BURY HIM IN THE CHURCHYARD AND NOT HAVE TO WORRY ABOUT HUNTING FOR NO KILLER.

SO THE HOPE WAS THAT TACK COULD TELL THEM SOMETHING ABOUT WHAT HAPPENED IN THIS CLEARING.

YOU BOYS SHOULDN'T HAVE GOT SO MAD HERE. ALL I CAN SEE IS YOU ALL JAWING...

IT DON'T LOOK TOO GOOD. I KEEP SEEING THEM RED FACES. KNIFE, ALL KINDS OF KNIVES GETTING SLASHED ON FOLKS' SKIN. A HATCHET FALLING...

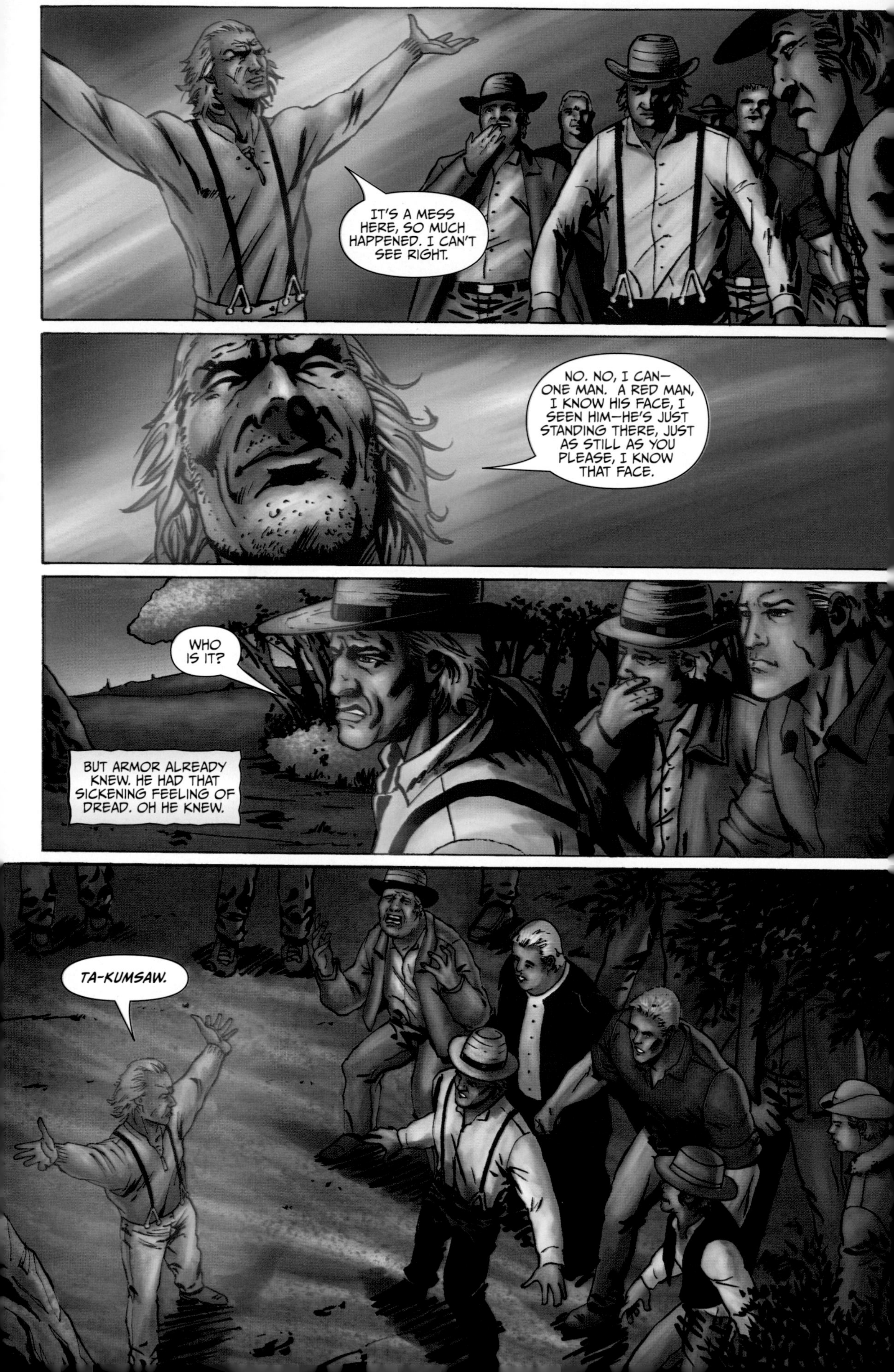
IT'S A MESS HERE, SO MUCH HAPPENED. I CAN'T SEE RIGHT.
NO. NO, I CAN— ONE MAN. A RED MAN, I KNOW HIS FACE, I SEEN HIM—HE'S JUST STANDING THERE, JUST AS STILL AS YOU PLEASE, I KNOW THAT FACE.
WHO IS IT?
BUT ARMOR ALREADY KNEW. HE HAD THAT SICKENING FEELING OF DREAD. OH HE KNEW.
TA-KUMSAW.

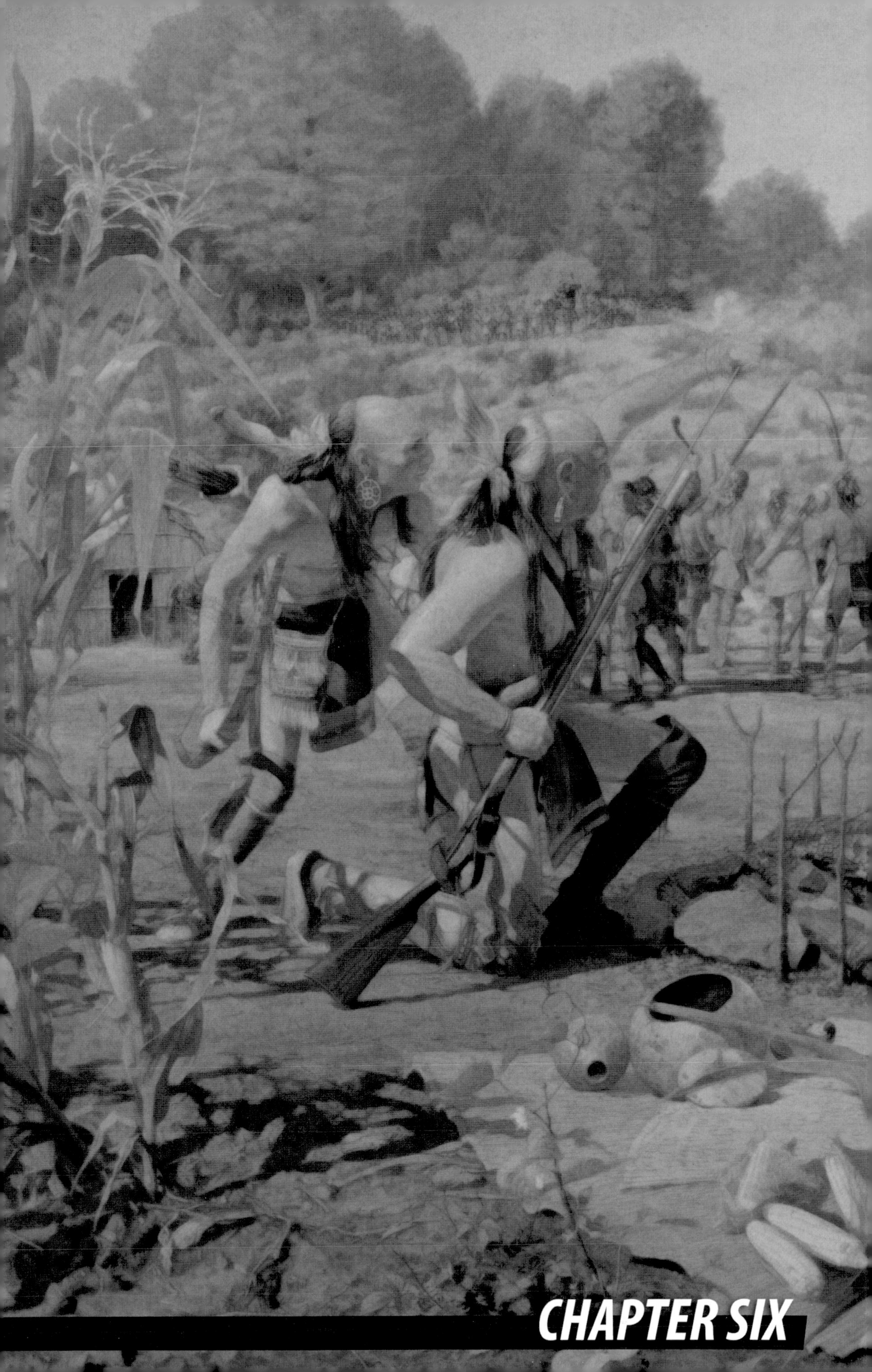

CHAPTER SIX

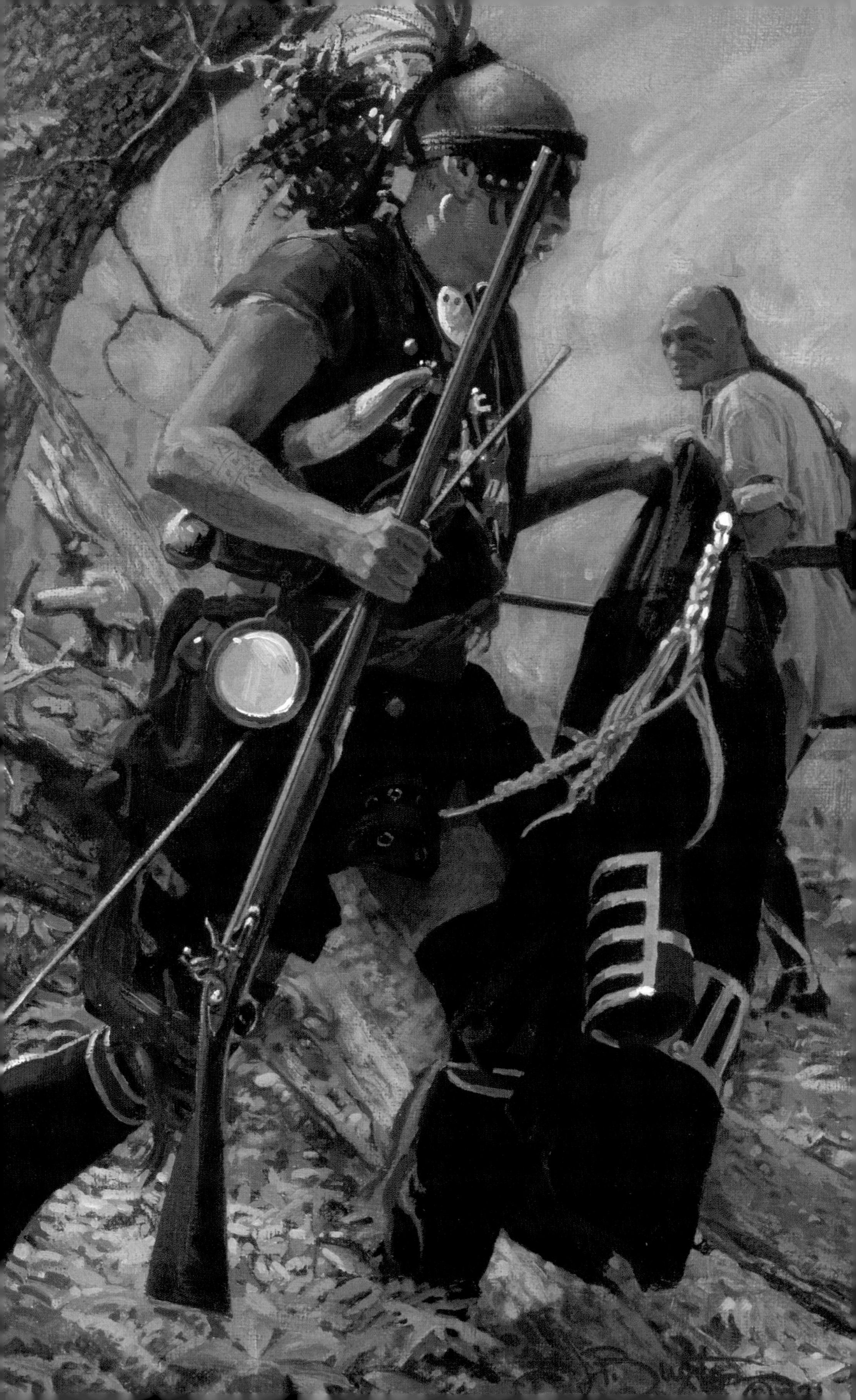

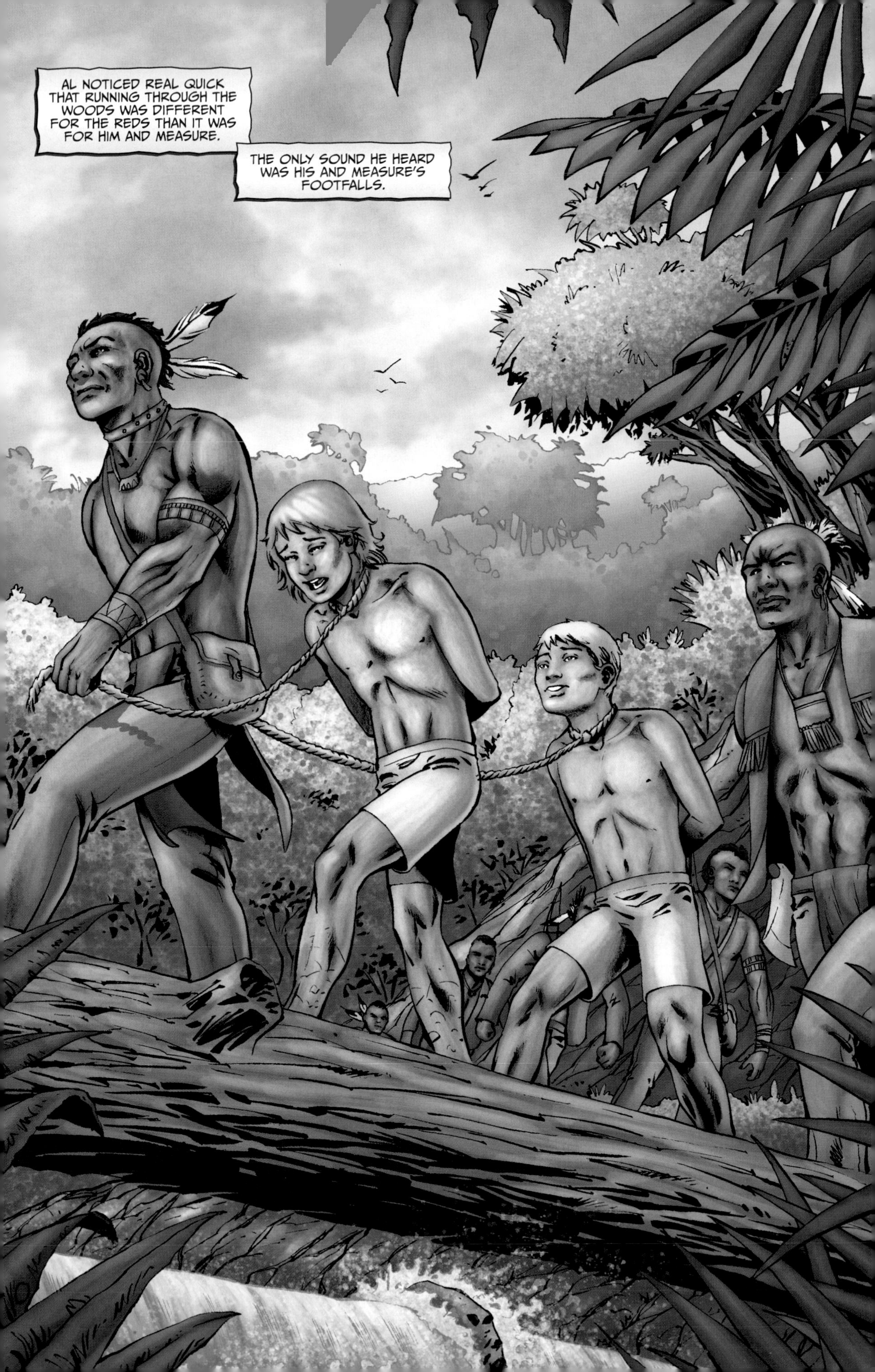
AL NOTICED REAL QUICK THAT RUNNING THROUGH THE WOODS WAS DIFFERENT FOR THE REDS THAN IT WAS FOR HIM AND MEASURE.
THE ONLY SOUND HE HEARD WAS HIS AND MEASURE'S FOOTFALLS.

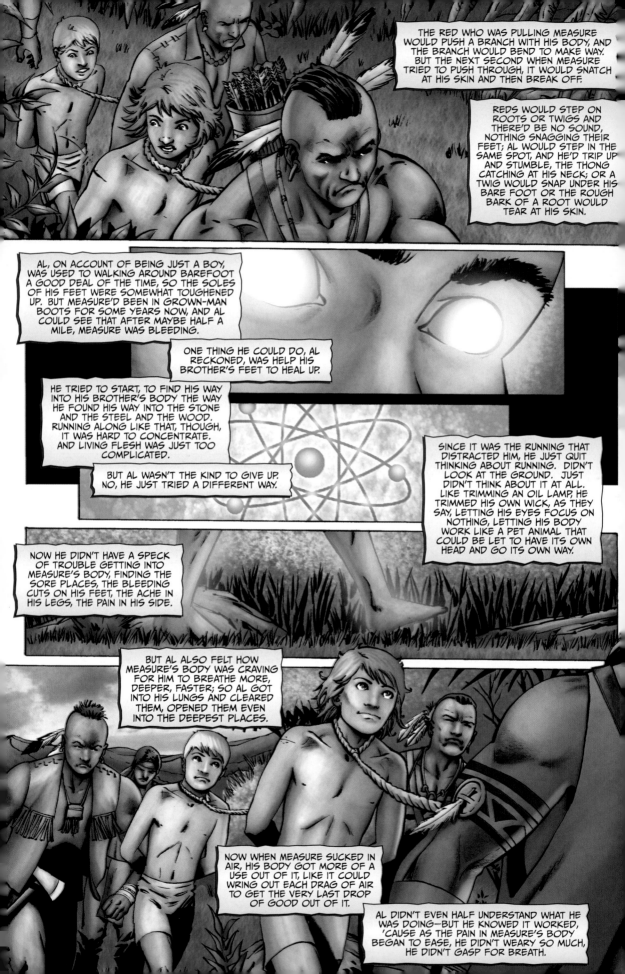

THE RED WHO WAS PULLING MEASURE WOULD PUSH A BRANCH WITH HIS BODY, AND THE BRANCH WOULD BEND TO MAKE WAY. BUT THE NEXT SECOND WHEN MEASURE TRIED TO PUSH THROUGH, IT WOULD SNATCH AT HIS SKIN AND THEN BREAK OFF.

REDS WOULD STEP ON ROOTS OR TWIGS AND THERE'D BE NO SOUND, NOTHING SNAGGING THEIR FEET; AL WOULD STEP IN THE SAME SPOT, AND HE'D TRIP UP AND STUMBLE, THE THONG CATCHING AT HIS NECK; OR A TWIG WOULD SNAP UNDER HIS BARE FOOT OR THE ROUGH BARK OF A ROOT WOULD TEAR AT HIS SKIN.

AL, ON ACCOUNT OF BEING JUST A BOY, WAS USED TO WALKING AROUND BAREFOOT A GOOD DEAL OF THE TIME, SO THE SOLES OF HIS FEET WERE SOMEWHAT TOUGHENED UP. BUT MEASURE'D BEEN IN GROWN-MAN BOOTS FOR SOME YEARS NOW, AND AL COULD SEE THAT AFTER MAYBE HALF A MILE, MEASURE WAS BLEEDING.

ONE THING HE COULD DO, AL RECKONED, WAS HELP HIS BROTHER'S FEET TO HEAL UP.

HE TRIED TO START, TO FIND HIS WAY INTO HIS BROTHER'S BODY THE WAY HE FOUND HIS WAY INTO THE STONE AND THE STEEL AND THE WOOD. RUNNING ALONG LIKE THAT, THOUGH, IT WAS HARD TO CONCENTRATE. AND LIVING FLESH WAS JUST TOO COMPLICATED.

BUT AL WASN'T THE KIND TO GIVE UP. NO, HE JUST TRIED A DIFFERENT WAY.

SINCE IT WAS THE RUNNING THAT DISTRACTED HIM, HE JUST QUIT THINKING ABOUT RUNNING. DIDN'T LOOK AT THE GROUND. JUST DIDN'T THINK ABOUT IT AT ALL. LIKE TRIMMING AN OIL LAMP, HE TRIMMED HIS OWN WICK, AS THEY SAY, LETTING HIS EYES FOCUS ON NOTHING, LETTING HIS BODY WORK LIKE A PET ANIMAL THAT COULD BE LET TO HAVE ITS OWN HEAD AND GO ITS OWN WAY.

NOW HE DIDN'T HAVE A SPECK OF TROUBLE GETTING INTO MEASURE'S BODY, FINDING THE SORE PLACES, THE BLEEDING CUTS ON HIS FEET, THE ACHE IN HIS LEGS, THE PAIN IN HIS SIDE.

BUT AL ALSO FELT HOW MEASURE'S BODY WAS CRAVING FOR HIM TO BREATHE MORE, DEEPER, FASTER; SO AL GOT INTO HIS LUNGS AND CLEARED THEM, OPENED THEM EVEN INTO THE DEEPEST PLACES.

NOW WHEN MEASURE SUCKED IN AIR, HIS BODY GOT MORE OF A USE OUT OF IT, LIKE IT COULD WRING OUT EACH DRAG OF AIR TO GET THE VERY LAST DROP OF GOOD OUT OF IT.

AL DIDN'T EVEN HALF UNDERSTAND WHAT HE WAS DOING—BUT HE KNEWED IT WORKED, 'CAUSE AS THE PAIN IN MEASURE'S BODY BEGAN TO EASE, HE DIDN'T WEARY SO MUCH, HE DIDN'T GASP FOR BREATH.

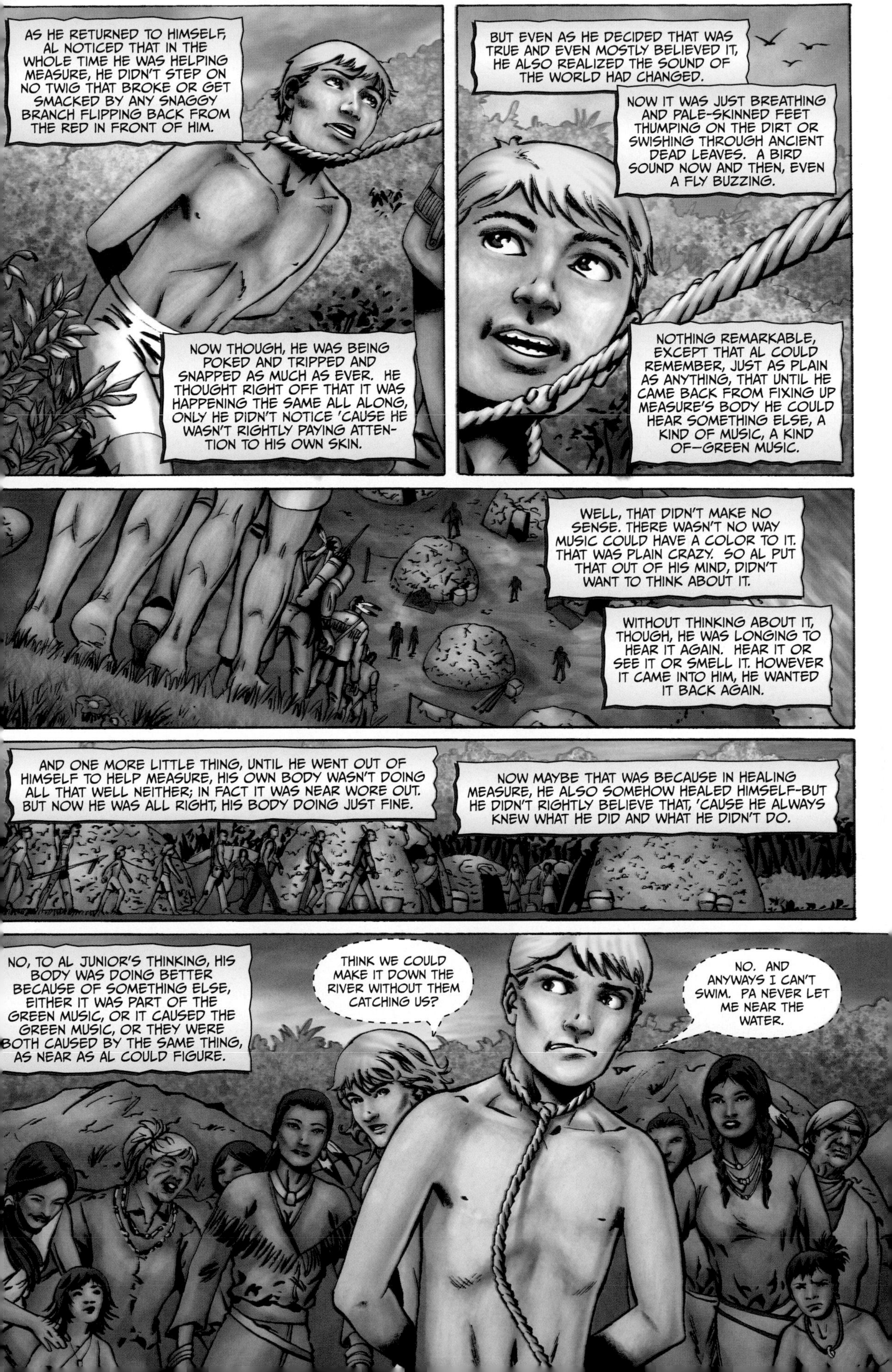
AS HE RETURNED TO HIMSELF, AL NOTICED THAT IN THE WHOLE TIME HE WAS HELPING MEASURE, HE DIDN'T STEP ON NO TWIG THAT BROKE OR GET SMACKED BY ANY SNAGGY BRANCH FLIPPING BACK FROM THE RED IN FRONT OF HIM.
NOW THOUGH, HE WAS BEING POKED AND TRIPPED AND SNAPPED AS MUCH AS EVER. HE THOUGHT RIGHT OFF THAT IT WAS HAPPENING THE SAME ALL ALONG, ONLY HE DIDN'T NOTICE 'CAUSE HE WASN'T RIGHTLY PAYING ATTEN-TION TO HIS OWN SKIN.
BUT EVEN AS HE DECIDED THAT WAS TRUE AND EVEN MOSTLY BELIEVED IT, HE ALSO REALIZED THE SOUND OF THE WORLD HAD CHANGED.
NOW IT WAS JUST BREATHING AND PALE-SKINNED FEET THUMPING ON THE DIRT OR SWISHING THROUGH ANCIENT DEAD LEAVES. A BIRD SOUND NOW AND THEN, EVEN A FLY BUZZING.
NOTHING REMARKABLE, EXCEPT THAT AL COULD REMEMBER, JUST AS PLAIN AS ANYTHING, THAT UNTIL HE CAME BACK FROM FIXING UP MEASURE'S BODY HE COULD HEAR SOMETHING ELSE, A KIND OF MUSIC, A KIND OF—GREEN MUSIC.
WELL, THAT DIDN'T MAKE NO SENSE. THERE WASN'T NO WAY MUSIC COULD HAVE A COLOR TO IT. THAT WAS PLAIN CRAZY. SO AL PUT THAT OUT OF HIS MIND, DIDN'T WANT TO THINK ABOUT IT.
WITHOUT THINKING ABOUT IT, THOUGH, HE WAS LONGING TO HEAR IT AGAIN. HEAR IT OR SEE IT OR SMELL IT. HOWEVER IT CAME INTO HIM, HE WANTED IT BACK AGAIN.
AND ONE MORE LITTLE THING, UNTIL HE WENT OUT OF HIMSELF TO HELP MEASURE, HIS OWN BODY WASN'T DOING ALL THAT WELL NEITHER; IN FACT IT WAS NEAR WORE OUT. BUT NOW HE WAS ALL RIGHT, HIS BODY DOING JUST FINE.
NOW MAYBE THAT WAS BECAUSE IN HEALING MEASURE, HE ALSO SOMEHOW HEALED HIMSELF–BUT HE DIDN'T RIGHTLY BELIEVE THAT, 'CAUSE HE ALWAYS KNEW WHAT HE DID AND WHAT HE DIDN'T DO.
NO, TO AL JUNIOR'S THINKING, HIS BODY WAS DOING BETTER BECAUSE OF SOMETHING ELSE, EITHER IT WAS PART OF THE GREEN MUSIC, OR IT CAUSED THE GREEN MUSIC, OR THEY WERE BOTH CAUSED BY THE SAME THING, AS NEAR AS AL COULD FIGURE.
THINK WE COULD MAKE IT DOWN THE RIVER WITHOUT THEM CATCHING US?
NO. AND ANYWAYS I CAN'T SWIM. PA NEVER LET ME NEAR THE WATER.

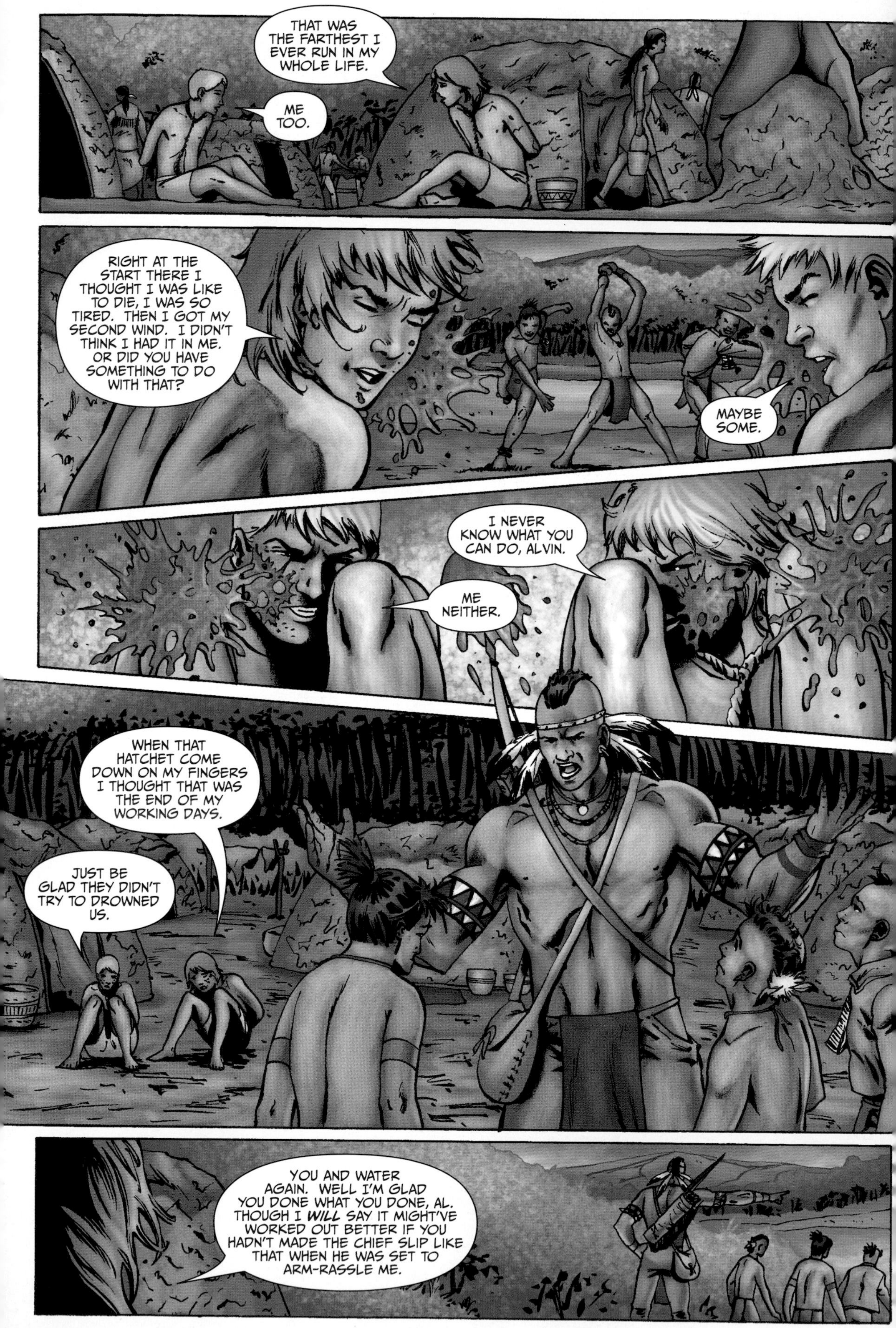
THAT WAS THE FARTHEST I EVER RUN IN MY WHOLE LIFE.
ME TOO.
RIGHT AT THE START THERE I THOUGHT I WAS LIKE TO DIE, I WAS SO TIRED. THEN I GOT MY SECOND WIND. I DIDN'T THINK I HAD IT IN ME. OR DID YOU HAVE SOMETHING TO DO WITH THAT?
MAYBE SOME.
I NEVER KNOW WHAT YOU CAN DO, ALVIN.
ME NEITHER.
WHEN THAT HATCHET COME DOWN ON MY FINGERS I THOUGHT THAT WAS THE END OF MY WORKING DAYS.
JUST BE GLAD THEY DIDN'T TRY TO DROWNED US.
YOU AND WATER AGAIN. WELL I'M GLAD YOU DONE WHAT YOU DONE, AL. THOUGH I *WILL* SAY IT MIGHT'VE WORKED OUT BETTER IF YOU HADN'T MADE THE CHIEF SLIP LIKE THAT WHEN HE WAS SET TO ARM-RASSLE ME.

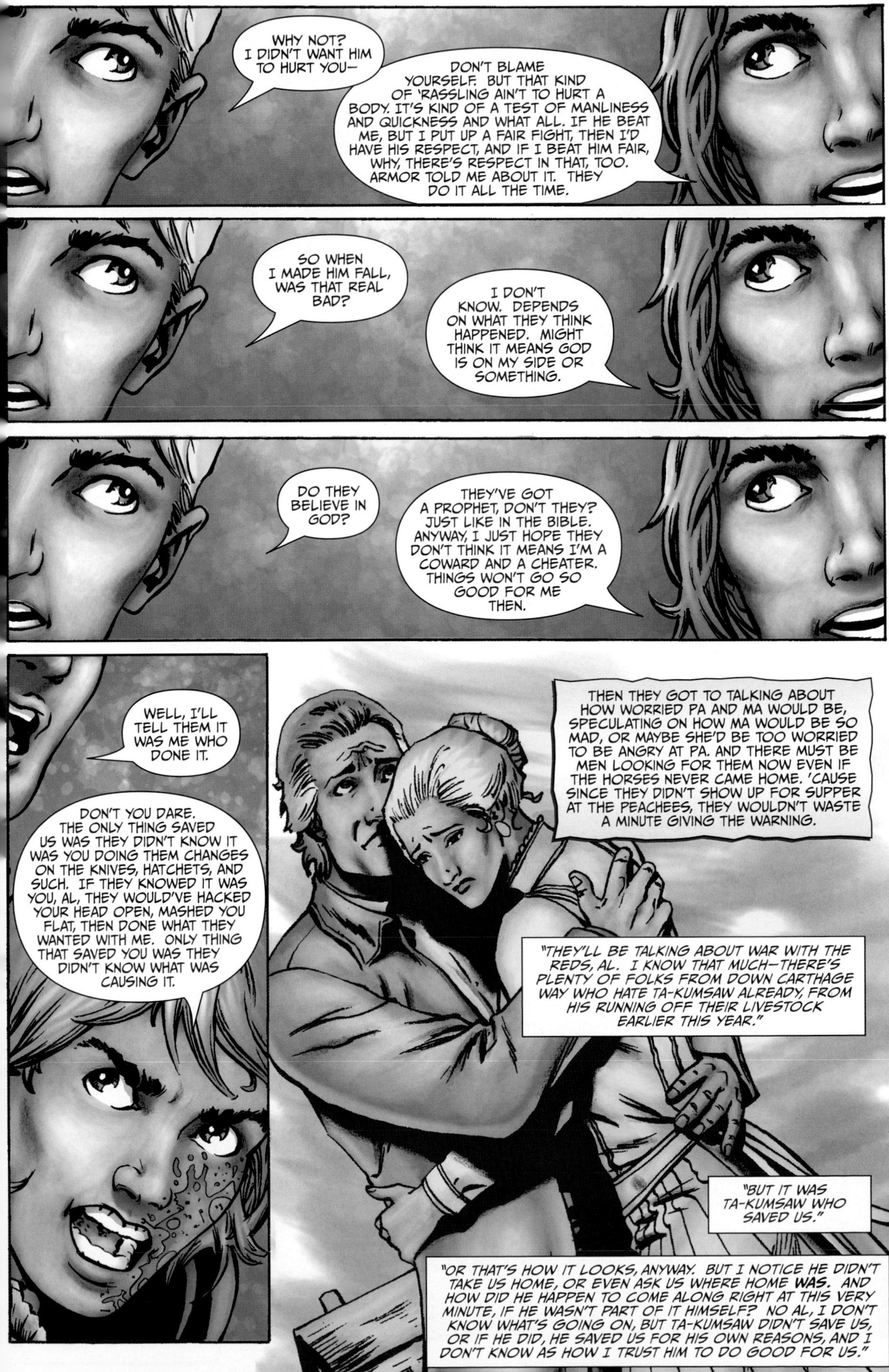
WHY NOT? I DIDN'T WANT HIM TO HURT YOU—
DON'T BLAME YOURSELF. BUT THAT KIND OF 'RASSLING AIN'T TO HURT A BODY. IT'S KIND OF A TEST OF MANLINESS AND QUICKNESS AND WHAT ALL. IF HE BEAT ME, BUT I PUT UP A FAIR FIGHT, THEN I'D HAVE HIS RESPECT, AND IF I BEAT HIM FAIR, WHY, THERE'S RESPECT IN THAT, TOO. ARMOR TOLD ME ABOUT IT. THEY DO IT ALL THE TIME.
SO WHEN I MADE HIM FALL, WAS THAT REAL BAD?
I DON'T KNOW. DEPENDS ON WHAT THEY THINK HAPPENED. MIGHT THINK IT MEANS GOD IS ON MY SIDE OR SOMETHING.
DO THEY BELIEVE IN GOD?
THEY'VE GOT A PROPHET, DON'T THEY? JUST LIKE IN THE BIBLE. ANYWAY, I JUST HOPE THEY DON'T THINK IT MEANS I'M A COWARD AND A CHEATER. THINGS WON'T GO SO GOOD FOR ME THEN.
WELL, I'LL TELL THEM IT WAS ME WHO DONE IT.
DON'T YOU DARE. THE ONLY THING SAVED US WAS THEY DIDN'T KNOW IT WAS YOU DOING THEM CHANGES ON THE KNIVES, HATCHETS, AND SUCH. IF THEY KNOWED IT WAS YOU, AL, THEY WOULD'VE HACKED YOUR HEAD OPEN, MASHED YOU FLAT, THEN DONE WHAT THEY WANTED WITH ME. ONLY THING THAT SAVED YOU WAS THEY DIDN'T KNOW WHAT WAS CAUSING IT.
THEN THEY GOT TO TALKING ABOUT HOW WORRIED PA AND MA WOULD BE, SPECULATING ON HOW MA WOULD BE SO MAD, OR MAYBE SHE'D BE TOO WORRIED TO BE ANGRY AT PA. AND THERE MUST BE MEN LOOKING FOR THEM NOW EVEN IF THE HORSES NEVER CAME HOME. 'CAUSE SINCE THEY DIDN'T SHOW UP FOR SUPPER AT THE PEACHEES, THEY WOULDN'T WASTE A MINUTE GIVING THE WARNING.
"THEY'LL BE TALKING ABOUT WAR WITH THE REDS, AL. I KNOW THAT MUCH—THERE'S PLENTY OF FOLKS FROM DOWN CARTHAGE WAY WHO HATE TA-KUMSAW ALREADY, FROM HIS RUNNING OFF THEIR LIVESTOCK EARLIER THIS YEAR."
"BUT IT WAS TA-KUMSAW WHO SAVED US."
"OR THAT'S HOW IT LOOKS, ANYWAY. BUT I NOTICE HE DIDN'T TAKE US HOME, OR EVEN ASK US WHERE HOME **WAS.** AND HOW DID HE HAPPEN TO COME ALONG RIGHT AT THIS VERY MINUTE, IF HE WASN'T PART OF IT HIMSELF? NO AL, I DON'T KNOW WHAT'S GOING ON, BUT TA-KUMSAW DIDN'T SAVE US, OR IF HE DID, HE SAVED US FOR HIS OWN REASONS, AND I DON'T KNOW AS HOW I TRUST HIM TO DO GOOD FOR US."

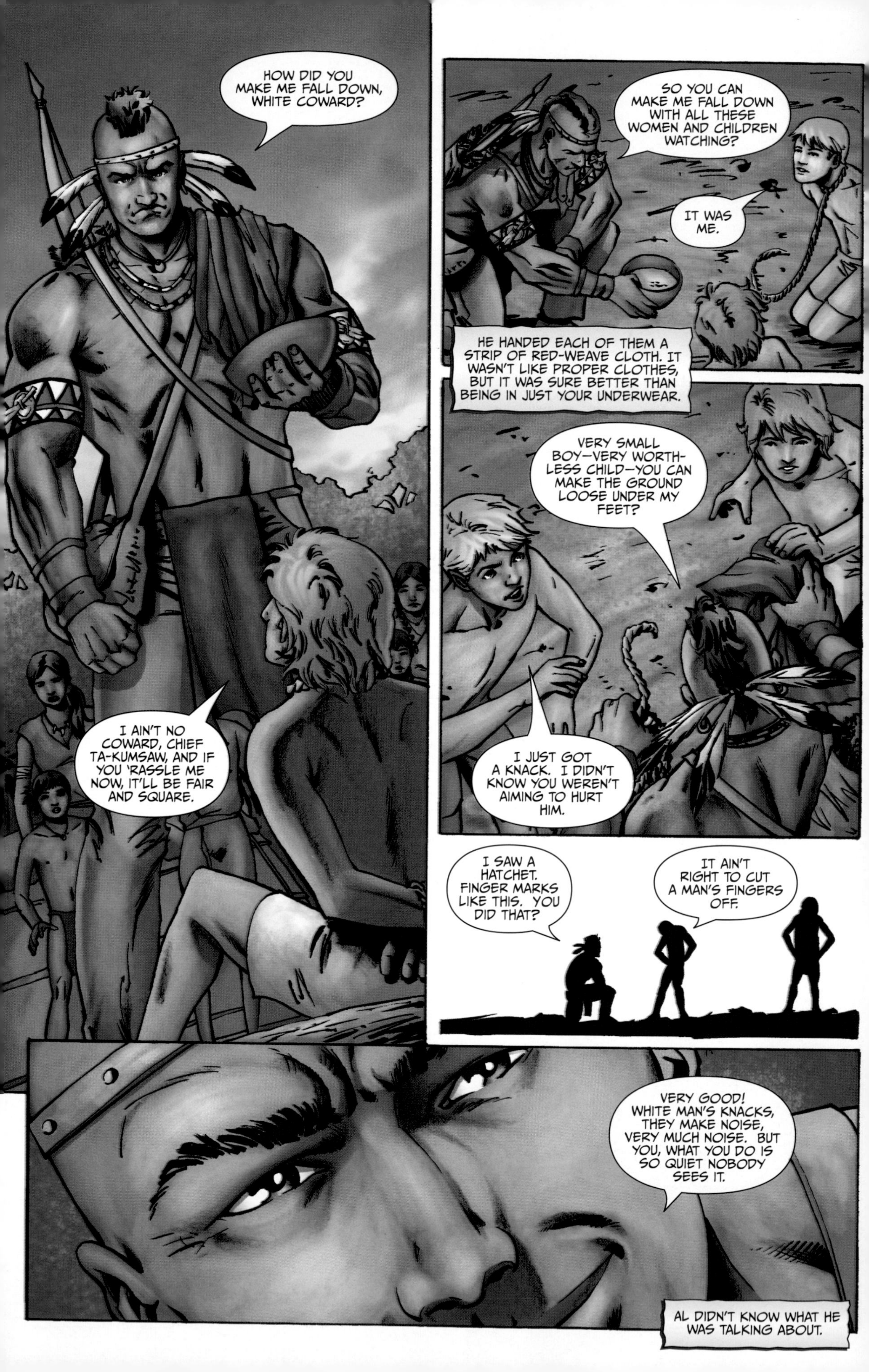

HOW DID YOU MAKE ME FALL DOWN, WHITE COWARD?
I AIN'T NO COWARD, CHIEF TA-KUMSAW, AND IF YOU 'RASSLE ME NOW, IT'LL BE FAIR AND SQUARE.
SO YOU CAN MAKE ME FALL DOWN WITH ALL THESE WOMEN AND CHILDREN WATCHING?
IT WAS ME.
HE HANDED EACH OF THEM A STRIP OF RED-WEAVE CLOTH. IT WASN'T LIKE PROPER CLOTHES, BUT IT WAS SURE BETTER THAN BEING IN JUST YOUR UNDERWEAR.
VERY SMALL BOY—VERY WORTH-LESS CHILD—YOU CAN MAKE THE GROUND LOOSE UNDER MY FEET?
I JUST GOT A KNACK. I DIDN'T KNOW YOU WEREN'T AIMING TO HURT HIM.
I SAW A HATCHET. FINGER MARKS LIKE THIS. YOU DID THAT?
IT AIN'T RIGHT TO CUT A MAN'S FINGERS OFF.
VERY GOOD! WHITE MAN'S KNACKS, THEY MAKE NOISE, VERY MUCH NOISE. BUT YOU, WHAT YOU DO IS SO QUIET NOBODY SEES IT.
AL DIDN'T KNOW WHAT HE WAS TALKING ABOUT.

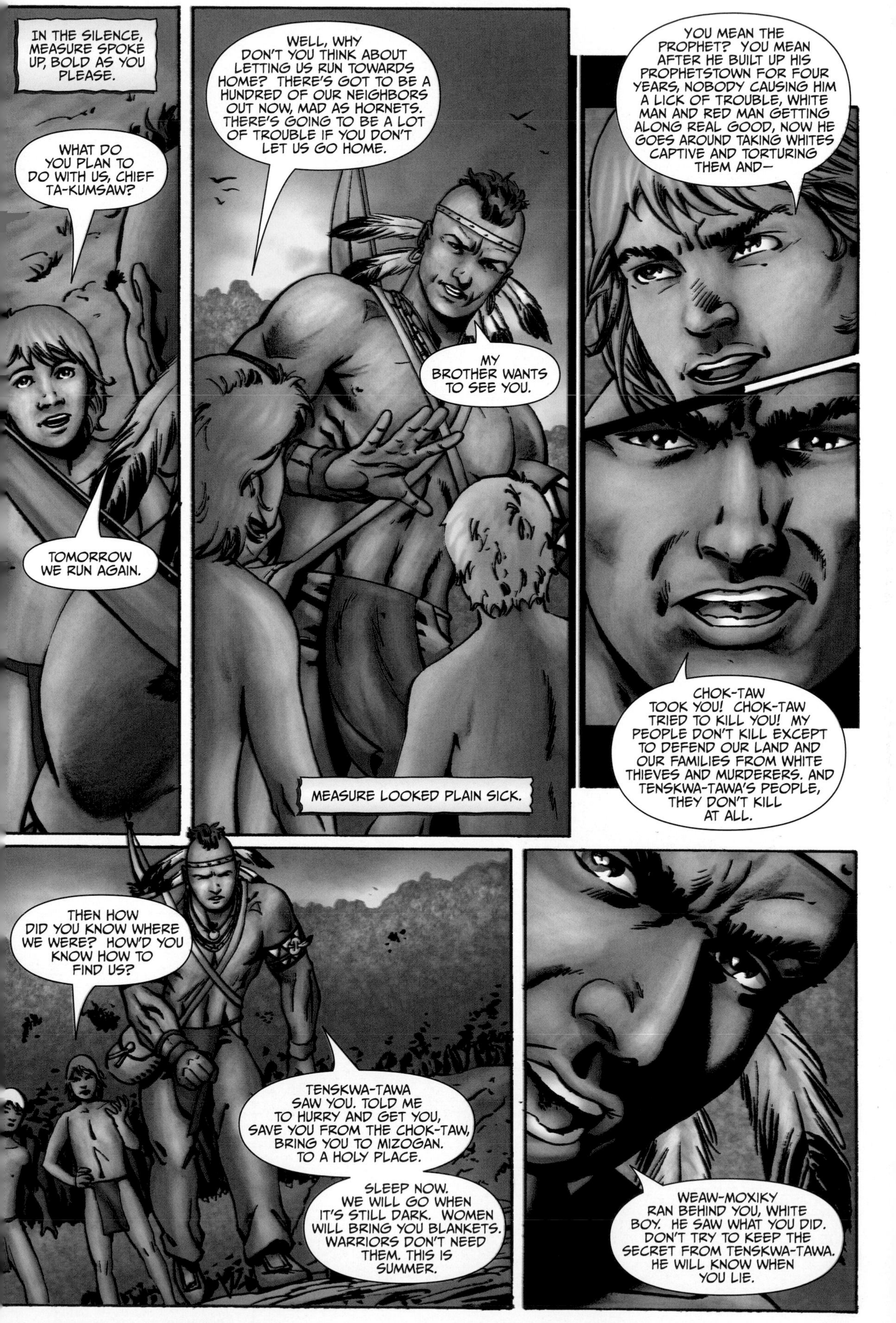

IN THE SILENCE, MEASURE SPOKE UP, BOLD AS YOU PLEASE.
WHAT DO YOU PLAN TO DO WITH US, CHIEF TA-KUMSAW?
TOMORROW WE RUN AGAIN.
WELL, WHY DON'T YOU THINK ABOUT LETTING US RUN TOWARDS HOME? THERE'S GOT TO BE A HUNDRED OF OUR NEIGHBORS OUT NOW, MAD AS HORNETS. THERE'S GOING TO BE A LOT OF TROUBLE IF YOU DON'T LET US GO HOME.
MY BROTHER WANTS TO SEE YOU.
MEASURE LOOKED PLAIN SICK.
YOU MEAN THE PROPHET? YOU MEAN AFTER HE BUILT UP HIS PROPHETSTOWN FOR FOUR YEARS, NOBODY CAUSING HIM A LICK OF TROUBLE, WHITE MAN AND RED MAN GETTING ALONG REAL GOOD, NOW HE GOES AROUND TAKING WHITES CAPTIVE AND TORTURING THEM AND—
CHOK-TAW TOOK YOU! CHOK-TAW TRIED TO KILL YOU! MY PEOPLE DON'T KILL EXCEPT TO DEFEND OUR LAND AND OUR FAMILIES FROM WHITE THIEVES AND MURDERERS. AND TENSKWA-TAWA'S PEOPLE, THEY DON'T KILL AT ALL.
THEN HOW DID YOU KNOW WHERE WE WERE? HOW'D YOU KNOW HOW TO FIND US?
TENSKWA-TAWA SAW YOU. TOLD ME TO HURRY AND GET YOU, SAVE YOU FROM THE CHOK-TAW, BRING YOU TO MIZOGAN. TO A HOLY PLACE.
SLEEP NOW. WE WILL GO WHEN IT'S STILL DARK. WOMEN WILL BRING YOU BLANKETS. WARRIORS DON'T NEED THEM. THIS IS SUMMER.
WEAW-MOXIKY RAN BEHIND YOU, WHITE BOY. HE SAW WHAT YOU DID. DON'T TRY TO KEEP THE SECRET FROM TENSKWA-TAWA. HE WILL KNOW WHEN YOU LIE.

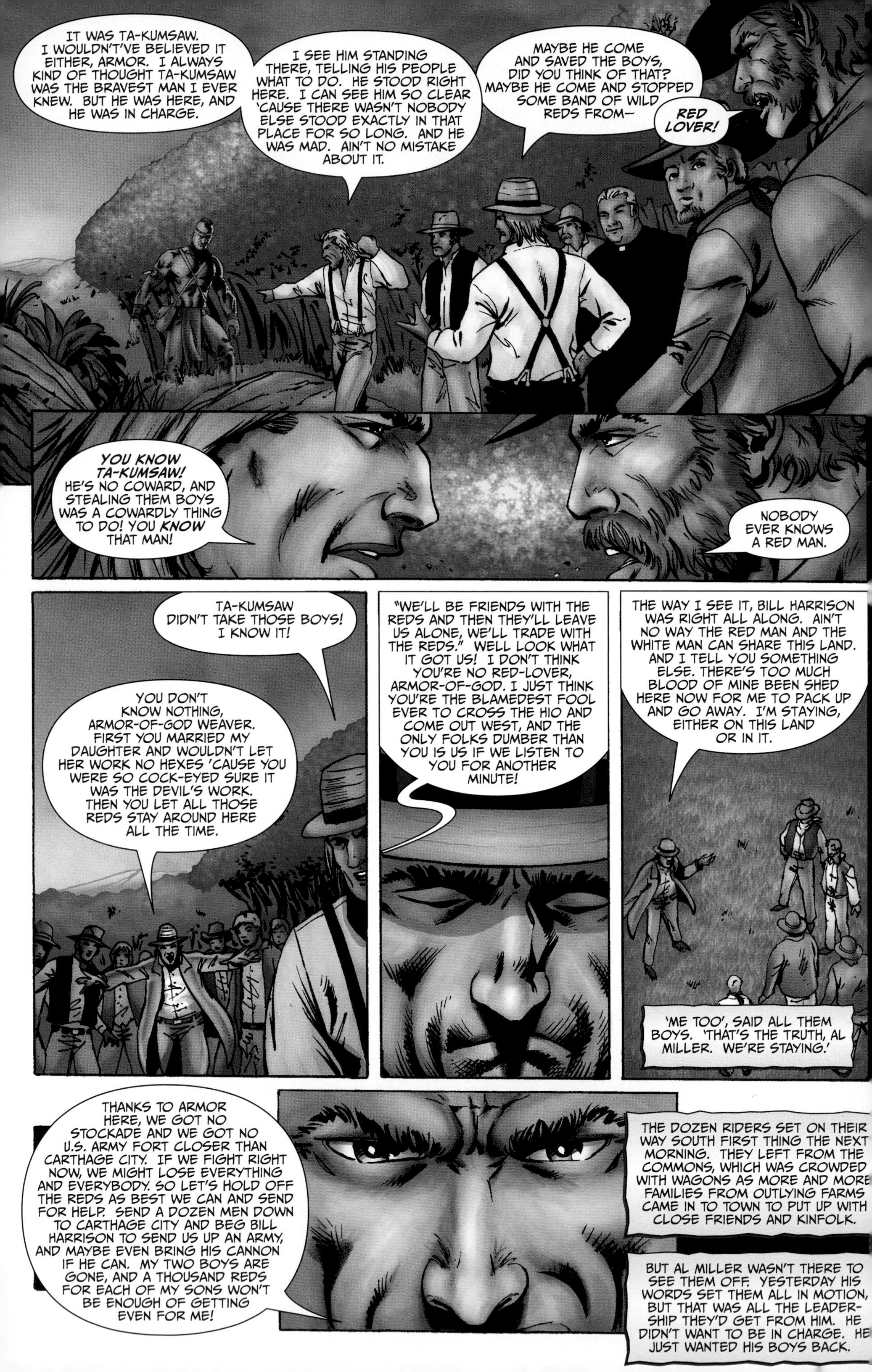

IT WAS TA-KUMSAW. I WOULDN'T'VE BELIEVED IT EITHER, ARMOR. I ALWAYS KIND OF THOUGHT TA-KUMSAW WAS THE BRAVEST MAN I EVER KNEW. BUT HE WAS HERE, AND HE WAS IN CHARGE.
I SEE HIM STANDING THERE, TELLING HIS PEOPLE WHAT TO DO. HE STOOD RIGHT HERE. I CAN SEE HIM SO CLEAR 'CAUSE THERE WASN'T NOBODY ELSE STOOD EXACTLY IN THAT PLACE FOR SO LONG. AND HE WAS MAD. AIN'T NO MISTAKE ABOUT IT.
MAYBE HE COME AND SAVED THE BOYS, DID YOU THINK OF THAT? MAYBE HE COME AND STOPPED SOME BAND OF WILD REDS FROM—
RED LOVER!
YOU KNOW TA-KUMSAW! HE'S NO COWARD, AND STEALING THEM BOYS WAS A COWARDLY THING TO DO! YOU KNOW THAT MAN!
NOBODY EVER KNOWS A RED MAN.
TA-KUMSAW DIDN'T TAKE THOSE BOYS! I KNOW IT!
YOU DON'T KNOW NOTHING, ARMOR-OF-GOD WEAVER. FIRST YOU MARRIED MY DAUGHTER AND WOULDN'T LET HER WORK NO HEXES 'CAUSE YOU WERE SO COCK-EYED SURE IT WAS THE DEVIL'S WORK. THEN YOU LET ALL THOSE REDS STAY AROUND HERE ALL THE TIME.
"WE'LL BE FRIENDS WITH THE REDS AND THEN THEY'LL LEAVE US ALONE, WE'LL TRADE WITH THE REDS." WELL LOOK WHAT IT GOT US! I DON'T THINK YOU'RE NO RED-LOVER, ARMOR-OF-GOD. I JUST THINK YOU'RE THE BLAMEDEST FOOL EVER TO CROSS THE HIO AND COME OUT WEST, AND THE ONLY FOLKS DUMBER THAN YOU IS US IF WE LISTEN TO YOU FOR ANOTHER MINUTE!
THE WAY I SEE IT, BILL HARRISON WAS RIGHT ALL ALONG. AIN'T NO WAY THE RED MAN AND THE WHITE MAN CAN SHARE THIS LAND. AND I TELL YOU SOMETHING ELSE. THERE'S TOO MUCH BLOOD OF MINE BEEN SHED HERE NOW FOR ME TO PACK UP AND GO AWAY. I'M STAYING, EITHER ON THIS LAND OR IN IT.
'ME TOO', SAID ALL THEM BOYS. 'THAT'S THE TRUTH, AL MILLER. WE'RE STAYING.'
THANKS TO ARMOR HERE, WE GOT NO STOCKADE AND WE GOT NO U.S. ARMY FORT CLOSER THAN CARTHAGE CITY. IF WE FIGHT RIGHT NOW, WE MIGHT LOSE EVERYTHING AND EVERYBODY. SO LET'S HOLD OFF THE REDS AS BEST WE CAN AND SEND FOR HELP. SEND A DOZEN MEN DOWN TO CARTHAGE CITY AND BEG BILL HARRISON TO SEND US UP AN ARMY, AND MAYBE EVEN BRING HIS CANNON IF HE CAN. MY TWO BOYS ARE GONE, AND A THOUSAND REDS FOR EACH OF MY SONS WON'T BE ENOUGH OF GETTING EVEN FOR ME!
THE DOZEN RIDERS SET ON THEIR WAY SOUTH FIRST THING THE NEXT MORNING. THEY LEFT FROM THE COMMONS, WHICH WAS CROWDED WITH WAGONS AS MORE AND MORE FAMILIES FROM OUTLYING FARMS CAME IN TO TOWN TO PUT UP WITH CLOSE FRIENDS AND KINFOLK.
BUT AL MILLER WASN'T THERE TO SEE THEM OFF. YESTERDAY HIS WORDS SET THEM ALL IN MOTION, BUT THAT WAS ALL THE LEADERSHIP THEY'D GET FROM HIM. HE DIDN'T WANT TO BE IN CHARGE. HE JUST WANTED HIS BOYS BACK.

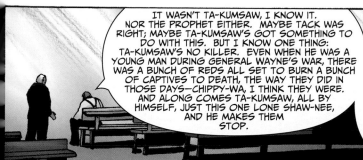

IT WASN'T TA-KUMSAW, I KNOW IT. NOR THE PROPHET EITHER. MAYBE TACK WAS RIGHT; MAYBE TA-KUMSAW'S GOT SOMETHING TO DO WITH THIS. BUT I KNOW ONE THING: TA-KUMSAW'S NO KILLER. EVEN WHEN HE WAS A YOUNG MAN DURING GENERAL WAYNE'S WAR, THERE WAS A BUNCH OF REDS ALL SET TO BURN A BUNCH OF CAPTIVES TO DEATH, THE WAY THEY DID IN THOSE DAYS—CHIPPY-WA, I THINK THEY WERE. AND ALONG COMES TA-KUMSAW, ALL BY HIMSELF, JUST THIS ONE LONE SHAW-NEE, AND HE MAKES THEM STOP.

"WE WANT THE WHITE MAN TO RESPECT US, TO TREAT US AS A NATION," HE SAYS TO THEM. "WHITE MAN WON'T RESPECT US IF WE ACT LIKE THIS! WE GOT TO BE CIVILIZED. NO SCALPS, NO TORTURE, NO BURNING, NO KILLING CAPTIVES." THAT'S WHAT HE SAYS TO THEM. HE'S STUCK TO THAT EVER SINCE. HE KILLS IN BATTLE, YES, BUT IN ALL HIS RAIDS DOWN SOUTH HE DIDN'T KILL ONE SOUL. DO YOU REALIZE THAT? IF TA-KUMSAW'S GOT THEM BOYS, THEY'RE AS SAFE AS IF THEIR MAMA HAD THEM HOME IN BED.

I KNOW THESE REDS BETTER THAN ANYBODY. SO THEY CALL ME "RED-LOVER" AND DON'T LISTEN TO A WORD I SAY. NO MATTER WHAT HE DOES, HE'LL BE A HERO. THEY'LL MAKE HIM GOVERNOR FOR REAL THEN. HECK, THEY'LL PROBABLY MAKE HIM PRESIDENT, IF WOBBISH EVER JOINS THE U.S.A.

I DON'T KNOW THIS HARRISON. HE CAN'T BE THE DEVIL YOU MAKE HIM OUT TO BE.

SOMETIMES, REVEREND, I THINK YOU ARE AS TRUSTING AS A LITTLE CHILD.

WHICH IS HOW THE LORD TOLD US TO BE, ARMOR-OF-GOD. BE PATIENT. ALL THINGS WILL WORK OUT AS THE LORD INTENDS.

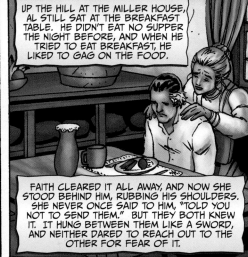

UP THE HILL AT THE MILLER HOUSE, AL STILL SAT AT THE BREAKFAST TABLE. HE DIDN'T EAT NO SUPPER THE NIGHT BEFORE, AND WHEN HE TRIED TO EAT BREAKFAST, HE LIKED TO GAG ON THE FOOD.

FAITH CLEARED IT ALL AWAY, AND NOW SHE STOOD BEHIND HIM, RUBBING HIS SHOULDERS. SHE NEVER ONCE SAID TO HIM, "TOLD YOU NOT TO SEND THEM." BUT THEY BOTH KNEW IT. IT HUNG BETWEEN THEM LIKE A SWORD, AND NEITHER DARED TO REACH OUT TO THE OTHER FOR FEAR OF IT.

THE SILENCE BROKE WHEN WASTENOT CAME IN, A RIFLE OVER HIS SHOULDER.

SINCE WHEN DID YOU LEARN TO USE THAT THING?

ME AND WANTNOT BEEN PRACTICING.

AND YOU'RE GOING TO KILL REDS WITH IT?

I SURE HOPE SO.

AND WHEN ALL THE REDS ARE DEAD, AND YOU PILE ALL THEIR BODIES TOGETHER, WILL MEASURE AND ALVIN SOMEHOW WRIGGLE OUT OF THAT PILE AND COME ON HOME TO ME?

WASTENOT SHOOK HIS HEAD.

LAST NIGHT SOME RED WENT HOME TO HIS FAMILY, ALL PROUD BECAUSE HE KILLED HIM SOME WHITE BOYS YESTERDAY.

HER VOICE CAUGHT WHEN SHE SAID IT, BUT SHE WENT ON ALL THE SAME, 'CAUSE WHEN FAITH MILLER HAD AUGHT TO SAY, IT GOT SAID.

AND MAYBE HIS WIFE OR HIS MAMA PATTED HIM AND KISSED HIM AND MADE HIM SUPPER. BUT DON'T YOU EVER WALK THROUGH THAT DOOR AND TELL ME YOU KILLED A RED MAN. 'CAUSE YOU WON'T GET NO SUPPER, BOY, AND YOU WON'T GET NO KISS, AND YOU WON'T GET NO PAT, AND NO WORD, AND NO HOME, AND NO MAMA. YOU HEAR ME?

YOU THINK WHAT YOU LIKE, MAMA, BUT THIS IS WAR, AND I AM GOING TO KILL ME SOME REDS, AND I'M GOING TO COME BACK HOME, AND I'M GOING TO OWN UP TO IT, PROUD AS CAN BE.

AND IF THAT MEANS YOU DON'T WANNA BE MY MAMA NO MORE, THEN YOU MAY AS WELL STOP BEING MY MAMA NOW, AND NOT WAIT TILL I COME BACK.

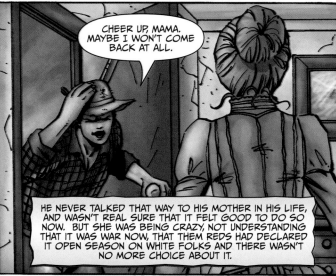

CHEER UP, MAMA. MAYBE I WON'T COME BACK AT ALL.

HE NEVER TALKED THAT WAY TO HIS MOTHER IN HIS LIFE, AND WASN'T REAL SURE THAT IT FELT GOOD TO DO SO NOW. BUT SHE WAS BEING CRAZY, NOT UNDERSTANDING THAT IT WAS WAR NOW, THAT THEM REDS HAD DECLARED IT OPEN SEASON ON WHITE FOLKS AND THERE WASN'T NO MORE CHOICE ABOUT IT.

WHAT BOTHERED HIM MOST, THOUGH, AS HE GOT ON HIS HORSE AND RODE OUT TO DAVID'S PLACE, WAS THAT HE COULDN'T EXACTLY BE SURE, BUT HE THOUGHT, HE JUST SUSPECTED ANYWAY, THAT PAPA WAS CRYING. IF THAT DIDN'T BEAT ALL. YESTERDAY PAPA WAS SO HOT AGAINST THE REDS, AND NOW MAMA TALKED AGAINST FIGHTING, AND PAPA JUST SAT THERE AND CRIED.

MAYBE IT WAS GETTING OLD THAT MADE PAPA LIKE THAT. BUT THAT WASN'T WASTENOT'S BUSINESS, NOT NOW.

MAYBE PAPA AND MAMA DIDN'T WANT TO KILL THEM AS TOOK THEIR SONS—BUT WASTENOT KNEW WHAT HE WAS GOING TO DO TO THEM AS TOOK HIS BROTHERS.

SLAM!

THEIR BLOOD WAS HIS BLOOD, AND WHOEVER SHED HIS BLOOD WAS GOING TO SHED SOME OF THEIR OWN TOO, A GALLON FOR EVERY DROP.

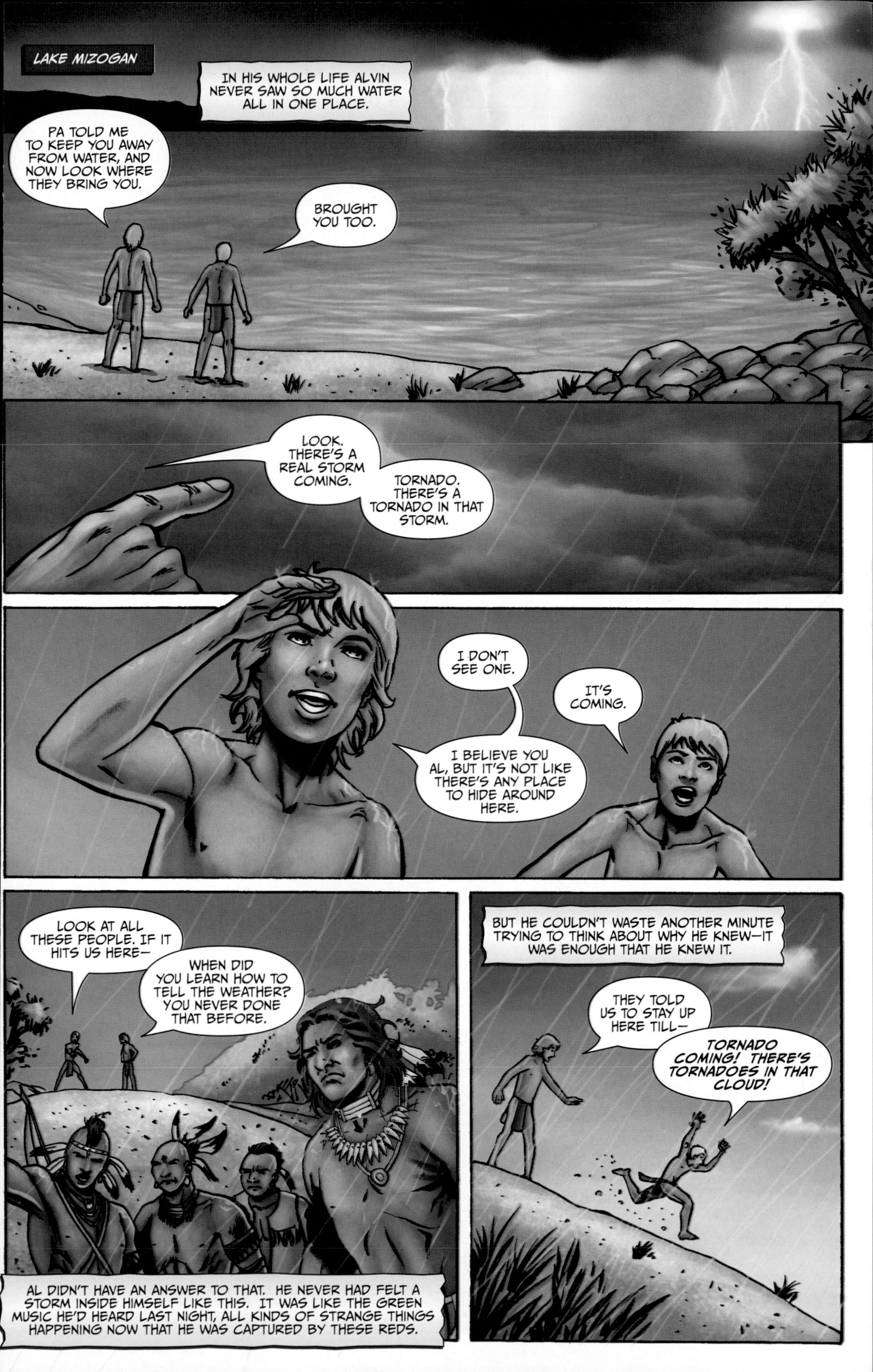

LAKE MIZOGAN
IN HIS WHOLE LIFE ALVIN NEVER SAW SO MUCH WATER ALL IN ONE PLACE.
PA TOLD ME TO KEEP YOU AWAY FROM WATER, AND NOW LOOK WHERE THEY BRING YOU.
BROUGHT YOU TOO.
LOOK. THERE'S A REAL STORM COMING.
TORNADO. THERE'S A TORNADO IN THAT STORM.
I DON'T SEE ONE.
IT'S COMING.
I BELIEVE YOU AL, BUT IT'S NOT LIKE THERE'S ANY PLACE TO HIDE AROUND HERE.
LOOK AT ALL THESE PEOPLE. IF IT HITS US HERE—
WHEN DID YOU LEARN HOW TO TELL THE WEATHER? YOU NEVER DONE THAT BEFORE.
AL DIDN'T HAVE AN ANSWER TO THAT. HE NEVER HAD FELT A STORM INSIDE HIMSELF LIKE THIS. IT WAS LIKE THE GREEN MUSIC HE'D HEARD LAST NIGHT, ALL KINDS OF STRANGE THINGS HAPPENING NOW THAT HE WAS CAPTURED BY THESE REDS.
BUT HE COULDN'T WASTE ANOTHER MINUTE TRYING TO THINK ABOUT WHY HE KNEW—IT WAS ENOUGH THAT HE KNEW IT.
THEY TOLD US TO STAY UP HERE TILL—
TORNADO COMING! THERE'S TORNADOES IN THAT CLOUD!

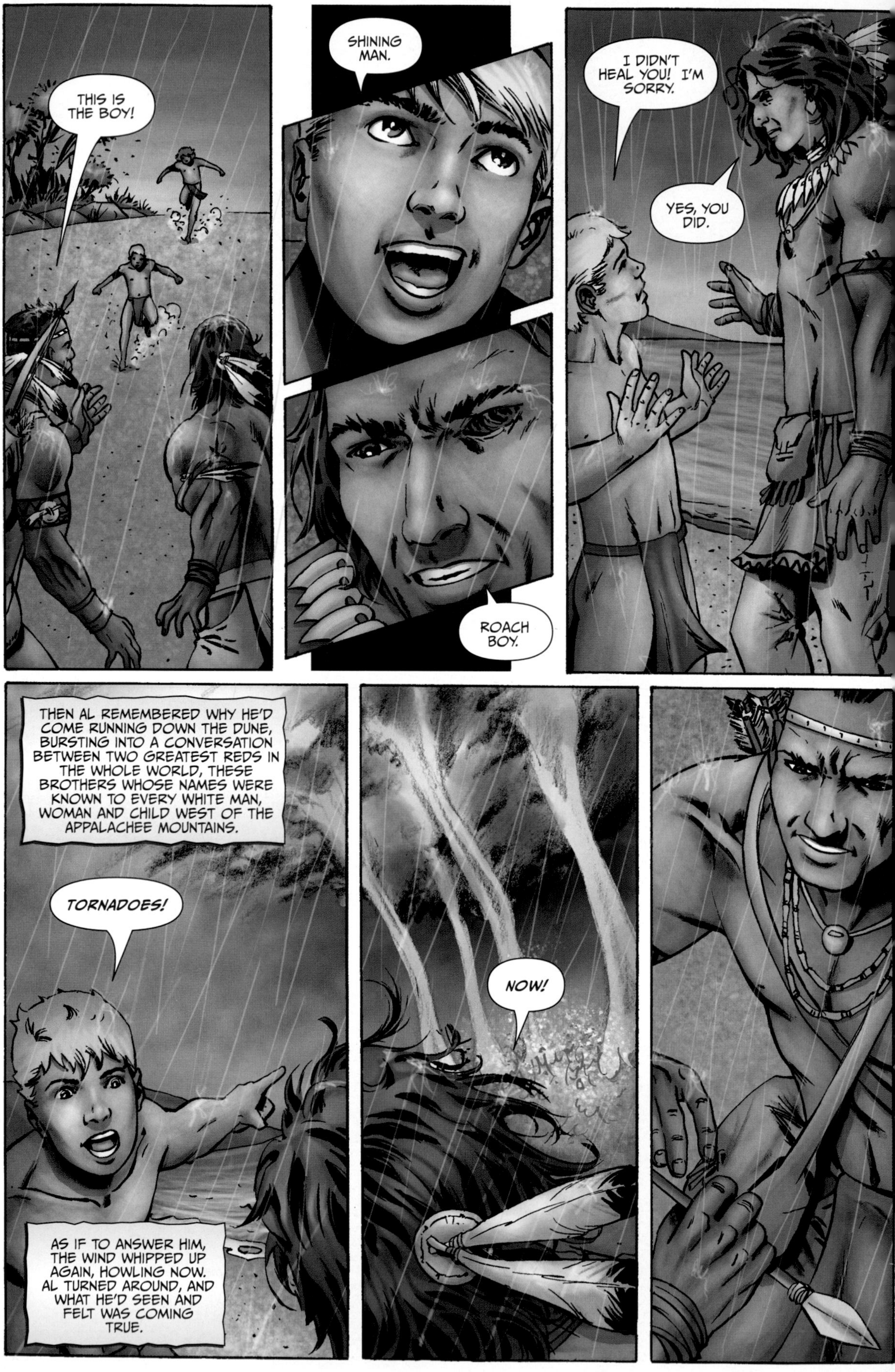
THIS IS THE BOY!
SHINING MAN.
ROACH BOY.
I DIDN'T HEAL YOU! I'M SORRY.
YES, YOU DID.
THEN AL REMEMBERED WHY HE'D COME RUNNING DOWN THE DUNE, BURSTING INTO A CONVERSATION BETWEEN TWO GREATEST REDS IN THE WHOLE WORLD, THESE BROTHERS WHOSE NAMES WERE KNOWN TO EVERY WHITE MAN, WOMAN AND CHILD WEST OF THE APPALACHEE MOUNTAINS.
TORNADOES!
AS IF TO ANSWER HIM, THE WIND WHIPPED UP AGAIN, HOWLING NOW. AL TURNED AROUND, AND WHAT HE'D SEEN AND FELT WAS COMING TRUE.
NOW!

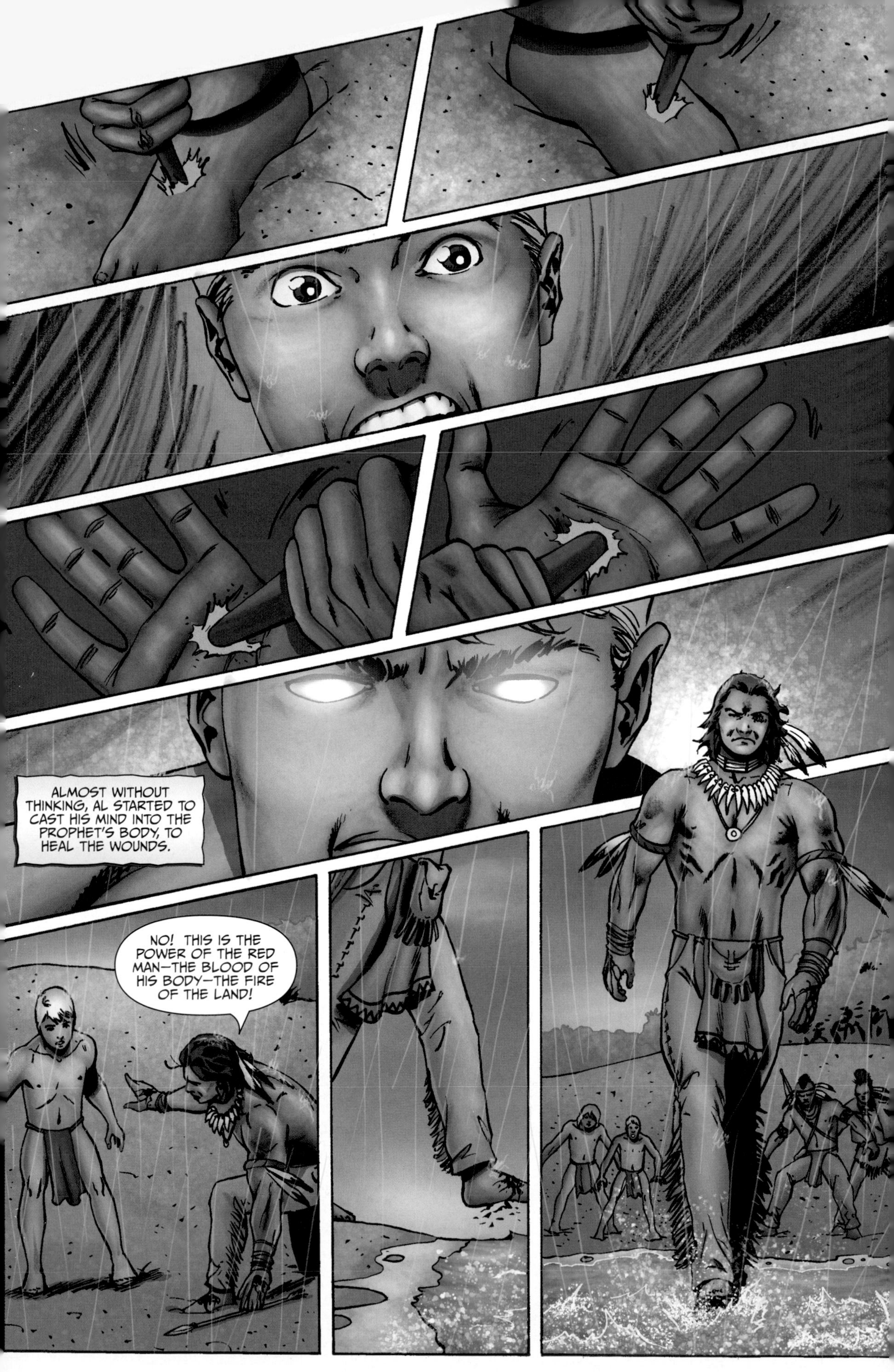
ALMOST WITHOUT THINKING, AL STARTED TO CAST HIS MIND INTO THE PROPHET'S BODY, TO HEAL THE WOUNDS.
NO! THIS IS THE POWER OF THE RED MAN—THE BLOOD OF HIS BODY—THE FIRE OF THE LAND!

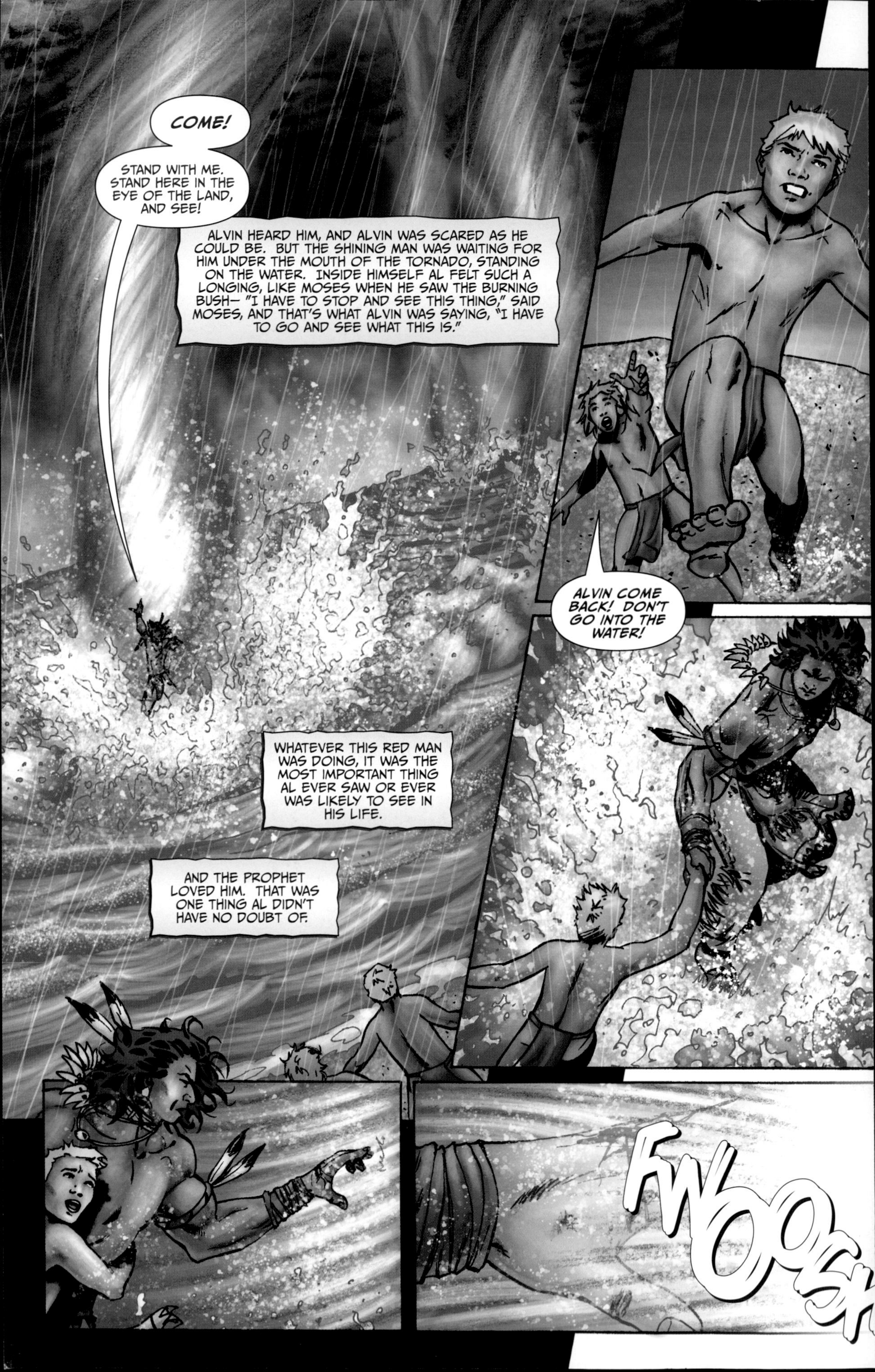
COME!
STAND WITH ME. STAND HERE IN THE EYE OF THE LAND, AND SEE!
ALVIN HEARD HIM, AND ALVIN WAS SCARED AS HE COULD BE. BUT THE SHINING MAN WAS WAITING FOR HIM UNDER THE MOUTH OF THE TORNADO, STANDING ON THE WATER. INSIDE HIMSELF AL FELT SUCH A LONGING, LIKE MOSES WHEN HE SAW THE BURNING BUSH– "I HAVE TO STOP AND SEE THIS THING," SAID MOSES, AND THAT'S WHAT ALVIN WAS SAYING, "I HAVE TO GO AND SEE WHAT THIS IS."
WHATEVER THIS RED MAN WAS DOING, IT WAS THE MOST IMPORTANT THING AL EVER SAW OR EVER WAS LIKELY TO SEE IN HIS LIFE.
AND THE PROPHET LOVED HIM. THAT WAS ONE THING AL DIDN'T HAVE NO DOUBT OF.
ALVIN COME BACK! DON'T GO INTO THE WATER!
FWOOSH

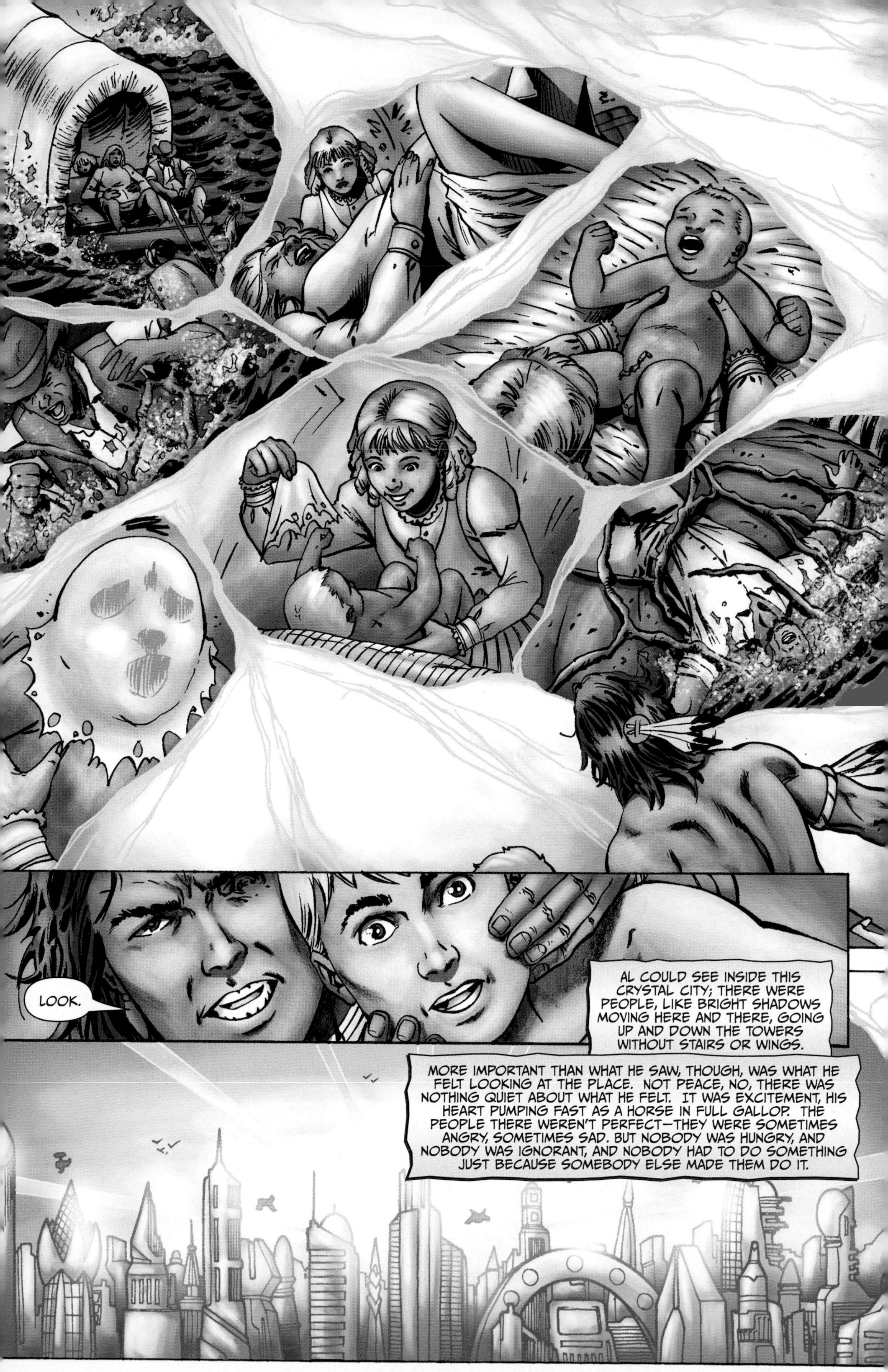
LOOK.
AL COULD SEE INSIDE THIS CRYSTAL CITY; THERE WERE PEOPLE, LIKE BRIGHT SHADOWS MOVING HERE AND THERE, GOING UP AND DOWN THE TOWERS WITHOUT STAIRS OR WINGS.
MORE IMPORTANT THAN WHAT HE SAW, THOUGH, WAS WHAT HE FELT LOOKING AT THE PLACE. NOT PEACE, NO, THERE WAS NOTHING QUIET ABOUT WHAT HE FELT. IT WAS EXCITEMENT, HIS HEART PUMPING FAST AS A HORSE IN FULL GALLOP. THE PEOPLE THERE WEREN'T PERFECT—THEY WERE SOMETIMES ANGRY, SOMETIMES SAD. BUT NOBODY WAS HUNGRY, AND NOBODY WAS IGNORANT, AND NOBODY HAD TO DO SOMETHING JUST BECAUSE SOMEBODY ELSE MADE THEM DO IT.

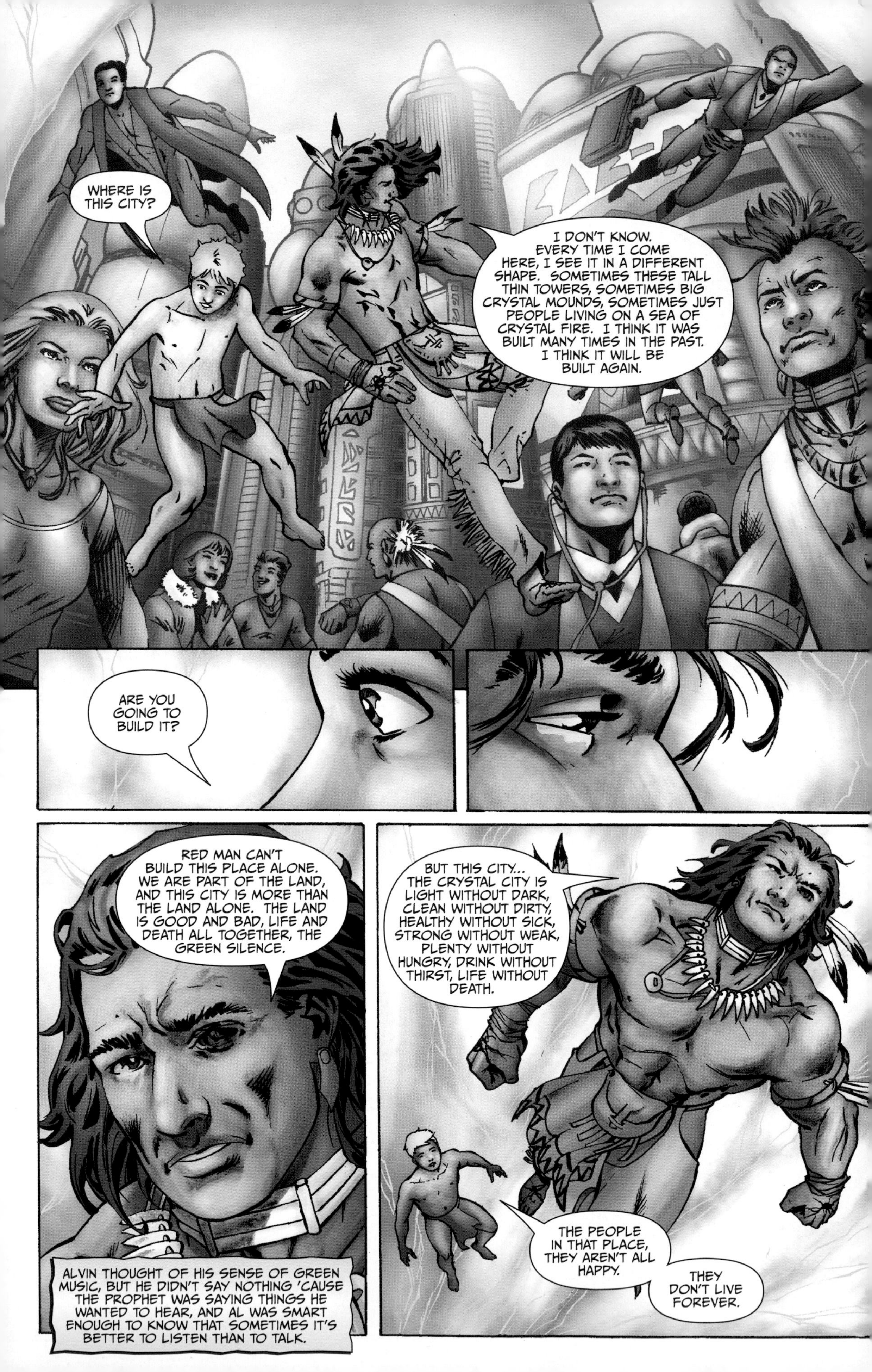
WHERE IS THIS CITY?
I DON'T KNOW. EVERY TIME I COME HERE, I SEE IT IN A DIFFERENT SHAPE. SOMETIMES THESE TALL THIN TOWERS, SOMETIMES BIG CRYSTAL MOUNDS, SOMETIMES JUST PEOPLE LIVING ON A SEA OF CRYSTAL FIRE. I THINK IT WAS BUILT MANY TIMES IN THE PAST. I THINK IT WILL BE BUILT AGAIN.
ARE YOU GOING TO BUILD IT?
RED MAN CAN'T BUILD THIS PLACE ALONE. WE ARE PART OF THE LAND, AND THIS CITY IS MORE THAN THE LAND ALONE. THE LAND IS GOOD AND BAD, LIFE AND DEATH ALL TOGETHER, THE GREEN SILENCE.
ALVIN THOUGHT OF HIS SENSE OF GREEN MUSIC, BUT HE DIDN'T SAY NOTHING 'CAUSE THE PROPHET WAS SAYING THINGS HE WANTED TO HEAR, AND AL WAS SMART ENOUGH TO KNOW THAT SOMETIMES IT'S BETTER TO LISTEN THAN TO TALK.
BUT THIS CITY... THE CRYSTAL CITY IS LIGHT WITHOUT DARK, CLEAN WITHOUT DIRTY, HEALTHY WITHOUT SICK, STRONG WITHOUT WEAK, PLENTY WITHOUT HUNGRY, DRINK WITHOUT THIRST, LIFE WITHOUT DEATH.
THE PEOPLE IN THAT PLACE, THEY AREN'T ALL HAPPY.
THEY DON'T LIVE FOREVER.

AH, YOU DON'T SEE THE SAME THAT I SEE.

WHAT I SEE IS, THEY'RE BUILDING IT, AND AT THE OTHER END IT'S FALLING DOWN.

AH, THE CITY I SEE WILL NEVER FALL.

WELL, WHAT'S THE DIFFERENCE? HOW COME WE DON'T SEE THE SAME THING?

I DON'T KNOW, ROACH BOY. I NEVER SHOWED THIS TO ANYBODY. NOW GO BACK DOWN. WAIT FOR ME BELOW. I HAVE THINGS TO SEE BEFORE TIME STARTS AGAIN.

JUST THINKING ABOUT GOING DOWN MADE ALVIN START TO SINK, UNTIL HE WAS CLEAR TO THE BOTTOM, ON THE SHINY CLEAR FLOOR.

FLOOR? IT COULD HAVE BEEN THE CEILING FOR ALL HE KNOWED. THERE WAS LIGHT COMING UP FROM THERE JUST LIKE IT WAS SHINING THROUGH THE OTHER WALLS, AND HE SAW PICTURES THERE TOO.

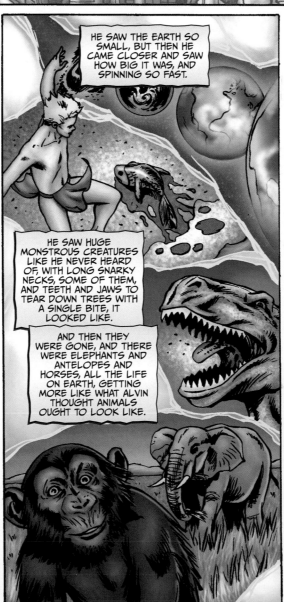

HE SAW THE EARTH SO SMALL, BUT THEN HE CAME CLOSER AND SAW HOW BIG IT WAS, AND SPINNING SO FAST.

HE SAW HUGE MONSTROUS CREATURES LIKE HE NEVER HEARD OF, WITH LONG SNARKY NECKS, SOME OF THEM, AND TEETH AND JAWS TO TEAR DOWN TREES WITH A SINGLE BITE, IT LOOKED LIKE.

AND THEN THEY WERE GONE, AND THERE WERE ELEPHANTS AND ANTELOPES AND HORSES, ALL THE LIFE ON EARTH, GETTING MORE LIKE WHAT ALVIN THOUGHT ANIMALS OUGHT TO LOOK LIKE.

AND HE DID SEE SOME FOLKS, THOUGH HE WASN'T SURE AT FIRST 'CAUSE THEY WERE BLACK AND HE HADN'T SEEN BUT ONE BLACK MAN IN HIS LIFE, A SLAVE OWNED BY A PEDDLER FROM THE CROWN COLONIES, WHO HAPPENED TO COME THROUGH VIGOR CHURCH MAYBE TWO YEARS BACK.

BUT THEY LOOKED LIKE PEOPLE ALL RIGHT, BLACK OR NOT, AND THEY WERE PULLING FRUIT DOWN OUT OF THE TREES AND BERRIES OFF BUSHES, FEEDING EACH OTHER, A PASSEL OF PICKANINNIES FOLLOWING IN THEIR TRACKS.

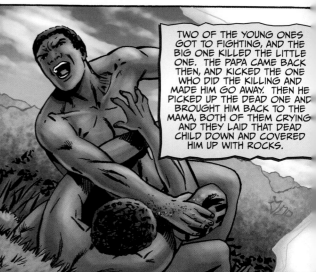

TWO OF THE YOUNG ONES GOT TO FIGHTING, AND THE BIG ONE KILLED THE LITTLE ONE. THE PAPA CAME BACK THEN, AND KICKED THE ONE WHO DID THE KILLING AND MADE HIM GO AWAY. THEN HE PICKED UP THE DEAD ONE AND BROUGHT HIM BACK TO THE MAMA, BOTH OF THEM CRYING AND THEY LAID THAT DEAD CHILD DOWN AND COVERED HIM UP WITH ROCKS.

THEN THEY JUST GATHERED UP THEIR FAMILY AND WALKED ON, AND AFTER JUST A FEW STEPS THEY WERE EATING AGAIN, AND THE TEARS STOPPED, AND THEY WENT ON, JUST WENT ON.

THESE ARE FOLKS, THAT'S SURE, THOUGHT ALVIN. THIS IS JUST THE WAY HUMAN PEOPLE ARE.

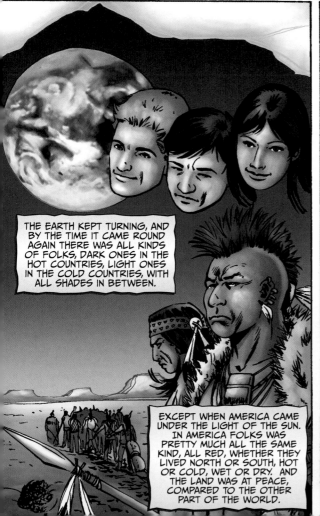

THE EARTH KEPT TURNING, AND BY THE TIME IT CAME ROUND AGAIN THERE WAS ALL KINDS OF FOLKS, DARK ONES IN THE HOT COUNTRIES, LIGHT ONES IN THE COLD COUNTRIES, WITH ALL SHADES IN BETWEEN.

EXCEPT WHEN AMERICA CAME UNDER THE LIGHT OF THE SUN. IN AMERICA FOLKS WAS PRETTY MUCH ALL THE SAME KIND, ALL RED, WHETHER THEY LIVED NORTH OR SOUTH, HOT OR COLD, WET OR DRY. AND THE LAND WAS AT PEACE, COMPARED TO THE OTHER PART OF THE WORLD.

IT WAS STRANGE FOR HIM TO SEE, BECAUSE WHEN THE BIG PART OF THE LAND CAME BY, WITH ALL ITS DIFFERENT RACES AND NATIONS, IT CHANGED WITH EVERY SWEEP OF THE EARTH. WHOLE COUNTRIES MOVED FROM ONE PLACE TO ANOTHER, EVERYTHING ALWAYS SHUFFLING AROUND, AND WARS EVERY MINUTE, EVERYWHERE.

THE SMALLER LAND, AMERICA, IT HAD SOME WARS TOO, BUT IT WAS SLOWER, GENTLER. THE PEOPLE LIVED IN A DIFFERENT RHYTHM. THE LAND HAD ITS OWN HEARTBEAT, ITS OWN LIFE.

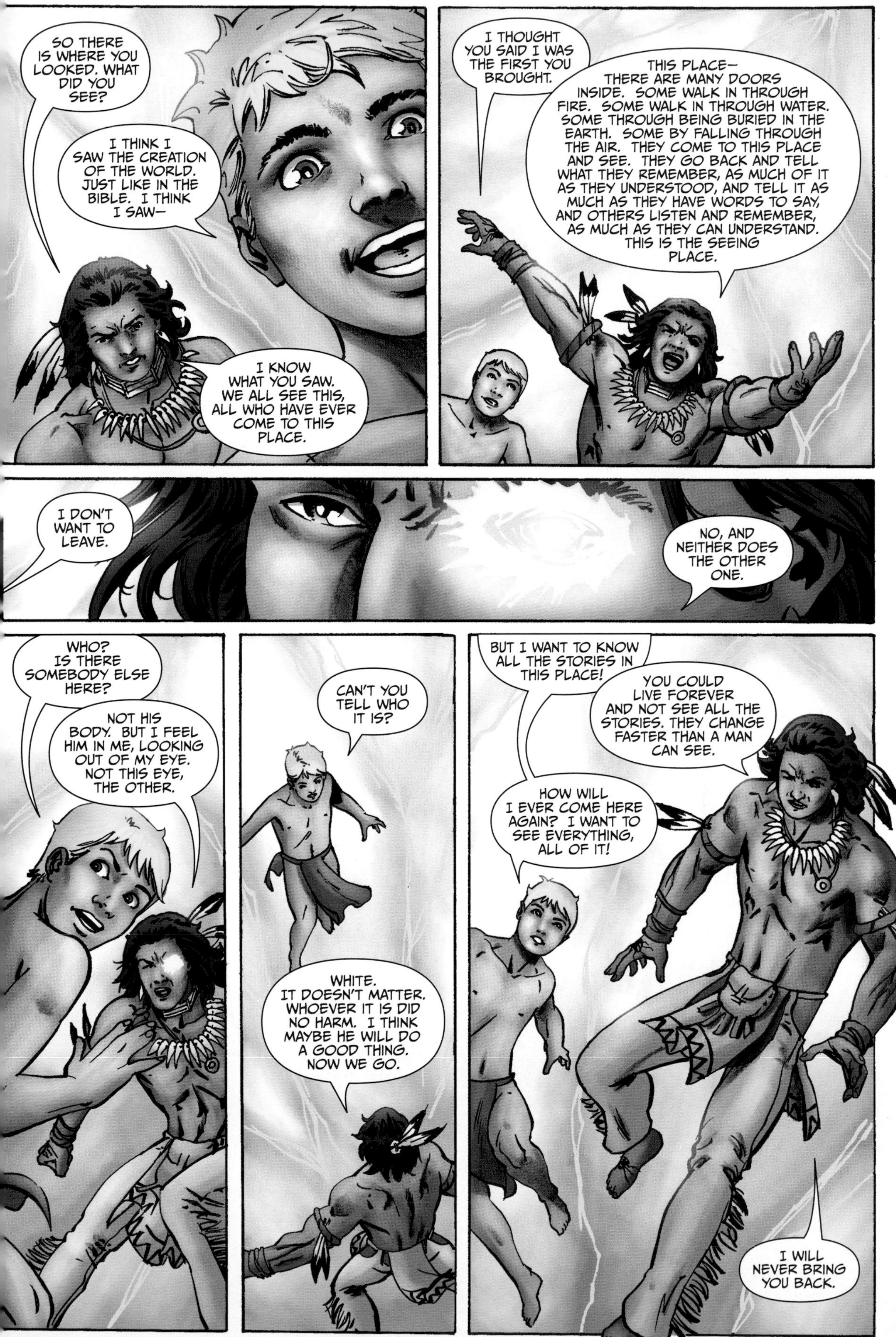
SO THERE IS WHERE YOU LOOKED. WHAT DID YOU SEE?
I THINK I SAW THE CREATION OF THE WORLD. JUST LIKE IN THE BIBLE. I THINK I SAW—
I KNOW WHAT YOU SAW. WE ALL SEE THIS, ALL WHO HAVE EVER COME TO THIS PLACE.
I THOUGHT YOU SAID I WAS THE FIRST YOU BROUGHT.
THIS PLACE— THERE ARE MANY DOORS INSIDE. SOME WALK IN THROUGH FIRE. SOME WALK IN THROUGH WATER. SOME THROUGH BEING BURIED IN THE EARTH. SOME BY FALLING THROUGH THE AIR. THEY COME TO THIS PLACE AND SEE. THEY GO BACK AND TELL WHAT THEY REMEMBER, AS MUCH OF IT AS THEY UNDERSTOOD, AND TELL IT AS MUCH AS THEY HAVE WORDS TO SAY, AND OTHERS LISTEN AND REMEMBER, AS MUCH AS THEY CAN UNDERSTAND. THIS IS THE SEEING PLACE.
I DON'T WANT TO LEAVE.
NO, AND NEITHER DOES THE OTHER ONE.
WHO? IS THERE SOMEBODY ELSE HERE?
NOT HIS BODY. BUT I FEEL HIM IN ME, LOOKING OUT OF MY EYE. NOT THIS EYE, THE OTHER.
CAN'T YOU TELL WHO IT IS?
WHITE. IT DOESN'T MATTER. WHOEVER IT IS DID NO HARM. I THINK MAYBE HE WILL DO A GOOD THING. NOW WE GO.
BUT I WANT TO KNOW ALL THE STORIES IN THIS PLACE!
YOU COULD LIVE FOREVER AND NOT SEE ALL THE STORIES. THEY CHANGE FASTER THAN A MAN CAN SEE.
HOW WILL I EVER COME HERE AGAIN? I WANT TO SEE EVERYTHING, ALL OF IT!
I WILL NEVER BRING YOU BACK.

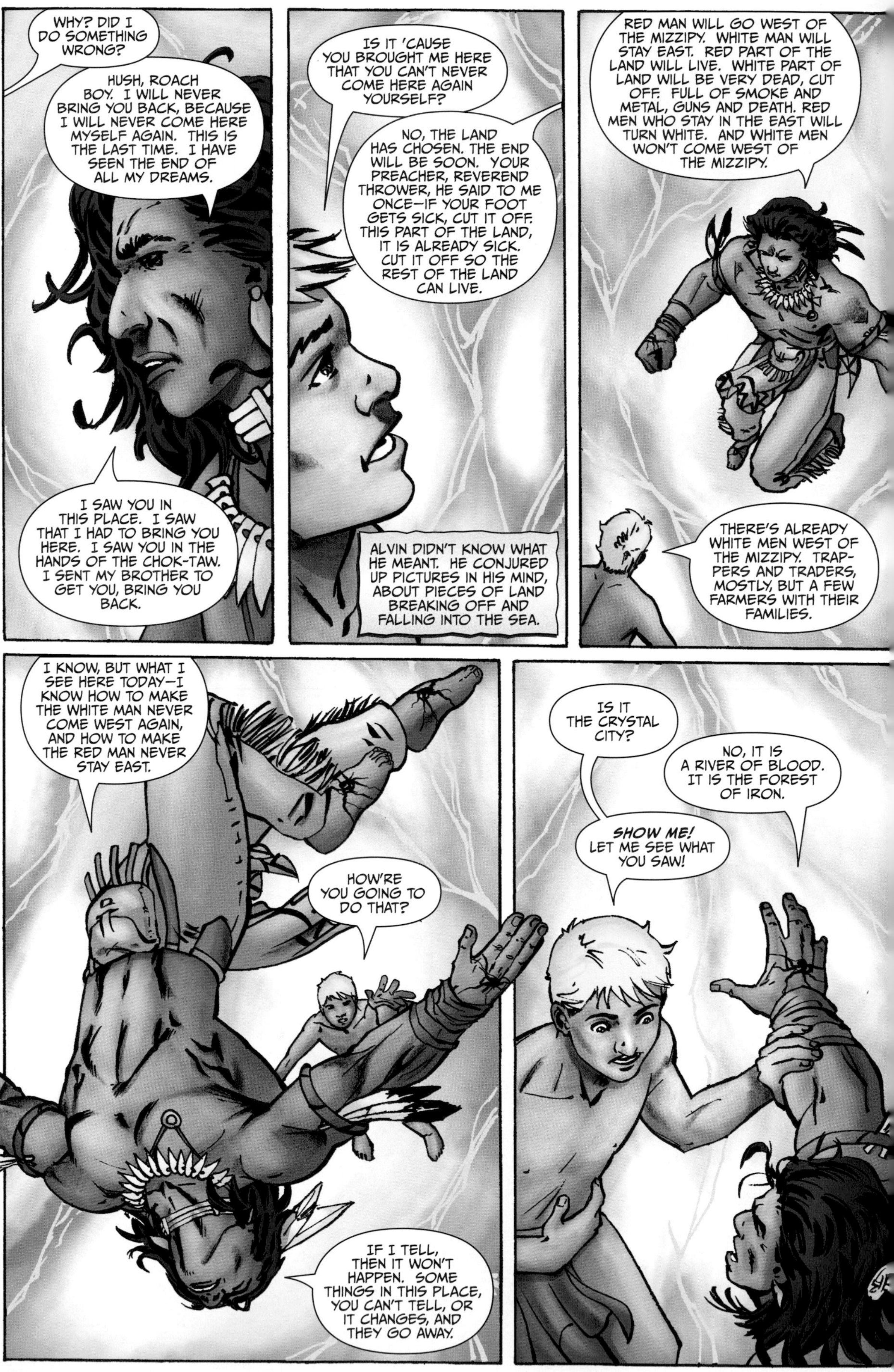
WHY? DID I DO SOMETHING WRONG?
HUSH, ROACH BOY. I WILL NEVER BRING YOU BACK, BECAUSE I WILL NEVER COME HERE MYSELF AGAIN. THIS IS THE LAST TIME. I HAVE SEEN THE END OF ALL MY DREAMS.
I SAW YOU IN THIS PLACE. I SAW THAT I HAD TO BRING YOU HERE. I SAW YOU IN THE HANDS OF THE CHOK-TAW. I SENT MY BROTHER TO GET YOU, BRING YOU BACK.
IS IT 'CAUSE YOU BROUGHT ME HERE THAT YOU CAN'T NEVER COME HERE AGAIN YOURSELF?
NO, THE LAND HAS CHOSEN. THE END WILL BE SOON. YOUR PREACHER, REVEREND THROWER, HE SAID TO ME ONCE—IF YOUR FOOT GETS SICK, CUT IT OFF. THIS PART OF THE LAND, IT IS ALREADY SICK. CUT IT OFF SO THE REST OF THE LAND CAN LIVE.
ALVIN DIDN'T KNOW WHAT HE MEANT. HE CONJURED UP PICTURES IN HIS MIND, ABOUT PIECES OF LAND BREAKING OFF AND FALLING INTO THE SEA.
RED MAN WILL GO WEST OF THE MIZZIPY. WHITE MAN WILL STAY EAST. RED PART OF THE LAND WILL LIVE. WHITE PART OF LAND WILL BE VERY DEAD, CUT OFF. FULL OF SMOKE AND METAL, GUNS AND DEATH. RED MEN WHO STAY IN THE EAST WILL TURN WHITE. AND WHITE MEN WON'T COME WEST OF THE MIZZIPY.
THERE'S ALREADY WHITE MEN WEST OF THE MIZZIPY. TRAPPERS AND TRADERS, MOSTLY, BUT A FEW FARMERS WITH THEIR FAMILIES.
I KNOW, BUT WHAT I SEE HERE TODAY—I KNOW HOW TO MAKE THE WHITE MAN NEVER COME WEST AGAIN, AND HOW TO MAKE THE RED MAN NEVER STAY EAST.
HOW'RE YOU GOING TO DO THAT?
IF I TELL, THEN IT WON'T HAPPEN. SOME THINGS IN THIS PLACE, YOU CAN'T TELL, OR IT CHANGES, AND THEY GO AWAY.
IS IT THE CRYSTAL CITY?
NO, IT IS A RIVER OF BLOOD. IT IS THE FOREST OF IRON.
SHOW ME! LET ME SEE WHAT YOU SAW!

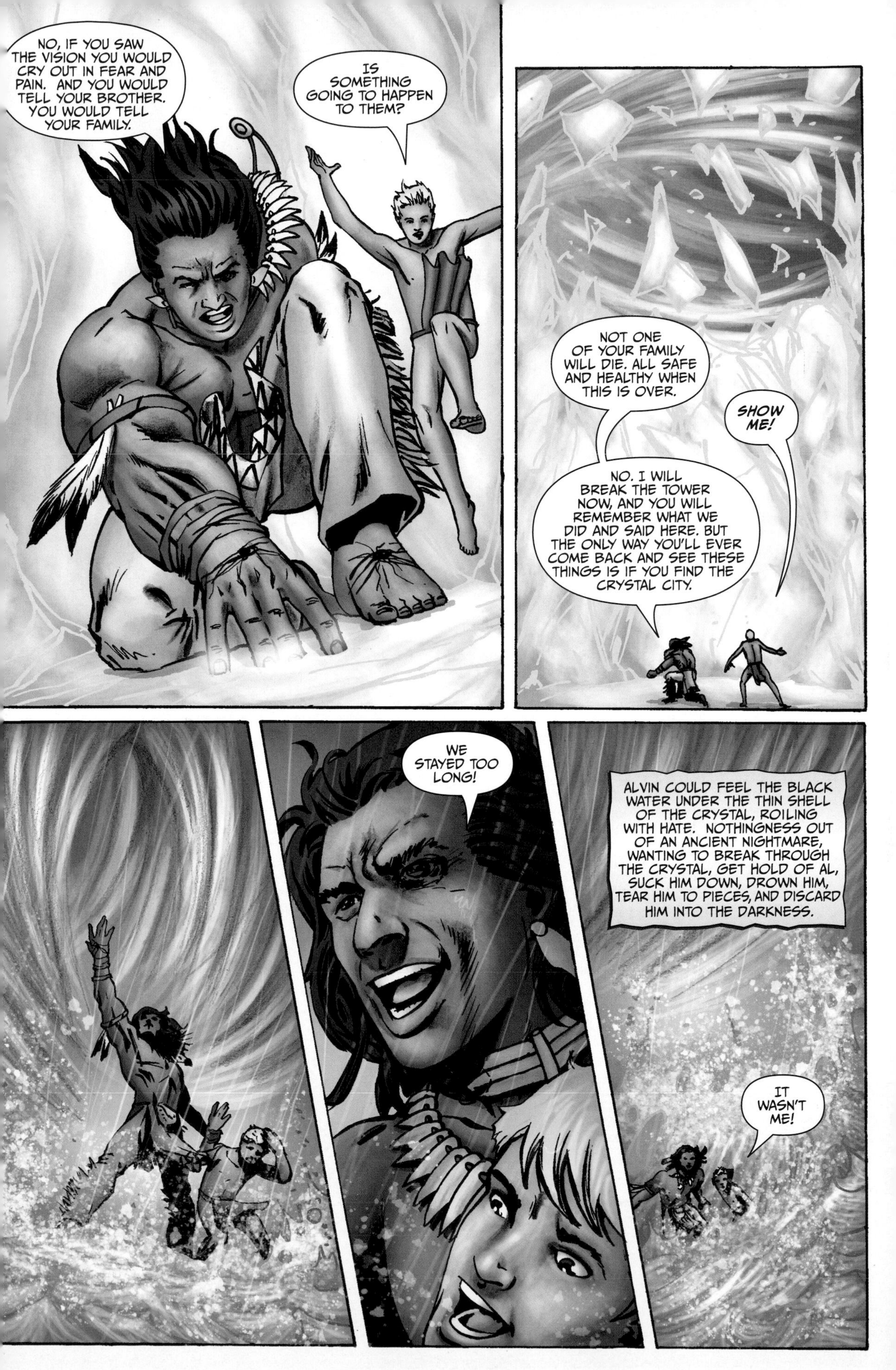
NO, IF YOU SAW THE VISION YOU WOULD CRY OUT IN FEAR AND PAIN. AND YOU WOULD TELL YOUR BROTHER. YOU WOULD TELL YOUR FAMILY.
IS SOMETHING GOING TO HAPPEN TO THEM?
NOT ONE OF YOUR FAMILY WILL DIE. ALL SAFE AND HEALTHY WHEN THIS IS OVER.
SHOW ME!
NO. I WILL BREAK THE TOWER NOW, AND YOU WILL REMEMBER WHAT WE DID AND SAID HERE. BUT THE ONLY WAY YOU'LL EVER COME BACK AND SEE THESE THINGS IS IF YOU FIND THE CRYSTAL CITY.
WE STAYED TOO LONG!
ALVIN COULD FEEL THE BLACK WATER UNDER THE THIN SHELL OF THE CRYSTAL, ROILING WITH HATE. NOTHINGNESS OUT OF AN ANCIENT NIGHTMARE, WANTING TO BREAK THROUGH THE CRYSTAL, GET HOLD OF AL, SUCK HIM DOWN, DROWN HIM, TEAR HIM TO PIECES, AND DISCARD HIM INTO THE DARKNESS.
IT WASN'T ME!

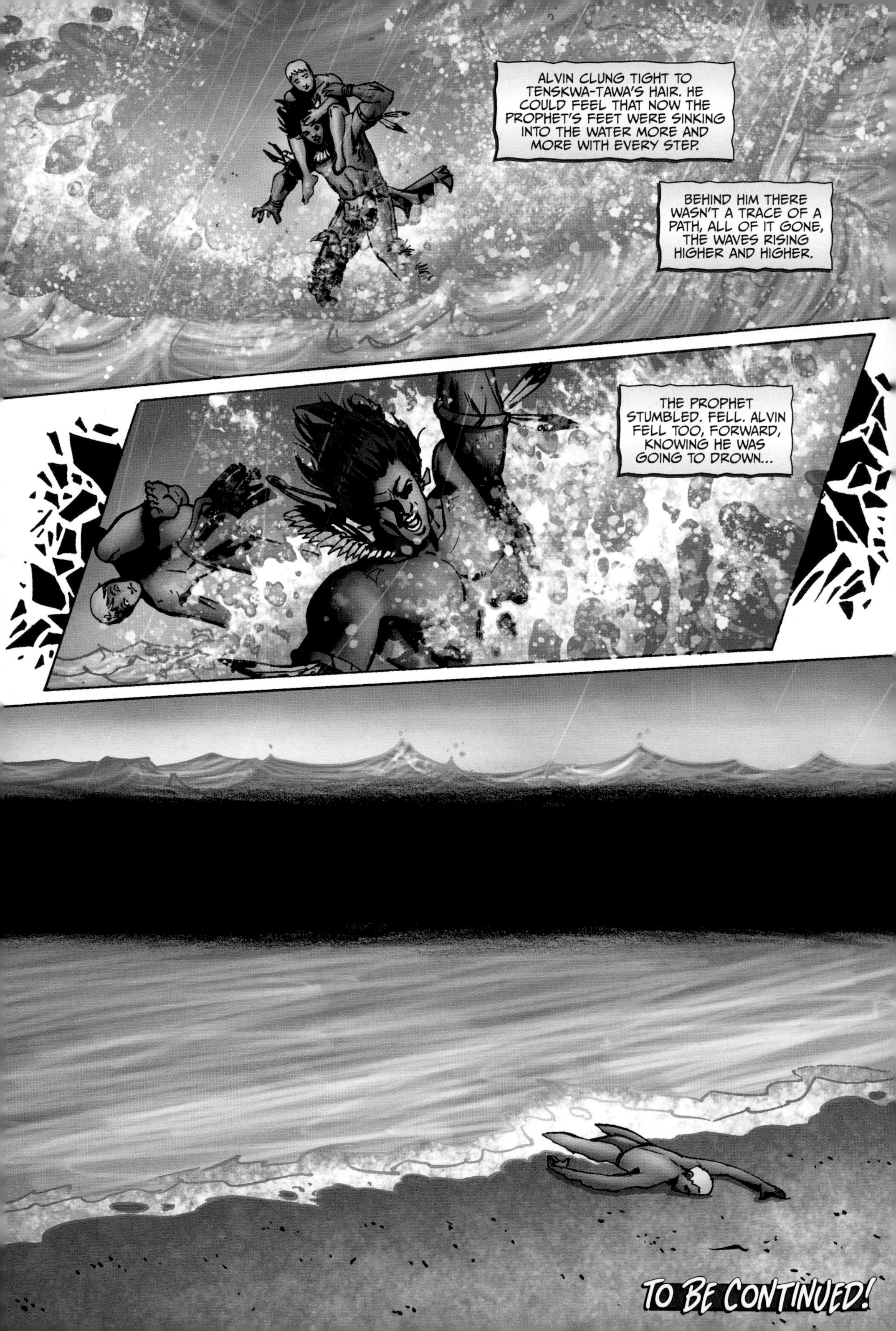
ALVIN CLUNG TIGHT TO TENSKWA-TAWA'S HAIR. HE COULD FEEL THAT NOW THE PROPHET'S FEET WERE SINKING INTO THE WATER MORE AND MORE WITH EVERY STEP.
BEHIND HIM THERE WASN'T A TRACE OF A PATH, ALL OF IT GONE, THE WAVES RISING HIGHER AND HIGHER.
THE PROPHET STUMBLED. FELL. ALVIN FELL TOO, FORWARD, KNOWING HE WAS GOING TO DROWN...
TO BE CONTINUED!

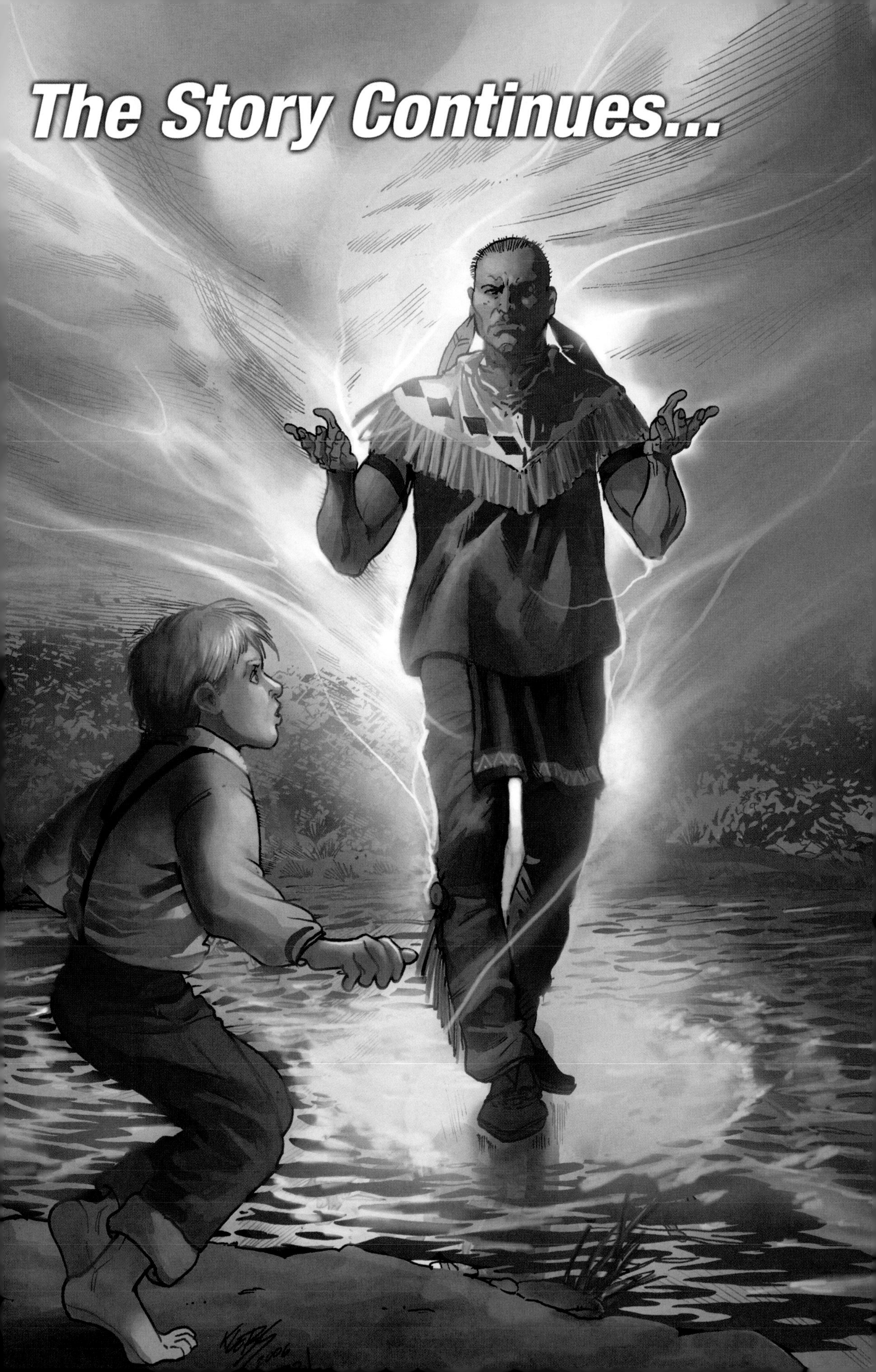
The Story Continues...

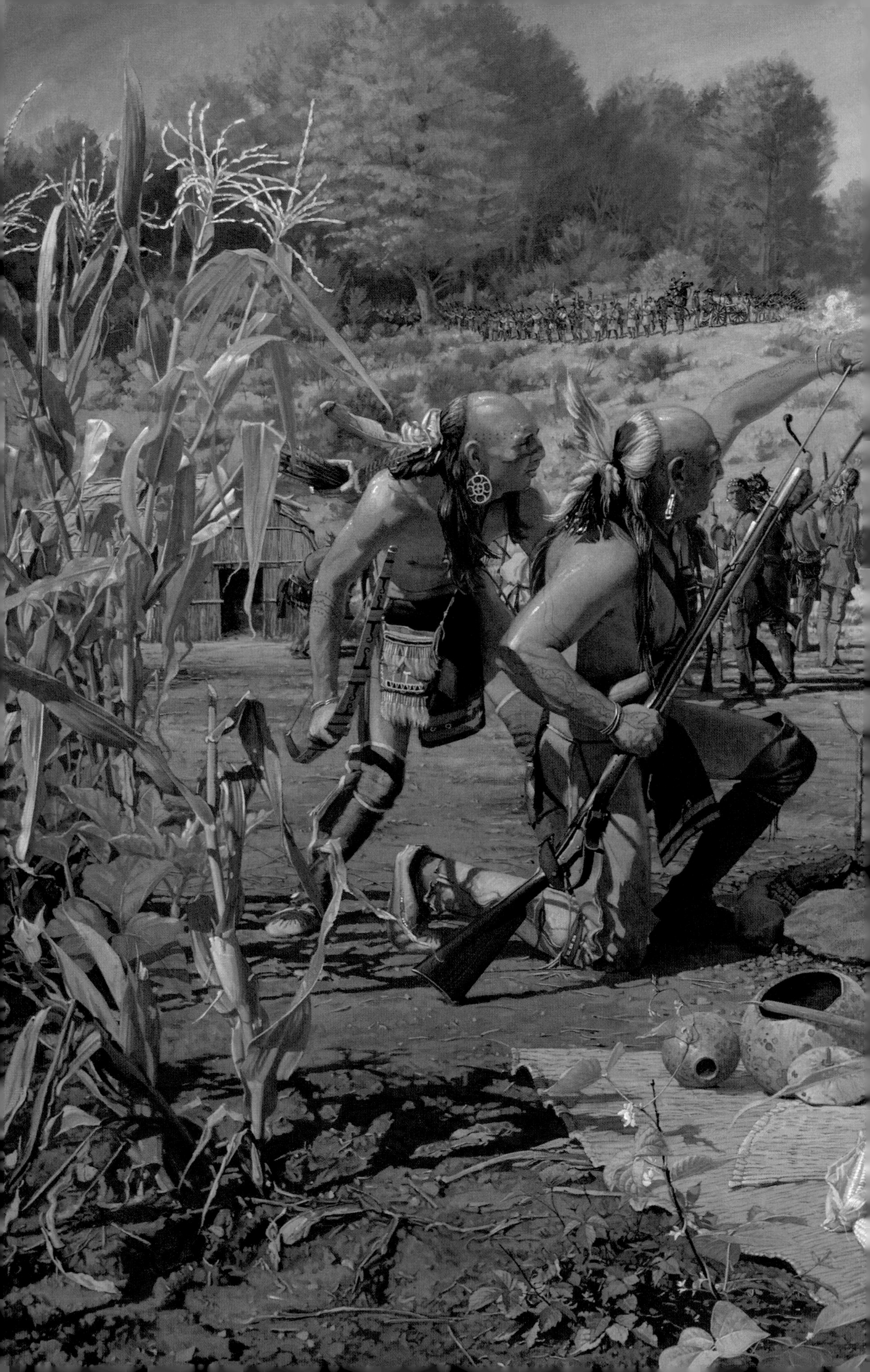

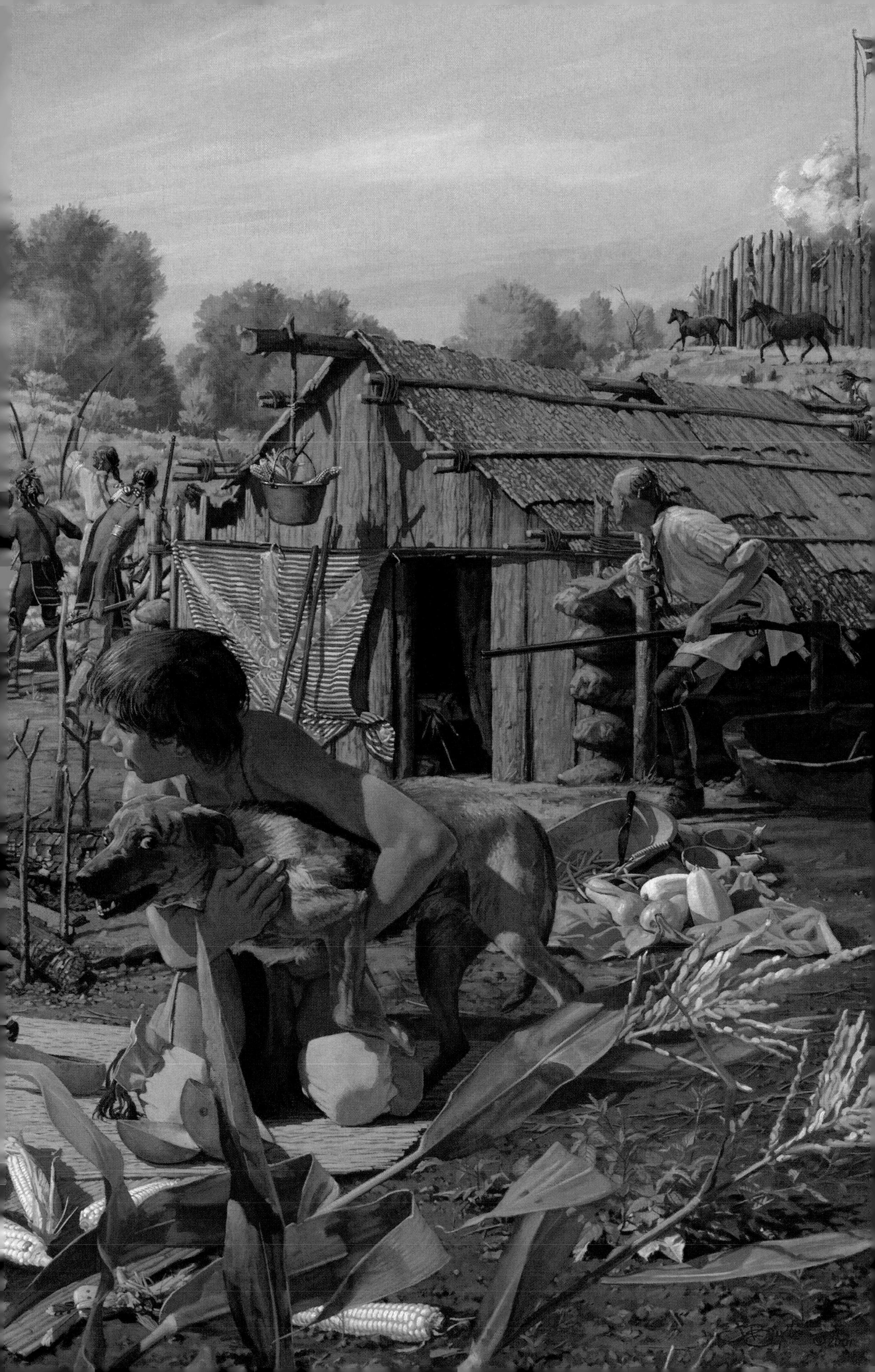

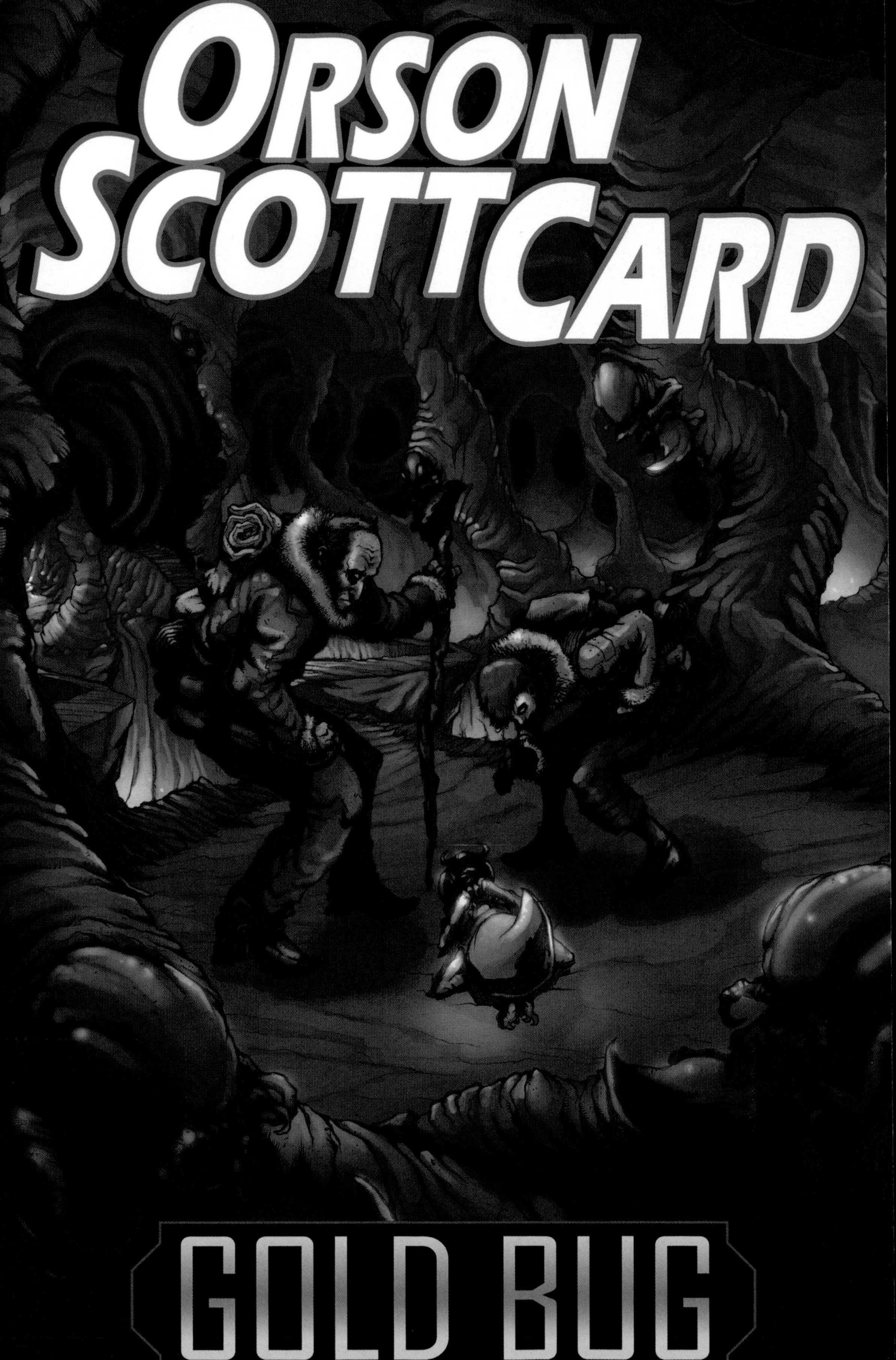
ORSON
SCOTT CARD
GOLD BUG

Decades ago, the Formics—a bug-like alien species—attacked Earth in an attempt to eradicate humanity. The nations of our world united together and sent fleets of military spaceships into the heart of the galaxy, striking back against this enemy. Fleet after fleet of spaceships were sent to the far reaches of known space, traveling for years at light speed, attacking the different Formic worlds.

Their mission: defeat the Formics and establish human colonies on the former Formic worlds. These armies depended on the guidance and leadership of a child named Ender Wiggin. The hope of humanity was a twelve-year-old boy who, though a brilliant military strategist, thought the war was nothing more than an elaborate game. Yet the soldiers loyally followed Ender and his squadron of youthful friends, looking to save mankind from the Formics, and to settle new worlds throughout the galaxy...

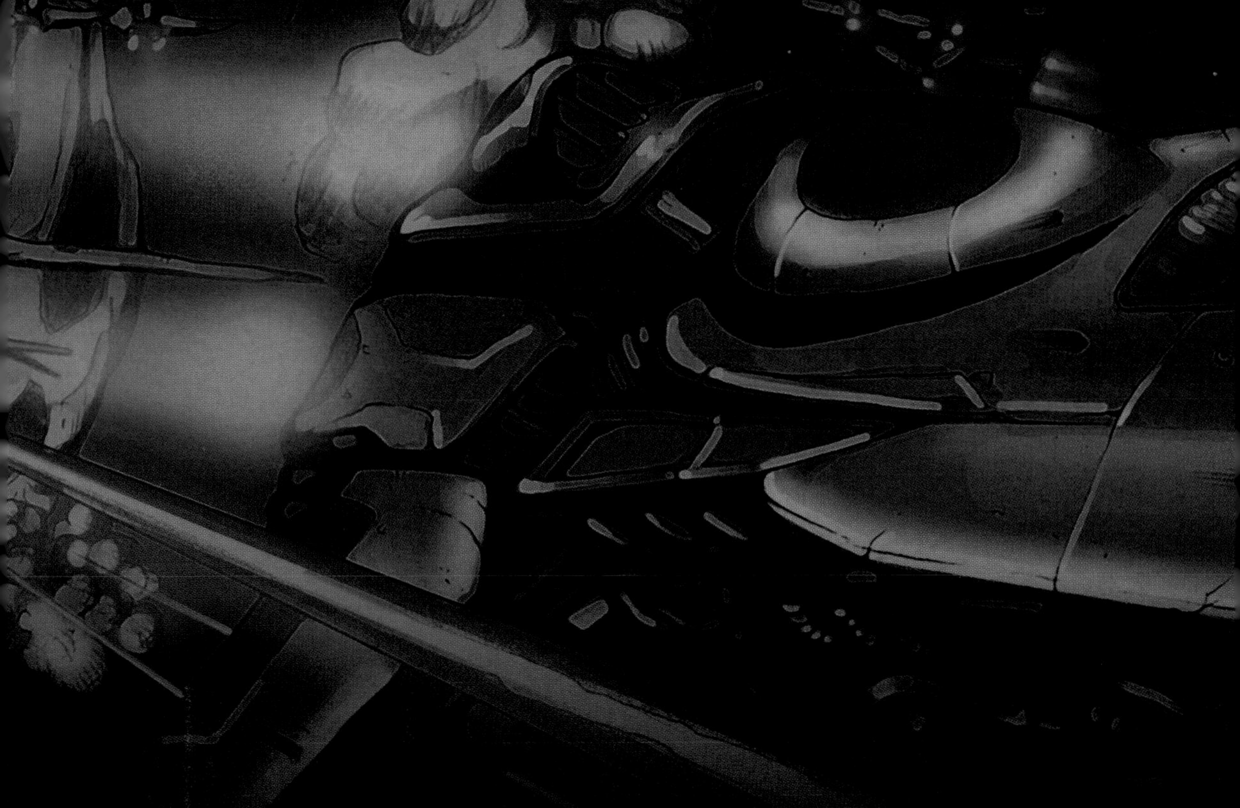

WRITER **ORSON SCOTT CARD**

ADAPTATION **JAKE BLACK** ARTWORK **JIN HAN**

COLORS **ROB RUFFOLO** LETTERS **SIMON BOWLAND**

EDITOR **MATT HANSEN**

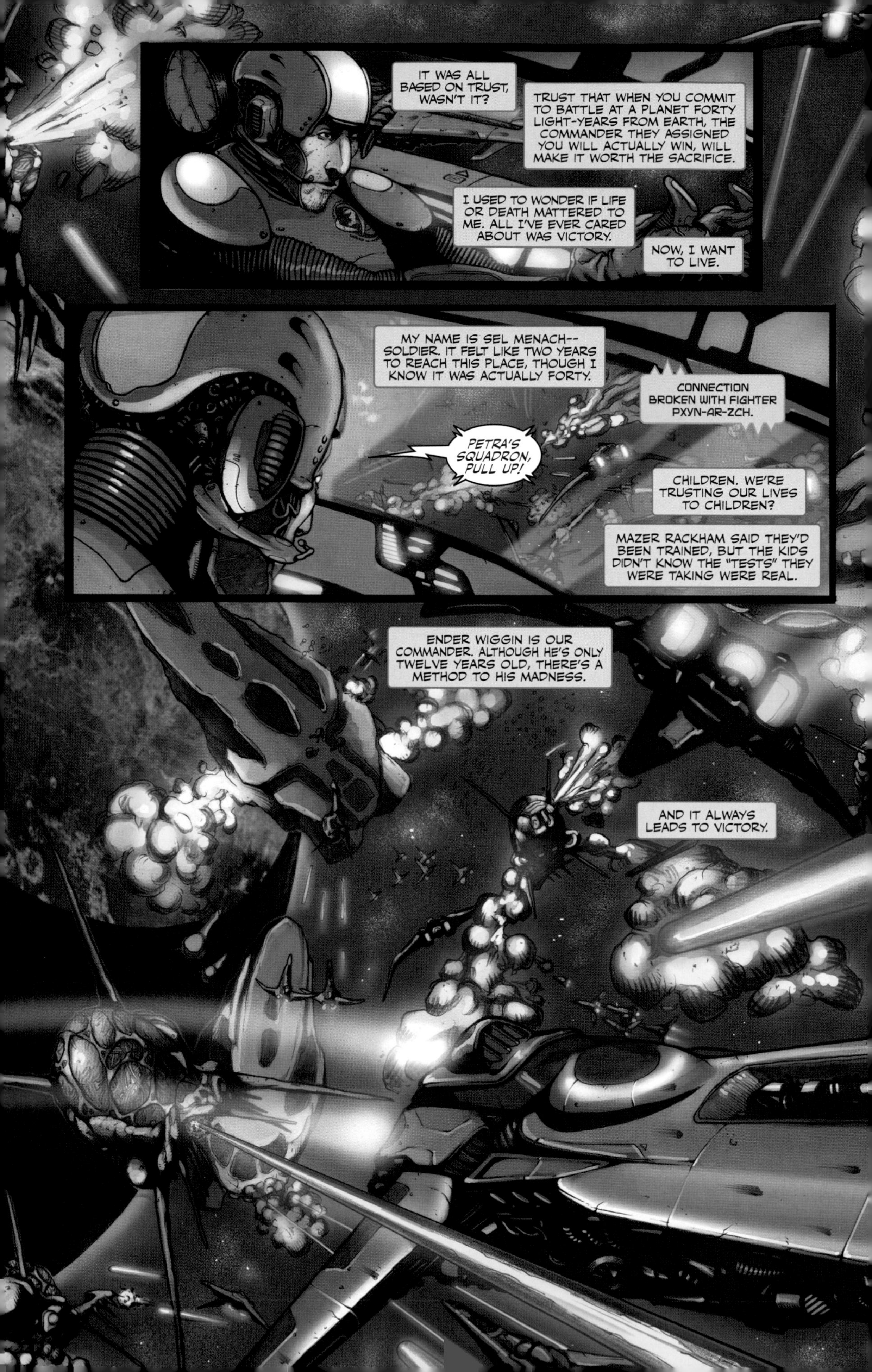
IT WAS ALL BASED ON TRUST, WASN'T IT?
TRUST THAT WHEN YOU COMMIT TO BATTLE AT A PLANET FORTY LIGHT-YEARS FROM EARTH, THE COMMANDER THEY ASSIGNED YOU WILL ACTUALLY WIN, WILL MAKE IT WORTH THE SACRIFICE.
I USED TO WONDER IF LIFE OR DEATH MATTERED TO ME. ALL I'VE EVER CARED ABOUT WAS VICTORY.
NOW, I WANT TO LIVE.
MY NAME IS SEL MENACH-- SOLDIER. IT FELT LIKE TWO YEARS TO REACH THIS PLACE, THOUGH I KNOW IT WAS ACTUALLY FORTY.
CONNECTION BROKEN WITH FIGHTER PXYN-AR-ZCH.
PETRA'S SQUADRON, PULL UP!
CHILDREN. WE'RE TRUSTING OUR LIVES TO CHILDREN?
MAZER RACKHAM SAID THEY'D BEEN TRAINED, BUT THE KIDS DIDN'T KNOW THE "TESTS" THEY WERE TAKING WERE REAL.
ENDER WIGGIN IS OUR COMMANDER. ALTHOUGH HE'S ONLY TWELVE YEARS OLD, THERE'S A METHOD TO HIS MADNESS.
AND IT ALWAYS LEADS TO VICTORY.

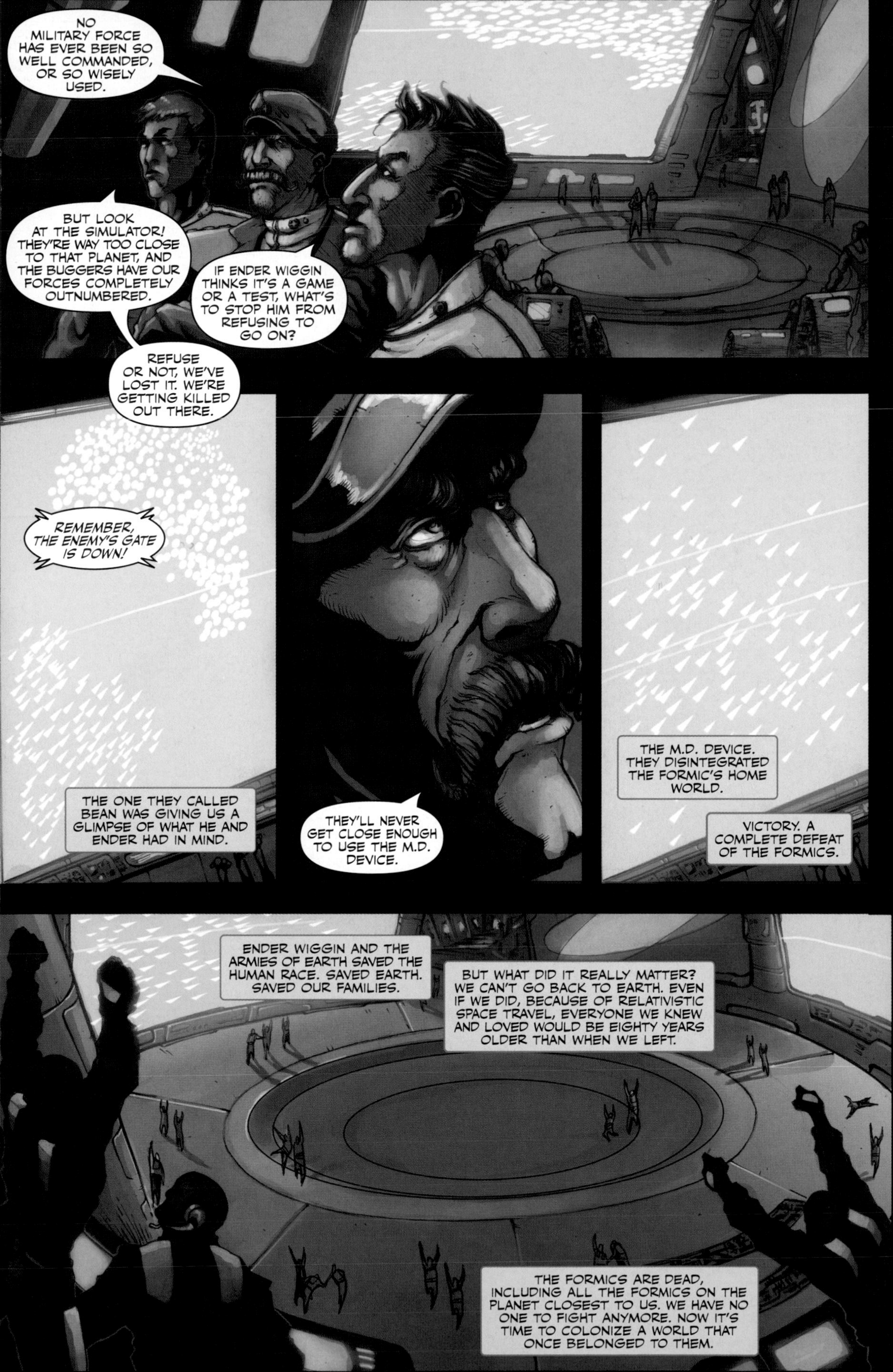
NO MILITARY FORCE HAS EVER BEEN SO WELL COMMANDED, OR SO WISELY USED.
BUT LOOK AT THE SIMULATOR! THEY'RE WAY TOO CLOSE TO THAT PLANET, AND THE BUGGERS HAVE OUR FORCES COMPLETELY OUTNUMBERED.
IF ENDER WIGGIN THINKS IT'S A GAME OR A TEST, WHAT'S TO STOP HIM FROM REFUSING TO GO ON?
REFUSE OR NOT, WE'VE LOST IT. WE'RE GETTING KILLED OUT THERE.
REMEMBER, THE ENEMY'S GATE IS DOWN!
THE ONE THEY CALLED BEAN WAS GIVING US A GLIMPSE OF WHAT HE AND ENDER HAD IN MIND.
THEY'LL NEVER GET CLOSE ENOUGH TO USE THE M.D. DEVICE.
THE M.D. DEVICE. THEY DISINTEGRATED THE FORMIC'S HOME WORLD.
VICTORY. A COMPLETE DEFEAT OF THE FORMICS.
ENDER WIGGIN AND THE ARMIES OF EARTH SAVED THE HUMAN RACE. SAVED EARTH. SAVED OUR FAMILIES.
BUT WHAT DID IT REALLY MATTER? WE CAN'T GO BACK TO EARTH. EVEN IF WE DID, BECAUSE OF RELATIVISTIC SPACE TRAVEL, EVERYONE WE KNEW AND LOVED WOULD BE EIGHTY YEARS OLDER THAN WHEN WE LEFT.
THE FORMICS ARE DEAD, INCLUDING ALL THE FORMICS ON THE PLANET CLOSEST TO US. WE HAVE NO ONE TO FIGHT ANYMORE. NOW IT'S TIME TO COLONIZE A WORLD THAT ONCE BELONGED TO THEM.

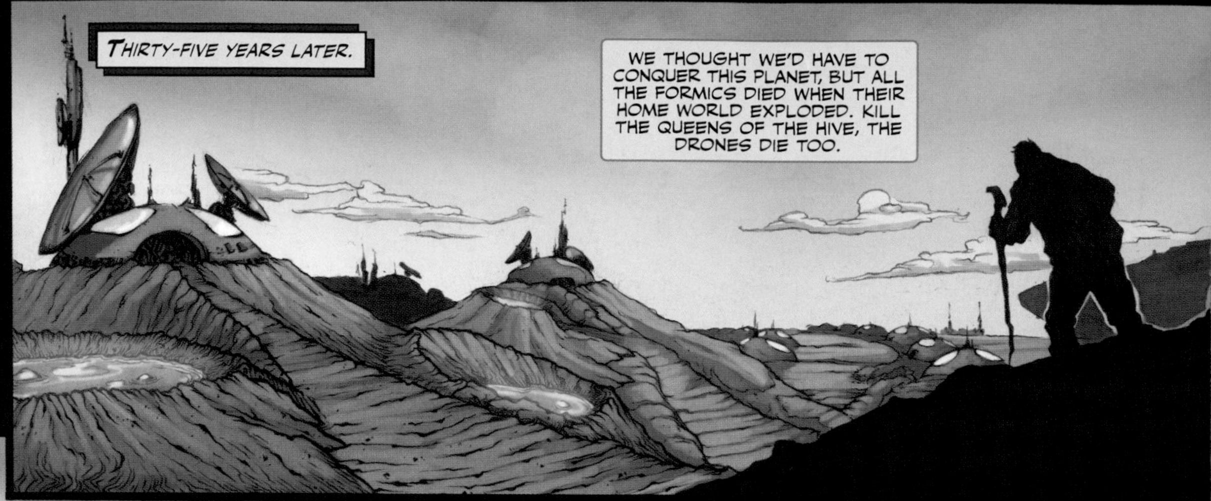
THIRTY-FIVE YEARS LATER.
WE THOUGHT WE'D HAVE TO CONQUER THIS PLANET, BUT ALL THE FORMICS DIED WHEN THEIR HOME WORLD EXPLODED. KILL THE QUEENS OF THE HIVE, THE DRONES DIE TOO.

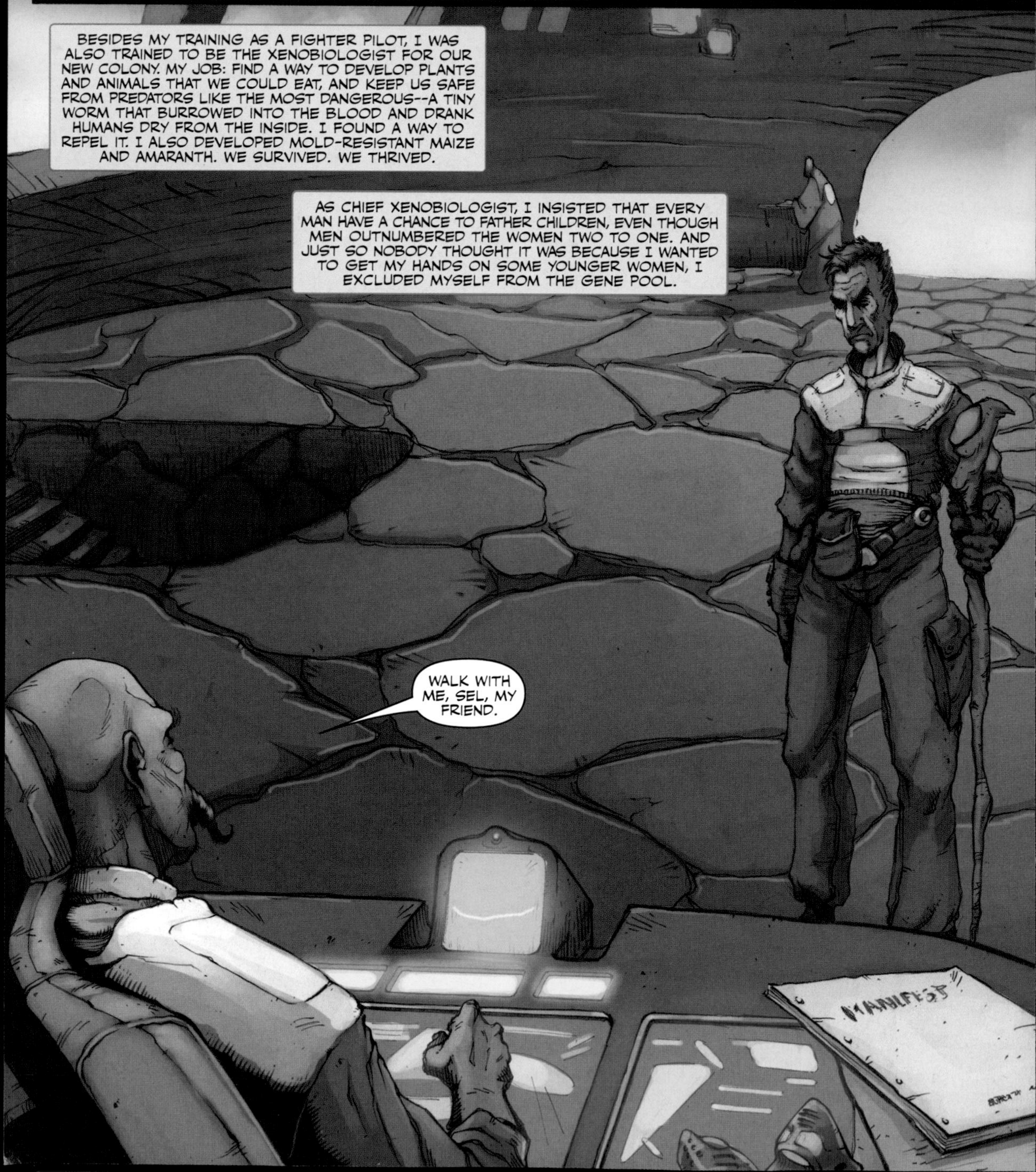
BESIDES MY TRAINING AS A FIGHTER PILOT, I WAS ALSO TRAINED TO BE THE XENOBIOLOGIST FOR OUR NEW COLONY. MY JOB: FIND A WAY TO DEVELOP PLANTS AND ANIMALS THAT WE COULD EAT, AND KEEP US SAFE FROM PREDATORS LIKE THE MOST DANGEROUS--A TINY WORM THAT BURROWED INTO THE BLOOD AND DRANK HUMANS DRY FROM THE INSIDE. I FOUND A WAY TO REPEL IT. I ALSO DEVELOPED MOLD-RESISTANT MAIZE AND AMARANTH. WE SURVIVED. WE THRIVED.
AS CHIEF XENOBIOLOGIST, I INSISTED THAT EVERY MAN HAVE A CHANCE TO FATHER CHILDREN, EVEN THOUGH MEN OUTNUMBERED THE WOMEN TWO TO ONE. AND JUST SO NOBODY THOUGHT IT WAS BECAUSE I WANTED TO GET MY HANDS ON SOME YOUNGER WOMEN, I EXCLUDED MYSELF FROM THE GENE POOL.
WALK WITH ME, SEL, MY FRIEND.

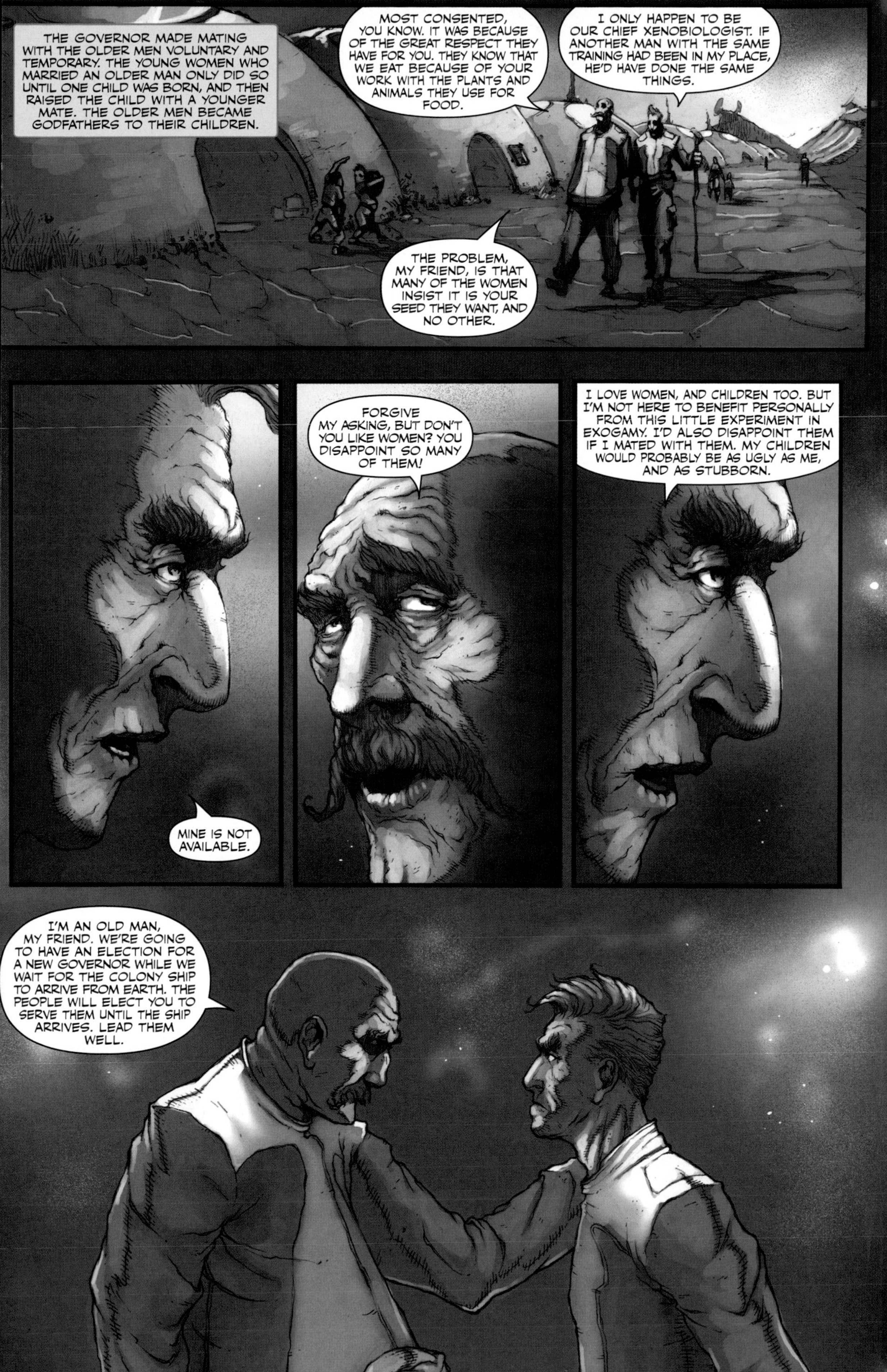
THE GOVERNOR MADE MATING WITH THE OLDER MEN VOLUNTARY AND TEMPORARY. THE YOUNG WOMEN WHO MARRIED AN OLDER MAN ONLY DID SO UNTIL ONE CHILD WAS BORN, AND THEN RAISED THE CHILD WITH A YOUNGER MATE. THE OLDER MEN BECAME GODFATHERS TO THEIR CHILDREN.
MOST CONSENTED, YOU KNOW. IT WAS BECAUSE OF THE GREAT RESPECT THEY HAVE FOR YOU. THEY KNOW THAT WE EAT BECAUSE OF YOUR WORK WITH THE PLANTS AND ANIMALS THEY USE FOR FOOD.
I ONLY HAPPEN TO BE OUR CHIEF XENOBIOLOGIST. IF ANOTHER MAN WITH THE SAME TRAINING HAD BEEN IN MY PLACE, HE'D HAVE DONE THE SAME THINGS.
THE PROBLEM, MY FRIEND, IS THAT MANY OF THE WOMEN INSIST IT IS YOUR SEED THEY WANT, AND NO OTHER.
MINE IS NOT AVAILABLE.
FORGIVE MY ASKING, BUT DON'T YOU LIKE WOMEN? YOU DISAPPOINT SO MANY OF THEM!
I LOVE WOMEN, AND CHILDREN TOO. BUT I'M NOT HERE TO BENEFIT PERSONALLY FROM THIS LITTLE EXPERIMENT IN EXOGAMY. I'D ALSO DISAPPOINT THEM IF I MATED WITH THEM. MY CHILDREN WOULD PROBABLY BE AS UGLY AS ME, AND AS STUBBORN.
I'M AN OLD MAN, MY FRIEND. WE'RE GOING TO HAVE AN ELECTION FOR A NEW GOVERNOR WHILE WE WAIT FOR THE COLONY SHIP TO ARRIVE FROM EARTH. THE PEOPLE WILL ELECT YOU TO SERVE THEM UNTIL THE SHIP ARRIVES. LEAD THEM WELL.

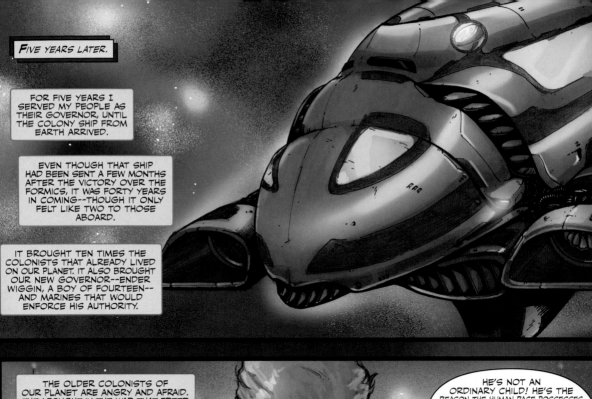

FIVE YEARS LATER.

FOR FIVE YEARS I SERVED MY PEOPLE AS THEIR GOVERNOR, UNTIL THE COLONY SHIP FROM EARTH ARRIVED.

EVEN THOUGH THAT SHIP HAD BEEN SENT A FEW MONTHS AFTER THE VICTORY OVER THE FORMICS, IT WAS FORTY YEARS IN COMING--THOUGH IT ONLY FELT LIKE TWO TO THOSE ABOARD.

IT BROUGHT TEN TIMES THE COLONISTS THAT ALREADY LIVED ON OUR PLANET. IT ALSO BROUGHT OUR NEW GOVERNOR--ENDER WIGGIN, A BOY OF FOURTEEN-- AND MARINES THAT WOULD ENFORCE HIS AUTHORITY.

THE OLDER COLONISTS OF OUR PLANET ARE ANGRY AND AFRAID. THEY FOUGHT IN THE WAR THAT FREED THIS PLANET AND SETTLED IT. IT'S THEIR HOME. AND YET THEY'RE ABOUT TO BE RULED BY A CHILD.

HE'S NOT AN ORDINARY CHILD! HE'S THE REASON THE HUMAN RACE POSSESSES THIS WORLD AND THE ENEMY DOES NOT. HE'S THE REASON HUMAN BEINGS ARE SPREADING THROUGHOUT THIS CORNER OF THE GALAXY, INSTEAD OF STRUGGLING TO SURVIVE IN THE BACK HILLS OF OUR OWN WORLD, HUNTED DOWN BY FORMICS.

BEFORE WE EVER LEFT ON THIS EXPEDITION, WE WERE TRAINED IN THE SKILLS AND SCIENCES THAT WOULD GIVE US THE BEST CHANCE OF SURVIVAL ON THIS PLANET. WE THOUGHT WE MIGHT HAVE TO FIGHT FOR EVERY INCH OF IT--THANKS TO ENDER WIGGIN'S VICTORY, WE DID NOT. BUT WE STILL STRUGGLED, AND WHY? WE'RE OLD NOW. WE WORKED SO HARD IN ORDER TO GIVE THIS COLONY TO OTHER PEOPLE, PEOPLE WE DIDN'T KNOW, PEOPLE WHO HADN'T BEEN BORN WHEN WE ARRIVED.

THAT'S WHAT CIVILIZATION IS. YOU LABOR ALL YOUR LIFE TO CREATE A GIFT, LARGE OR SMALL, WHICH YOU THEN HAND TO STRANGERS TO BUILD ON AND IMPROVE FOR GENERATIONS AFTER. SOME OF THEM MIGHT BE GENETICALLY RELATED TO US--MOST OF THEM WILL NOT. WE'VE BUILT SOMETHING FINE HERE, BUT WITH FAR LARGER NUMBERS, EACH OF OUR LITTLE COLONIES CAN NOW BECOME TOWNS.

WE CAN MAKE OF THIS A WORLD AS DIVERSE AND RICH AS EARTH. AND WE NEED THEIR GENES TO MAKE OUR FUTURE GENERATIONS COMPETITIVE WITH THE HUMANS BEING BORN ON EARTH. WE ARE BROTHERS AND SISTERS ON A PLANET WHERE THE LIFEFORMS HAVE NO KINSHIP WITH US AT ALL.

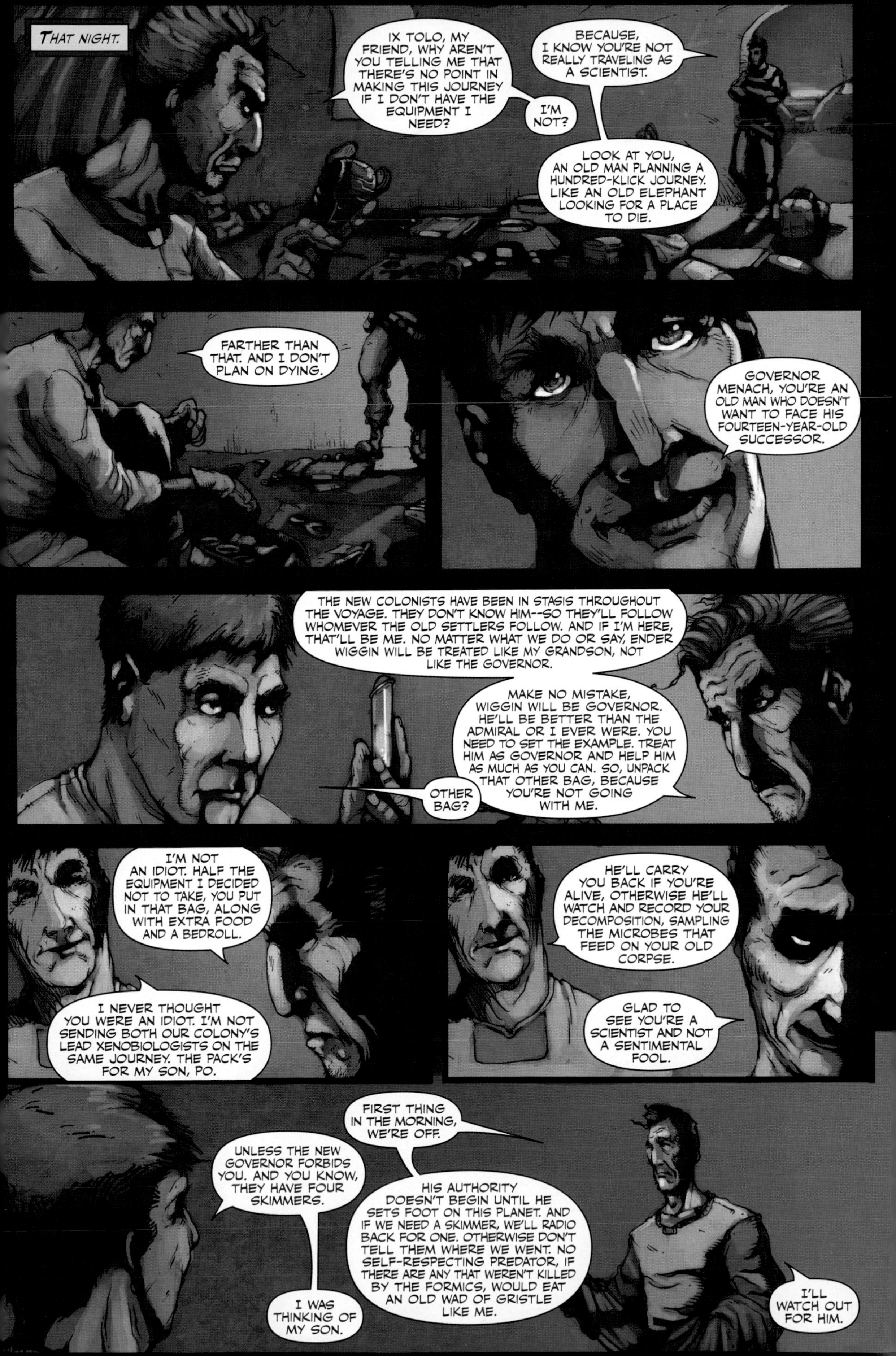
THAT NIGHT.
IX TOLO, MY FRIEND, WHY AREN'T YOU TELLING ME THAT THERE'S NO POINT IN MAKING THIS JOURNEY IF I DON'T HAVE THE EQUIPMENT I NEED?
BECAUSE, I KNOW YOU'RE NOT REALLY TRAVELING AS A SCIENTIST.
I'M NOT?
LOOK AT YOU, AN OLD MAN PLANNING A HUNDRED-KLICK JOURNEY. LIKE AN OLD ELEPHANT LOOKING FOR A PLACE TO DIE.
FARTHER THAN THAT. AND I DON'T PLAN ON DYING.
GOVERNOR MENACH, YOU'RE AN OLD MAN WHO DOESN'T WANT TO FACE HIS FOURTEEN-YEAR-OLD SUCCESSOR.
THE NEW COLONISTS HAVE BEEN IN STASIS THROUGHOUT THE VOYAGE. THEY DON'T KNOW HIM--SO THEY'LL FOLLOW WHOMEVER THE OLD SETTLERS FOLLOW. AND IF I'M HERE, THAT'LL BE ME. NO MATTER WHAT WE DO OR SAY, ENDER WIGGIN WILL BE TREATED LIKE MY GRANDSON, NOT LIKE THE GOVERNOR.
MAKE NO MISTAKE, WIGGIN WILL BE GOVERNOR. HE'LL BE BETTER THAN THE ADMIRAL OR I EVER WERE. YOU NEED TO SET THE EXAMPLE. TREAT HIM AS GOVERNOR AND HELP HIM AS MUCH AS YOU CAN. SO, UNPACK THAT OTHER BAG, BECAUSE YOU'RE NOT GOING WITH ME.
OTHER BAG?
I'M NOT AN IDIOT. HALF THE EQUIPMENT I DECIDED NOT TO TAKE, YOU PUT IN THAT BAG, ALONG WITH EXTRA FOOD AND A BEDROLL.
I NEVER THOUGHT YOU WERE AN IDIOT. I'M NOT SENDING BOTH OUR COLONY'S LEAD XENOBIOLOGISTS ON THE SAME JOURNEY. THE PACK'S FOR MY SON, PO.
HE'LL CARRY YOU BACK IF YOU'RE ALIVE, OTHERWISE HE'LL WATCH AND RECORD YOUR DECOMPOSITION, SAMPLING THE MICROBES THAT FEED ON YOUR OLD CORPSE.
GLAD TO SEE YOU'RE A SCIENTIST AND NOT A SENTIMENTAL FOOL.
FIRST THING IN THE MORNING, WE'RE OFF.
UNLESS THE NEW GOVERNOR FORBIDS YOU. AND YOU KNOW, THEY HAVE FOUR SKIMMERS.
HIS AUTHORITY DOESN'T BEGIN UNTIL HE SETS FOOT ON THIS PLANET. AND IF WE NEED A SKIMMER, WE'LL RADIO BACK FOR ONE. OTHERWISE DON'T TELL THEM WHERE WE WENT. NO SELF-RESPECTING PREDATOR, IF THERE ARE ANY THAT WEREN'T KILLED BY THE FORMICS, WOULD EAT AN OLD WAD OF GRISTLE LIKE ME.
I WAS THINKING OF MY SON.
I'LL WATCH OUT FOR HIM.

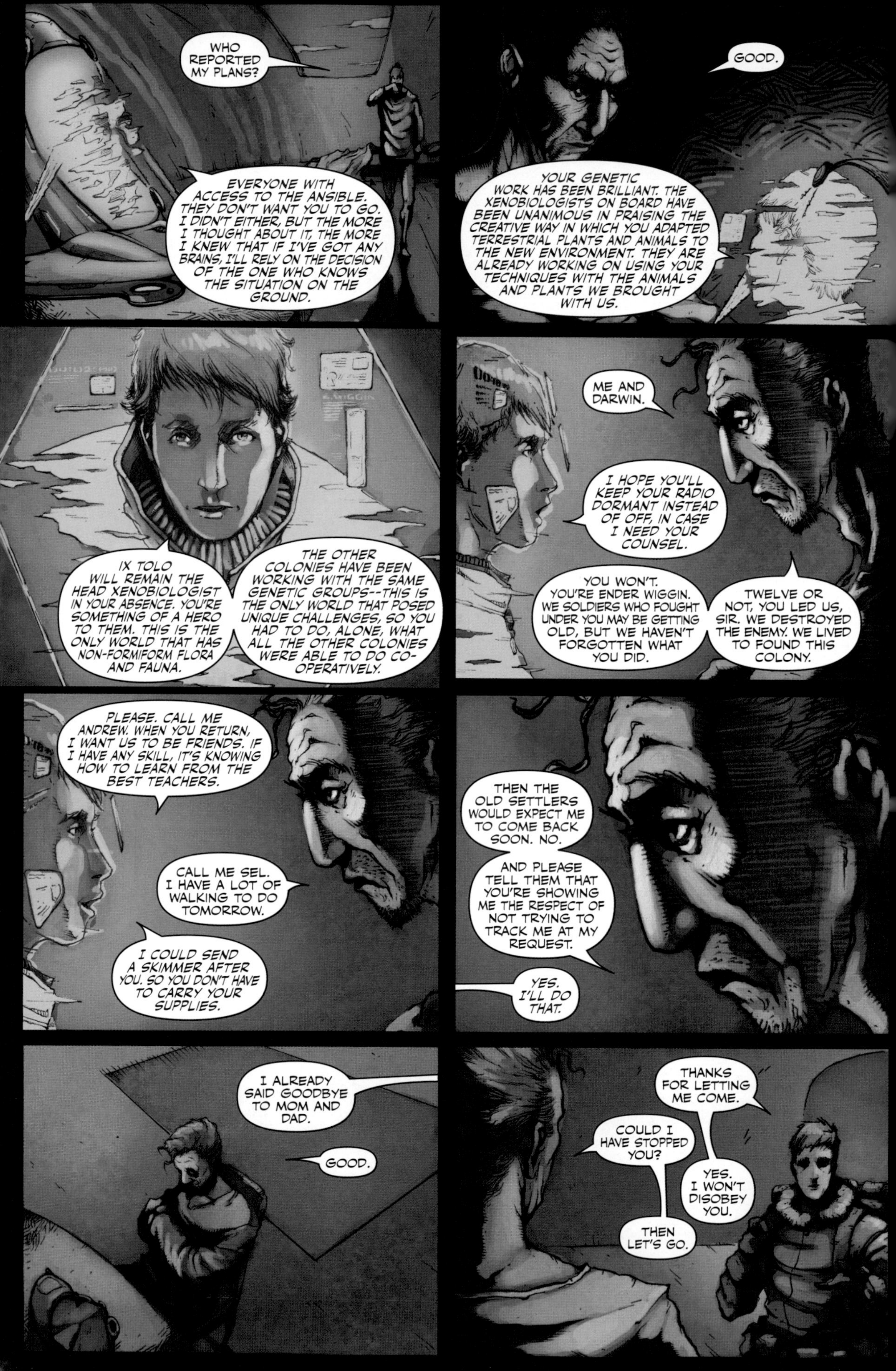
WHO REPORTED MY PLANS?
EVERYONE WITH ACCESS TO THE ANSIBLE. THEY DON'T WANT YOU TO GO. I DIDN'T EITHER, BUT THE MORE I THOUGHT ABOUT IT, THE MORE I KNEW THAT IF I'VE GOT ANY BRAINS, I'LL RELY ON THE DECISION OF THE ONE WHO KNOWS THE SITUATION ON THE GROUND.
GOOD.
YOUR GENETIC WORK HAS BEEN BRILLIANT. THE XENOBIOLOGISTS ON BOARD HAVE BEEN UNANIMOUS IN PRAISING THE CREATIVE WAY IN WHICH YOU ADAPTED TERRESTRIAL PLANTS AND ANIMALS TO THE NEW ENVIRONMENT. THEY ARE ALREADY WORKING ON USING YOUR TECHNIQUES WITH THE ANIMALS AND PLANTS WE BROUGHT WITH US.
IX TOLO WILL REMAIN THE HEAD XENOBIOLOGIST IN YOUR ABSENCE. YOU'RE SOMETHING OF A HERO TO THEM. THIS IS THE ONLY WORLD THAT HAS NON-FORMIFORM FLORA AND FAUNA.
THE OTHER COLONIES HAVE BEEN WORKING WITH THE SAME GENETIC GROUPS--THIS IS THE ONLY WORLD THAT POSED UNIQUE CHALLENGES, SO YOU HAD TO DO, ALONE, WHAT ALL THE OTHER COLONIES WERE ABLE TO DO CO-OPERATIVELY.
ME AND DARWIN.
I HOPE YOU'LL KEEP YOUR RADIO DORMANT INSTEAD OF OFF, IN CASE I NEED YOUR COUNSEL.
YOU WON'T. YOU'RE ENDER WIGGIN. WE SOLDIERS WHO FOUGHT UNDER YOU MAY BE GETTING OLD, BUT WE HAVEN'T FORGOTTEN WHAT YOU DID.
TWELVE OR NOT, YOU LED US, SIR. WE DESTROYED THE ENEMY. WE LIVED TO FOUND THIS COLONY.
PLEASE. CALL ME ANDREW. WHEN YOU RETURN, I WANT US TO BE FRIENDS. IF I HAVE ANY SKILL, IT'S KNOWING HOW TO LEARN FROM THE BEST TEACHERS.
CALL ME SEL. I HAVE A LOT OF WALKING TO DO TOMORROW.
I COULD SEND A SKIMMER AFTER YOU. SO YOU DON'T HAVE TO CARRY YOUR SUPPLIES.
THEN THE OLD SETTLERS WOULD EXPECT ME TO COME BACK SOON. NO.
AND PLEASE TELL THEM THAT YOU'RE SHOWING ME THE RESPECT OF NOT TRYING TO TRACK ME AT MY REQUEST.
YES. I'LL DO THAT.
I ALREADY SAID GOODBYE TO MOM AND DAD.
GOOD.
THANKS FOR LETTING ME COME.
COULD I HAVE STOPPED YOU?
YES. I WON'T DISOBEY YOU.
THEN LET'S GO.

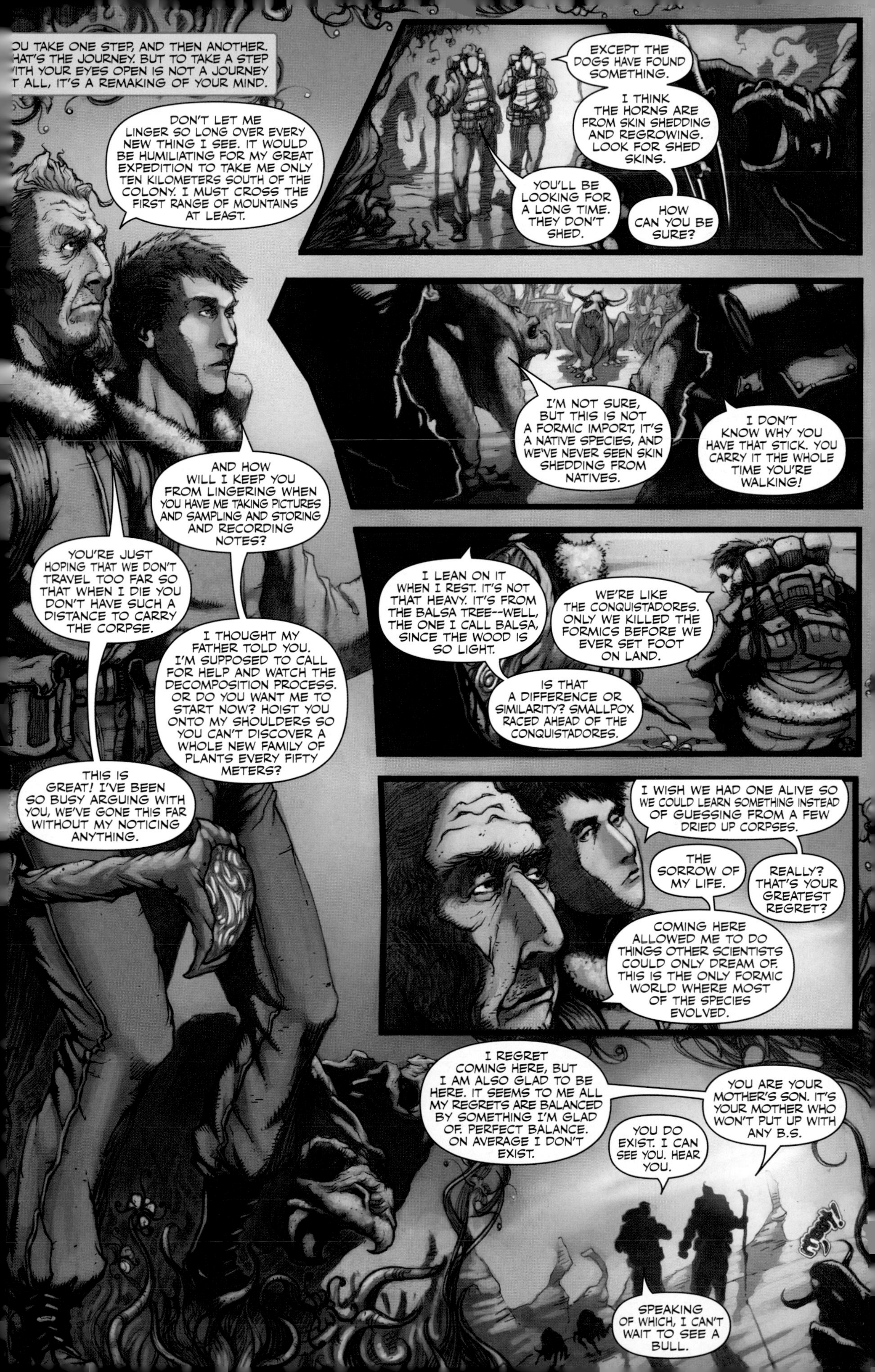
OU TAKE ONE STEP, AND THEN ANOTHER. HAT'S THE JOURNEY. BUT TO TAKE A STEP ITH YOUR EYES OPEN IS NOT A JOURNEY T ALL, IT'S A REMAKING OF YOUR MIND.
DON'T LET ME LINGER SO LONG OVER EVERY NEW THING I SEE. IT WOULD BE HUMILIATING FOR MY GREAT EXPEDITION TO TAKE ME ONLY TEN KILOMETERS SOUTH OF THE COLONY. I MUST CROSS THE FIRST RANGE OF MOUNTAINS AT LEAST.
EXCEPT THE DOGS HAVE FOUND SOMETHING.
I THINK THE HORNS ARE FROM SKIN SHEDDING AND REGROWING. LOOK FOR SHED SKINS.
YOU'LL BE LOOKING FOR A LONG TIME. THEY DON'T SHED.
HOW CAN YOU BE SURE?
I'M NOT SURE, BUT THIS IS NOT A FORMIC IMPORT, IT'S A NATIVE SPECIES, AND WE'VE NEVER SEEN SKIN SHEDDING FROM NATIVES.
I DON'T KNOW WHY YOU HAVE THAT STICK. YOU CARRY IT THE WHOLE TIME YOU'RE WALKING!
AND HOW WILL I KEEP YOU FROM LINGERING WHEN YOU HAVE ME TAKING PICTURES AND SAMPLING AND STORING AND RECORDING NOTES?
YOU'RE JUST HOPING THAT WE DON'T TRAVEL TOO FAR SO THAT WHEN I DIE YOU DON'T HAVE SUCH A DISTANCE TO CARRY THE CORPSE.
I THOUGHT MY FATHER TOLD YOU. I'M SUPPOSED TO CALL FOR HELP AND WATCH THE DECOMPOSITION PROCESS. OR DO YOU WANT ME TO START NOW? HOIST YOU ONTO MY SHOULDERS SO YOU CAN'T DISCOVER A WHOLE NEW FAMILY OF PLANTS EVERY FIFTY METERS?
THIS IS GREAT! I'VE BEEN SO BUSY ARGUING WITH YOU, WE'VE GONE THIS FAR WITHOUT MY NOTICING ANYTHING.
I LEAN ON IT WHEN I REST. IT'S NOT THAT HEAVY. IT'S FROM THE BALSA TREE--WELL, THE ONE I CALL BALSA, SINCE THE WOOD IS SO LIGHT.
WE'RE LIKE THE CONQUISTADORES. ONLY WE KILLED THE FORMICS BEFORE WE EVER SET FOOT ON LAND.
IS THAT A DIFFERENCE OR SIMILARITY? SMALLPOX RACED AHEAD OF THE CONQUISTADORES.
I WISH WE HAD ONE ALIVE SO WE COULD LEARN SOMETHING INSTEAD OF GUESSING FROM A FEW DRIED UP CORPSES.
THE SORROW OF MY LIFE.
REALLY? THAT'S YOUR GREATEST REGRET?
COMING HERE ALLOWED ME TO DO THINGS OTHER SCIENTISTS COULD ONLY DREAM OF. THIS IS THE ONLY FORMIC WORLD WHERE MOST OF THE SPECIES EVOLVED.
I REGRET COMING HERE, BUT I AM ALSO GLAD TO BE HERE. IT SEEMS TO ME ALL MY REGRETS ARE BALANCED BY SOMETHING I'M GLAD OF. PERFECT BALANCE. ON AVERAGE I DON'T EXIST.
YOU ARE YOUR MOTHER'S SON. IT'S YOUR MOTHER WHO WON'T PUT UP WITH ANY B.S.
YOU DO EXIST. I CAN SEE YOU. HEAR YOU.
SPEAKING OF WHICH, I CAN'T WAIT TO SEE A BULL.

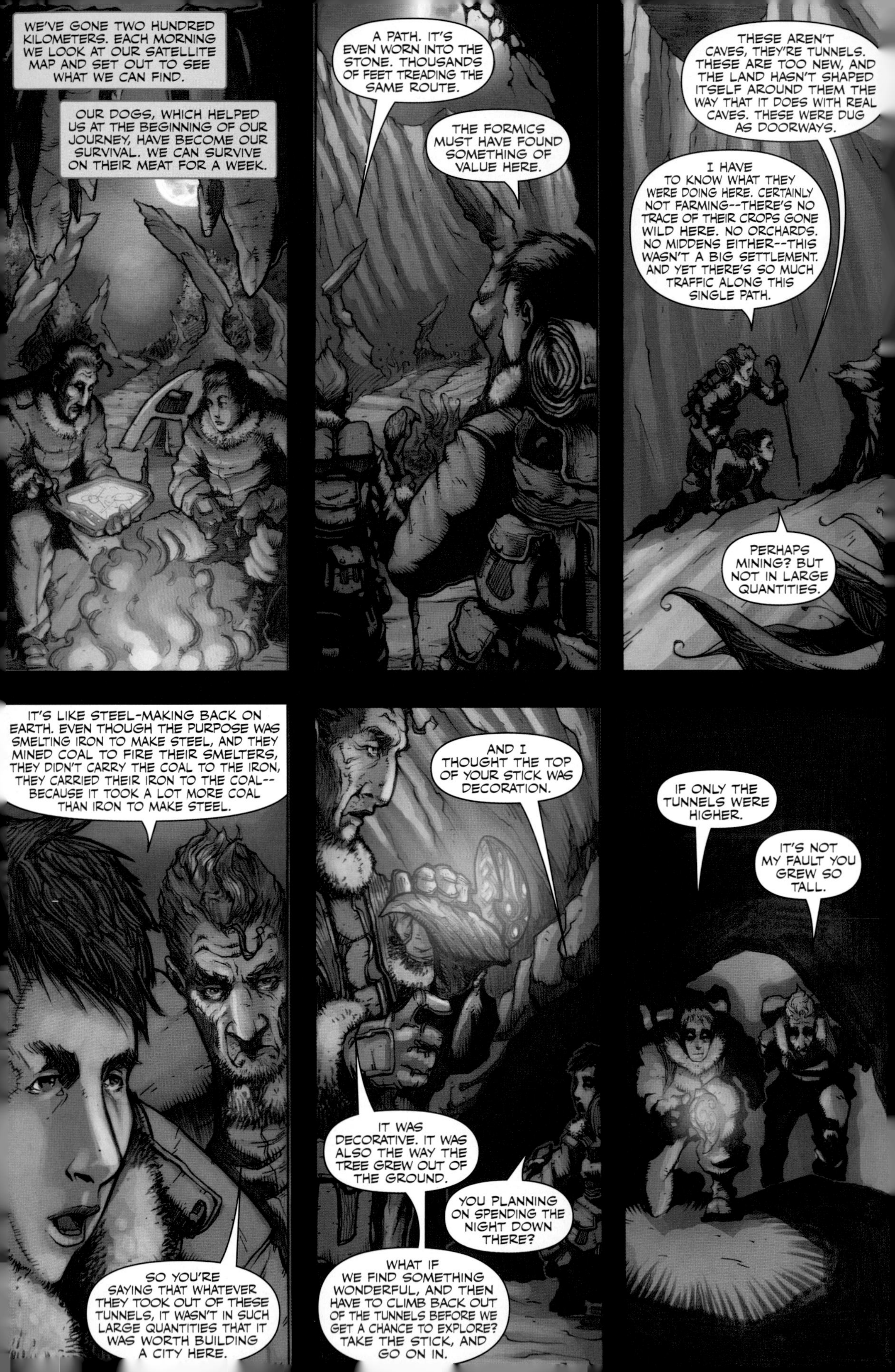
WE'VE GONE TWO HUNDRED KILOMETERS. EACH MORNING WE LOOK AT OUR SATELLITE MAP AND SET OUT TO SEE WHAT WE CAN FIND.
OUR DOGS, WHICH HELPED US AT THE BEGINNING OF OUR JOURNEY, HAVE BECOME OUR SURVIVAL. WE CAN SURVIVE ON THEIR MEAT FOR A WEEK.
A PATH. IT'S EVEN WORN INTO THE STONE. THOUSANDS OF FEET TREADING THE SAME ROUTE.
THE FORMICS MUST HAVE FOUND SOMETHING OF VALUE HERE.
THESE AREN'T CAVES, THEY'RE TUNNELS. THESE ARE TOO NEW, AND THE LAND HASN'T SHAPED ITSELF AROUND THEM THE WAY THAT IT DOES WITH REAL CAVES. THESE WERE DUG AS DOORWAYS.
I HAVE TO KNOW WHAT THEY WERE DOING HERE. CERTAINLY NOT FARMING--THERE'S NO TRACE OF THEIR CROPS GONE WILD HERE. NO ORCHARDS. NO MIDDENS EITHER--THIS WASN'T A BIG SETTLEMENT. AND YET THERE'S SO MUCH TRAFFIC ALONG THIS SINGLE PATH.
PERHAPS MINING? BUT NOT IN LARGE QUANTITIES.
IT'S LIKE STEEL-MAKING BACK ON EARTH. EVEN THOUGH THE PURPOSE WAS SMELTING IRON TO MAKE STEEL, AND THEY MINED COAL TO FIRE THEIR SMELTERS, THEY DIDN'T CARRY THE COAL TO THE IRON, THEY CARRIED THEIR IRON TO THE COAL--BECAUSE IT TOOK A LOT MORE COAL THAN IRON TO MAKE STEEL.
SO YOU'RE SAYING THAT WHATEVER THEY TOOK OUT OF THESE TUNNELS, IT WASN'T IN SUCH LARGE QUANTITIES THAT IT WAS WORTH BUILDING A CITY HERE.
AND I THOUGHT THE TOP OF YOUR STICK WAS DECORATION.
IT WAS DECORATIVE. IT WAS ALSO THE WAY THE TREE GREW OUT OF THE GROUND.
YOU PLANNING ON SPENDING THE NIGHT DOWN THERE?
WHAT IF WE FIND SOMETHING WONDERFUL, AND THEN HAVE TO CLIMB BACK OUT OF THE TUNNELS BEFORE WE GET A CHANCE TO EXPLORE? TAKE THE STICK, AND GO ON IN.
IF ONLY THE TUNNELS WERE HIGHER.
IT'S NOT MY FAULT YOU GREW SO TALL.

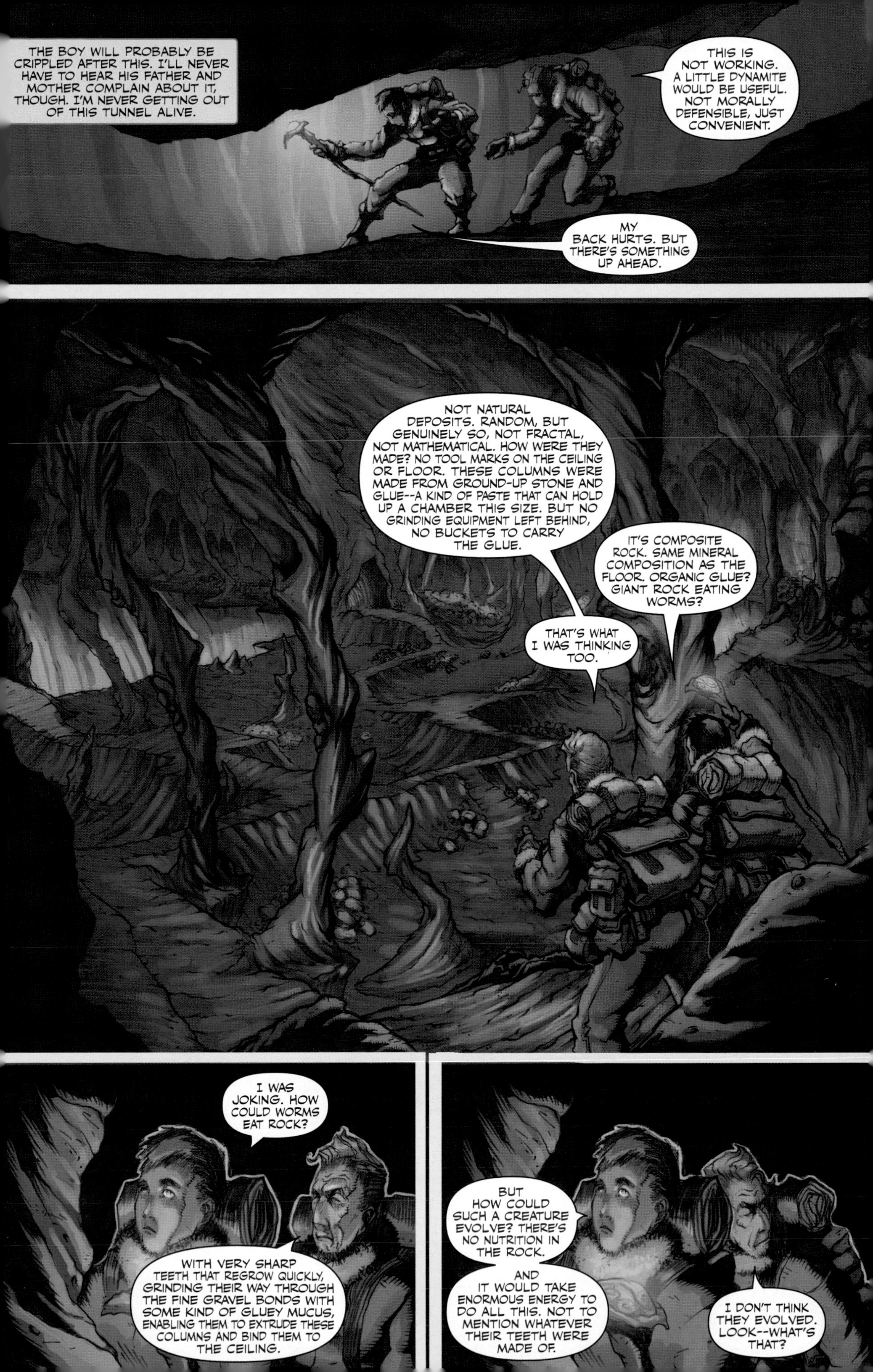
THE BOY WILL PROBABLY BE CRIPPLED AFTER THIS. I'LL NEVER HAVE TO HEAR HIS FATHER AND MOTHER COMPLAIN ABOUT IT, THOUGH. I'M NEVER GETTING OUT OF THIS TUNNEL ALIVE.
THIS IS NOT WORKING. A LITTLE DYNAMITE WOULD BE USEFUL. NOT MORALLY DEFENSIBLE, JUST CONVENIENT.
MY BACK HURTS. BUT THERE'S SOMETHING UP AHEAD.
NOT NATURAL DEPOSITS. RANDOM, BUT GENUINELY SO, NOT FRACTAL, NOT MATHEMATICAL. HOW WERE THEY MADE? NO TOOL MARKS ON THE CEILING OR FLOOR. THESE COLUMNS WERE MADE FROM GROUND-UP STONE AND GLUE--A KIND OF PASTE THAT CAN HOLD UP A CHAMBER THIS SIZE. BUT NO GRINDING EQUIPMENT LEFT BEHIND, NO BUCKETS TO CARRY THE GLUE.
IT'S COMPOSITE ROCK. SAME MINERAL COMPOSITION AS THE FLOOR. ORGANIC GLUE? GIANT ROCK EATING WORMS?
THAT'S WHAT I WAS THINKING TOO.
I WAS JOKING. HOW COULD WORMS EAT ROCK?
WITH VERY SHARP TEETH THAT REGROW QUICKLY, GRINDING THEIR WAY THROUGH THE FINE GRAVEL BONDS WITH SOME KIND OF GLUEY MUCUS, ENABLING THEM TO EXTRUDE THESE COLUMNS AND BIND THEM TO THE CEILING.
BUT HOW COULD SUCH A CREATURE EVOLVE? THERE'S NO NUTRITION IN THE ROCK.
AND IT WOULD TAKE ENORMOUS ENERGY TO DO ALL THIS. NOT TO MENTION WHATEVER THEIR TEETH WERE MADE OF.
I DON'T THINK THEY EVOLVED. LOOK--WHAT'S THAT?

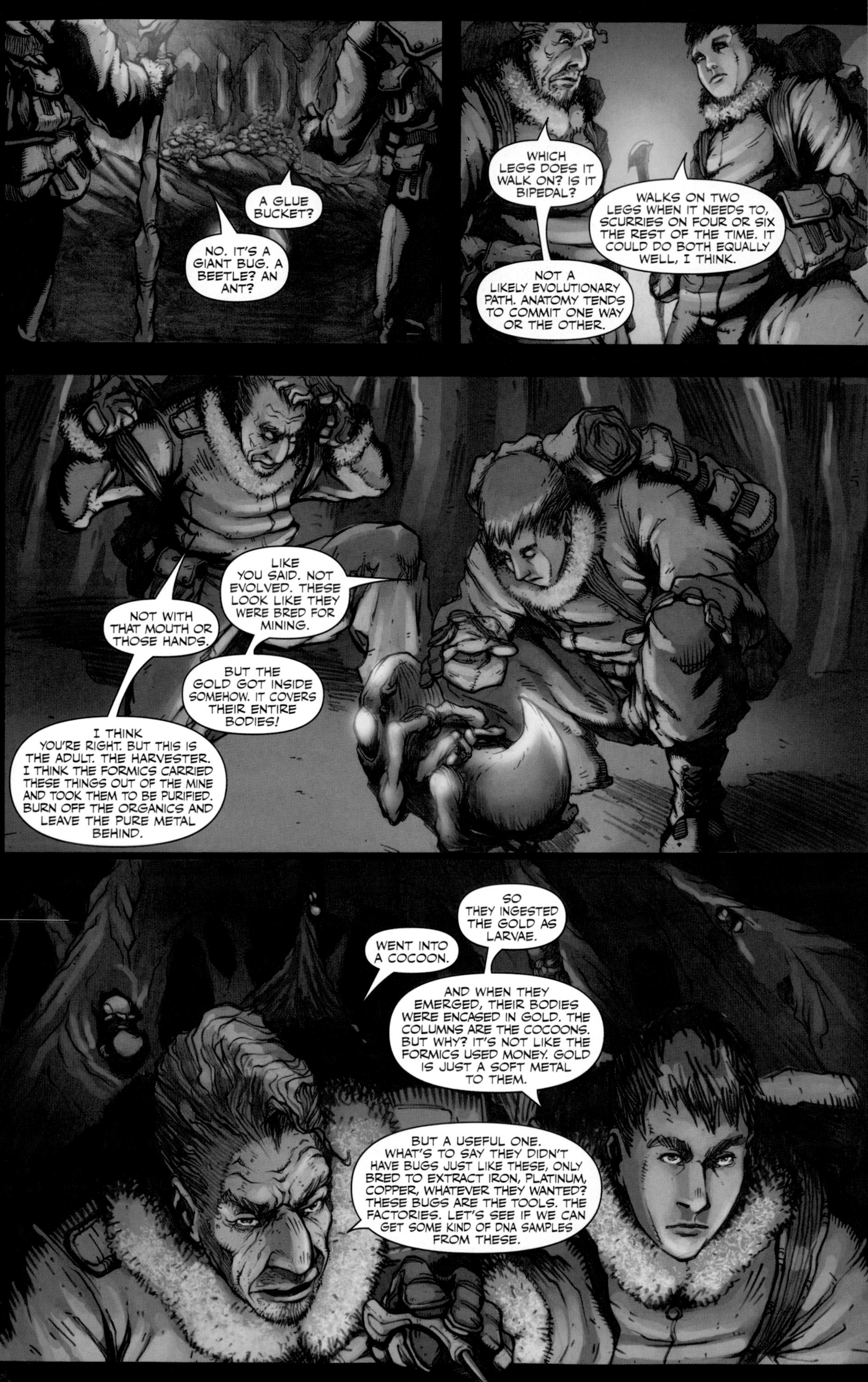
A GLUE BUCKET?
NO. IT'S A GIANT BUG. A BEETLE? AN ANT?
WHICH LEGS DOES IT WALK ON? IS IT BIPEDAL?
WALKS ON TWO LEGS WHEN IT NEEDS TO, SCURRIES ON FOUR OR SIX THE REST OF THE TIME. IT COULD DO BOTH EQUALLY WELL, I THINK.
NOT A LIKELY EVOLUTIONARY PATH. ANATOMY TENDS TO COMMIT ONE WAY OR THE OTHER.
NOT WITH THAT MOUTH OR THOSE HANDS.
LIKE YOU SAID. NOT EVOLVED. THESE LOOK LIKE THEY WERE BRED FOR MINING.
BUT THE GOLD GOT INSIDE SOMEHOW. IT COVERS THEIR ENTIRE BODIES!
I THINK YOU'RE RIGHT. BUT THIS IS THE ADULT. THE HARVESTER. I THINK THE FORMICS CARRIED THESE THINGS OUT OF THE MINE AND TOOK THEM TO BE PURIFIED. BURN OFF THE ORGANICS AND LEAVE THE PURE METAL BEHIND.
SO THEY INGESTED THE GOLD AS LARVAE.
WENT INTO A COCOON.
AND WHEN THEY EMERGED, THEIR BODIES WERE ENCASED IN GOLD. THE COLUMNS ARE THE COCOONS. BUT WHY? IT'S NOT LIKE THE FORMICS USED MONEY. GOLD IS JUST A SOFT METAL TO THEM.
BUT A USEFUL ONE. WHAT'S TO SAY THEY DIDN'T HAVE BUGS JUST LIKE THESE, ONLY BRED TO EXTRACT IRON, PLATINUM, COPPER, WHATEVER THEY WANTED? THESE BUGS ARE THE TOOLS. THE FACTORIES. LET'S SEE IF WE CAN GET SOME KIND OF DNA SAMPLES FROM THESE.

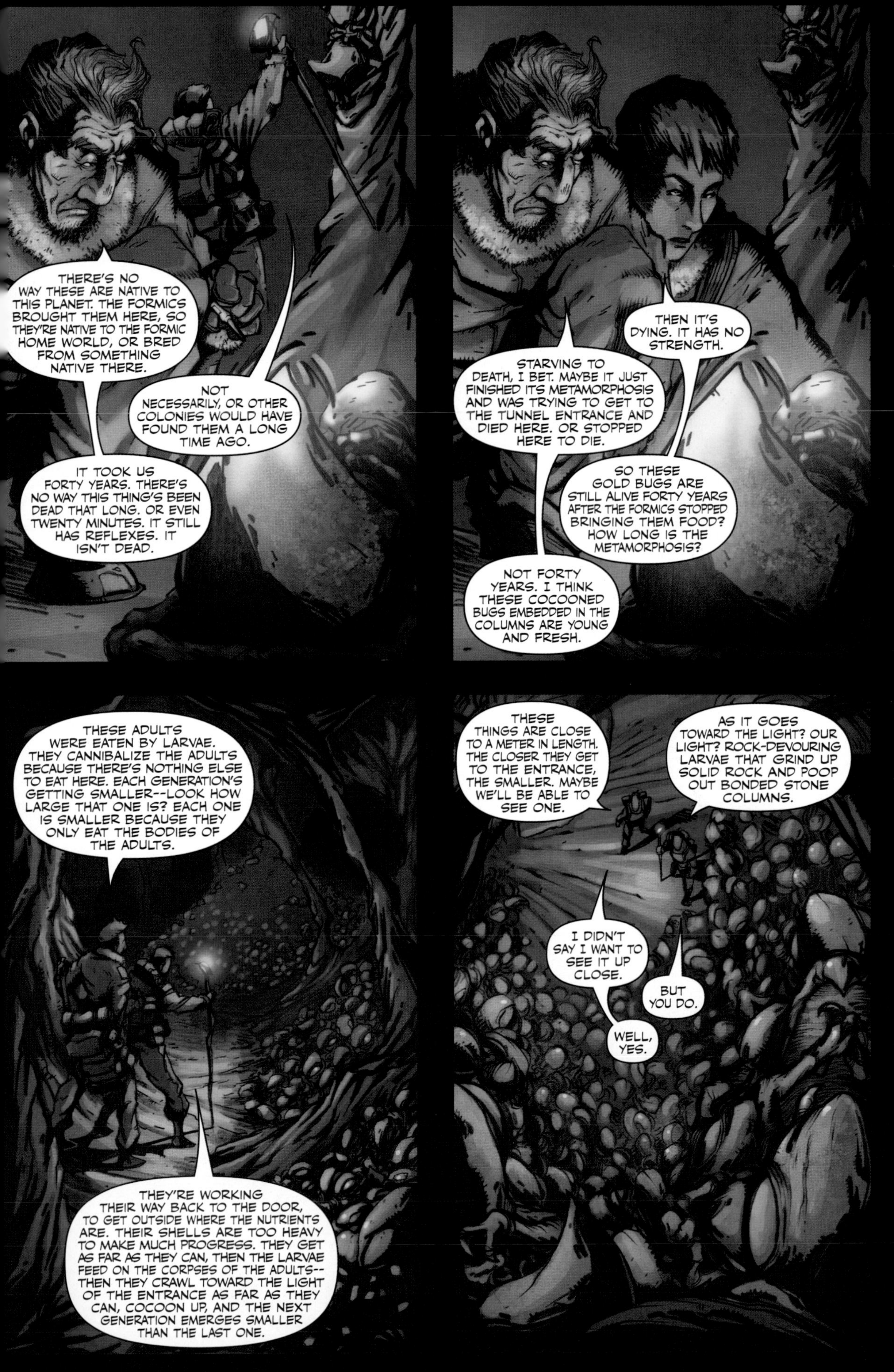
THERE'S NO WAY THESE ARE NATIVE TO THIS PLANET. THE FORMICS BROUGHT THEM HERE, SO THEY'RE NATIVE TO THE FORMIC HOME WORLD, OR BRED FROM SOMETHING NATIVE THERE.
NOT NECESSARILY, OR OTHER COLONIES WOULD HAVE FOUND THEM A LONG TIME AGO.
IT TOOK US FORTY YEARS. THERE'S NO WAY THIS THING'S BEEN DEAD THAT LONG. OR EVEN TWENTY MINUTES. IT STILL HAS REFLEXES. IT ISN'T DEAD.
THEN IT'S DYING. IT HAS NO STRENGTH.
STARVING TO DEATH, I BET. MAYBE IT JUST FINISHED ITS METAMORPHOSIS AND WAS TRYING TO GET TO THE TUNNEL ENTRANCE AND DIED HERE. OR STOPPED HERE TO DIE.
SO THESE GOLD BUGS ARE STILL ALIVE FORTY YEARS AFTER THE FORMICS STOPPED BRINGING THEM FOOD? HOW LONG IS THE METAMORPHOSIS?
NOT FORTY YEARS. I THINK THESE COCOONED BUGS EMBEDDED IN THE COLUMNS ARE YOUNG AND FRESH.
THESE ADULTS WERE EATEN BY LARVAE. THEY CANNIBALIZE THE ADULTS BECAUSE THERE'S NOTHING ELSE TO EAT HERE. EACH GENERATION'S GETTING SMALLER--LOOK HOW LARGE THAT ONE IS? EACH ONE IS SMALLER BECAUSE THEY ONLY EAT THE BODIES OF THE ADULTS.
THEY'RE WORKING THEIR WAY BACK TO THE DOOR, TO GET OUTSIDE WHERE THE NUTRIENTS ARE. THEIR SHELLS ARE TOO HEAVY TO MAKE MUCH PROGRESS. THEY GET AS FAR AS THEY CAN, THEN THE LARVAE FEED ON THE CORPSES OF THE ADULTS-- THEN THEY CRAWL TOWARD THE LIGHT OF THE ENTRANCE AS FAR AS THEY CAN, COCOON UP, AND THE NEXT GENERATION EMERGES SMALLER THAN THE LAST ONE.
THESE THINGS ARE CLOSE TO A METER IN LENGTH. THE CLOSER THEY GET TO THE ENTRANCE, THE SMALLER. MAYBE WE'LL BE ABLE TO SEE ONE.
AS IT GOES TOWARD THE LIGHT? OUR LIGHT? ROCK-DEVOURING LARVAE THAT GRIND UP SOLID ROCK AND POOP OUT BONDED STONE COLUMNS.
I DIDN'T SAY I WANT TO SEE IT UP CLOSE.
BUT YOU DO.
WELL, YES.

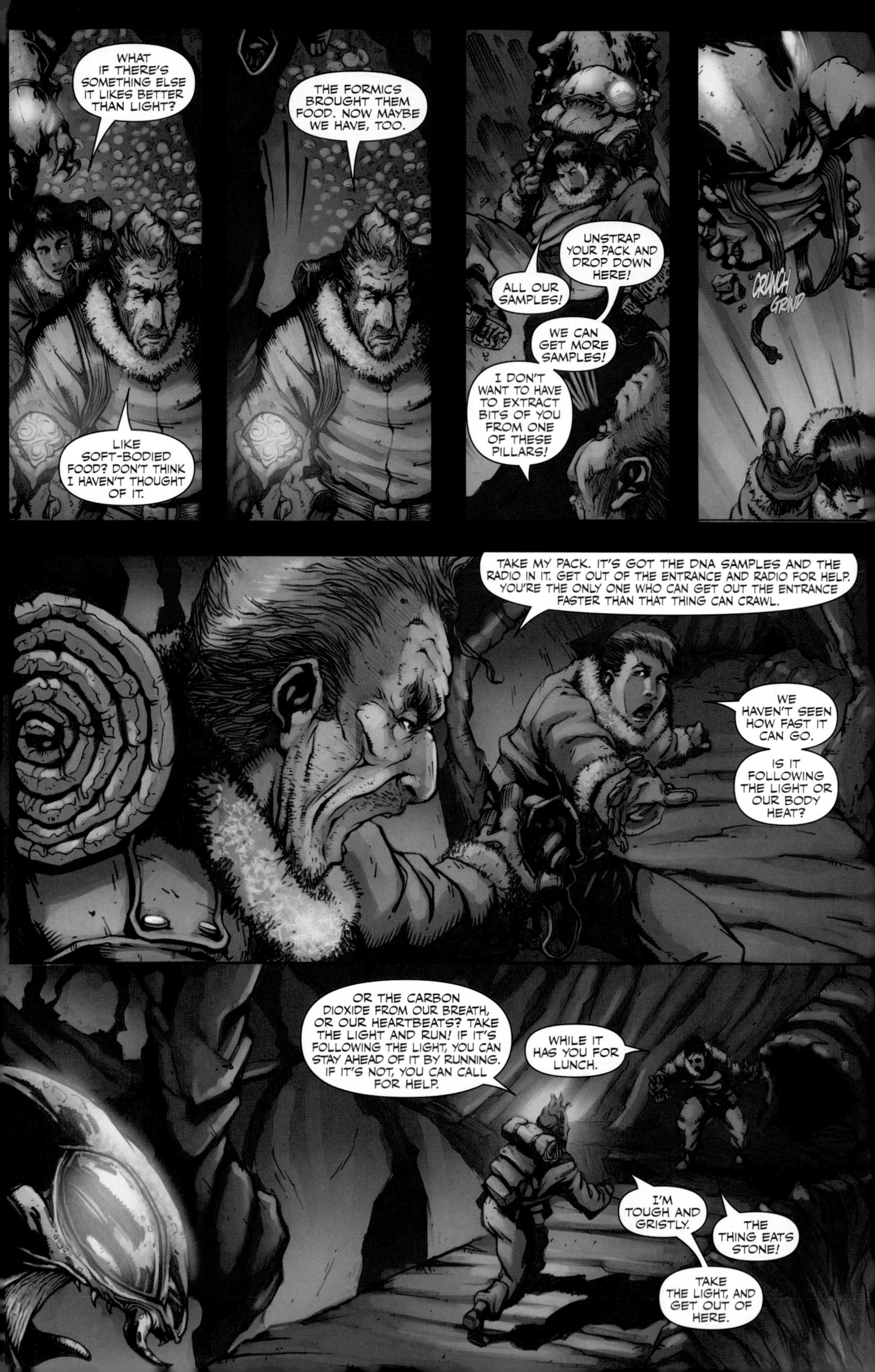

WHAT IF THERE'S SOMETHING ELSE IT LIKES BETTER THAN LIGHT?
LIKE SOFT-BODIED FOOD? DON'T THINK I HAVEN'T THOUGHT OF IT.
THE FORMICS BROUGHT THEM FOOD. NOW MAYBE WE HAVE, TOO.
UNSTRAP YOUR PACK AND DROP DOWN HERE!
ALL OUR SAMPLES!
WE CAN GET MORE SAMPLES!
I DON'T WANT TO HAVE TO EXTRACT BITS OF YOU FROM ONE OF THESE PILLARS!
CRUNCH
GRIND
TAKE MY PACK. IT'S GOT THE DNA SAMPLES AND THE RADIO IN IT. GET OUT OF THE ENTRANCE AND RADIO FOR HELP. YOU'RE THE ONLY ONE WHO CAN GET OUT THE ENTRANCE FASTER THAN THAT THING CAN CRAWL.
WE HAVEN'T SEEN HOW FAST IT CAN GO.
IS IT FOLLOWING THE LIGHT OR OUR BODY HEAT?
OR THE CARBON DIOXIDE FROM OUR BREATH, OR OUR HEARTBEATS? TAKE THE LIGHT AND RUN! IF IT'S FOLLOWING THE LIGHT, YOU CAN STAY AHEAD OF IT BY RUNNING. IF IT'S NOT, YOU CAN CALL FOR HELP.
WHILE IT HAS YOU FOR LUNCH.
I'M TOUGH AND GRISTLY.
THE THING EATS STONE!
TAKE THE LIGHT, AND GET OUT OF HERE.

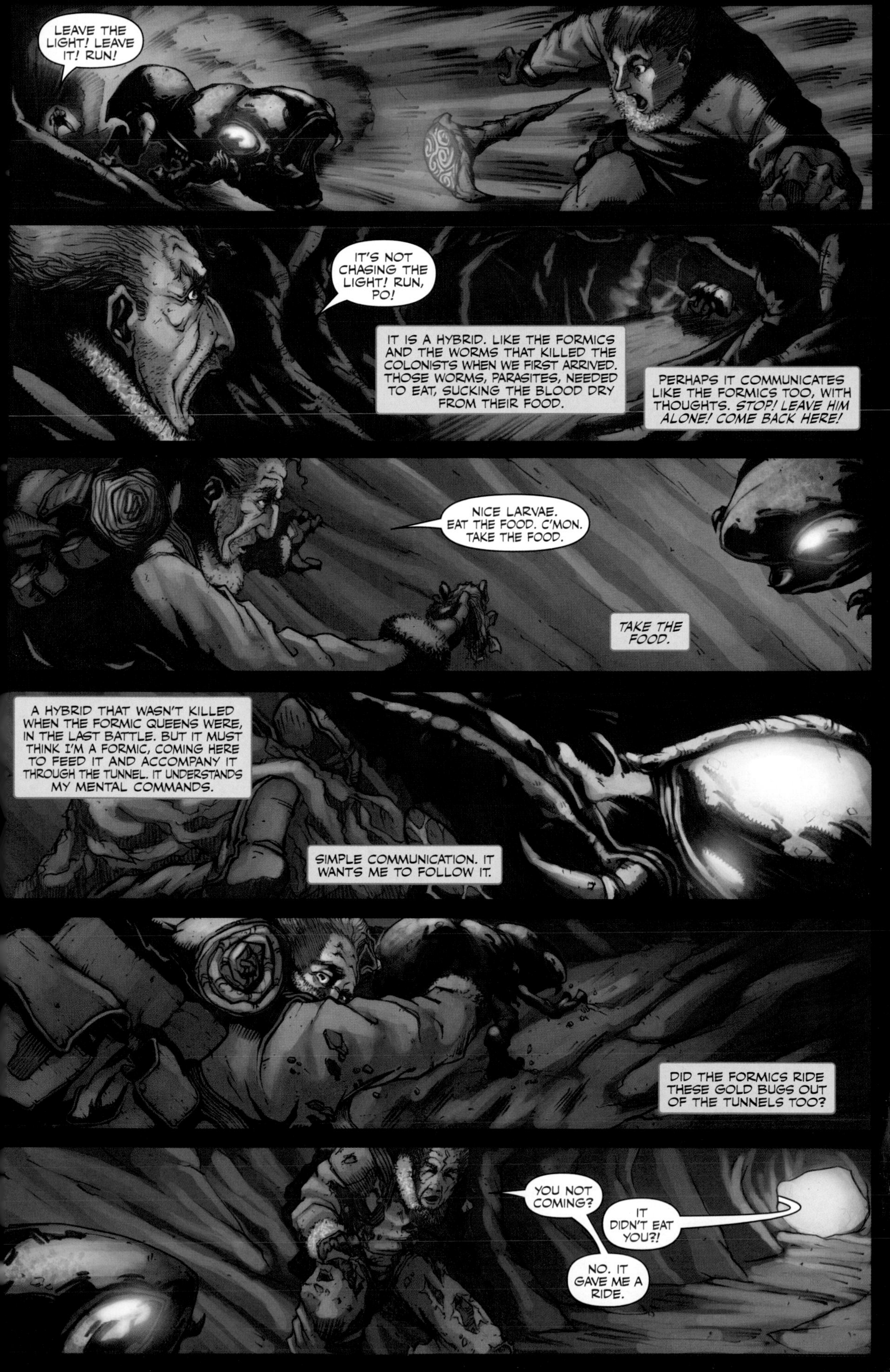

LEAVE THE LIGHT! LEAVE IT! RUN!
IT'S NOT CHASING THE LIGHT! RUN, PO!
IT IS A HYBRID. LIKE THE FORMICS AND THE WORMS THAT KILLED THE COLONISTS WHEN WE FIRST ARRIVED. THOSE WORMS, PARASITES, NEEDED TO EAT, SUCKING THE BLOOD DRY FROM THEIR FOOD.
PERHAPS IT COMMUNICATES LIKE THE FORMICS TOO, WITH THOUGHTS. STOP! LEAVE HIM ALONE! COME BACK HERE!
NICE LARVAE. EAT THE FOOD. C'MON. TAKE THE FOOD.
TAKE THE FOOD.
A HYBRID THAT WASN'T KILLED WHEN THE FORMIC QUEENS WERE, IN THE LAST BATTLE. BUT IT MUST THINK I'M A FORMIC, COMING HERE TO FEED IT AND ACCOMPANY IT THROUGH THE TUNNEL. IT UNDERSTANDS MY MENTAL COMMANDS.
SIMPLE COMMUNICATION. IT WANTS ME TO FOLLOW IT.
DID THE FORMICS RIDE THESE GOLD BUGS OUT OF THE TUNNELS TOO?
YOU NOT COMING?
IT DIDN'T EAT YOU?!
NO. IT GAVE ME A RIDE.

WE NEED TO GET THEM MORE FOOD. IF I'M RIGHT, THIS THING'S HALF-NATIVE TO THIS WORLD, AND IT CAN PROBABLY METABOLIZE THE LOCAL VEGETATION.

ENDER WIGGIN.

SEL MENACH. PO RADIOED. SAID YOU HAD A GIANT WORM SITUATION GOING ON.

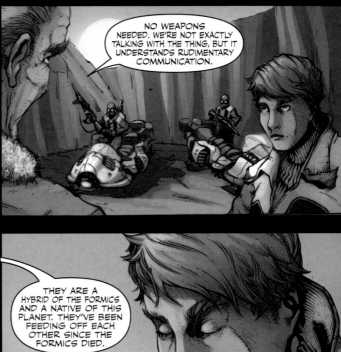

NO WEAPONS NEEDED. WE'RE NOT EXACTLY TALKING WITH THE THING, BUT IT UNDERSTANDS RUDIMENTARY COMMUNICATION.

THEY ARE A HYBRID OF THE FORMICS AND A NATIVE OF THIS PLANET. THEY'VE BEEN FEEDING OFF EACH OTHER SINCE THE FORMICS DIED.

SO THESE AREN'T ACTUALLY FORMICS?

NONE OF THE FORMICS COULD HAVE SURVIVED, BUT THESE BUGS ARE LIKE FORMICS. WHEN WE GET BACK TO THE COLONY, WE CAN DO THE GENE COMPARISON AND SEE JUST HOW THESE THINGS WERE MADE. AND WE CAN ALSO GET ALL THE GOLD WE WOULD EVER WANT.

THERE MIGHT BE IRON BUGS, AND SILVER BUGS, AND COPPER BUGS ELSEWHERE. WE NEED TO DO A SEARCH FOR THE LIKELY SITES. FORTY YEARS OF SURVIVING BY CANNIBALIZING EACH OTHER IS A LONG TIME, AND THEY MAY BE ON THEIR LAST LEGS, SO TO SPEAK.

COUNT ON IT. WE'LL DO IT AT ONCE.

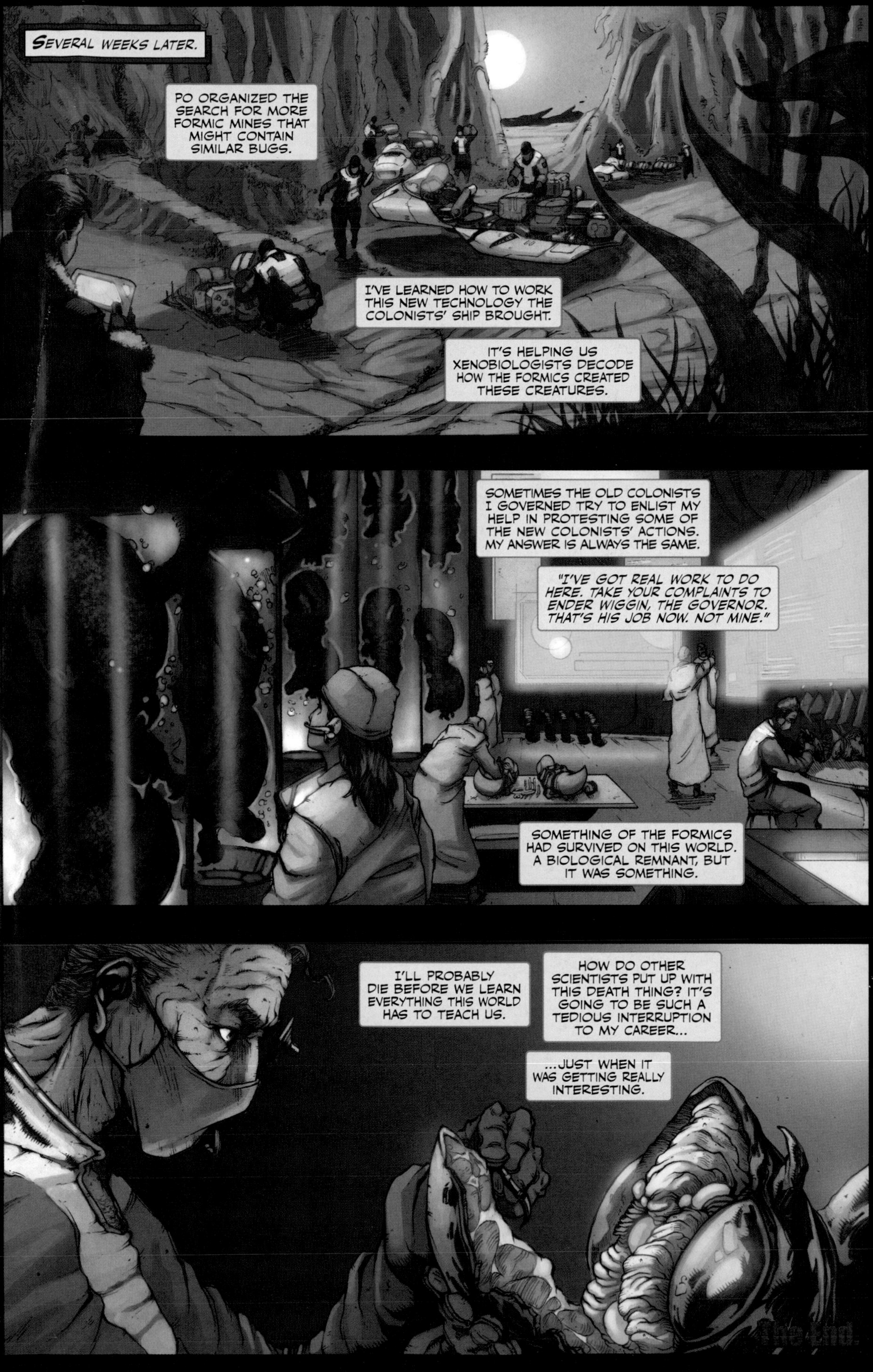
SEVERAL WEEKS LATER.
PO ORGANIZED THE SEARCH FOR MORE FORMIC MINES THAT MIGHT CONTAIN SIMILAR BUGS.
I'VE LEARNED HOW TO WORK THIS NEW TECHNOLOGY THE COLONISTS' SHIP BROUGHT.
IT'S HELPING US XENOBIOLOGISTS DECODE HOW THE FORMICS CREATED THESE CREATURES.
SOMETIMES THE OLD COLONISTS I GOVERNED TRY TO ENLIST MY HELP IN PROTESTING SOME OF THE NEW COLONISTS' ACTIONS. MY ANSWER IS ALWAYS THE SAME.
"I'VE GOT REAL WORK TO DO HERE. TAKE YOUR COMPLAINTS TO ENDER WIGGIN, THE GOVERNOR. THAT'S HIS JOB NOW. NOT MINE."
SOMETHING OF THE FORMICS HAD SURVIVED ON THIS WORLD. A BIOLOGICAL REMNANT, BUT IT WAS SOMETHING.
I'LL PROBABLY DIE BEFORE WE LEARN EVERYTHING THIS WORLD HAS TO TEACH US.
HOW DO OTHER SCIENTISTS PUT UP WITH THIS DEATH THING? IT'S GOING TO BE SUCH A TEDIOUS INTERRUPTION TO MY CAREER...
...JUST WHEN IT WAS GETTING REALLY INTERESTING.
The End.

ORSON SCOTT CARD

RED PROPHET

TALES OF ALVIN MAKER